THE
ARCHAEOLOGY
OF GREECE

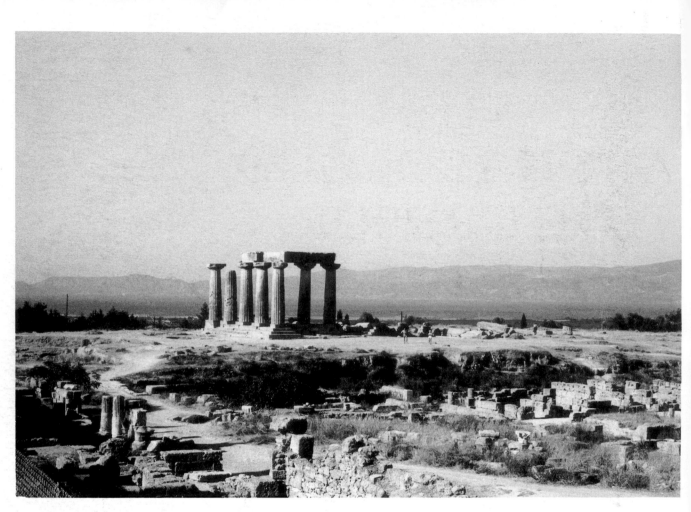

View of ancient Corinth and the Temple of Apollo from the southwest. Photo: William R. Biers.

THE ARCHAEOLOGY OF GREECE

AN INTRODUCTION

WILLIAM R. BIERS

SECOND EDITION

Cornell University Press

ITHACA AND LONDON

First published 1980 by Cornell University Press
First printing, revised edition, cloth and paperback, 1987
First printing, second edition, cloth and paperback, 1996

Illustrations from *Zakros* by Nicholas Platon are used with the permission of Charles Scribner's Sons. Copyright © 1971 by Nicholas Platon.

Illustrations are reproduced from *The Architecture of Ancient Greece* by William Bell Dinsmoor with the permission of W. W. Norton & Company, Inc. Copyright © 1975 by W. W. Norton & Company, Inc.

Printed in the United States of America

Library of Congress Cataloging-in-Publication Data

Biers, William R., 1938–
    The archaeology of Greece : an introduction / William R. Biers.—2nd ed.
      p.   cm.
    Includes bibliographical references and index.
      ISBN 0-8014-3173-5 (cloth : alk. paper). — ISBN 0-8014-8280-1 (pbk. : alk. paper)
      1. Greece—Antiquities. 2. Excavations (Archaeology)—Greece. I. Title.
DF77.B58 1996
938—dc20   95-48905

Cornell University Press strives to use environmentally responsible suppliers and materials to the fullest extent possible in the publishing of its books. Such materials include vegetable-based, low-VOC inks and acid-free papers that are recycled, totally chlorine-free, or partly composed of nonwood fibers.

Cloth printing   10 9 8 7 6 5 4 3 2 1

Paperback printing   10 9 8 7 6 5 4 3

Contents

Maps

Preface

IN WRITING THIS BOOK I have attempted to produce a work that will be useful to beginning students and teachers exploring the world of ancient Greece, and one that will also be useful to all readers with an interest in archaeology and the beginnings of our Western heritage. It is intended to be a brief overall view of the subject and to provide a framework for further study.

The first chapter briefly explores classical archaeology in Greece. Each of the following chapters begins with a brief historical and artistic summary. Then the major monuments of architecture, sculpture, and painting are discussed. These discussions are followed by short sections on typical archaeological finds, which vary from period to period. By including minor objects commonly found at archaeological sites—metalwork, lamps, and the like, as well as pottery—I attempt to show that stylistic development is to be seen in artifacts as well as in the major arts.

Footnotes have been kept to a minimum and refer only to sources in English. They are generally designed to lead the reader further into subjects or controversies, and thus selected references to scholarly journals are given. Readers with competence in foreign languages can find their way to other works through the studies cited there and in the Suggestions for Further Reading at the end of the text—highly selective groups of studies, concerned mainly with the period with which each chapter deals. The Select Bibliography lists basic handbooks.

In my decisions as to what to include and what to exclude, a number of biases will be evident to the reader, as they are to the author. I have chosen to exclude some works that scholars may expect to see and to include some recent finds that have not previously found their way into general works. An Attic bias is fairly general in classical archaeology and is reflected in these pages. This bias can hardly be avoided in a discussion of Greek art, but I hope the broader view does come through to some extent. I also acknowledge a strong emphasis on mainland and eastern sites at the expense of the archaeology and art of Sicily and Magna Graecia. I must plead limitations of space; a separate book should be devoted to those areas, as distinct manifestations of Greek art and archaeology.

I have benefited greatly from the suggestions of colleagues who kindly agreed to take time from their own hectic schedules to read this work in early drafts and who saved me from a number of silly mistakes. Those that are left are my own responsibility. A simple listing of names must suffice, although my debt to these colleagues and friends is great: Gerald Cadogan, Christine Havelock, Steven Lattimore, Fordyce Mitchel, Elizabeth Pemberton, Evelyn Smithson. In addition, Homer and Dorothy Thompson, D. A. Amyx, and T. Leslie Shear, Jr., shared their enthusiasm and their wisdom with me at the beginning of this project.

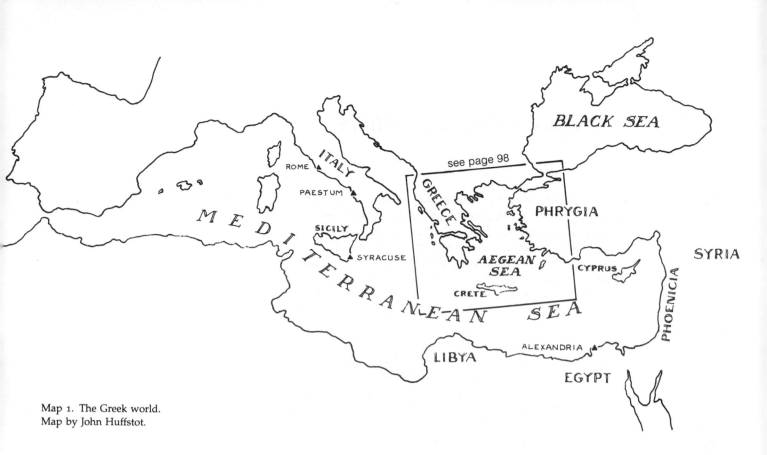

Map 1. The Greek world.
Map by John Huffstot.

see page 98

Special thanks go also to those who helped with my large and sometimes disorganized photo orders: D. M. Bailey, the British Museum; Nancy Bookides, American School of Classical Studies at Athens, Corinth Excavations; Irmgard Ernstmeier, Hirmer Verlag; Alison Frantz; Lucy Krystallis, American School of Classical Studies at Athens, Agora Excavations; Michael Maass, Staatliche Antikensammlungen und Glyptothek, Munich; Werner Schmaltz and Gerhild Hübner, Deutsches Archäologisches Institut, Athens; and the Curator of Ancient Art at the Museum of Art and Archaeology of the University of Missouri–Columbia.

Many scholars selflessly provided illustrations or were instrumental in their acquisition. Most of these people are acknowledged in the captions, but Michael Jameson, Angeliki Lebesi, George Mylonas, Elisabeth Rhode, and Anthony Snodgrass were particularly helpful.

Finally, I thank the editors and staff of Cornell University Press for their patience and understanding.

WILLIAM R. BIERS

Columbia, Missouri

Preface to the Second Edition

THE FIELD OF GREEK ARCHAEOLOGY, broadly defined, may seem to be conservative and slow moving, but it has undergone major changes since the first edition of *The Archaeology of Greece* appeared, especially in respect to the Bronze Age. This edition brings the information on all areas up to date, reflecting the most recent research, and includes new illustrations—some of new finds, some of improved plans, others of new examples to enhance an explanation or illustrate a point. As in the first edition, the choice of illustrations has been a personal one and will surely not please everyone. I have again tried to cite accessible sources in English in the hope that they may serve as starting points for further research.

New to the second edition are references to *Perseus II*, the interactive electronic data base on Archaic and Classical Greece, published by Yale University Press. A superscript P in a figure caption indicates that the reader can find additional information or illustrations having to do with that particular object, building, or site in *Perseus II*. When more than one illustration of a site or object is provided, the reference appears only in the caption accompanying the first illustration.

I am grateful to the individuals and institutions that provided the illustrations for this edition; they are noted in the individual captions. Special thanks also go to Jeremy Rutter, without whom the rewriting of the early chapters would have been nearly impossible. I have once again bothered colleagues for corrections and suggestions, and it is a pleasure to express my appreciation for their interest and their time. A bald listing of names must suffice: Eugene Borza, Elizabeth Gebhard, Jeffrey Hurwit, Susan Langdon, Stella Miller-Collett, Gullög Nordquist, Erik Østby, Nancy Reed, Joe Shaw, Kathleen Warner Slane, Neel Smith, Jeffrey Soles, Anne Stewart, Tasos Tanoulas, Mary Voyatsis, and Nancy Winter.

W. R. B.

DATES: All dates, unless otherwise indicated, represent years before Christ (B.C.). When a specific date cannot be given, the approximate date is preceded by "c.," for *circa*, about.

MEASUREMENTS: Measurements of length are given in the metric system. A conversion table is given below:

Metric unit	Abbreviation	Metric equivalent	U.S. equivalent
Kilometer	km.	1,000 meters	0.62 miles
Meter	m.	1	39.37 inches
Centimeter	cm.	0.01 meter	0.39 inches

P: A superscript P in a figure caption indicates that more illustrations and perhaps a description of the subject are available in *Perseus II*, the interactive electronic data base on Archaic and Classical Greece published by Yale University Press.

PERIODICALS:

AA	*Archäologischer Anzeiger*
AAA	*Athens Annals of Archaeology*
AD	*Archaiologikon Deltion*
AJA	*American Journal of Archaeology*
Ath. Mitt.	*Mitteilungen des Deutschen Archäologischen Instituts, Athenische Abteilung*
BCH	*Bulletin de correspondance hellénique*
BSA	*Annual of the British School of Archaeology at Athens*
JDI	*Jahrbuch des Deutschen Archäologischen Instituts*
JHS	*Journal of Hellenic Studies*

THE

ARCHAEOLOGY

OF GREECE

1

Archaeology in Greece

ARCHAEOLOGY has been defined as "the scientific study of the material remains of past cultures." There are almost as many kinds of archaeology as of archaeologists, but all basically conform to the general definition. Whether working with Indian mounds in the American midwest or city mounds in the Near East, archaeologists work primarily with the objects or artifacts they uncover, seeking to fit them into the cultural and historical framework of the area. Cultures differ, as does the evidence available to archaeologists in reconstructing them, but certain techniques, especially in excavation, are the same or similar everywhere, for wherever one works, the central goal is to gain knowledge about the human past.

Classical archaeologists—those who deal with the remains of the classical civilizations of Greece and Rome—have one great advantage over those who work in other areas: they have at their command a great wealth of evidence concerning the civilizations with which they are dealing in the writings of the ancients themselves. This great mass of material, from Homer and Hesiod to the early church fathers, has been studied and analyzed by generations of scholars and of course stands at the beginnings of our Western tradition. Thus classical archaeologists begin with much greater knowledge of the society whose artifacts they are uncovering than do those who work with more primitive societies or with cultures that have not left behind such great bodies of literature as have Greece and Rome. This advantage is not available, however, to the archaeologist who specializes in the prehistoric periods of Greek culture, during the Bronze Age and earlier. Archaeology has provided almost all we know about these societies, for they have left few, if any, written records.

It is important to emphasize that an archaeologist is not only someone who actually digs up artifacts from the ground. Only a few positions in the profession, in fact, are limited to the activities of excavating and publishing reports of finds. Most archaeologists teach or hold positions in museums and carry out their research in their spare time or during leaves of absence. This research may or may not include actual digging or fieldwork. The responsibilities of the discipline include the dissemination of knowledge gained through archaeological work. Study and analysis of material from excavations and publication of findings absorb most of the time of any archaeological enterprise. Some archaeologists become experts in particular subjects or in particular areas without having engaged in excavation themselves. Here the realms of the archaeologist and the art historian begin to merge. Some experts in Greek sculpture, for instance, consider themselves to be ancient art historians rather than archaeologists, while scholars whose main interests reside in such artifacts as loom weights or amphora handles consider themselves to be archaeologists. As far as recognition and consideration of changes in the shapes of objects are concerned, either label could apply. The point is that one need not actually dig to be an archaeologist.

Under the general heading of archaeology stand a great number of specialties, all of which add to the overall picture. To such major divisions as painting, sculpture, and architecture one must add numismatics (the study of coins) epigraphy (the study of inscriptions and letter forms), and other, more highly complex and specialized fields: palaeobotany, physical anthropology, and the like.

Since field archaeologists are the most widely known, however, it might be instructive to outline briefly what they do. Their activities can be summarized conveniently as recovery and preservation, study and classification, and publication. The following remarks apply particularly to Greece but are in general representative of all archaeological activity.

Sites to be excavated are generally chosen as a result of careful surveys carried out not only in the traditional way—ground-level inspection for sherds (fragments of pottery) or remains of constructions—but also by such comparatively new techniques as aerial photography and resistivity surveys. Surface survey has recently become an end in itself, particularly for regional studies, and much information has been derived from survey projects that have not been overtly connected with excavations.[1] Once a site is chosen, the money raised, the necessary permission secured, the staff assembled, and the land purchased, the fieldwork begins. Excavators are faced with two problems: removing the earth and debris without endangering the objects within and interpreting the evidence their spades uncover. Much of it appears contradictory and senseless at first. If it is not to remain so, the archaeologist must record, as meticulously as possible, everything that is found.

The importance of careful, even meticulous recording cannot be overstated, because when an area is cleared from top to bottom it is literally destroyed as superimposed features are pulled down to yield access to lower levels. Often it is only at the end of the fieldwork or even years later that what has been found begins to make sense through close study of the records.

In Greece the general practice now is to work with trained local workers, many of them professional excavators, though economic considerations are leading to the use of volunteer excavators to the extent that local conditions allow. The basis of any excavation is stratigraphy, or the study of the arrangement of cultural remains in layers or strata, each covered up and buried by succeeding generations. In cultures that built mainly with such perishable materials as wood and mud brick, continuous rebuilding on the same site, abandonment, destruction, climatic changes, and a dozen other factors allow structures to be buried quite quickly. Upon excavation, the various strata are often easy to identify by their contrasting colors or consistencies, the results of their differing composition. Records of the makeup of each level and everything found there must be kept both horizontally, in such things as ground plans, which can show an area or a building as it is now (actual state plan) or as it was (restored plan), and vertically, as in the theoretical cross section shown in Figure 1.1.

Study of Figure 1.1 will reveal that stratigraphy is not always easy; only with

[1] Archaeological survey is discussed in Colin Renfrew and Paul Bahn, *Archaeology: Theories, Methods, and Practice* (New York, 1991), pp. 61–90; also in Irwin Scollar, *Archaeological Prospecting and Remote Sensing* (Cambridge, 1990), and P. Nick Kardulias, ed., *Beyond the Site: Regional Studies in the Aegean Area* (Lanham, Md., and London, 1994).

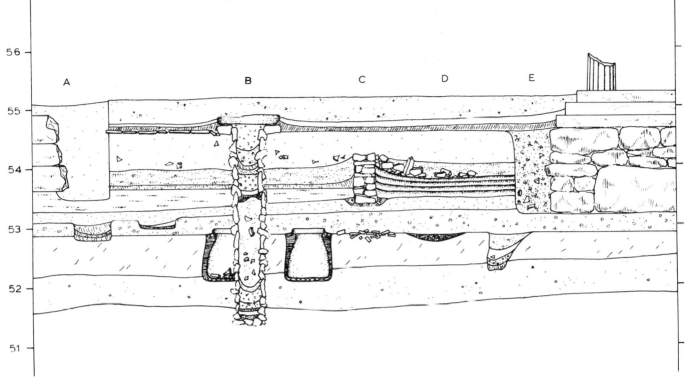

57 — M. ABOVE SEA LEVEL

56 —

A   B   C   D   E

55 —

54 —

53 —

52 —

51 —

experience does one become adept at recognizing what one sees. Layers can disappear into one another or be disturbed by intrusions from above. These intrusions of later artifacts into earlier layers, if not detected, muddle the historical sequences. Thus the modern pit at A in Figure 1.1 has broken through a pavement and destroyed a wall, and the earlier well at B has destroyed a storage vessel deep below its mouth while missing another slightly to the right. In making the trench at E to lay the foundation stones of a building, the construction workers dug down through earlier levels. The softer fill in the trench must be recognized by the excavator and the finds from it kept separate, for they may include objects from the period during which the building was erected, things that were dropped by the workmen or that fell in while the foundation stones were being put in place. The digging part of archaeology is a skill that must be acquired; no one should consider himself an archaeologist until he has undergone the necessary discipline and training.

The archaeologist's responsibility does not end with digging things up and recording the locations of their discovery. Often conservation work must be undertaken to preserve buildings and walls so that, once rid of their protective mantle of earth, they can be consolidated to retard deterioration and be seen by visitors. Buildings may be partially or completely rebuilt along original lines, either to protect them or to permit them to be seen as they once were.

During and particularly after the actual fieldwork, the finds are analyzed. The director must then make the results of the work available to other scholars as one or more contribution to the overall study of the ancient society. During the fieldwork phase the excavation staff normally includes such experts as

1.1 Theoretical stratigraphical cross section: A, modern trench dug by looters; B, well; C, wall, partially collapsed; D, superimposed road levels; E, "footing" trench for foundations. Drawing by John Huffstot.

photographers, artists, architects, draftsmen, cataloguers, restorers, menders, and perhaps numismatists and epigraphers. Each excavation has its particular needs. The work of all of these staff members must be brought together in a statement of the overall results of the fieldwork. This statement can usually be ready for publication by the end of the excavation season, but the detailed analysis of the finds and the placement of the site in the historical and cultural framework of the area may take years. During this phase various experts in the field who may or may not have belonged to the primary excavation staff are called upon. Thus experts in, say, various phases of pottery or minor finds or architecture collaborate. Although the director has the overall responsibility for publishing the results of the work, he is usually not an expert in every phase of it and so must assign material to those who are; some of this work may be assigned to students, who receive valuable training in this way.

One of the principal problems in archaeology is determining the age or date of the buildings and objects that are found. Often a single article found in the right place—for instance, in association with the foundations of a building—can provide at least an approximate date for the building, and then for a whole complex or perhaps even an entire site. In Greece, dates have traditionally been assigned in accordance with the stylistic development of specific classes of material, especially ceramics. The most well-known pottery styles have been so carefully studied that the presence of pottery in an excavation often serves to date the site within a fairly short range. Recent advances in technology have provided such scientific dating methods as radiocarbon and thermoluminescence dating, which lend precision to the dating of prehistoric finds. Although these methods and others like them are being used with increasing frequency in historical archaeology, stylistic chronology in conjunction with known historical dates is still considered the most reliable dating method because of the inherent variation factors of the scientific methods.[2]

Since pottery, then, is the primary time index, excavators must be well acquainted with the pottery of the areas they study. Pottery shapes and decoration change with time. The arrangement of these factors yields relative dates: by its shape and decoration a pot can be seen to stand at the beginning, middle, or end of a known series. Such a stylistic development in the Greek kylix, a drinking cup, is shown in Figure 1.2. It can be seen that the shape clearly changes within the time span as relatively short as one hundred years. The shape, together with knowledge of the development of kylix decoration, allows an expert to place a given kylix within a period of a very few years. The principle can be extended to architecture, as seen in Figure 1.3, which shows the development in shape and proportion of the Doric column over some 250 years. Once a relative chronology has been developed, dates can be assigned to individual objects in the series and then to others related to them. A number of dates in Greek history are known with certainty from historical sources, and thus can provide reference points for a given series. The destruction of the northern city of Olynthos by Philip of Macedon in 348 is one known reference point. Everything found in the excavation of this town should then date before 348. By examining the sherds in a specific level or associated with a given feature, a scholar can assign a reasonably accurate date to that level or feature.

[2] Dating methods in archaeology are discussed in Renfrew and Bahn, *Archaeology*, chap. 4, and in William R. Biers, *Art, Artefacts, and Chronology in Classical Archaeology* (London and New York, 1992).

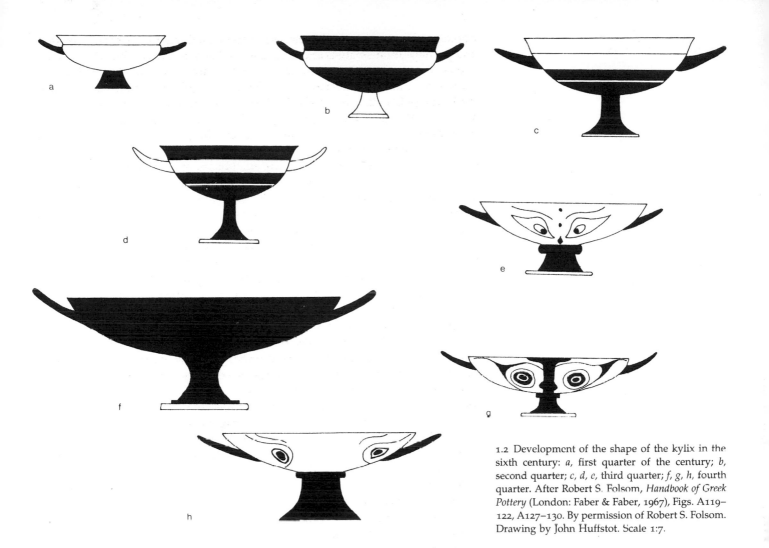

1.2 Development of the shape of the kylix in the sixth century: *a*, first quarter of the century; *b*, second quarter; *c*, *d*, *e*, third quarter; *f*, *g*, *h*, fourth quarter. After Robert S. Folsom, *Handbook of Greek Pottery* (London: Faber & Faber, 1967), Figs. A119–122, A127–130. By permission of Robert S. Folsom. Drawing by John Huffstot. Scale 1:7.

Archaeology in Greece has been affected, if in a somewhat minor way so far, by the great technological and scientific advances of recent years. Archaeologists working at prehistoric sites are enlisting the help of specialists in botany, anthropology, geology, and other disciplines in attempts to discover the total ancient environment. Even excavators of historic sites are taking advantage of modern techniques, which add precision and certainty when used in conjunction with traditional methods. Computer technology is rapidly invading the field of classical archaeology, as it is all areas of modern life, both for recording the day-to-day activity of an excavation and as a tool for analysis of finds. New methods of photography, surveying, technical analysis, and recovery of agricultural remains, such as seeds and grains, are constantly being employed. Theory has also begun to be discussed in the discipline—a relatively new development.[3]

[3] For a survey of the applications of science in archaeology in general, see Patrick E. McGovern, "Science in Archaeology: A Review," *AJA* 99 (1995): 79–142. For the various theories in archaeology, see K. R. Dark, *Theoretical Archaeology* (Ithaca, N.Y., 1995). Also see Stephen L. Dyson, "From New to New Age Archaeology: Archaeological Theory and Classical Archaeology—A 1990s Perspective," *AJA* 97 (1993): 195–206.

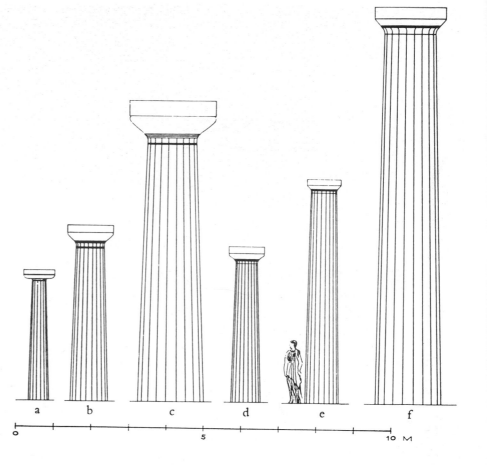

Get out of this class while you still can

Scientific advances have led to new subdisciplines. Underwater archaeology, in its infancy only a relatively short time ago, has already graduated from treasure hunting to careful excavation and recovery of sealed deposits from ancient wrecks and the study of submerged sites.[4] Underwater excavation and aerial photography are combined in Figure 1.4. Photographed by remote control from a balloon, the scene reveals the remains of a temple and other buildings, now underwater, at the site of Porto Cheli in the Peloponnesos.

Materials derived from excavation and survey, as well as Greek art, particularly sculpture and painting, are also being looked at in new ways. Here approaches influenced by such disciplines as anthropology, psychology, sociology, and even literary studies are employed to go beyond conventional explanations of subject matter and decode an image in the context of its time and place.[5]

Archaeology in Greece dates almost from Greek independence from the Turkish Empire in A.D. 1832. From the founding of the foreign schools of archaeology in the nineteenth century until today, foreign scholars have assisted their Greek hosts with investigations all over the country. Certain sites

[4] A vast literature on underwater archaeology has grown up. For a survey see Jeremy N. Green, *Maritime Archaeology: A Technical Handbook* (London and San Diego, 1990).
[5] Two examples of these differing approaches are Claude Berard and others, *City of Images* (Princeton, 1989), and Simon Goldhill and Robin Osborne, eds., *Art and Text in Ancient Greek Culture* (Cambridge, 1994).

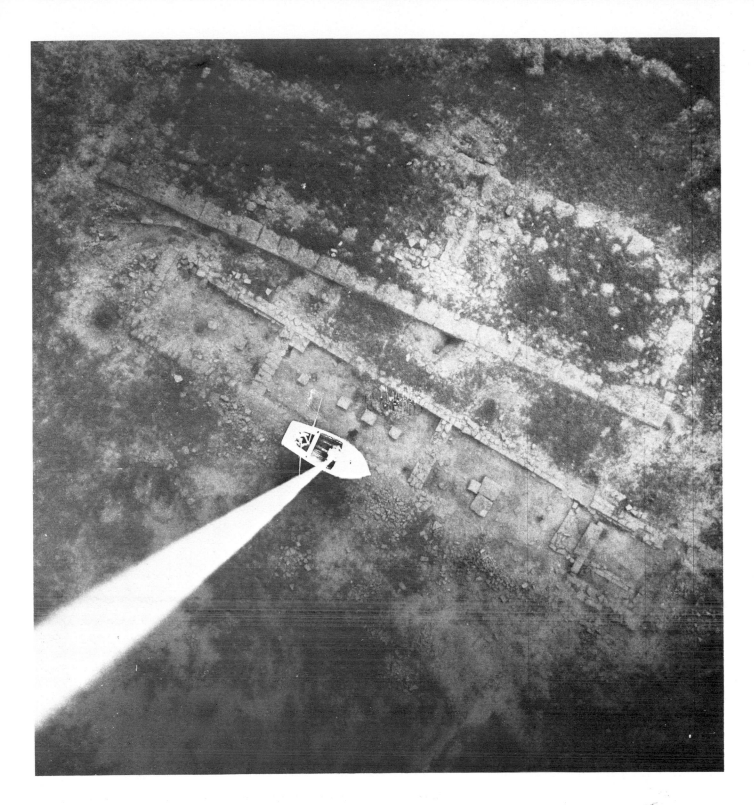

soon became the major responsibilities of individual foreign schools. Archaeology in Greece is truly an international undertaking, in which scholars of all nations have worked together to give the Western world a glimpse of its

1.4 Aerial view of submerged buildings at Porto Cheli. Photo: University of Pennsylvania/Indiana University and the Whittlesey Foundation.

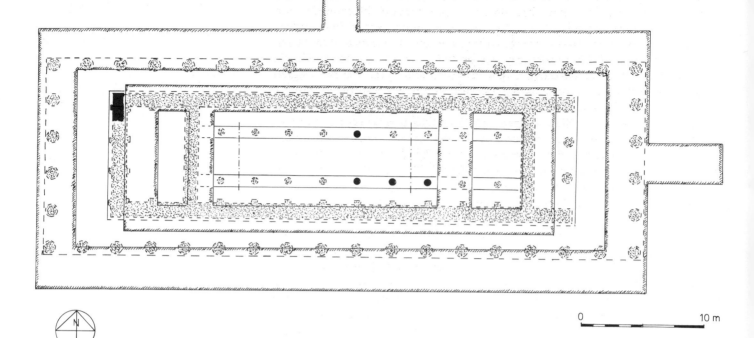

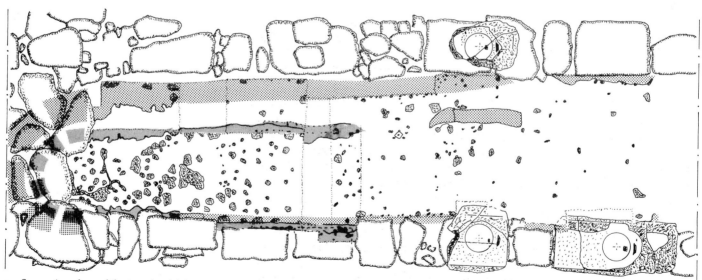

1.5 Successive plans of the temple of Athena Alea at Tegea.ᴾ At the top, the late seventh-century temple (stippled) is superimposed on the outline of the fourth-century temple, which lies above it. Below, the earlier (small gray apsidal shape) and later (larger dotted apsidal shape). Geometric buildings are seen between the outlines of the seventh-century temple they preceded. Courtesy of Erik Østby.

origins. An example of this cooperation is the modern excavation at the sanctuary of Athena Alea at Tegea in the Peloponnesos, the site of the great fourth-century temple described in Chapter 9. Here a project under the aegis of the Norwegian Institute in Athens has staff members from eight countries and funding from three. In other ways, too, this excavation exemplifies modern archaeological work in Greece, particularly in the return to sites that had been dug into in the past. This sanctuary was investigated by successive Greek, German, and French archaeologists between 1880 and 1910. The Norwegian project has changed a lot of what we thought we knew about the sanctuary. Walls that the earlier studies associated with the Byzantine period, for example, have now been identified as part of the archaic temple on the site (see Chapter 6), and two small structures beneath the temple remains (see Chapter 5) have been dated to the Geometric period. The superimposition of remains is a typical occurrence in Greece and elsewhere, at least in major urban areas and sanctuaries. Figure 1.5 shows the four superimposed architectural phases in plan, indicating how they relate to one another.[6]

Archaeology has almost singlehandedly revealed the Greek prehistoric world to modern eyes. Although Homer and the Greek myths were well known, it was through the explorations of such men as Heinrich Schliemann of Germany, Arthur Evans of England, and Carl Blegen of the United States that the several civilizations that flourished in this period were made known to the modern world. This rich and interesting period in Greece appears to have possessed no literature or history (or if it had any, it has completely disappeared), so our knowledge is dependent on what is recovered from the earth. This evidence is not always clear and there are many problems and misunderstandings; any day may see a new discovery that will change our ideas of the period.

The situation is somewhat different in regard to historic Greece. Here, apart from the obvious value of the recovery and study of the monuments of Western art, archaeology makes its major contribution by filling in details and adding to history. Excavations of private houses and residential districts yield evidence of the private lives of individuals, and our knowledge of public life and religion have been enhanced by the excavation of town centers, religious sanctuaries, and cemeteries. The everyday life of the people is being brought back to us in detail that one could not hope to grasp from literary sources. At the same time archaeology has added to our knowledge of the history of ancient Greece to a startling degree. A single example will suffice. In the fifth century the Athenians devised the practice of ostracism, according to which a citizen who was considered dangerous to the state could be banished for a period of ten years upon the vote of his fellow Athenians.[7] Each citizen voted by inscribing on a broken piece of pottery (*ostrakon*) the name of the person he wished to be banished. The excavations in the Athenian agora, or marketplace, and in the Kerameikos Cemetery and the surrounding area outside the city walls to the west, have uncovered some thousands of ostraka bearing the

[6] For the modern excavations at Tegea see Erik Østby, "Recent Excavations in the Sanctuary of Athena Alea at Tegea (1990–1993)," in *Archaeology in the Peloponnese: New Excavations and Research*, ed. K. A. Sheedy, Oxbow Monograph 48 (Oxford, 1994), pp. 39–63.
[7] A most readable account of ostracism and the ostraka can be found in Eugene Vanderpool, "Ostracism at Athens," *Lectures in Memory of Louise Taft Semple*, University of Cincinnati Classical Studies no. 2 (Norman, Okla., 1973), pp. 217–250.

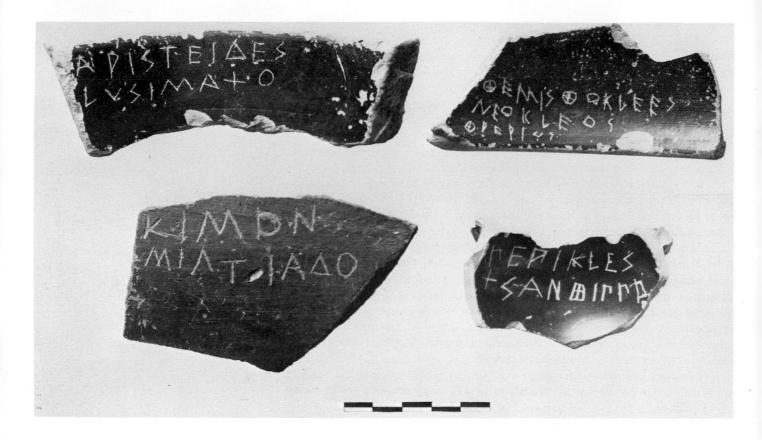

1.6 Ostraka from Athenian agora bearing the names of Aristeides, Themistokles, Kimon, and Perikles. Athens, Agora Museum. Photo: American School of Classical Studies at Athens: Agora Excavations.

names of participants in the various votes that were held throughout the fifth century (Fig. 1.6).

In ancient Greece a citizen's full name consisted of his given name plus that of his father and/or the place where he lived. Here, then, are original historical documents written by the hands of ordinary citizens. They not only provide evidence of a political process, but also yield information on the spelling, pronunciation, grammar, and styles of composition used by fifth-century Athenians. The appearance of names of people well known from the works of ancient authors and of some previously unknown, together with the excavation evidence and even the types of pottery used as ostraka, add to our knowledge of the social and political history of Athens.

Other scattered finds from excavations, such as a helmet dedicated at Olympia by the Athenian general Miltiades, a Spartan shield captured by the Athenians at Sphacteria in 425 and found in the Athenian agora, and a cup inscribed with the name of Phidias from Olympia, bring to life the people of antiquity and momentarily bring us closer to the "romance of archaeology."[8]

[8] An illustration of Miltiades' helmet and a Persian one, part of spoil from the Persians, can be seen in Ludwig Drees, *Olympia* (London, 1968), Plate 52. The cup of Phidias is shown in John Boardman, *Greek Art* (New York, 1964), p. 19, Fig. 9. The Spartan shield may be seen in Homer A. Thompson and R. E. Wycherley, *The Agora of Athens,* Athenian Agora series, vol. 14 (Princeton, 1972), p. 93, Fig. 26.

2

The Minoans

TWO GREAT CIVILIZATIONS flourished in the Greek Bronze Age. The earlier, based on the island of Crete, is known as the Minoan civilization, after the legendary king Minos. The later civilization, based on the Greek mainland, is called in its last phase Mycenaean, after Mycenae, one of its principal cities. For reasons of space, this book can deal only with the height of each civilization. Map 2 indicates the major sites. We shall begin with Crete.

The island of Crete lies southeast of the Greek mainland and is a convenient midpoint between the Near East, particularly Egypt, and Greece. The island measures some 250 kilometers from east to west and its greatest width is some 57 kilometers. It is quite fertile and must have been even more so in antiquity, but the arable land is broken up by mountain ranges. The high central range rises to the great Mount Ida in the center of the island.

The discovery of the great Bronze Age civilization of Crete is the story of Arthur Evans, who first visited the island in A.D. 1894, attracted by engraved seal stones that were known to have come from there. He began to dig at the site of Knossos in 1899 and eventually resurrected not only a great palace but an entire civilization whose existence had been only dimly known from later myths of the Greeks.[1] Evans's successors of many nations have continued to work on Crete to the present day. New and exciting discoveries are constantly being made; the island seems inexhaustible in its cultural richness.

The chronology of the Minoan civilization—or, more precisely, its terminology—is in a state of flux. Evans introduced a three-part division of the time in which it flourished, labeling the periods Early Minoan, Middle Minoan, and Late Minoan. Each of the three periods was subdivided three or more times (EM I, II, III, and so on) and then further subdivided into units indicated by letters of the alphabet (for example, LM IB). As excavation and study have proceeded, this system, based on pottery styles and stratigraphical evidence, has been criticized as too inflexible and partially inaccurate. A new system, first articulated on the basis of finds from the palace at Phaistos and revolving around the building and destruction of the palaces, has come into favor. The system is based on the belief that most of the palaces suffered major damages, perhaps by earthquake, around 1700 or slightly earlier. The palaces were then rebuilt in a more magnificent style, ushering in the great flowering of the civilization. Unfortunately, the chronological sequence is still uncertain. It appears, for instance, that a major period of rebuilding at some of the palaces must be dated later, and that perhaps Knossos was the only real palace in existence in the latter part of what is designated the New Palace period. We shall use the architectural classification, which is given below. It must be noted,

---

[1] For the story of Evans and Cretan civilization, see William A. McDonald and Carol G. Thomas, *The Rediscovery of Mycenaean Civilization*, 2d ed. (Bloomington, Ind., 1990), pp. 111–169.

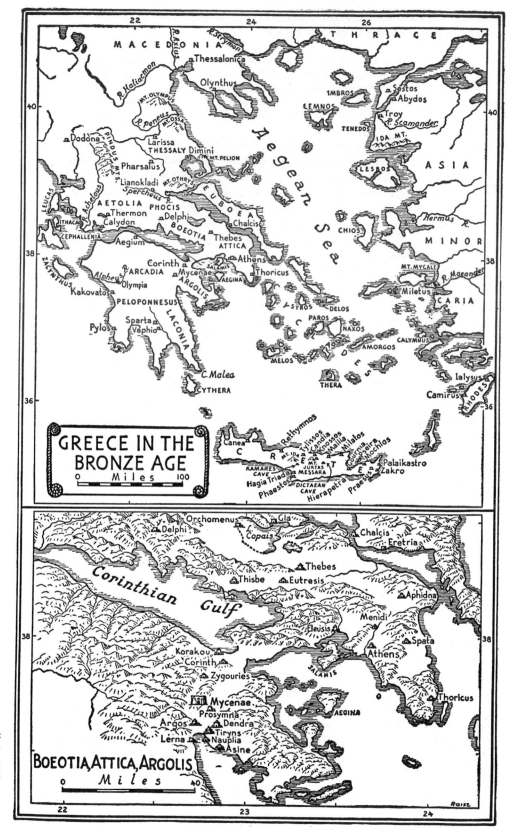

Map 2. Greece in the Bronze Age.
Reprinted with the permission of Simon &
Schuster, Inc., from the Macmillan College
text *Hellenic History*, 5th ed., by George W.
Botsford and Charles A. Robinson, revised
by Donald Kagan. Copyright © 1970
by Macmillan College Publishing Company, Inc.

24

however, that most scholars still retain the basic Early, Middle, and Late classifications when speaking of pottery styles.

Pre-Palace period (Early Minoan I through Middle Minoan IA)   c. 3100–1925
Old Palace period (Middle Minoan IB and II)   c. 1925–1725
New Palace period (Middle Minoan III and Late Minoan I, II, and IIIA1)   c. 1725–1380
Post-Palace period (Late Minoan IIIA2, IIIB, and IIIC)   c. 1380–1000

Humans first arrived in Crete, probably from the Near East, in the seventh millennium (7000–6000), near the beginning of the Neolithic or New Stone Age, a period in which metal was relatively unknown and tools were made of stone. Dwelling in caves and in villages of roughly built houses, they led a fairly settled existence as farmers and herdsmen. Their pottery and crude figurines of naked women of the type known as mother goddesses have been found at various sites in Crete, often below the later Bronze Age remains. Occupation of the sites was apparently continuous; unlike mainland Greece, Crete offers no evidence of a distinctive break in cultural development until the end of the New Palace period.

After many years, perhaps three thousand or more, the first knowledge of metallurgy, together with new types of pottery and other artifacts, initiated the Bronze Age in Crete. Many archaeologists see in the appearance of the new artifacts evidence of the arrival of new peoples from Asia Minor, but it is possible that the changes were self-generated, stimulated by the introduction of metallurgy. The Pre-Palace period or Early Bronze Age is one of rapid developments in the arts and probably of increased overseas contact. By the end of the period, a homogeneous and relatively rich civilization had established itself on the island.

After another thousand years or so, changes are again recorded in artistic styles and made outstandingly evident by the erection of the great palaces. The extent of the foreign influence that may be reflected in these undertakings is disputed; once again, they may simply represent a sudden flowering of culture with the centralization of authority after the long years of development. We know comparatively little about the earlier palaces, for all of them were probably destroyed in the great earthquake or series of earthquakes that was felt throughout the Mediterranean about 1700.[2] They were quickly rebuilt, and with no break in the cultural tradition Minoan civilization entered into its greatest and richest stage, the New Palace period. It is the remains of this period that will be investigated here.

Cretan civilization still holds many mysteries, primarily because of the lack of intelligible written records to give us information on the political and social history of the times. Almost all we know is derived from archaeology, and the physical record is open to differing interpretations. The remains do permit plausible suggestions, however, and the scattered references in later Greek tradition, although difficult, can be used as evidence, but with caution. That the Minoans themselves wrote there can be no doubt. With the rise of the first palaces hieroglyphic scripts came into use; they have been found on seals and other objects. They consist of drawings of common objects and have not been

---

[2] For the archaeology of Crete up to the New Palace period, see L. Vance Watrous, "Review of Aegean Prehistory III: Crete from Earliest Prehistory through the Protopalatial Period," *AJA* 98 (1994): 695–753.

deciphered. Two scripts appear to have been developed out of the hieroglyphic by the process of simplification. They are called linear scripts because the hieroglyphic pictures have become simplified, sketchily rendered signs, with little attention to pictorial representation. One of these scripts, Linear A, was used during the New Palace period and is most commonly found inscribed on clay tablets. It consists of some seventy-five signs and a number of ideograms as a help to the reader. The script is largely syllabic—that is, the signs represent syllables—but it has not yet been deciphered, either. The second script, Linear B, is found mainly at Knossos, on tablets dating from the palace's last days, and on the Greek mainland in contexts dated between c. 1340 and 1190. Probably adapted from Linear A, it employs some eighty-seven signs and a number of ideograms. This script has been translated by Michael Ventris and is recognized by most scholars as an early form of Greek. Although the nature of the script makes translation extremely hazardous, all of the tablets so far found consist of inventories, lists of dedications, and records of deposits and withdrawals from the palace's stores of agricultural produce, military supplies, and the like. Incised on soft clay tablets by scribes as daily records, the lists survive because the tablets were baked in the fire that destroyed the palace. More will be said about the Linear B tablets and the information they convey to us in our discussion of the mainland evidence; suffice it to say here that they give evidence of the last days of Knossos and reflect the administration of Crete under the rule of mainland Mycenaean Greeks.[3]

The impression gained from these various sources is one of a populous, complex, and highly civilized culture. A unique feature of this civilization is the large architectural complex, traditionally called a "palace" and considered to be the living quarters of rulers. As additional large complexes have been discovered, the automatic designation of "palace" has been questioned. It seems clear that at least the larger examples functioned as administrative, ceremonial, manufacturing, and storage centers and thus indicate the existence of one or more central authorities. Knossos was traditionally the primary seat of government. Its great size, two and a half times that of any other palace, and its opulence tend to confirm the tradition. A great number of people were associated with the palaces, which appear to have been similar to small independent cities with their own manufacturing areas, flocks, and so on. No doubt they exacted tribute from the surrounding countryside. There were also towns, isolated farm complexes, hamlets, and larger provincial manors that may have figured in the administrative complex centered in the palaces. It would seem that the island was densely populated in Minoan times.

At the top of the social scale was the king, perhaps called Minos, or a queen-priestess, or both. Courtiers, who lived in palatial villas near the main palaces, and perhaps a priestly caste came next in line. Officials attached to the courts, the military, artisans, farmers, and slaves made up the rest of the population.

The religion of the Minoans is difficult to grasp, for the illustrations of what we consider to be religious scenes are open to many interpretations. Some scholars see religious significance in almost every object depicted in Cretan art and in every anomaly of architecture, and construct a society in which ritual and cult were ubiquitous and all-pervading. How far this approach can be carried is not known, but certain recurring features give us some general outlines. Emphasis appears to be on fertility, with the female principle clearly

---

[3] See Chapter 3.

in the ascendant. The mother goddess, her aspect perhaps varying from place to place, and her worshipers are seen again and again. Certain animals, especially the bull, seem to have great significance in Cretan civilization, as do sacred trees, birds, and a host of other animate and inanimate objects, depending on one's interpretation of the evidence. Various "demons" crowd into religious scenes. Obviously fertility, the death and rebirth of vegetation, and attendant primitive beliefs serve as the basis of Minoan religion.

An often observed fact is the general lack of military architecture in palatial Crete and of military themes in the art of the period. The wealth that the palaces attained would have made them tempting targets for greedy neighbors. Archaeological evidence of widespread Cretan cultural influence in the Aegean, together with finds of Cretan pottery outside Crete and foreign imports within it, combine with the literary tradition of thalassocracy (supremacy on the sea) to suggest that Crete was one of the international powers of its day. Doubts have been expressed as to the date and makeup of this thalassocracy, but some sort of control of the sea fits the facts as we know them, and the spectacular frescoes recently found on the island of Thera (Santorini) could at least support the supposition. Claims of a Cretan empire in the New Palace period and of organized trade may be overblown, in view of the simple conditions of the time, but it is certain that the Minoan civilization was known to its neighbors, for New Kingdom Egyptian tomb paintings depict men in Cretan dress bearing gifts. The extent and nature of contact between the Bronze Age cultures of the eastern Mediterranean are shown to be complex by the apparently Minoan wall paintings that have been found in Egypt and elsewhere (see Fig. 2.22).

This vibrant and unified civilization fell in fire and destruction at the beginning of the fourteenth century B.C. The circumstances, chronology, and reasons for the collapse of the Minoan civilization make one of the most tangled and confused problems in Greek prehistoric archaeology, and one that has heated tempers and spawned a huge bibliography. The arguments swirl around the interpretation of archaeological evidence on the one hand and the development, distribution, and chronology of pottery styles on the other. A detailed examination of the chronological problems involved in the New Palace period would require the remainder of the book. The following synopsis is intended simply to sketch the problem.

Recent excavations and studies on the island of Santorini, ninety-six kilometers north of Crete, have uncovered major buildings buried in volcanic ash and belonging to a Bronze Age settlement with affinities to the art and architecture of that great island. The site was destroyed by an immense volcanic explosion that blew out the center of the island and left it in the sickle shape it has today.

Since the emission of large quantities of ash may be presumed to precede a volcanic eruption, the explosion of the island, or rather its implosion, would have occurred after the fall of ash, and indeed there is some evidence that the inhabitants returned for a time before the final disaster. Most vulcanologists, however, believe the explosion followed the ash fall within a very short time, perhaps only a year. The assumed size of the destruction impressed scholars, and it was postulated that this natural disaster might have had something to do with destruction levels in Crete during the New Palace period.

Since Evans's time, evidence has accumulated that a major catastrophe affected practically all the major sites in Crete at a time when LM IB Marine-style pottery was in use. Destruction took place not only in Crete but throughout the

Aegean, in such places as Rhodes, Kea, and Melos. It is now generally agreed that the Thera destruction took place during an advanced stage of the LM IA ceramic phase on Crete, well before the LM IB devastations of so many Cretan sites. The exact cause of these destructions is still unknown, although invaders from the mainland are still popular culprits.[4]

The difference between the character of Knossos just before its destruction and that of the other Cretan sites was recognized by Evans and received strong corroboration when the Linear B tablets found at the destruction levels were deciphered as an early form of Greek.[5] At this time, especially at Knossos, a number of significant innovations appear, including a new style of pottery, typical of the mainland and christened Palace style on Crete. Also new is the appearance of military themes in paintings and military equipment in graves, new tomb types, and characteristic weapons. These changes are interpreted as indicating the arrival of Mycenaean Greek invaders. This period, known as LM II, and characterized by close connections between the mainland and Crete, has been considered, with a few dissenters, as a chronological period.

The palace of Minos suffered less than the other sites at the end of the period characterized by the use of LM IB pottery. It continued along for sixty or seventy years on a reduced scale under Mycenaean control and then suffered destruction by a native Cretan uprising or perhaps by the Mycenaeans themselves near the beginning of the ceramic phase called Late Minoan IIIA2, c. 1380. This may not have been the final destruction, and many scholars believe that the palace continued to function on some level down into the thirteenth century.

These chronological niceties have been dwelt upon here to demonstrate the fluidity of the field. Our knowledge of what happened after the LM IB destructions on Crete, especially the character of the reoccupation period, is constantly changing. Recent discoveries at Chania in western Crete (including Linear B tablets, one of them written in the same hand as one from Knossos) and in the Phaistos area suggest that there was major regional development beginning in the fourteenth century B.C. At Ayia Triadha and Kommos, west of Phaistos, especially, there is evidence for a major economic center (see Fig. 2.18). The evidence at Knossos for Mycenaean occupation, not yet documented elsewhere, together with the fact that the Mycenaeans immediately step into the vacuum created by the collapse of Crete wherever we can see it abroad, certainly leads one to suspect that, Santorini apart, men must have had a hand in the destruction of Minoan Crete.

The period from the final destruction of Knossos early in the fourteenth century to the end of the Bronze Age in Crete in the tenth is still not completely understood. It appears to have been more prosperous in its earlier years than previously thought, with many of the towns, such as those at Knossos,

[4] For a statement and extensive bibliography on the date of the Thera volcano, see Jack L. Davis, "Review of Aegean Prehistory I: The Islands of the Aegean," *AJA* 96 (1992): 699–756, especially 735–736. The problems surrounding any attempt to assign absolute dates to Aegean chronology are well illustrated in two works that summarize the evidence: Peter Warren and Vronwy Hankey, *Aegean Bronze Age Chronology* (Bristol, 1989); Sturt W. Manning, *The Absolute Chronology of the Aegean Early Bronze Age: Archaeology, Radiocarbon, and History* (Sheffield, 1995). The alternatives for the absolute date of the Thera destruction appear to be either the late seventeenth or late sixteenth century B.C. Each chronology has its adherents.

[5] On the other hand, the decipherment brought doubts as to the date of the destruction, since the only other known tablets were from mainland sites destroyed 200 years later. These doubts were articulated by the English philologist L. R. Palmer, whose reconstruction of events sparked a bitter and divisive scholarly argument that is still continuing.

Phaestos, and Mallia, returning to normal, new settlements founded, and new settlers arriving from the mainland. The culture was now a mixed Minoan-Mycenaean one, with some mainland features.

ART

A unique feature of this culture is its art, which stands in great contrast to that of contemporary civilizations, even though some motifs or technical processes may ultimately have been derived from them. The monumental character of so much of Egyptian art is not to be found here, but Cretan artistic expression found outlets in vivid representations of nature and of religious and court life in many media. Although a certain freedom from restraint can be seen, a number of conventions are also in force, particularly in the frescoes, which are discussed below. An interest in nature is also evident in the decoration of the many minor objects known from the Cretan civilization, which represent some of the finest and most characteristic artistic expressions of the culture. In a sense, Minoan art was primarily a miniature art.

ARCHITECTURE

The great palaces are the characteristic monuments of this civilization. Small cities in themselves, they and their dependencies sprawl in what at first appears to be an unorganized jumble of courtyards, rooms, and narrow corridors. Influences from similar palaces in the Near East have been seen in the ground plans and some details, but the Minoan palace in its final manifestation must be of mainly local inspiration.

Ancient architecture in Greek lands until at least the late Hellenistic period is based on the post-and-lintel system—in other words, verticals and horizontals. It was within this austere formula that Minoan and Mycenaean architects operated. In looking at the ground plans of the known palaces, we must remember that the drawings represent lower or basement floors; usually at least one other story lay above.

Every major palace had a central point of focus, a rectangular paved court around which the palace buildings were grouped (Fig. 2.1). The courts vary in size from those at Knossos and Phaistos, which measure about 49 by 27 meters, to the smallest at Kato Zakro, which is approximately one-third as large. The court, which occupied a considerable portion of the total space in each palace, was obviously important and was the first element laid out by the architect. Apart from being the focus of everyday life in the palace and providing light and warmth in winter to the buildings all around it, the court may have served as the site of processions, religious rituals, and other ceremonial functions, and perhaps of the bull games that we know from artistic representations. Around the court the main rooms of the palace were grouped, including the major living quarters, religious areas, reception and banquet rooms, storerooms, and so on.

Stone blocks cut in set shapes (dressed masonry), rubble, and mud brick were used for wall construction. Often these materials were laid either singly or in combination in a framework of wooden beams laid both vertically and horizontally. The purpose of this half-timbering was to provide strength and at the same time some elasticity to withstand earthquakes. Wood was used extensively in Minoan construction, not only in the walls but also for interior door-

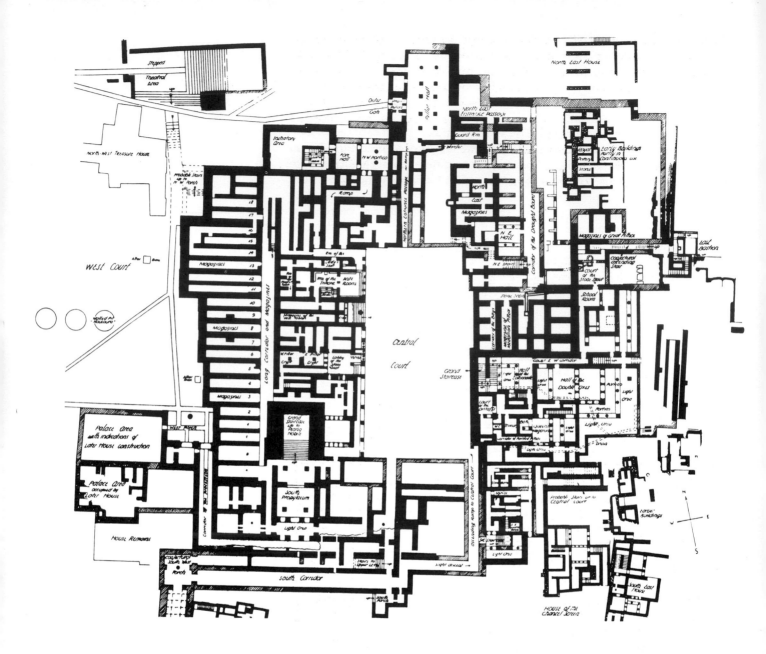

2.1 Ground plan of the palace at Knossos.ᴾ From Arthur Evans, *The Palace of Minos at Knossos*, vol. 4, pt. 1 (London: Macmillan, 1935), p. xxvi. By permission of the trustees of the estate of Sir Arthur Evans.

frames, moldings, sheathings, and columns, which we know from excavation evidence were of wood. Minoan pillars and columns came in a variety of shapes. Columns could be fluted or unfluted; one of the most distinctive types had a downward taper and a swelling upper member, like a later Greek echinus, to cover the transition from the shaft to the horizontal beam that it supported. At Knossos, Ayia Triadha, and a few other palatial establishments, the interior walls of some rooms were plastered and painted with decorative designs or scenes in bright and gay colors above dadoes either of stone or painted to resemble stone. There is even some evidence that the exterior facades may have been painted.

Characteristic features of Minoan architecture, which are encountered not only in the palaces but also in smaller buildings, include rambling flat-roofed complexes containing a number of rooms often entered off center, light wells to provide light and air to lower stories, pier and door partitions (doors set between piers which could be opened singly or in series to increase ventilation or conserve heat), lustral or bathroom areas, hydraulic engineering, porticoes, corridors, and staircases, and such construction materials as wood, dressed masonry, mud brick, rubble, and plaster.

Four large major palaces have been identified and excavated: Knossos, on the north coast of the island and the largest and first discovered (Fig. 2.1); Mallia, some thirty kilometers east of Knossos (Fig. 2.2); Phaistos, on the

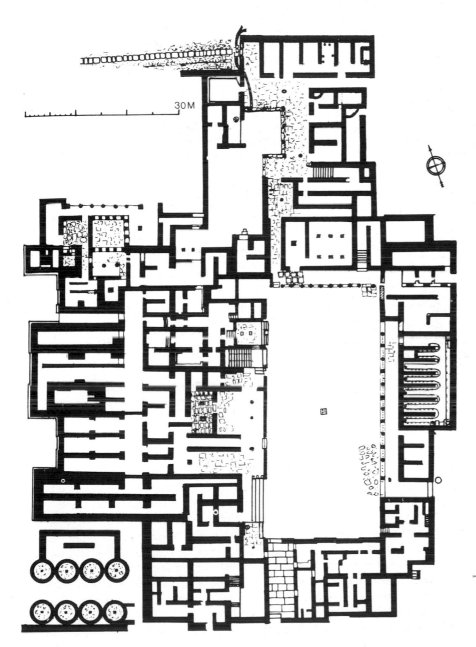

2.2 Plan of the palace at Mallia.ᴾ From James Walter Graham, *The Palaces of Crete*, copyright © 1962 by Princeton University Press (Princeton Paperback, 1969), Fig. 6. Reprinted by permission of Princeton University Press.

31

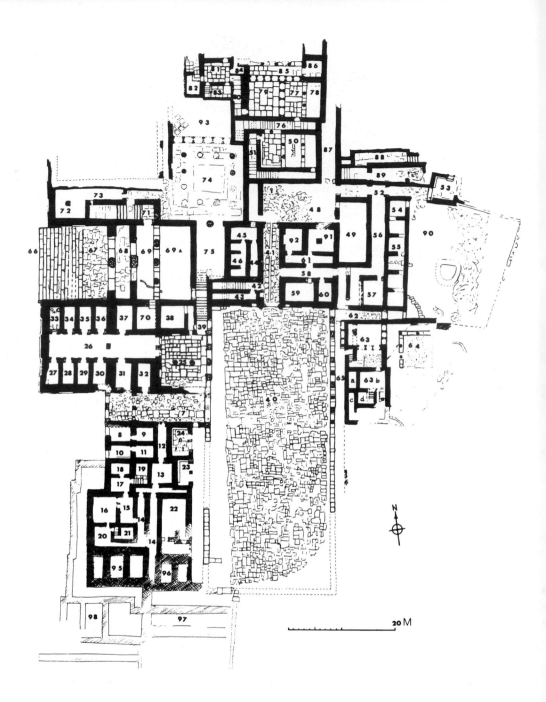

2.3 Plan of the palace at Phaistos.[P] From James Walter Graham, *The Palaces of Crete*, copyright © 1962 by Princeton University Press (Princeton Paperback, 1969), Fig. 4. Reprinted by permission of Princeton University Press.

Mesara Plain to the south (Fig. 2.3); and Kato Zakro, at the east end of the island (Fig. 2.4). A comparison of the ground plans of the palaces shows obvious similarities, especially the central court, although this feature may not be confined to "palaces." Other buildings with central courts have been identified elsewhere on Crete and are being investigated. Knossos can be used as a representative example of the Minoan palace. Arthur Evans, who excavated it in the early years of the twentieth century, also restored parts of it to an extent frowned upon today. The reconstructions, however, have made it easier for the visitor to visualize how the palace once looked. Figure 2.5 shows a recent

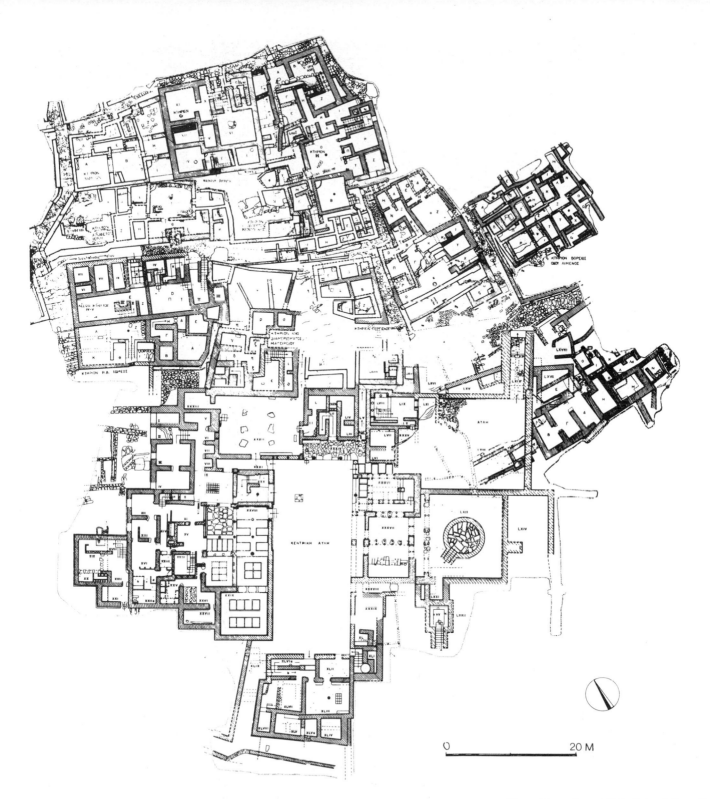

2.4 Plan of the palace at Kato Zakro.[P] From Spyridon Marinatos, *Kreta, Thera, und Das Mykenische Hellas*, 3d ed. (Munich: Hirmer Verlag, 1976), p. 133, Fig. 15. Reproduced by permission.

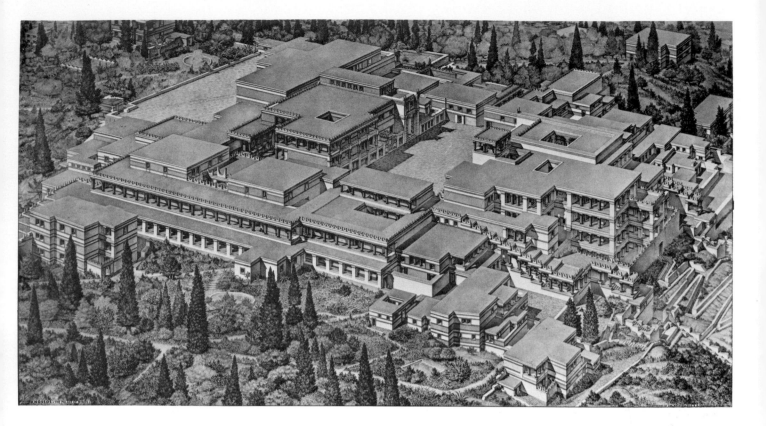

2.5 Reconstruction of the palace at Knossos. Copyright N. Gouvoussis, 1977, Athens, Greece. Reproduced by permission.

attempt at reconstructing the palace which at least conveys its great size and sprawling nature, even if the setting seems rather too lush. Evans started digging at Knossos in 1900 and a year later announced he would need another twelve months; he spent his whole life at it, and excavations by the British School of Archaeology at Athens are still going on there. The palace itself covers some three acres; the whole complex, including the outlying dependencies, covers some six acres. The palace was entered at three rather narrow points, but there is no evidence of fortifications here or at any of the other sites, with the possible exception of a defense wall in the town of Mallia. Minos' legendary rule of the sea is usually given as the main reason for this situation. The visitor now approaches the palace from the west across the paved west court on narrow raised causeways that are thought to have offered a dry route when the rest of the court was flooded after a heavy rain, and may also have had a ceremonial use. The west facade of the palace, which borders the west court on the east, was originally built as part of the first palace and was constructed of large gypsum blocks forming an orthostate (high first course), from the top of which rose the rest of the wall, perhaps made of rubble (Fig. 2.6). The outer and inner faces of the wall were connected by wooden clamps that passed through a filling of rubble. The line of the facade was uneven, some sections projecting farther to the west, and the vertical surfaces were decorated with shallow recesses 12 to 18 centimeters in depth. This surface treatment, which is characteristic of the main west facades of the palaces, was no doubt carried above the orthostate level into the upper portions of the walls. The projection of sections of wall has been variously explained as an aesthetic device, as an element inherited from earlier periods when buildings

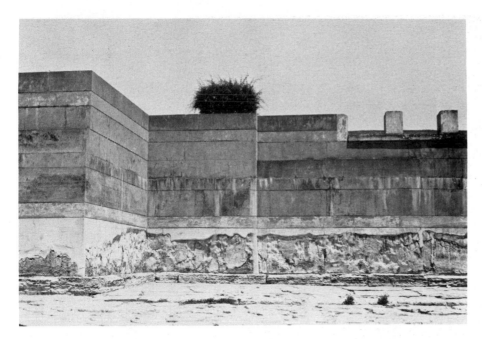

2.6 West facade of the palace at Knossos, partially reconstructed by Arthur Evans. Photo: William R. Biers.

were constructed of less durable materials, as a structural necessity to avoid long straight stretches, and as a function of the varying importance of the architectural units themselves. The niches have also been thought to indicate the locations of windows in upper stories.

The raised walkway led to a porch whose roof was held up by a single massive column, perhaps 7.6 meters high and almost 1.2 meters in diameter, whose raised plinth (base) is still preserved. The use of a single column placed in the center of the opening rather than two columns, one on either side, was a peculiarity of Minoan architecture. The east wall of this propylon, or porch, bore a painted fresco depicting a bull-vaulting scene and opened to a corridor whose walls were decorated with life-sized frescoes of a procession. This passage once led into the central court, joining an elaborate processional entrance through which one entered the palace from the south after passing over the valley on a raised bridge. A short passageway could alternately carry the visitor to a large flight of steps that led to the upper rooms of the west wing.

The basement level of the west wing of the palace contained two sets of rooms connected by a long north-south corridor. Those on the west, immediately behind the west facade, were long and narrow and were used for storage of the wealth of the palace (Fig. 2.7). Similar storerooms are found in most of the other palaces. Rectangular boxes were set into the floors of these rooms for the storage of valuables; against the walls on either side stood great storage jars, or pithoi, almost two meters high, which held olive oil and other agricultural products. The total capacity of these magazines may have been as much as 60,000 gallons.[6] To the east of the central corridor on the lower level lay a series of cult rooms that will be discussed in relation to the central court. Features of the construction of this lower area, especially the thickening of its walls and heavy pier foundations, indicate the existence of an upper story containing large rooms, probably banquet and state reception chambers, which

[6] J. Walter Graham, *Minoan Crete* (Athens, n.d.), p. 21.

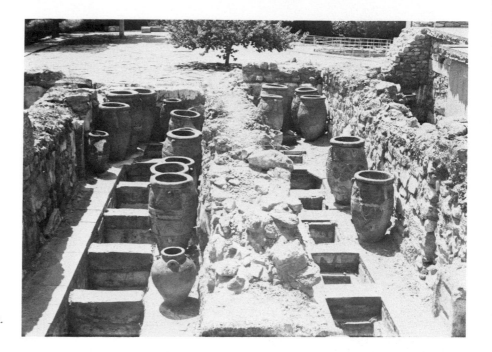

2.7 West storerooms at Knossos. Photo: William R. Biers.

must have been very grand indeed and highly decorated. Except for some furnishings and decorations that were recovered from the basements below, these rooms have vanished. They were approached by two broad staircases, one certainly leading up from the central court and the other probably located behind a large propylon on the south which was approached through the procession corridor already mentioned.

The great courtyard is rectangular, measuring some 49 by 27 meters and oriented north-south, as are all the central courts. It was originally paved and could be left directly, off center, to the north and the south. The north exit is by means of a narrow ramp that was bordered at an upper level by two colonnades whose back walls bore great charging bulls in painted plaster relief. Figure 2.8 shows a reconstruction of this area as it is thought to have appeared in Minoan times; Figure 2.9 shows it as it appears today, partially reconstructed. The ramp led down through a large rectangular building containing two rows of pillars and then turned west to meet a road that led from the coast. This Royal Road, as Evans called it, has a narrow raised causeway similar to the one in the west court and terminates in an open paved area flanked on the east by a flight of low flat steps and on the south by another but smaller flight. At the end of this flight on the east and facing the larger flight is a rectangular podium constructed of squared masonry (Fig. 2.10). Evans interpreted this area as a "theatral" area, where sacred dances or other activities took place under the eyes of the rulers, seated on the podium.

The courtyard is bounded on the west by a series of rooms considered to be of cult character. A reconstruction of the facade of this part of the palace is shown in Figure 2.11. A conspicuous feature of this facade is the great staircase that gives access to the state apartments on the upper floor. A wooden column on a round base stands in typical Minoan fashion right in the middle of the flight of stairs. To the right, or north, a simple partitioned entrance leads down a short flight of steps to a room whose walls are lined with benches. Beyond

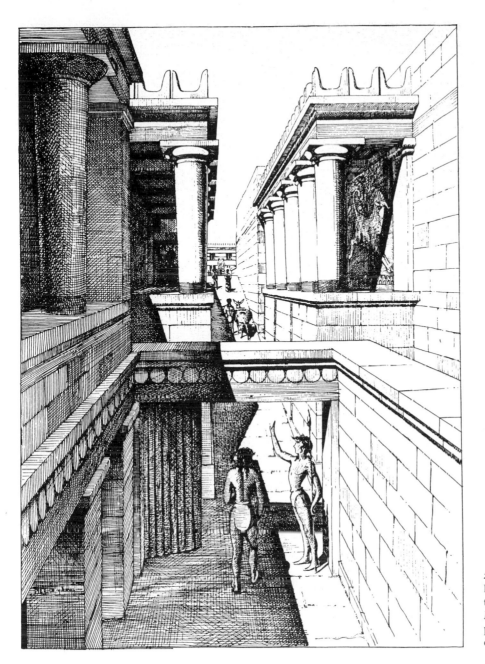

2.8 The ramp leading to the central court at Knossos, with bull relief, as it appeared in Minoan times. From Arthur Evans, *The Palace of Minos at Knossos*, vol. 4, pt. 1 (London: Macmillan, 1935), p. 9, Fig. 3. By permission of the trustees of the estate of Sir Arthur Evans.

this room is the "throne room," another room with benches built around the walls but with the central position on the north wall occupied by a high-backed carved stone seat, the "throne" (Fig. 2.12). On the wall to the right and left of the throne, two painted heraldic griffons symbolically guarded the occupant of the seat. The person who actually sat on the "oldest throne in Europe" is not known, but it may have been a priestess or queen and the complex may have been a shrine rather than a throne room, which, if it existed, is more likely to have been on an upper floor. Before the seat a sunken rectangular chamber, approached by a short flight of steps and cut off from the throne room by a parapet bearing a single column, was termed a "lustral area" by Evans, indicat-

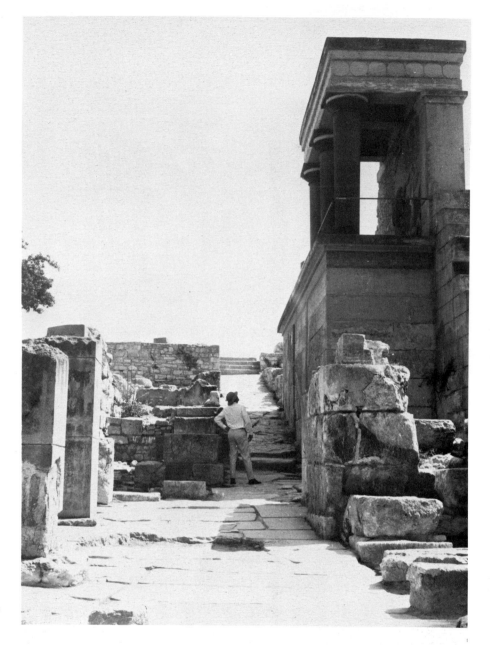

2.9 The north ramp at Knossos as it appears today.
Photo: William R. Biers.

ing some cult purpose, placed as it is in the religious area of the palace. Similar constructions are known elsewhere in Minoan architecture; some, especially those located in the living quarters, were simply bathing areas.

On the other side of the staircase the foundations of a shrine facing the central court were found. Its upper portion is restored on the basis of more or less contemporary frescoes, especially the Grandstand fresco (see Fig. 2.24). Behind the facade lies a suite of rooms in which cult finds, including the faience snake goddesses, were found (see Figs. 2.43 and 2.44). These finds, together with small rooms containing pillars on which liquid offerings were poured, indicated the religious nature of the area.

The actual living quarters for the principal inhabitants of the palace are on

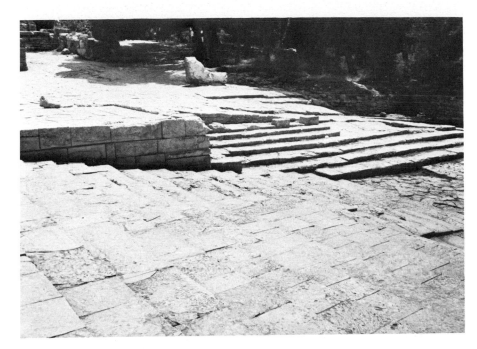

2.10 Theatral area at Knossos, from the northeast. The podium is at the left. Photo: William R. Biers.

2.11 The west side of the central court at Knossos as reconstructed by Thomas Phanourakis. Photo: Ekdotike Athenon S. A.

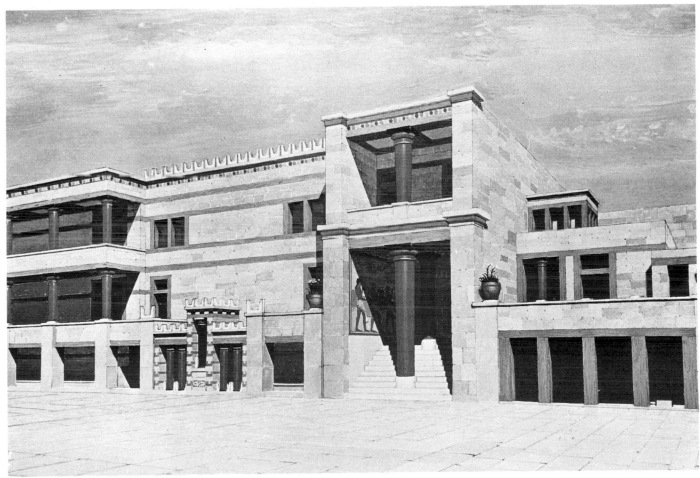

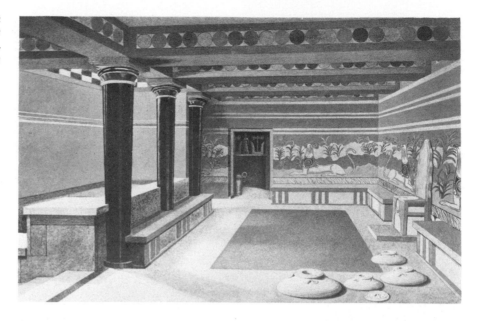

2.12 Reconstruction of the throne room at Knossos. From Arthur Evans, *The Palace of Minos at Knossos*, vol. 4, pt. 2 (London: Macmillan, 1935), Plate 33. By permission of the trustees of the estate of Sir Arthur Evans.

the east side of the central court. Here the rooms have actually been cut into the slope of the low hill on which the palace stands, so that the ground level of this residential quarter is below the level of the central court. On this side the palace was at least three stories high and may have been even taller. A monumental staircase in two sections illuminated by a light well leads down from the central court to residential suites. This staircase was found well preserved and has been restored on good evidence (Fig. 2.13). The typical tapered Minoan columns with their rounded capitals and red-and-black color scheme have been restored on the basis of wall paintings. The staircase opens to a corridor

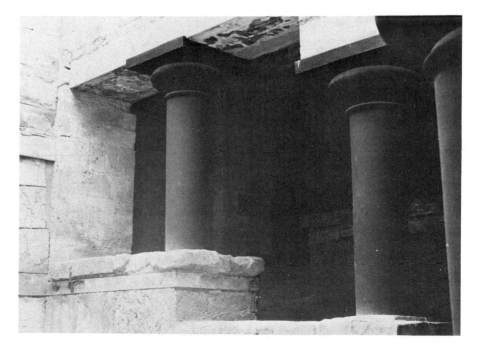

2.13 Staircase in the residential quarter at Knossos. Photo: William R. Biers.

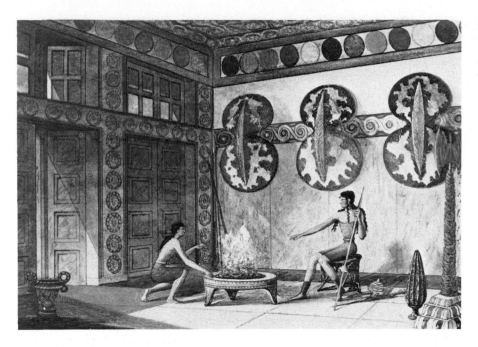

2.14 Reconstruction of the east end of the Hall of the Double Axes at Knossos. From Arthur Evans, *The Palace of Minos at Knossos*, vol. 3 (London: Macmillan, 1930), Plate 24. By permission of the trustees of the estate of Sir Arthur Evans.

that runs along beside a large hall called by Evans the Hall of the Double Axes, after the design carved on the walls of the light well at the west end (Fig. 2.14). The room, which must have been one of the principal living rooms of the domestic quarter, had a system of pier and door partitions and opened onto a portico that perhaps faced a private garden. Portable braziers were commonly used for heat during the winter, but it is possible that the Hall of the Double Axes was in use only during the summer months. A suite of rooms above the hall and entered by a small staircase leading from it would have been warmer in winter, and there is evidence that such rooms existed, seemingly similar in plan to the area below them. Low pedestals against the walls of the Hall of the Double Axes perhaps supported wooden thrones. The walls were plastered and painted above a high dado constructed of thin slabs of gypsum. Much of the painted decoration in the domestic quarters belongs to the latest periods of the palace, the period of Mycenaean influence; such influence can also be seen in the painted bull's-hide shields that adorned the walls in this wing.

Next to the Hall of the Double Axes is a smaller apartment, lighted by another light well and restored as containing the famous Dolphin fresco (Fig. 2.15). Evans considered this to be the queen's apartment, but this designation is conjectural. A small room, separated from the main area by a parapet that bore a fluted column, was called a bathroom by Evans. He restored a bathtub here, though it was not actually found in place but nearby.

Near the small hall and connected with it by a narrow corridor, a tiny room contains a privy: a wooden seat apparently covered an opening into a drain. Such sanitary arrangements were relatively common in Minoan Crete, though nothing similar appeared in the Western world until well over a thousand years later. In general, the Minoans were highly skilled in hydraulic engineering and the palace was well provided with drains, which ran beneath it and chiefly drained water away from the numerous light wells. The rest of the

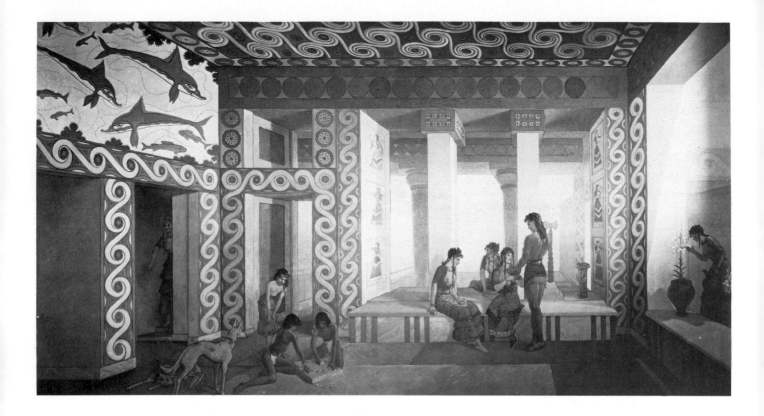

2.15 Reconstruction of the queen's apartment at Knossos, with Dolphin fresco. Mural by Sylvia Hahn. Photo: Royal Ontario Museum, Toronto.

palace is in fragmentary condition, but it is known that it contained more storerooms, workrooms, and other areas.

In the other palaces, the same general divisions into cult complexes, domestic quarters, storage areas, and so on are to be found, though occasionally grouped differently than in the Palace of Minos. The characteristics of Minoan architecture that have been outlined here are repeated in the many smaller houses that have been found, both in association with the major palaces and set apart as private homes. A plan of one of these buildings, House Δa at Mallia, is shown in Figure 2.16. Here we find a hall, a bathroom, light wells—in fact, all the characteristic features of the palaces on the smaller scale of a private house.

A few examples of even more modest dwellings exist, and even an almost completely excavated town, Gournia, east of Mallia (Fig. 2.17). This little town covers a small hill and consists of paved, narrow, often stepped streets bordered by numerous small and simple houses of irregular plan. Excavations indicate that this small village was the home of peasants who engaged in farming, fishing, and simple crafts. A small palace existed near the top of the hill, perhaps an indication that this site was the center of an independent political entity.[7]

New types of buildings are also being identified. At Kommos, southwest of Phaistos on the south coast, excavators recently found a rectangular building divided into six wide galleries, open to the seashore, which have been interpreted as having been used to house ships during the nonsailing months of the winter (Fig. 2.18). This structure was built about the same time as a large

[7] Jeffrey S. Soles, "The Gournia Palace," AJA 95 (1991): 17–78.

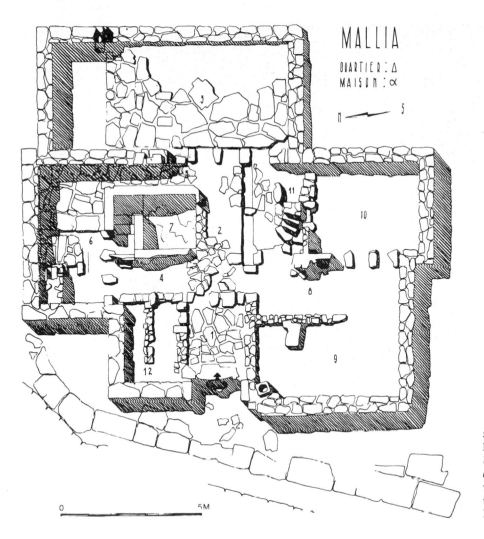

MALLIA
QUARTIER : Δ
MAISON : α

2.16 Actual state plan of house Δα at Mallia. From Pierre Demargne and Hubert Gallet de Santerre, *Fouilles exécutées à Mallia: Exploration des maisons et quartiers d'habitation* (1921–1948), Études Crétoises, vol. 9, no. 1 (Paris: Librairie Orientaliste Paul Geuthner, 1953), Plate 63. By permission of the Ecole Française d'Archéologie, Athens.

rectangular building and stoa at Ayia Triadha and is part of the new evidence for regional activity in the Post-Palace period.[8]

Minoan burial practices were varied but generally of a communal nature. In the Mesara Plain circular stone tombs built aboveground in the Pre-Palatial period were still used in the later periods, and burials in rock-cut chambers, sometimes in pithoi or oval larnakes (bathtub-shaped containers), are known. A few monumental royal tombs associated with cult places have been found, but such tombs are not common.[9]

PAINTING

Reconstructions of the interior rooms of the palace of Minos at Knossos show them to have been highly decorated. Above the stone dadoes the walls were

[8] For the new building at Kommos, see Joseph W. Shaw and Maria C. Shaw, "Excavations at Kommos (Crete) during 1986–1992," *Hesperia* 62 (1993): 129–190, especially 185–188.
[9] A general outline of Minoan burial customs in the context of the Bronze Age in general is found in Oliver Dickinson, *The Aegean Bronze Age* (Cambridge, 1994), pp. 212–220.

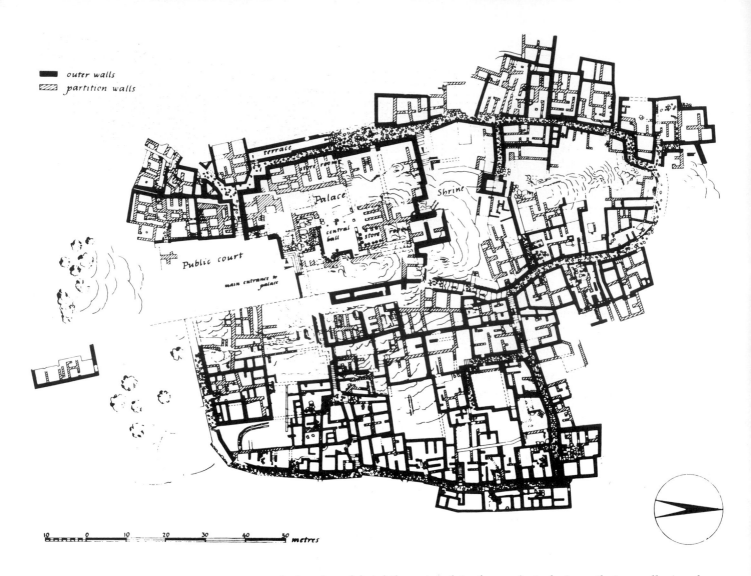

outer walls
partition walls

terrace

Palace

Shrine

central
hall

P
store

Public court

main entrance to
palace

10   0   10   20   30   40   50 metres

2.17 Plan of Gournia[P] at the beginning of the Late Minoan period, c. 1500. From Sinclair Hood, *The Home of the Heroes: The Aegean before the Greeks* (New York: McGraw-Hill, 1967), p. 84, Fig. 69. By permission of Thames & Hudson Ltd.

plastered and brightly painted in fresco (a technique that usually involves brushing natural earth colors on wet plaster; much painting at Knossos was done after the wall had dried).[10] In Minoan paintings, spontaneity and love of life are expressed in bright colors. They are naturalistic but the artist was not afraid of changing colors or distorting natural shapes in order to convey feeling or emotion. Many of the frescoes exhibit a quick, sketchy technique that forced the artist to concentrate on the particular parts of the picture that were most important to him. This selective detail can be seen in such fragments as La Parisienne, which dates to the last palace and is probably a divinity, in which the outline of the face, the red lips, and the great eye are heavily emphasized while the ear is left without delineation (Fig. 2.19).

Evidence of solid-color wall painting, especially in terra cotta red, goes back to the Pre-Palace period; figured scenes are associated only with the palaces

[10] Technique is discussed in chap. 2 of Sara A. Immerwahr, *Aegean Painting in the Bronze Age* (University Park, Pa., 1989), which is a good survey of the art of painting in the Bronze Age. Also useful, but shorter, is the coverage in Sinclair Hood, *The Arts in Prehistoric Greece* (Harmondsworth, 1978), pp. 47–87.

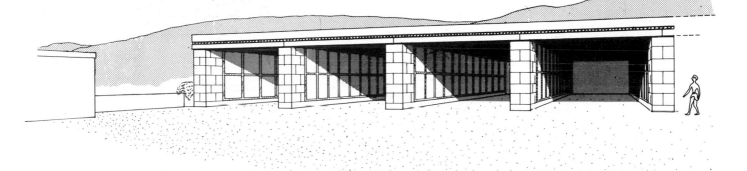

2.18 The view from the seashore looking east at LM III Building P at Kommos. Four of the six galleries are shown. Drawing courtesy of Joseph W. Shaw.

and mostly with Knossos, although a few examples have come from a site in the south, Ayia Triadha, and from one or two other sites on Crete. Phylakopi on Melos has produced one famous example, known as the Flying Fish fresco, and the buried city of Thera is producing frescoes of astonishing originality.

Paintings found on Crete vary in size from life-sized figures to miniature frescoes in which the figures are quite small. Floors may also have been painted; it has been suggested that the famous Dolphin fresco from Evans's queen's apartment at Knossos originally may have been on the floor of an upper room. The fire that destroyed Knossos caused upper stories to fall into basements, hopelessly mixing remains from all the rooms in one giant pile. Excavators are thus faced with an extremely arduous task when they attempt to piece together the original compositions, and once they have succeeded in reassembling a frescoed surface, it is by no means certain where in the building the fresco once appeared.

The Flying Fish fresco (Fig. 2.20) represents one of the two main categories of subjects illustrated in the frescoes, scenes from nature. Here flying fish in blue, white, and yellow swim through water in which seaweed floats. The fish appear to swoop through the sea with their winglike fins. The borders of the picture consist of odd shapes unusually colored—Minoan free-form rocks meant to represent the bottom of the sea. Scattered here and there are multicolored egg-shaped objects, perhaps pebbles. The use of color and the mixture of realistic and impressionistic renderings are typical of Minoan nature scenes.

Scenes from Minoan court and religious life make up the second category of themes in Minoan painting. The procession fresco from the entrance to the south corridor at Knossos has already been mentioned. Here life-sized figures carrying ritual objects approach a central female figure. Although badly preserved, the procession scene can be seen to owe something to Egypt, where such scenes were common. Bull-vaulting scenes were numerous at Knossos, and the one in Figure 2.21 was part of a frieze of such scenes that decorated a single room. In a sense it is representative of all of them, combining as it does observation of nature and a probable court and religious ritual. The great bull is shown in full charge with all four feet off the ground and the body fully stretched into a flying gallop, an artistic convention to indicate the speed and fury of the animal's charge. A closer examination shows that the artist has further distorted the bull's shape to emphasize its power, especially in the neck

45

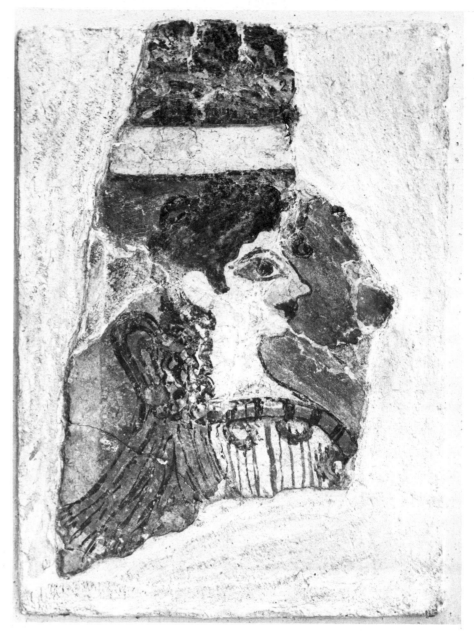

2.19 La Parisienne, Knossos. Heraklion Museum, Crete. Photo: Alison Frantz.

and shoulders, which are very thick in comparison with the stubby legs. The bull is painted more or less naturalistically in brown and white, while the human figures, large in relation to the animal to emphasize their importance, are painted white and red. The use of red for men and white for women is generally thought, on the basis of Egyptian usage, to be another Minoan convention, and it leads to the suggestion that women dressed as men took part in the bull games. They are shown in profile but again the artist has distorted for effect. The figure over the bull's back at first glance seems to be in a perfectly natural position. It is only on close examination that the physical impossibility of the pose can be seen. The decorative border of overlapping varicolored ovals

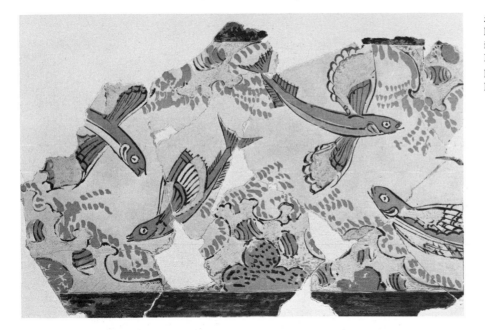

2.20 Watercolor of the Flying Fish fresco at Phylakopi. From Robert Bosanquet, "The Wall Paintings," in *Excavations at Phylakopi*, Society for the Promotion of Hellenic Studies, Supplementary Paper no. 4 (London: Macmillan, 1904), Plate 3. By permission of Charles Bosanquet.

2.21 Bull-vaulting fresco at Knossos. Heraklion Museum, Crete. Photo: Alison Frantz.

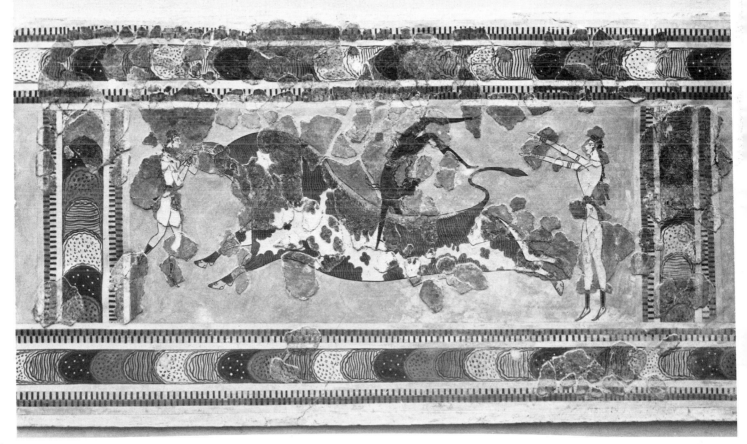

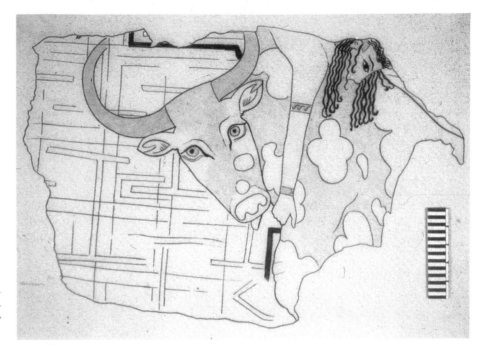

2.22 A detail of a fresco fragment from Tell el-Dab'a in Egypt. Copyright Manfred Bietak, Austrian Archaeological Institute, Cairo. Drawing by L. P. Brock. Courtesy of Manfred Bietak.

is thought to represent Minoan free-form rendering of a rocky landscape, similar to the sea bottom in the Flying Fish fresco. That the dangerous bull sports took place elsewhere than within the confines of the central court has been suggested, and this border is cited to support the supposition.

Excavations in the Nile Delta in Egypt are continuing to produce fragments of frescoes, painted in Minoan style and technique and showing some typical Minoan themes, including bull vaulting. The fragment shown in Figure 2.22 depicts a leaper or grappler on the back of a bull, whose head is turned toward the viewer. The figures are shown against a distinctive background that can be paralleled at Knossos, where of course representations of bulls and bull "games" are plentiful. The significance of these finds, which may indicate close connections between the Minoans and Egyptians at one time, is being studied.

One miniature fresco from the palace shows female figures apparently dancing while a crowd of male figures, impressionistically shown with white splotches for eyes and necklaces, occupy the background (Fig. 2.23). Crossing the area are long narrow constructions that Evans called walls but which remind one of the raised causeways, especially those in the theatral area. Another fresco, known as the Grandstand fresco, shows a crowd of people seated around a tripartite shrine whose elevation in the painting agrees well enough with the remains found to allow it to be restored next to the staircase on the west side of the central court (Fig. 2.24).

The majority of the frescoes from Knossos were painted on flat surfaces, but a few experiments were made with surfaces raised here and there by added plaster. This concept is similar to that of relief figures, fragments of which were found in the palace. The charging bull that flanked the north corridor entrance (to the right in Fig. 2.8) and parts of other large-scale figures found in the palace are essentially relief frescoes.

A final example of Cretan frescoes is the Ayia Triadha sarcophagus, found in a tomb at that site and dated at the end of the New Palace period. The lime-

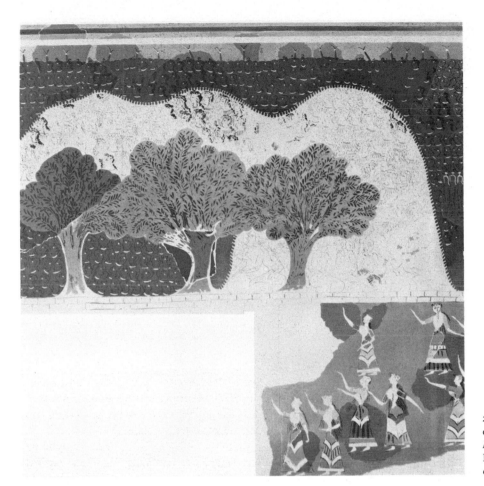

2.23 Portion of a reconstruction of the Dance fresco at Knossos. From Arthur Evans, *The Palace of Minos at Knossos*, vol. 3 (London: Macmillan, 1930), Plate 18. By permission of the trustees of the estate of Sir Arthur Evans.

stone sarcophagus was covered with a layer of plaster on which seemingly religious scenes were painted, but interpretation is difficult in the present state of knowledge. Stylistically, the painting shows some parallels in its subsidiary decoration to the latest period at Knossos and thus to mainland Greece, but Cretan elements are of course predominant. On one side (Fig. 2.25) a bull is trussed on a table as a sacrifice, his blood pouring into a container that may be a conical rhyton set into the floor below the table while a priestess(?) dressed in an animal skin worships in front of an altar and a man plays double flutes in the background. The other side (Fig. 2.26) shows a liquid being poured into a bowl between two stands bearing double axes while three men carry models of two bulls and a boat(?) to a shrouded figure that stands in front of a building. The most recent interpretation has the figure as the spirit of the deceased watching the ceremonies designed to speed his way to the underworld.[11] The bull sacrifice on the other side would then also be part of funerary practice. An exciting discovery supports the interpretation as far as the sacrifice is concerned. A bull's skull was found built into the blocking door of a side chamber of a tomb dated to about the same period at Arkhanes.[12] A bull sacrifice in connection with a funerary cult is thus very likely.

[11] An attempt to interpret these scenes is Charlotte Long, *The Ayia Triadha Sarcophagus*, Studies in Mediterranean Archaeology 41 (Gothenburg, 1974).
[12] Efi and John A. Sakellarakis, *Archanes* (Athens, 1991).

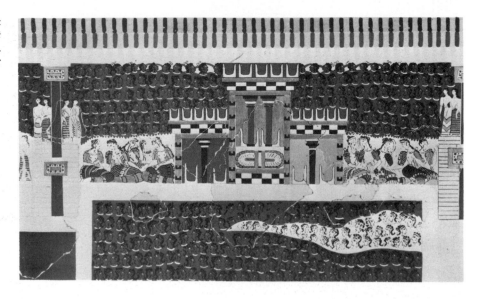

2.24 Reconstruction of the Grandstand fresco at Knossos. From Arthur Evans, *The Palace of Minos at Knossos*, vol. 3 (London: Macmillan, 1930), Plate 16. By permission of the trustees of the estate of Sir Arthur Evans.

2.25 Bull sacrifice, Ayia Triadha[P] sarcophagus. Heraklion Museum, Crete. Photo: Alison Frantz.

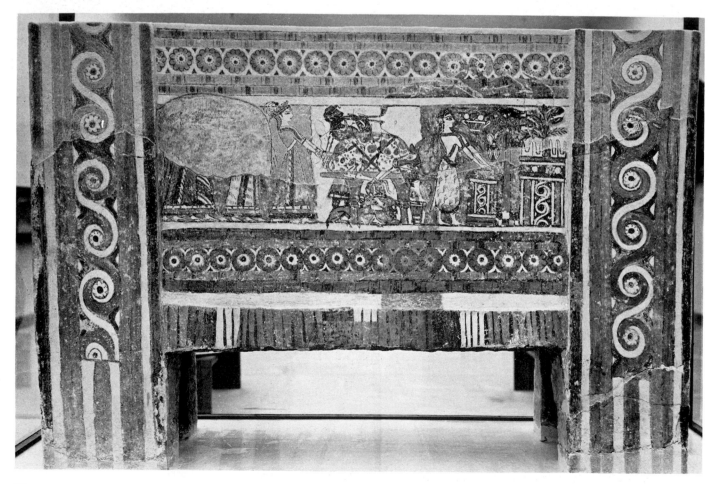

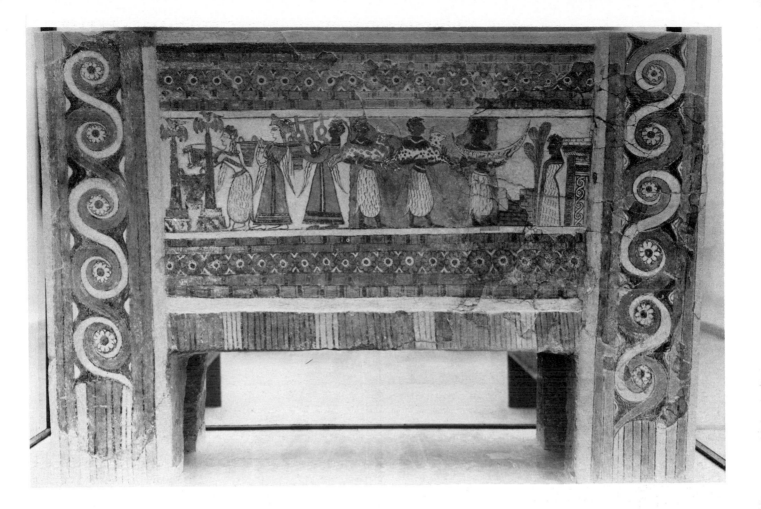

2.26 Procession, Ayia Triadha sarcophagus. Heraklion Museum, Crete. Photo: Alison Frantz.

The finds from the site of Thera, on modern Santorini, continue to provide information about what must have been a prosperous settlement. Recent and continuing excavations by the Greek Archaeological Service have recovered much of the settlement from the debris of the eruption. Some of the buildings, which are preserved to a height of several stories, were painted with frescoes, technically similar to and influenced by Crete but astonishingly original and vibrant. The same love of nature is to be seen on Thera, sometimes in overpowering colors, as in the room of the blue monkeys (Fig. 2.27). Human figures are also to be found, most often three-fourths life size. The boxing children of Figure 2.28 must be the earliest representation of childish anatomy in Western art and was not paralleled until Hellenistic times. Comparison of the treatment of the features of a brightly attired woman from Thera (Color Plate 1, following p. 96) with that of La Parisienne (Fig. 2.19) shows interesting similarities and contrasts. Contrasts abound, too, among Thera's many frescoes. Two women, with differing hair styles, gather crocuses on the east wall of a house known as Xeste 3 (Color Plate 2); the north wall shows an enthroned female figure attended by a griffin and a blue monkey, probably an indication that the women are engaged in an act that can be interpreted as religious. An extraordinary find in another house, known as the West House, is a miniature painting showing a landscape that encompasses four cities, a sea battle(?), and a great

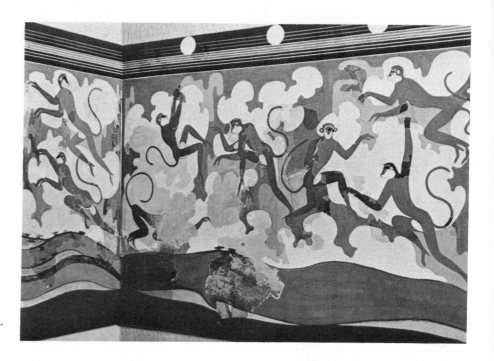

2.27 Room of the monkeys at Thera. Photo: National Archaeological Museum, Athens.

fleet of ships (Fig. 2.29). The interpretation of the subject matter of these newly discovered frescoes of Thera will engage scholars for years to come.[13]

POTTERY

The most common find in any archaeological excavation is pottery, and in such a period as the Bronze Age, which left few written records, it forms the most important source of evidence for chronology and movements of peoples as well as for the civilization that produced it. Minoan pottery attained a very high standard in both fabric and decoration and is found throughout the eastern Mediterranean world in the contexts of the years preceding the great destructions.[14] The New Palace period saw a number of styles of painting on pottery; it is the relationship of these changing styles to one another that forms the basis of our understanding of the chronology of the period.

Following the destruction of approximately 1700 B.C., pottery styles underwent a change, from the bright polychrome designs of the previous period,

[13] On the Thera frescoes see Immerwahr, *Aegean Painting in the Bronze Age*; Lyvia Morgan, *The Miniature Wall Paintings of Thera* (Cambridge, 1988); Christos Doumas, *The Wall-Paintings of Thera* (Athens, 1992). For a largely religious interpretation of the frescoes see Nanno Marinatos, *Art and Religion in Thera: Reconstructing a Bronze Age Society* (Athens, 1984). For a large collection of papers dealing with all aspects of the Thera finds, see the proceedings of the third international congress on the subject: D. A. Hardy and A. C. Renfrew, eds., *Thera and the Aegean World III*, 3 vols. (London, 1990). An excellent survey of the evidence, including the frescoe fragments from Egypt, for contact between various cultures in the Late Bronze Age is Ora Negbi, "The 'Libyan Landscape' from Thera: A Review of Aegean Enterprises Overseas in the Late Minoan IA Period," *Journal of Mediterranean Archaeology* 7 (1994): 73–112. For criticism of this article and different views, see Sturt W. Manning, Sarah J. Monks, Georgia Nakou, and Francis A. De Mita Jr., "The Fatal Shore, the Long Years, and the Geographical Unconscious: Considerations of Iconography, Chronology, and Trade in Response to Negbi's 'The "Libyan Landscape" from Thera: A Review of Aegean Enterprises Overseas in the Late Minoan IA Period' (*JMA* 7.1)," ibid., pp. 219–235.
[14] The basic handbook for Minoan pottery is Philip P. Betancourt, *The History of Minoan Pottery* (Princeton, 1985).

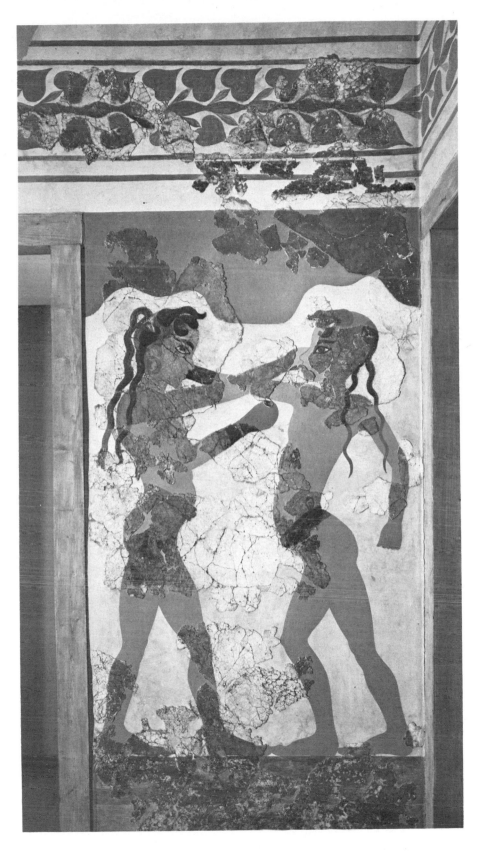

2.28 Boxing children, Thera. National Archaeological Museum, Athens. Photo: Hirmer Fotoarchiv, Munich.

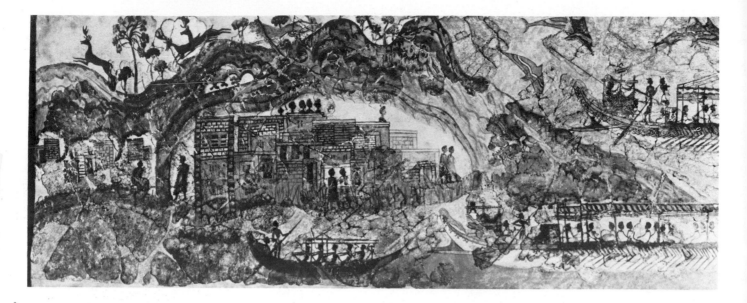

2.29 Detail of naval fresco from Thera. Photo: National Archaeological Museum, Athens.

associated with the first palaces, to a more sober black-and-white style with only occasional touches of red and yellow. Many types of pottery are found, ranging from the gigantic pithoi of the palace magazines to small cups and goblets, including both open and closed shapes designed for many uses, from storage to everyday table use.

Dark-on-light designs predominate in Late Minoan pottery. Often overall patterns of reeds or grasses completely cover the vase in the so-called Floral style that began in LM IA, with roots in the previous period, and continued into LM IB (Fig. 2.30). Abstract designs form the LM IA Pattern style (Fig. 2.31). Sometimes both types of decoration can be found on the same vase. Probably most famous of the Minoan pottery styles is the LM IB Marine style, which clearly reflects the style of the naturalistic frescoes, as indeed some of the LM IA designs must have done. Here sea creatures are shown floating over the surfaces of the pots, with little regard for the shape they cover. Figure 2.32 shows a stirrup jar (so called because the handles are shaped like stirrups), a Minoan invention with a favorite Minoan design, an octopus. The creature floats freely over the surface of the pot with its tentacles waving in water festooned with seaweed and floating plants, as in the Flying Fish fresco. The suckers on the tentacles, the great staring eyes, and the bulbous shape are emphasized. Nautiluses, fish, sea plants, and other forms of marine life make up the repertoire of this style, which is often found in the debris associated with the final destruction of Cretan sites.

Primarily at Knossos and now elsewhere, a distinctive pottery succeeds the Marine style, with some overlap. This is the Palace style, of the LM II period, found mainly in large three-handled amphoras of a shape very common on the mainland but uncommon on Crete. With the new shape comes a new style of decoration, in which the Minoan decorative motifs are stiffened and frozen into design elements (Fig. 2.33). Leaves, lilies, and other flora are forced to stand upright in a system that recognizes the vase form by emphasizing such things as the foot, the handles, and the neck. The octopus is at first taken over almost entirely from the Marine style and allowed to float on the mainland shapes, but soon it appears to go through a period of organization and is

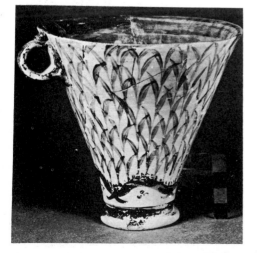

2.30 Floral-style cup from Kato Zakro. Heraklion Museum, Crete. From Nicholas Platon, *Zakros* (New York: Scribner, 1971), p. 112.

straightened up and stylized. Now it is placed vertically on the surface of the pot and its arms are heraldically arranged around its body (Fig. 2.34). We shall meet this passion for balance and symmetry again, for it seems to be a basic characteristic of the Greek artistic sense—and we have seen that the Mycenaeans are to be considered Greeks.

The progressive stylization of Minoan naturalistic designs proceeds into Late Minoan III, or the Post-Palace period, but can be more profitably followed on the mainland.

TERRA COTTA FIGURINES

Terra cotta of course had a number of domestic uses besides the making of pottery.[15] Figurines were a very common type of dedication or offering, and we shall be looking at objects of this sort throughout this book. Late Minoan figurines are typically standing "household goddesses." Many date from the

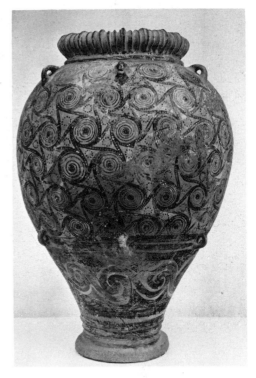

2.31 Pattern-style pithos from eastern Crete. Heraklion Museum, Crete. Photo: Deutsches Archäologisches Institut, Athens.

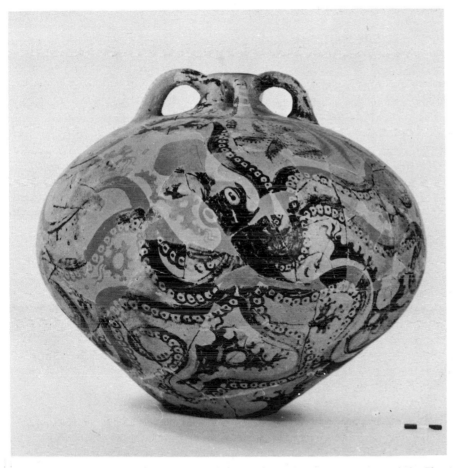

2.32 Marine-style stirrup jar from Kato Zakro. Heraklion Museum, Crete. From Nicholas Platon, *Zakros* (New York: Scribner, 1971), p. 121.

[15] Although pottery can generally be identified as Minoan or Mycenaean, minor finds are often less readily labeled. This situation is to be expected, since a certain unity of culture on a lower level must be assumed in the Late Bronze Age. A number of categories of minor finds will therefore be discussed in Chapter 3 as belonging to both the Minoan and the Mycenaean civilizations.

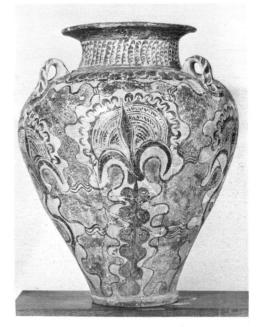

2.33 Palace-style amphora from Knossos. Heraklion Museum, Crete. Photo: Hirmer Fotoarchiv, Munich.

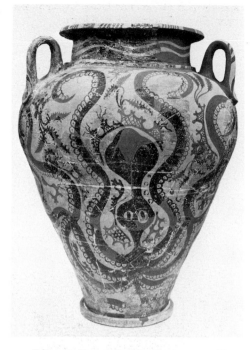

2.34 Palace-style amphora with octopus. Heraklion Museum, Crete. Photo: Deutsches Archäologisches Institut, Athens.

Post-Palace period and appear extremely crude in comparison with the faience figurines. The flaring skirt has been simplified into a wheel-turned tube and the natural curves of the human body have been almost completely suppressed. The goddess is shown with raised hands and has been found accompanied by smaller companions or worshipers, as shown in Figure 2.35, depicting figurines from a shrine at Knossos dated in the thirteenth century. The male figure shows some link with the more common and better made figurines of the Old Palace period, but in neither period was the manufacture of figurines a major art form. Larger household goddesses are known from a number of sites, and the type persists down into the Dark Ages.

A particularly interesting find from Arkhanes, near Knossos, is a large model of a Minoan building complete with an upper story, balcony, staircase ramp, and light well (Fig. 2.36). Dating to the beginning of the New Palace period, this model provides much information about the upper stories of Minoan buildings, which of course have seldom been preserved.

STONEWORK

The Minoans were excellent workers in stone, using techniques learned from Egypt.[16] From Pre-Palace times stone had been fashioned into many simple vase shapes, but more elaborate stone vessels were also in use in the later periods for religious and everyday use.

Several outstanding examples of stone carving from the palace at Kato Zakro are shown in Figures 2.37–2.40, including a typical Minoan stone lamp (Fig. 2.37). A number of ritual vases made of a soft stone known as serpentine and once covered with gold leaf also exist. The Sanctuary Rhyton from Kato Zakro (Fig. 2.40) shows a building set in a rocky landscape and wild goats

2.35 Figurines from a shrine at Knossos. Heraklion Museum, Crete. Photo: Hirmer Fotoarchiv, Munich.

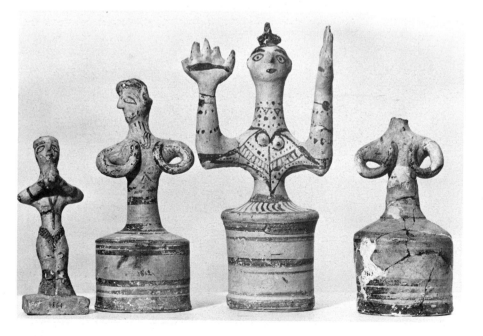

[16] A special study of Minoan stone carving is to be found in Peter Warren, *Minoan Stone Vases* (Cambridge, 1969).

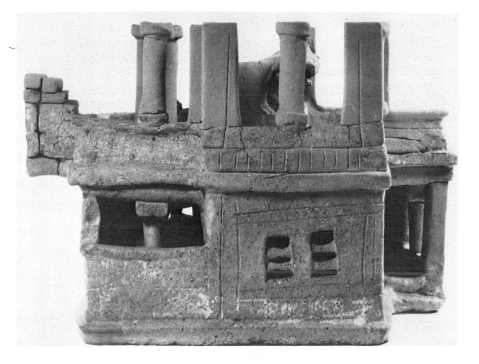

2.36 House model from Arkhanes. Heraklion Museum, Crete. Photo: Georgios Xuloures.

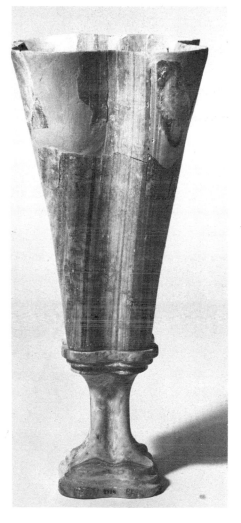

lounging on its roof. A similar but larger vase from Ayia Triadha is decorated with scenes of bull vaulting and boxing, and a small vessel from the same site, its lower portion missing, shows a harvest procession in which one of the men shakes a sistrum, an instrument we know from Egypt (Fig. 2.41). This Harvester Vase again illustrates the Minoans' interest in the world around them. The figures are most expressive and alive as they move rapidly around the circumference of the vase in their procession, carrying winnowing fans over

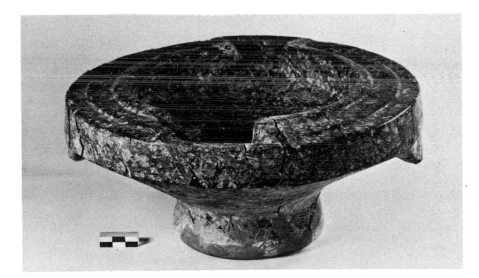

2.37 Stone lamp from Kato Zakro. Heraklion Museum, Crete. From Nicholas Platon, *Zakros* (New York: Scribner, 1971), p. 149.

2.38 Chalice from Kato Zakro. Heraklion Museum, Crete. Photo: Hirmer Fotoarchiv, Munich.

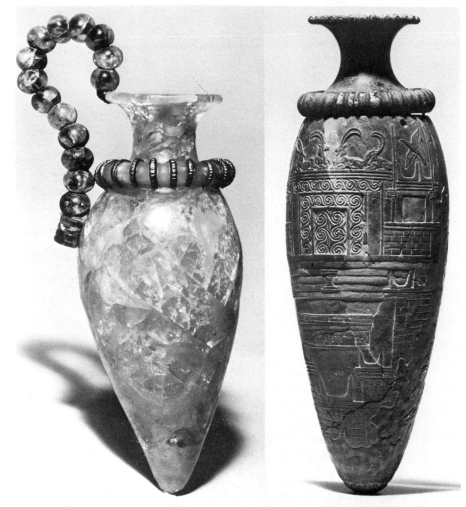

2.39 Rock-crystal rhyton from Kato Zakro. Heraklion Museum, Crete. Photo: Hirmer Fotoarchiv, Munich.

2.40 (far right) Rhyton from Kato Zakro. Heraklion Museum, Crete. Photo: Hirmer Fotoarchiv, Munich.

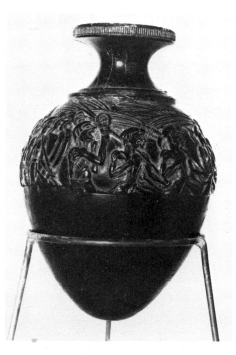

2.41 Harvester Vase from Ayia Triadha. Heraklion Museum, Crete. Photo: Alison Frantz.

their shoulders. Occasionally ritual stone vases were made in the shapes of animal heads. The most famous of these vases is the bull's-head rhyton from an outlying building at Knossos (Fig. 2.42). Only half the head was preserved, but enough remained to permit the reconstruction of the vase, which originally had rock-crystal eyes, shell inlay on the muzzle, and gilded wooden horns. A similar but smaller example was recovered from Kato Zakro; a silver example comes from the shaft graves at Mycenae; and a number of others are known from various sites in various materials. A hole at the nape of the neck was used for filling the vessel; the liquid must have poured out of the mouth.

Other products of the stonecutters were small seals in oval, almond, and lens shapes. They were incised with designs or scenes, often from nature or of a religious character. They were apparently used as marks of ownership to seal doors, clothes chests, and the like.[17]

[17] For a general survey of Bronze Age seals, see John Boardman, *Greek Gems and Finger Rings* (London, 1970), pp. 19–107, and John Younger, *A Bibliography for Aegean Glyptic in the Bronze Age* (Berlin, 1991).

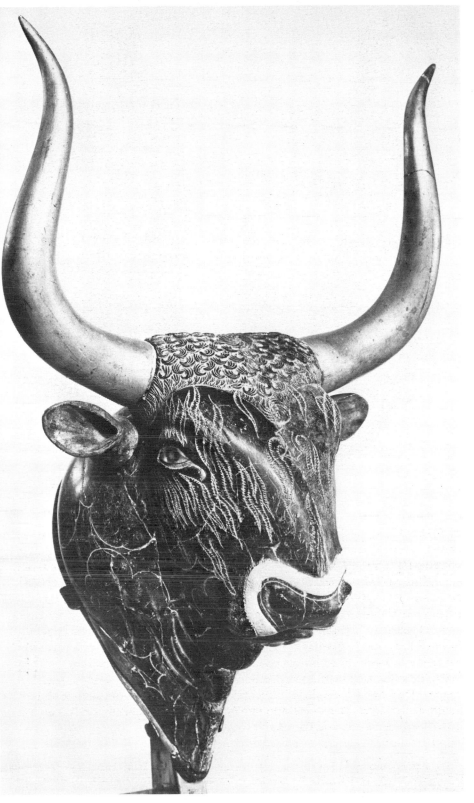

2.42 Bull's-head rhyton from the Little Palace, Knossos. Heraklion Museum, Crete. Photo: Alison Frantz.

2.43 Faience snake goddess from Knossos. Heraklion Museum, Crete. Photo: Hirmer Fotoarchiv, Munich.

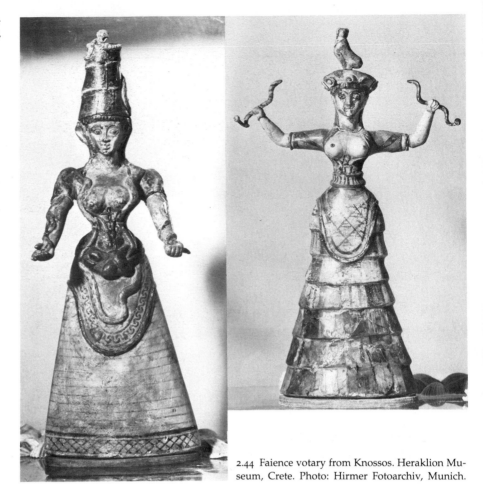

2.44 Faience votary from Knossos. Heraklion Museum, Crete. Photo: Hirmer Fotoarchiv, Munich.

FAIENCE

A technique probably imported from Egypt in the Pre-Palace period is that of the manufacture of faience, earthenware covered with an opaque glaze made mainly of crushed quartz. The glassy surface is formed when the object is fired. Its color, usually blue, is derived from the presence of copper oxide. At the rear of the pillar shrine at Knossos, Evans found a deposit of discarded material that included two large faience figurines. The larger (Fig. 2.43) is generally regarded as a snake goddess or mother goddess, the smaller (Fig. 2.44) as her daughter or a votary. Both wear the Minoan court costume seen in the frescoes, with wide flounced skirt and open bodice. The larger figure, over 34 centimeters high, is literally covered with snakes, which curl around her body and wind up her arms and even onto her high hat; the smaller figure holds two small snakes in her raised hands and wears a flat head covering on which sits a spotted feline. Also in faience is a series of small plaques from Knossos representing the houses of a town, datable to the Old Palace period (Fig. 2.45). The evidence they provide for the facades, construction methods, window placement, roof treatment, and other details has been used in many reconstructions.

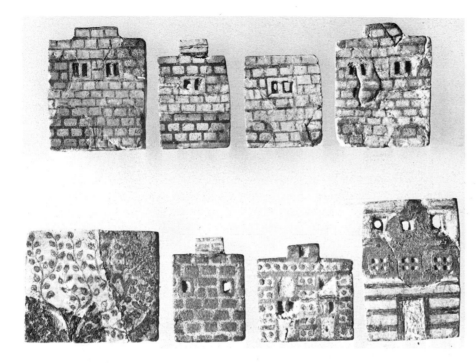

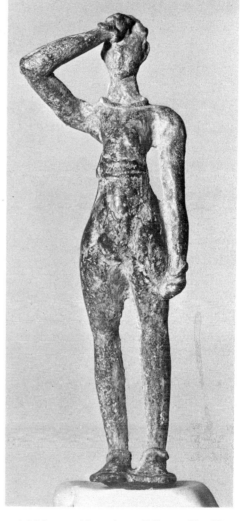

2.45 Faience town mosaic from Knossos Heraklion Museum, Crete. Photo: Alison Frantz.

METALWORK

Many bronze objects for daily use have been found in Crete. Some bronze figurines have also been discovered; a common type is that represented by the male figure shown in Figure 2.46, with his fist to his brow in an attitude of worship. Female figures also exist.

2.46 Male worshiper from Tylissos. Heraklion Museum, Crete. Photo: Hirmer Fotoarchiv, Munich.

3

The Mycenaeans

THE ARCHAEOLOGY OF the Bronze Age on the mainland and the discovery of the Mycenaean civilization can be said to have started in the 1870s with Heinrich Schliemann's discoveries at Mycenae, where work has continued down to the present day.[1] A great many Mycenaean sites have been discovered since Schliemann's day, and a number have been excavated. Researches have shown that, unlike Crete, the mainland did not enjoy a single, more or less uninterrupted period of development. At numerous sites archaeologists have detected evidence of destructions and changes, some of which may be purely local, while others perhaps indicate more widespread activity. Much of the evidence is obscure and difficult to interpret. A few of the changes, however, are so obvious and universal as to be generally recognized.[2]

The Bronze Age presents as many problems on the mainland as it does on Crete. The chronology follows the familiar tripartite scheme of Early, Middle, and Late. The mainland culture is labeled Helladic, a manufactured word to distinguish it from the Minoan of Crete. A similar convention is used for the islands, whose Bronze Age culture is termed Cycladic; it is less well known generally than either of the other two. The mainland chronology is further divided into three periods by the use of Roman numerals and subdivided by the use of letters of the alphabet in a manner identical to that used for Crete. Thus one can have Late Helladic IIIB, while more detailed pottery designations further divide the periods by the addition of Arabic numerals, as in LH IIIB2.

Although this terminology has met with some of the same objections as those raised by the Minoan series, it has been less vigorously attacked and will be employed here. The final phases of the period, Late Helladic I, II, and III, are often called Mycenaean after the site of Mycenae in the Argolid, one of the earliest centers investigated and one of the most important. The following list gives the major chronological divisions:

Early Helladic	c. 3000–2000
Middle Helladic	c. 2000–1675
Late Helladic I and II (Mycenaean)	c. 1675–1425
Late Helladic IIIA (Mycenaean)	c. 1425–1340
Late Helladic IIIB (Mycenaean)	c. 1340–1190
Late Helladic IIIC and Sub-Mycenaean	c. 1190–1020

---

[1] An account of Schliemann's archaeological work and life may conveniently be found in William A. McDonald and Carol G. Thomas, *Progress into the Past: The Rediscovery of Mycenaean Civilization,* 2d ed. (Bloomington, Ind., 1990). A biography that gives a balanced view of his entire life is Leo Deuel, *Memoirs of Heinrich Schliemann* (New York, 1977).

[2] The prehistoric mainland is covered in Oliver Dickinson, *The Aegean Bronze Age* (Cambridge, 1994). See also Richard Hope Simpson and O. T. P. K. Dickinson, *A Gazetteer of Civilization in the Bronze Age,* vol. 1 (Göteborg, 1979). Now a little out of date but still worth reading is Emily T. Vermeule, *Greece in the Bronze Age,* fifth printing with new introduction (Chicago, 1972). For the Cycladic islands see Jack Davis, "Review of Aegean Prehistory I: The Islands of the Aegean," *AJA* 96 (1992): 699–756.

A long Neolithic period of some three thousand years on the mainland was succeeded by an early Bronze Age culture (Early Helladic) with new and characteristic features in architecture, pottery, and so on. The Early Helladic period is a rich and important phase on the mainland, with walled towns, monumental architecture, increasing use of metals, foreign trade connections, and some wealth. It lasted roughly a thousand years. The end of the period is marked by disturbances in the Aegean and on the Greek mainland. The evidence for what happened at the end of the Early Helladic is so difficult to interpret that it has been the subject of much controversy, and no consensus has been reached. Early Helladic is followed by the distinctive culture of the Middle Bronze Age, or Middle Helladic. This culture, distinguished by the so-called Minyan and Matt Painted ceramics, by some differences in architecture, and by a seemingly lower stage of civilization than the culture it displaced, is still not well known.[3]

Its significance lies in the fact that it is the direct precursor of the Mycenaean period. No major break can be detected between the establishment of Middle Helladic culture and the disintegration of the Mycenaean in the twelfth century. The now generally accepted view that the Linear B script of the later palaces is an early form of Greek pushes the Greek language back into Middle Helladic times and thus makes the Middle Helladic peoples Greeks.

Although no break as such can be detected from about 2000 to the end of the Bronze Age, certainly changes can be noted, and dramatic ones too, around 1700, just before the beginning of the Late Helladic period. Here are the astonishing shaft graves at Mycenae, whose wealth is not equalled by any other remains from the period, and whose origin and artistic connections are subject to endless theories and suggestions. The finds from the graves appear to reflect a sudden increase in the tempo of culture and civilization at Mycenae, but whether this flowering is the result of an infusion of new blood from elsewhere, loot, payment for mercenary service, or riches derived from the metal trade with central Europe is not known.

The period from the shaft graves to the fall of Knossos is called the Early Mycenaean period (Late Helladic I–IIIA1). The eclipse of the Minoan civilization in the fourteenth century marks the beginning of the most flourishing period of the Mycenaean civilization—and in fact it has been called the Mycenaean Empire. The juxtaposition of Minoan decline and Mycenaean rise to prominence is of course significant, and evidence that the Mycenaeans may have had a hand in Crete's misfortunes has already been mentioned.

Much of our knowledge of the Mycenaeans is based on two kinds of written evidence, which exist in greater abundance for the Mycenaean civilization than for the Minoan. The Linear B tablets have already been touched on as providing evidence of Mycenaean occupation of Knossos. The great majority of the tablets have come from mainland sites. Although many problems remain after some forty years of intense scholarly work on these "account books of anonymous clerks," as John Chadwick has called them, they have yielded invaluable

[3] Monochrome Minyan ware is named after the legendary king of Orchomenos in Boiotia, where it was first recognized. Matt Painted ware is a class of pottery in which brown to black designs were applied in lusterless paint on a light background. For a recent survey of the cultures of the mainland before the rise of the Mycenaean palaces, and particularly of the question of the events surrounding the change from the Early Helladic culture to that of the succeeding Middle Helladic, see Jeremy Rutter, "Review of Aegean Prehistory II: The Prepalatial Bronze Age of the Southern and Central Greek Mainland," *AJA* 97 (1993): 745–797. Dickinson, *Aegean Bronze Age,* is now also basic.

information on the day-to-day workings of the great Mycenaean palace centers.[4] Before the tablets were deciphered, the only written sources that were thought to apply to the Bronze Age were the Homeric epics and the myths and stories told by later Greek writers. The difficulties in using this kind of material are many and obvious, and various degrees of acceptance of the information supplied by these sources can be found among scholars. The discoveries of archaeologists, beginning with Schliemann at Troy and Mycenae, gave great satisfaction to those who would like to see the Homeric poems as reflections of the Mycenaean Age, and some scholars have accepted the mythological rulers of Attica and the Peloponnesos as historical figures. Others reject the myths as historical sources and regard Homer's evidence as more clearly reflecting his own time, although there is general agreement that of the material in the epics some could date back to the Mycenaean period.[5] It is also possible to search among the later sources for a story or a myth that fits a particular hypothesis and then reject any others that do not fit. The historical veracity of stories repeated by later writers is probably incapable of absolute proof, but some startling archaeological correspondences with literary statements indicate at least some historical value in the later stories, even if they are badly distorted by time and circumstance. A third source of information is the records of other nations, particularly of the Hittites, in which we find mention of people who have been identified as Mycenaeans, but the evidence is hard to interpret, finds little agreement among scholars, and deals only peripherally with the Mycenaeans in any case.

The picture of the Mycenaean civilization in the fourteenth and thirteenth centuries given by archaeological and other sources is that of a number of kingdoms, probably independent, possibly recognizing one or another of the larger centers as suzerain. Each kingdom had a central administrative capital, usually fortified, which was the home of the king and a bureaucratic and possibly religious center as well. From this center the king controlled the surrounding countryside, which consisted of farmland, towns, and sometimes even other fortified citadels. There appears to have been no subsidiary network of villas as on Crete. The Linear B tablets reveal a tremendous bureaucracy centered in the palaces, which were almost self-contained units with an elaborate social organization based on agriculture and to a lesser extent on trade. In this regard the mainland palaces were similar to those on Crete, but on a smaller scale. All evidence seems to indicate that the Mycenaeans were a warlike people, especially in their formative period; loot probably played a great part in their development.

It is exceedingly difficult to grasp the differences between Mycenaean and Minoan religion. Many of the gods of the later Greek pantheon are present in the Linear B tablets but cannot be identified in the religious art, which looks

[4] The story of the decipherment can be found in John Chadwick, *The Decipherment of Linear B*, 2d ed. (Cambridge, 1967). Many of the documents are reproduced in Michael Ventris and John Chadwick, *Documents in Mycenaean Greek*, 2d ed. (Cambridge, 1973). A historical interpretation of the texts is provided in Chadwick's *The Mycenaean World* (Cambridge, 1976). Although designed for students "with some knowledge of Greek," J. T. Hooker's *Linear B: An Introduction* (Bristol, 1980) can be profitably looked at by the "Greekless" as well. Also helpful is Anna Morpurgo Davies and Yves Duhoux, *Linear B: A 1984 Survey* (Louvain-la-Neuve, 1985).
[5] Two approaches to the Homeric evidence can be found in M. I. Finley, *The World of Odysseus*, rev. ed. (New York, 1978), and Denys Page, *History and the Homeric Iliad* (Berkeley, 1959; reprinted 1972). An interesting modern archaeological perspective on Homer can be found in E. S. Sherratt, "'Reading the Texts': Archaeology and the Homeric Question," *Antiquity* 64 (1990): 807–824.

almost wholly Minoan with only a few exceptions. Possibly the intrusive Mycenaean Greeks accepted the fertility and vegetation deities of the Minoans, identifying their gods with them in some cases. Others of their gods may have remained unrepresented. In any event, the tablets and art indicate numerous deities receiving offerings and sacrifices.

During the thirteenth century Mycenaean culture spread beyond the mainland to both east and west, and it is likely that more or less formalized relations were opened between one or more Mycenaean kingdoms and the great eastern powers, such as Egypt and the Hittite kingdom. Representations of Minoans and Mycenaeans appear in the art of Egypt, as has been mentioned, and Mycenaean pottery is found throughout the Near East, including Troy.[6]

The Mycenaean civilization and with it the Bronze Age came to an end in a series of catastrophes in the twelfth century, beginning with the destruction of the palace at Pylos about 1200 or a little later. The next hundred years saw many of the Mycenaean centers either destroyed or abandoned, with major shifts of population away from the traditional Mycenaean homeland and into new areas on the mainland, especially Achaia, the island of Kephallenia, Attica, and abroad (especially Cyprus). New evidence from Mycenae and elsewhere has shown considerable revival after the destructions and abandonments, although the settlements were fewer, more scattered, and less unified culturally than before. By the end of the twelfth century the last citadels were abandoned or destroyed and a general lowering of civilization can be seen. Greece passed into a dark age, which is the subject of the next chapter.

The reason for the end of the Bronze Age and the destruction of the Mycenaean civilization is one of the great problems of Greek prehistoric archaeology. Traditionally, an invasion of Greeks speaking a Dorian dialect and Mycenaean exiles were responsible, but despite the existence of the Dorian dialect in later Greece and the strength of the tradition, archaeologists look in vain for Dorian artifacts. The recent trend has been either to deny the Dorians any hand in the destructions or to see them as culturally indistinguishable from the peoples they overthrew. Various other suggestions have been made at one time or another in an attempt to explain the wave of destructions and abandonments at the turn of LH IIIB and IIIC: foreign raids or invasions by groups other than the Dorians (for instance, the sea peoples), climatic changes, internal disputes. Probably a combination of factors was responsible for the great upheavals in the Mediterranean world at this time.[7]

ART

In their early development the Mycenaeans were clearly influenced by Crete, which of course lies only a short distance to the south. Cretan influence is clear in the material recovered from the shaft graves and in the palaces and their

---

[6] The many problems surrounding the date and even the historicity of the Trojan War cannot be considered here. For surveys of the problem, see Donald Easton, "Has the Trojan War Been Found?" *Antiquity* 59 (1985): 188–196, and Michael Wood, *In Search of the Trojan War* (London, 1985).

[7] A useful summary of the various theories with an emphasis on at least partially economic factors may be found in Philip P. Betancourt, "The End of the Greek Bronze Age," *Antiquity* 50 (1976): 40–47. The destructions of the palaces did not signal the total end of the Mycenaean way of life; see Jeremy Rutter, "Cultural Novelties in the Post-Palatial Aegean World: Indices of Vitality or Decline?" in *The Crisis Years: The Twelfth Century B.C.*, ed. William A. Ward and Martha Sharp Joukowsky (Dubuque, Ia., 1992), pp. 61–78.

decoration. Although the Mycenaeans were clearly dependent on Crete, and probably on Cretan artists in their formative stage, Mycenaean art is not Cretan, or even a provincial Cretan art. It has a distinctive flavor of its own, to be seen in some choices of subject matter; in the conservatism and formulaic quality of some of the frescoes; in the formalism of its designs, which are progressively more abstract versions of motifs inherited from the Minoans; and in large-scale sculpture. In a sense Minoan-Mycenaean art is a unit, particularly where religious scenes are concerned, but one must be aware of the differences in the components. These differences are not always easy to see, however, and it is sometimes embarrassingly difficult, particularly in the early years of the Mycenaean period, to decide what is Mycenaean and what is Minoan.[8]

ARCHITECTURE

The period of LH IIIA and IIIB (1425–1190) saw the establishment on the mainland, and to a certain extent abroad, of Mycenaean power centers, each usually containing a fortified royal compound containing a central hall and other buildings surrounded by a great wall. Outside the wall, additional houses straggled down the hill below it. Of the major mainland centers, only Mycenae and Tiryns, in the Argolid, and Pylos, on the southwest coast of the Peloponnesos, have been excavated to an extent that provides overall plans. Here and elsewhere, Mycenaean architecture owes much to Minoan construction, and despite a few fundamental differences may be considered Minoan in its general outlines. A glance at the plans of Mycenae and of Pylos (Figs. 3.1

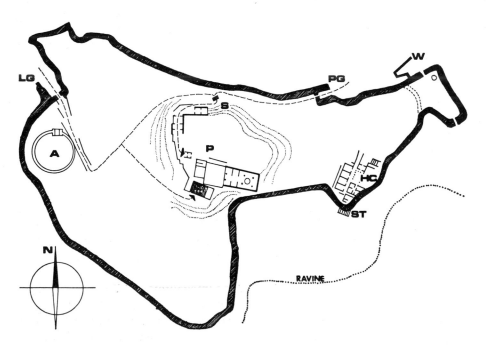

3.1 Sketch plan of third citadel, Mycenae:[P] *LG* = Lion Gate; *A* = Grave Circle A; *P* = Megaron; *PG* = Postern Gate; *W* = Secret Spring. From George E. Mylonas, *Mycenae and the Mycenaean Age* (copyright © 1956 by Princeton University Press), p. 31, Fig. 7. Reprinted by permission of Princeton University Press. LM III A

[8] For an illustration of the problem of differentiating "Minoan" from "Mycenaean" stylistically, see Jeffrey M. Hurwit, "The Dendra Octapus Cup and the Problems of Style in the Fifteenth-Century Aegean," *AJA* 83 (1979): 413–426.

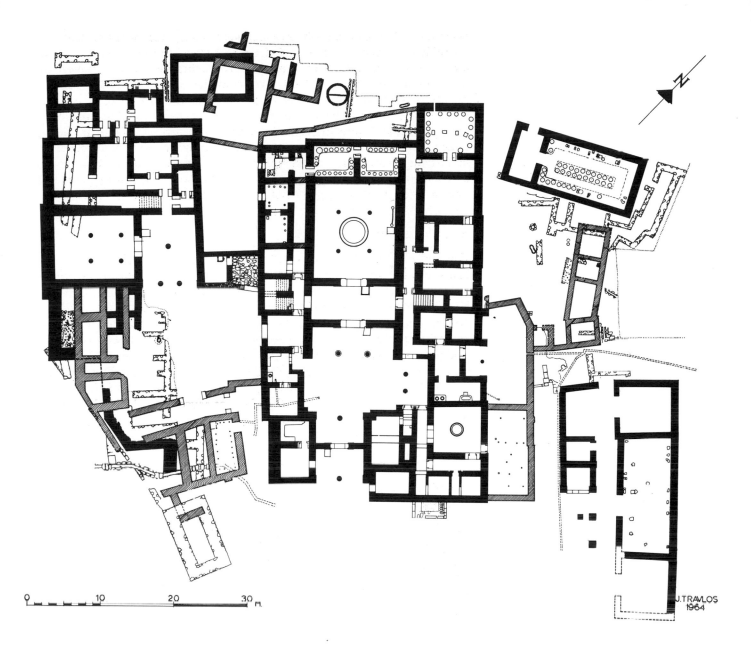

and 3.2), however, indicates the differences between the Mycenaean citadel and the Minoan palace. At Mycenae we find great fortification walls and a central hall of purely mainland style, the megaron. A Mycenaean citadel generally has a main gate, as at Mycenae, with one or two subsidiary smaller openings.

Ability to work with large blocks of stone (megalithic architecture) seems to have been a Mycenaean specialty. An example can be seen in the Cyclopean fortification walls, so called by later Greeks who thought they must have been built by those mythical creatures because of their huge size. The walls are constructed of great boulders only roughly trimmed; some of them are eight meters thick. Ashlar work (blocks laid in regular courses) is sometimes combined on the same massive scale with Cyclopean construction at entrances. A

3.2 Ground plan of Pylos.[P] From Carl W. Blegen and Marion Rawson, *The Palace of Nestor at Pylos in Western Messenia*, vol. 1, pt. 2 (Princeton: Princeton University Press, 1966), Fig. 417. Reprinted by permission of Princeton University Press and the University of Cincinnati.

3.3 The Lion Gate at Mycenae. Photo: Alison Frantz. ᒪᕼᛯ B

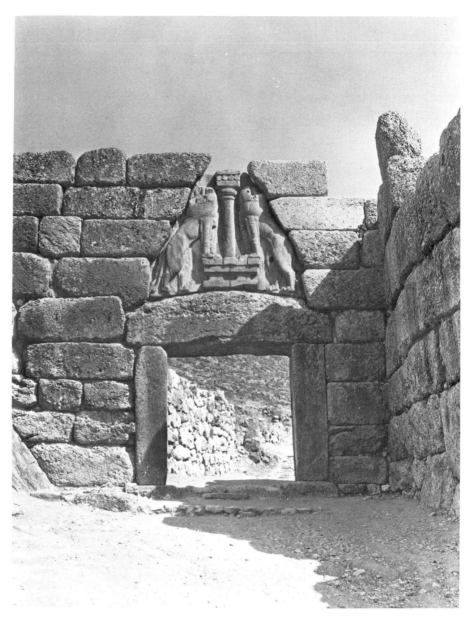

photo of the area of the main entrance at Mycenae, the Lion Gate, shows the use of ashlar work (Fig. 3.3).

Mycenaean megalithic construction is characterized by corbel vaulting, or the projection of each successive course of stones slightly beyond the course below, so that the wall is stepped upward and outward. This technique can be used to span both circular spaces, such as tholos tombs, and rectangular ones, such as the stairway to the "secret spring" at Mycenae (Fig. 3.4). Another conspicuous feature of Mycenaean megalithic construction is a "relieving trian-gle" above a lintel block. This is a triangular opening, designed to reduce the weight over the lintel. The space was filled with some lighter stone or other material, which occasionally was carved, as is the block in the relieving triangle over the Lion Gate at Mycenae (see Fig. 3.3).

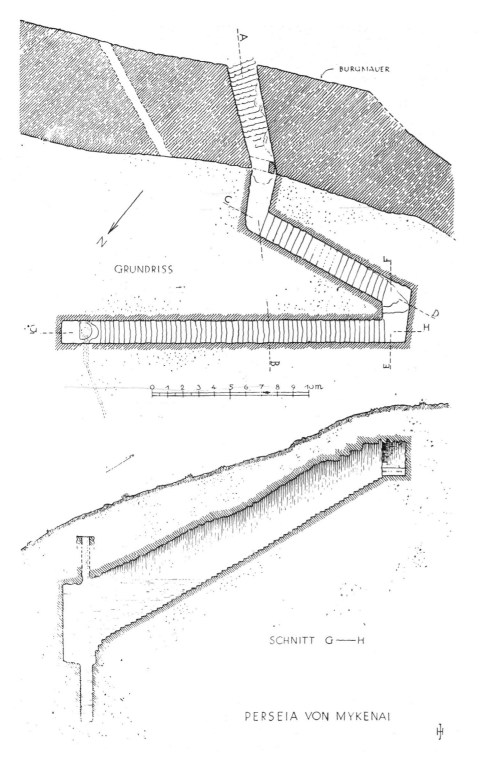

3.4 Plan and section of the Secret Spring, Mycenae. From Georg Karo, "Die Perseia von Mykenai," *American Journal of Archaeology* 38 (1934): 123–127, Plate 12.

Perhaps the most conspicuous and distinctive feature of Mycenaean architecture is the central hall, or megaron, which is found not only in the palaces but in private houses as well. A typical mainland form, traceable at least to Early Helladic and perhaps to Neolithic predecessors, it is almost unvarying in form. The megaron may be defined as a free-standing unit composed of a more or less square main room entered at one side through a porch with two columns and sometimes an anteroom of the same width as the main room. The principal room was dominated by a round fixed hearth, and a platform for a throne was situated against the wall opposite it. The hearth was surrounded by four columns, which held up the roof and stood at the four sides of an opening in the ceiling to allow the smoke from the hearth to escape. Megara were two stories high, and at least at Pylos a balcony surrounded the smoke opening, which was surmounted by a lantern with chimney pipes to draw off the smoke. Many archaeologists believe that megara, like Cretan buildings, had flat roofs.

The plan of Mycenae shows the citadel at its greatest extent (see Fig. 3.1). The earliest fortification wall, datable to early LH IIIA, enclosed a much smaller area at the top of the hill. Later additions swung the west wall out to enclose a previously existing circle of earlier graves, Grave Circle A, and established the Lion Gate, the bastion to the west of it, and later a north postern gate. Militarily, the bastion strengthened the citadel's defense, forcing an attacker into a narrow area where his unshielded right side was vulnerable, another typical Mycenaean feature. The Lion Gate itself is constructed of large conglomerate blocks cut to shape by hammer and saw (see Fig. 3.3). The great door revolved around a vertical beam that acted as a pivot; the pivot hole in the lintel is preserved, as are holes for the crossbeams in the doorjambs which secured the door when it was closed. The lintel is a single stone, or monolith, some 4.5 meters in length and weighing some eighteen tons. Above the lintel rests a relief sculpture of two lionesses in the relieving triangle. The addition of the Lion Gate and its bastion is dated by the latest excavator of Mycenae, George Mylonas, to mid-LH IIIB times (mid-thirteenth century).[9]

The final extension of the citadel to the northeast involved the construction of a corbel-vaulted stairway that went through the fortification wall to an underground cistern fed by a spring outside the citadel (see Fig. 3.4). This "secret spring" construction is similar to other hidden water sources known from Mycenaean palace sites at Athens and Tiryns toward the end of the thirteenth century and perhaps indicates military preparations to meet some impending threat.

A large portion of the central part of Mycenae was destroyed to make way for later building, so that only a part of the megaron is now preserved. One must imagine that there once were storerooms, workshops, and living quarters for the royal family, palace staff, and retainers.

It was formerly thought that Mycenaean religious practices must have been carried out in the megaron, for no buildings clearly designed exclusively for cult ritual had been found. Excavations in A.D. 1968 and 1969 on the south slope of the citadel at Mycenae, just within the walls, revealed a cult area containing a shrine in which terra cotta figurines were found, and in an adjoining room a wall painting of a female figure holding what appear to be sheaves of wheat. Other cult areas have come to light on the islands, specifically at Phylakopi on Melos and on the island of Kea, sometimes called Keos, in a late Cycladic town greatly influenced by Minoan culture. Large terra cotta female figurines are associated with the site on Kea (Fig. 3.13). The buildings at Mycenae and Kea are long and narrow, with one or more rooms behind or beside a

---

[9] George E. Mylonas, *Mycenae and the Mycenaean Age* (Princeton, 1966), pp. 19–22.

principal room. In both cases it was in the back room that the large clay figures were found.[10]

More is preserved at Tiryns, which has an even more heavily fortified citadel and two megara, a larger and a smaller, both facing courtyards. Recent work at this site by the German Archaeological Institute has uncovered interesting and important information by traditional excavation, such as an underground water tunnel like that at Mycenae (top left in Fig. 3.5), and also has found evidence of environmental changes in the area in the Late Helladic period by geoarchaeological investigations.[11]

The best preserved and the best excavated of the major palaces is Pylos. The location of the palace, in the west Peloponnesos on a low hill, matches the traditional location of the home of wise old King Nestor of the Homeric stories. It was excavated in recent times by Carl Blegen. Since it was not reinhabited after its destruction and has been carefully excavated, it has yielded a great amount of information.[12] The strong axial symmetry imparted by the megaron is very obvious from the plan (see Fig. 3.2). Upon entering the palace the visitor would notice on the left a suite of small rooms just off the entrance. These rooms appear to have been the archives center for the palace, or at least the area where the commodities that entered the palace were recorded; some 150 Linear B tablets were found there. Beyond, an open court led to the megaron, which was a typical example with a place for a wooden throne against the east wall. The large megaron (12.9 by 11.2 meters) was highly decorated; a reconstruction of it appears in Figure 3.6. Both the walls and the floor were painted in bright colors, as was the hearth, whose spiral and flame patterns had been repainted a number of times. The upper portions of the room, the beams, and the column capitals were also decorated, but here the evidence is less certain. Before the throne a stylized octopus was painted in one of the floor squares, perhaps representing the symbol of Pylos' ruling family. There was an upper floor, probably with a balcony over the hearth, as shown in the reconstruction. It is conjectured that smoke and gases escaped through a tall lantern that rose above the roofline and in which were placed terra cotta chimney pipes, examples of which were actually found in the debris over the hearth. The megaron was originally bordered on both sides by long, narrow corridors, off which opened a number of rooms (Fig. 3.7). Those to the northwest appear to have been the pantry of the palace, for a great number of pots of all shapes and sizes were found here; in fact, some 7,000 were recovered from eight pantries, including more than 2,800 stemmed drinking cups, or kylikes. Two more store rooms lay immediately behind the megaron, where olive oil was kept in large jars built into a plastered bench (Fig. 3.7); a similar storage room occupied the northeast corner of the complex. The rest of the east side of the palace was

[10] The cult area at Mycenae is described in Lord William Taylour, "New Light on Mycenaean Religion," *Antiquity* 44 (1970): 270–280, and George E. Mylonas, "The Cult Center of Mycenae," *Proceedings of the British Academy* 67 (1982): 307–320. For the area on Melos see Colin Renfrew, *The Archaeology of Cult: The Sanctuary at Phylakopi* (London, 1985). For the statues from Kea see Miriam Caskey, *Keos II*, vol. 1: *The Temple at Ayia Irini: The Statues* (Princeton, 1986).

[11] Eberhard Zangger, "Landscape Changes around Tiryns during the Bronze Age," *AJA* 98 (1994): 189–212.

[12] The results of the excavations are published by Princeton University Press in a series titled *The Palace of Nestor at Pylos in Western Messenia*. Three volumes have been published: vol. 1, *The Buildings*, by Carl W. Blegen and Marion Rawson (1966); vol. 2, *The Frescoes*, by Mabel Lang (1969); and vol. 3, *Acropolis, Tholoi, Etc.*, by Blegen and others (1973). See also C. W. Shelmerdine and T. G. Palaima, eds., *Pylos Comes Alive: Industry and Administration in a Mycenaean Palace* (New York, 1984).

3.5 Ground plan of the citadel of Tiryns[P] in the
LH IIIB period. Courtesy of Dr. Joseph Maran.

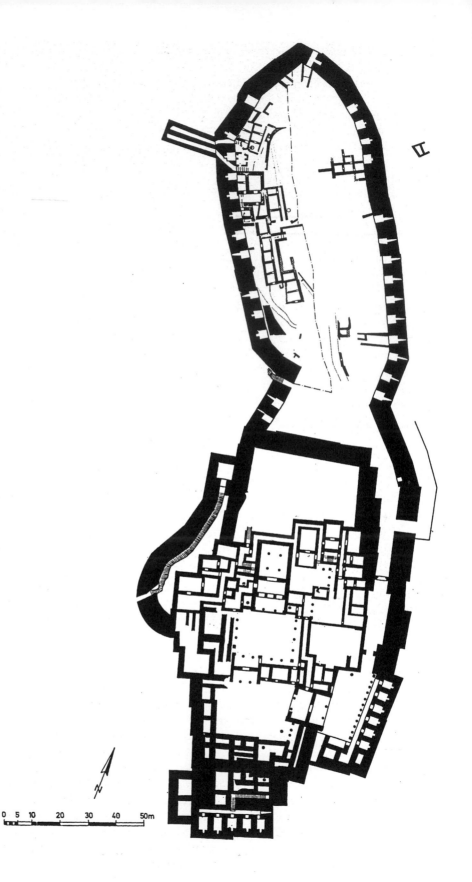

0 5 10   20   30   40   50m

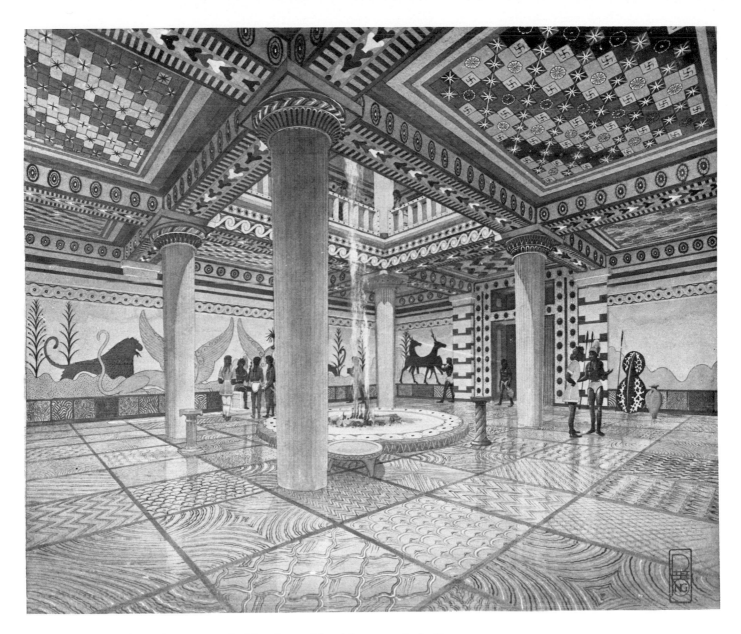

devoted to a number of rooms, probably of a residential nature, including a smaller but highly decorated megaron, dubbed the Queen's Megaron, with its own hearth. It had an exit into an open fenced courtyard similar to a slightly larger area to the north. Nearby, but not entered from the small megaron, a room that contained a built-in terra cotta bathtub was excavated (Fig. 3.8). A step next to it aided the bather in getting in, and the tub itself was painted with spiral designs. In a corner of the room stood two large jars, presumably for water, which were also built into a plaster bench. Rooms above can be inferred from the remains of staircases opening off both the east and west corridors, and it has often been possible to make intelligent guesses as to the functions of these rooms from some of the objects that have fallen into the lower areas. For instance, fragments of worked ivory found well above the floor in one of the rooms in the east wing suggest an upper room in which highly decorated small boxes or instruments were used, perhaps a boudoir.

3.6 Reconstruction of the throne room of the megaron at Pylos. Reprinted by permission of Princeton University Press and the University of Cincinnati.

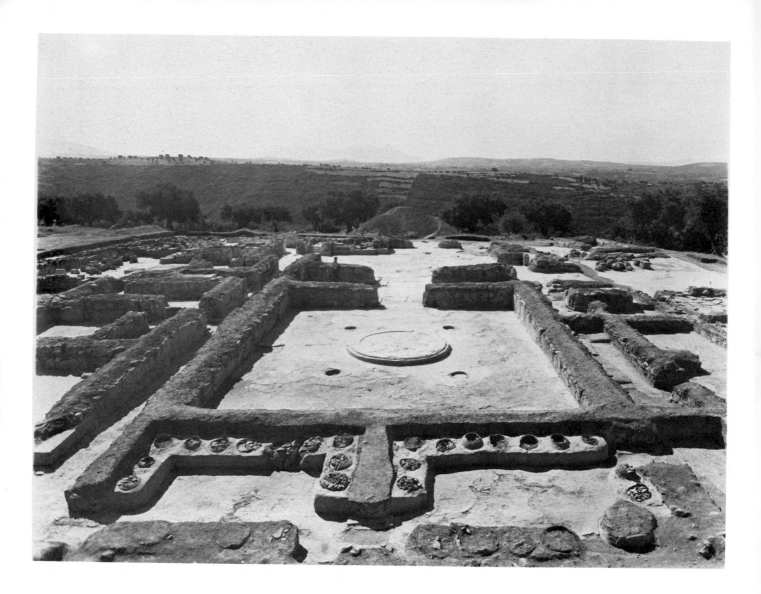

3.7 View of the throne room at Pylos and the surrounding area, from the northwest. Reprinted by permission of Princeton University Press and the University of Cincinnati.

Some private Mycenaean houses were sumptuous copies of the palaces; others were simple rectangular or apsidal buildings. A central room, or megaron, was a usual feature, but rooms were of various sizes and shapes.

Mycenaean engineering is to be seen not only in the great fortification walls of Mycenae and Tiryns but also in such things as the carefully maintained system of roads that connected major centers and the stone bridges over which they passed. Hydraulic engineering works, although generally not so extensive as in the Cretan palaces, brought water into the palaces on aqueducts and carried it out in drains. A great engineering project drained a large swamp in Boiotia, thus reclaiming valuable farmland.

Nowhere is Mycenaean construction seen to better advantage than in the great tholos or beehive tombs of the mainland, which were in fact the royal burial vaults associated with the palace sites. Before the tholos tombs came into use, at the end of the Middle Helladic period (about 1675), a particular type of grave made a sudden appearance at Mycenae, interrupting the normal MH practice of single burials in stone-lined cists. These graves are known as shaft graves from the manner of construction. A shaft was cut downward from the

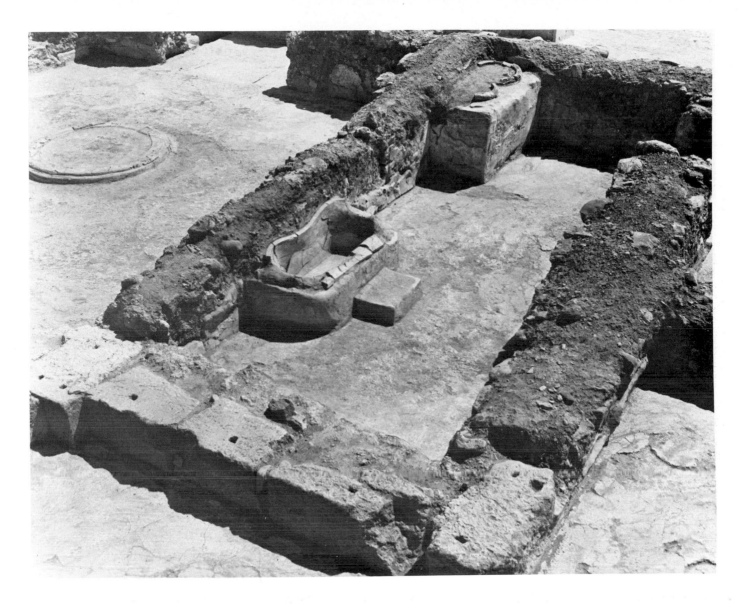

3.8 The Queen's Megaron and bathroom, Pylos, from the north. Reprinted by permission of Princeton University Press and the University of Cincinnati.

surface, sometimes as far as four meters into bedrock. Side walls were then built chest-high to form a chamber. The body and grave goods were laid on the floor of the shaft, which sometimes was covered with pebbles, and a roof of wooden beams and branches waterproofed with clay was placed on the walls before the shaft was filled with earth. These were communal graves, the shaft dug out and refilled each time a subsequent body was introduced. The most famous of these shaft graves are those found at Mycenae, which in date overlap the late Middle Helladic and early Late Helladic periods. Grave Circle A was included within the fortification walls of the thirteenth century, but Grave Circle B was outside the walls and was discovered by the Greek Archaeological Service some seventy-five years after Schliemann had found the first circle. Grave Circle A held nineteen skeletons (nine men, eight women, and two children) in six shaft graves and a group of Middle Helladic inhumations that were never counted; they have been dated as spanning up to three generations. Circle B is smaller, poorer, and older, containing some twenty-four graves (twenty-two men, eight women, and four children), fourteen of which were

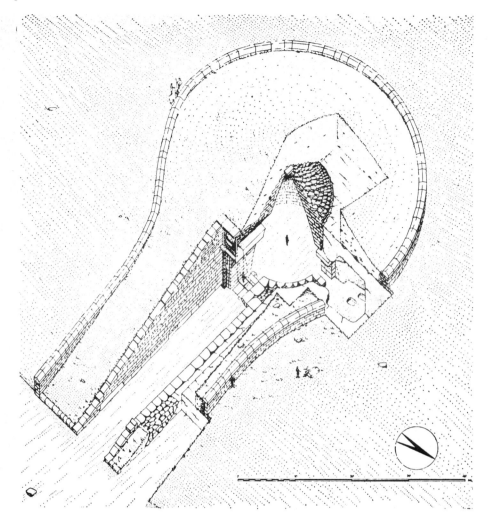

3.9 Isometric drawing of the Treasury of Atreus, Mycenae. From Reynold Higgins, *Minoan and Mycenaean Art*, rev. ed. (London, 1981), p. 88, Fig. 93. Reproduced by permission.

shaft graves and the remaining simple inhumations. The finds from the two circles include pottery, stone, and metalwork, especially objects of precious metals, and are our best source of information on Early Mycenaean minor arts.[13]

The principal methods of burial during the later Mycenaean period were interment in chamber tombs and, for the royal family, in tholos tombs. Chamber tombs are essentially caves cut horizontally into the side of a hill and approached by a long entrance passage, or dromos. They are family tombs, and many held generations of the dead. Tholos tombs were constructed of great blocks of cut stone and have been described as stonelined holes. A deep circular cut in a hillside was lined with blocks laid in corbel style, so that the diameter of the circle decreased until the final opening at the top could be closed with a capstone. An entrance constructed of large blocks is approached by a sloping dromos (Fig. 3.9). The dead were laid on the floor of the tholos or perhaps in single graves cut into its floor.

[13] Mylonas, *Mycenae and the Mycenaean Age*, chap. 4, contains a general discussion of the two grave circles. The finds are readably discussed in Emily Vermeule, *The Art of the Shaft Graves of Mycenae* (Norman, Okla., 1975).

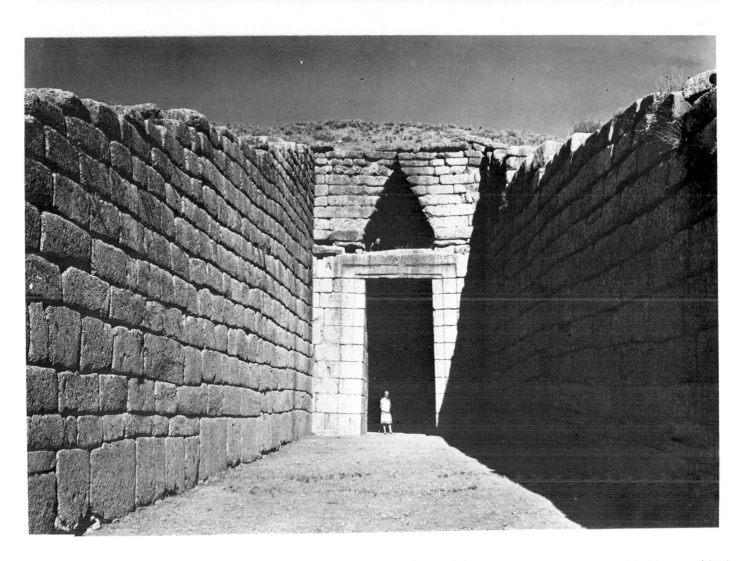

The tholos tomb is known throughout mainland Greece. Although its origin is not fully understood, it is now clear that the type extended into Protogeometric times. Although possibly a Mycenaean form, it may owe at least some inspiration to round communal graves on Crete.[14]

The best preserved and most famous of the tholoi is the so-called Treasury of Atreus at Mycenae (Fig. 3.9), dating to the mid-LH IIIB period or slightly earlier.[15] Here the dromos is gigantic, 6.0 meters wide and 36.0 meters long, and ends at a decorated doorway 5.4 meters high and 2.7 meters wide at the threshold (Fig. 3.10). Green limestone half columns with decorative zigzag relief carving originally stood on either side of the door, probably supporting smaller columns that flanked whatever fitted into the now empty relieving triangle above. The doorway is framed by great blocks of limestone 5.4 meters

3.10 Dromos and entrance of the Treasury of Atreus, Mycenae. Photo: Deutsches Archäologisches Institut, Athens.

[14] M. S. F. Hood, "Tholos Tombs of the Aegean," *Antiquity* 34 (1960): 166–176, is the basic reference on the subject of the origin of tholos tombs. See also Vermeule, *Greece in the Bronze Age*, pp. 120–136 and Bibliography. Dickinson, *Aegean Bronze Age*, discusses Mycenaean burial customs on pp. 222–233.
[15] Opinions vary on the date of this tholos. A summary of the evidence may be found in Mylonas, *Mycenae and the Mycenaean Age*, pp. 120–122.

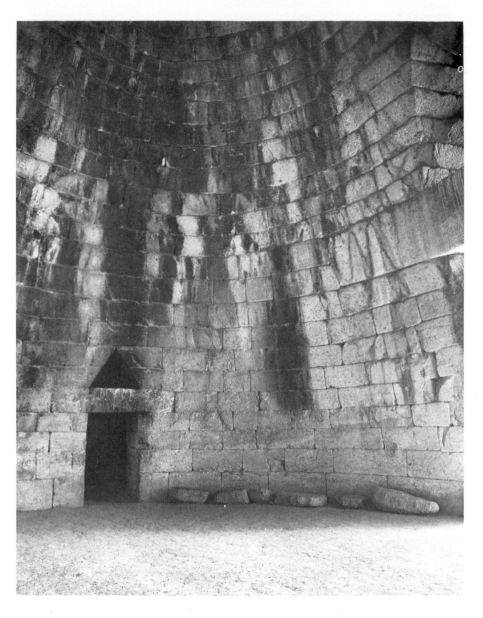

deep; the inner of the two massive lintels is a block 9.0 meters long, 5.0 meters wide, and 1.2 meters thick, and has been calculated to weigh 120 tons. The main room of the tholos measures 14.6 meters in diameter and the height to the vault is 13.5 meters. The walls are composed of thirty-three superimposed courses and contain holes and remnants of bronze nails for decorations of some kind, perhaps rosettes. A side room was attached to the Treasury of Atreus (Fig. 3.11). Only two other examples of such a room in a tholos are known.

SCULPTURE

Large-scale sculpture, generally unknown in Mycenaean art, is represented only by the high relief of the Lion Gate at Mycenae (see Fig. 3.3), although there surely must have been other examples, now lost. Two lionesses stand on either side of a tapering column that supports four circles between two horizontal bars, probably representing an entablature. The lionesses rest their front paws on either side of the base of the column above two altars with concave sides. Cuttings in their necks suggest that the heads were made of another material and then attached, probably facing out toward the visitor to the citadel. Although the subject of the relief is fairly clear, its meaning is disputed. It has variously been interpreted as a religious symbol, a political emblem, a heraldic device, and a purely decorative sculpture.[16]

A painted plaster head found at Mycenae is the one other object that can be considered to be large-scale sculpture, although it is only 16.8 centimeters in height (Fig. 3.12). The long white face is brightly picked out in black, blue, and red, with red lips and red rosettes formed of dots on both cheeks and the chin. It perhaps represents a sphinx. Although not strictly Mycenaean, the large terra cotta figures found in the shrine on Kea should probably be illustrated here (Fig. 3.13). Fragments of more than fifty female statues were found, representing at least nine distinct types within the general formula of a standing or dancing female wearing a flaring skirt, heavy girdle, and short, flaring jacket that exposes the breasts. Some wear a thick, heavy collar, perhaps representing a garland; others a flat band around the neck, possibly a necklace. They vary in height from only 70 centimeters to life size and were modeled in sections over wooden supports, which were left in the clay during firing. Traces of yellow, red, and white indicate they were brightly painted; no doubt the flesh parts of these female figures were white, as was the convention in the Bronze Age. Some of the earliest of the groups are conjectured to have been made as early as the Middle Bronze Age, the latest after the temple was destroyed at a period that in the Cyclades was contemporary with the end of Late Helladic II. The head of one of the statues was even reused in an eighth-century shrine to Dionysos built above the Mycenaean one.[17]

Relief sculpture evidently had its beginnings in Mycenaean Greece with the grave markers from the shaft graves. Undecorated gravestones were known in the Middle Helladic period; decorations appear on them at the end of the period. A number of stone markers have been found in association with both grave circles, some carved and others left plain. Those decorated are of local limestone, smooth on the back and incised or lightly carved on the front. Ornamental designs and scenes of animals, warriors in chariots, and the like reflect Mycenaean life. A typical example is the stele from Grave V in Circle A (Fig. 3.14), which shows a lion chasing a gazelle or other deerlike animal while above a figure with a sword in a chariot moves in the same direction as the animals. Under his horse and above the animals is a shape that has been interpreted as rocky ground or a fallen enemy under a bull's-hide figure-eight shield. Did the sculptor intend to suggest a relationship between the lion running down its prey and the warrior doing likewise, or is it simply a hunting scene? Chariot scenes may similarly be interpreted as battles or as funeral games for the dead. The crudeness of the carving makes interpretation difficult, but the themes portrayed seem to fit well with Mycenaean culture.[18]

[16] See ibid., pp. 173–176.
[17] See n. 10 above.
[18] These gravestones are discussed in Vermeule, *Greece in the Bronze Age*, pp. 90–94.

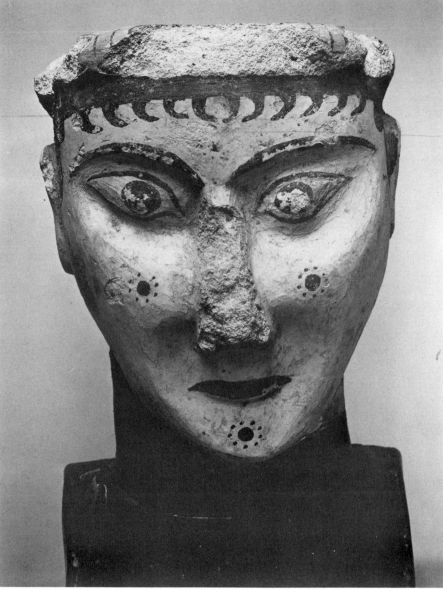

3.12 Plaster head from Mycenae. National Archaeological Museum, Athens. Photo: Deutsches Archäologisches Institut, Athens.

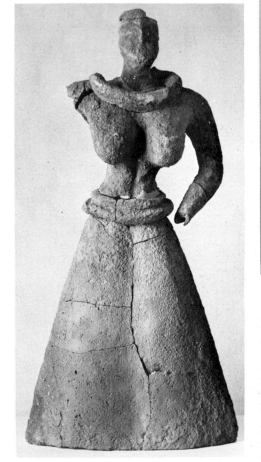

3.13 Terra cotta figure from Kea. Photo: J. L. Caskey.

PAINTING

The mainland palaces were heavily decorated, with painted floors, walls, and probably even ceilings. Fragments of paintings have been recovered from almost all palace sites and recent researches have shown that even some houses outside the fortification walls at Mycenae had wall paintings. Mycenaean walls were decorated with frescoes in Minoan style and technique. Minoan artists may have been responsible for them, at least in the initial stages, although there is no direct evidence. Some themes, such as that of the procession fresco, are taken over from the Minoan repertoire and are endlessly repeated. Mycenae and Tiryns even had bull-vaulting scenes, though their significance may have been entirely lost on the mainland lords who commissioned them. Where

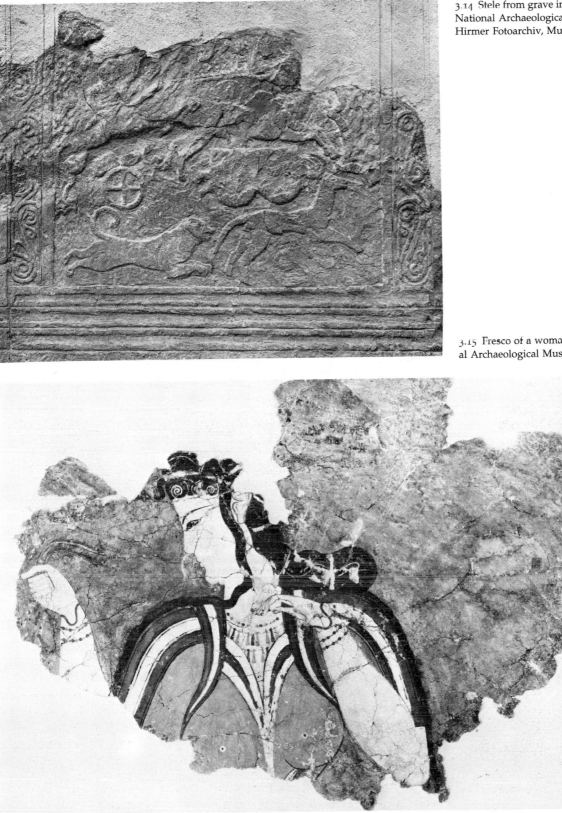

3.14 Stele from grave in Grave Circle A, Mycenae. National Archaeological Museum, Athens. Photo: Hirmer Fotoarchiv, Munich.

3.15 Fresco of a woman, Mycenae. Photo: National Archaeological Museum, Athens.

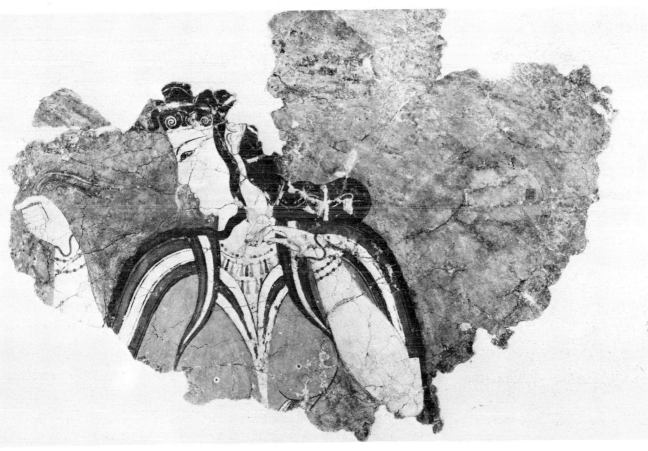

originality existed, it was in the themes with which the Mycenaeans felt at home and which were alien to the Minoans: heraldic animals, war, the hunt. The Minoan love of nature is missing from Mycenaean work; plants, trees, flowers, and so on are used only as stylized backgrounds or as adjuncts to human figures, who hold flowers in their hands in procession scenes. When animals appear, they are shown either as helpers of men (horses, hunting dogs), as their prey (stags, wild boar), or in rows of decorative friezes.

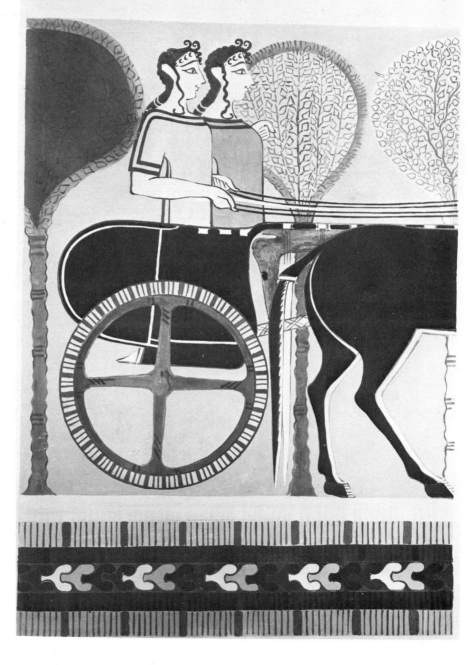

3.16 Reconstructed wall painting of women in a chariot, Tiryns. Photo: Deutsches Archäologisches Institut, Athens.

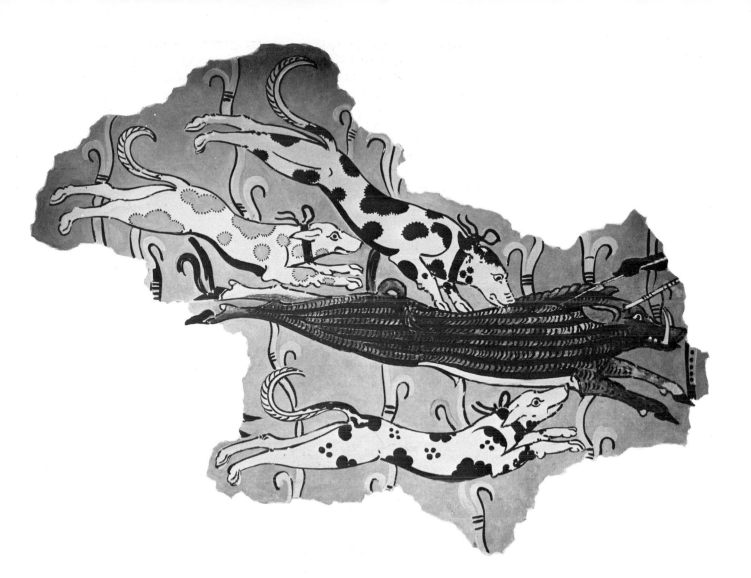

3.17 Reconstructed wall painting of a boar hunt. Tiryns. Photo: Deutsches Archäologisches Institut, Athens.

A recently found fresco fragment from Mycenae can be compared to La Parisienne from Knossos (Fig. 3.15). The Mycenaean figure is larger and heavier and lacks the subtlety of the Minoan. Note the heavy jewelry, the mannered position of the hands (both are right hands), and the great interest in details, as shown by the carefully drawn fingernails. Although this fresco was painted by an artist of some talent, not all Mycenaean painting is of such quality, as is evident in the representation of two women in a chariot from Tiryns (Fig. 3.16). Here the stiff, upright figures pass in front of baldly stylized trees, and the artist has lavished more attention on the chariot than he has on the humans. The Mycenaeans' accuracy in depicting equipment, in contrast to the sketchiness of Cretan paintings, is often achieved at the expense of figured work. The boar harried by hunting dogs in the same composition shows the treatment of animals, with the creatures carefully drawn despite their rather mechanical flying gallops (Fig. 3.17). In their flight through a stylized thicket, they seem unreal in their perfection and are somewhat strangely colored. The procession fresco from Pylos (Fig. 3.18) repeats a Minoan formula, this time acted out by

3.18 Restored procession fresco, Pylos. Reprinted by permission of Princeton University Press and the University of Cincinnati.

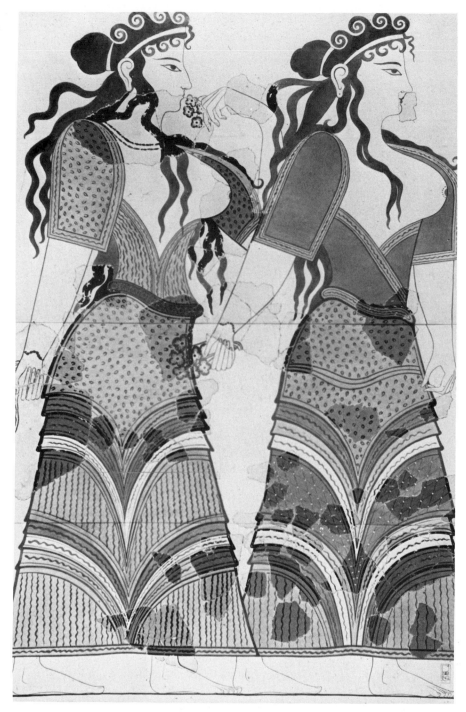

typically formal, austere, repetitive, and heavy Mycenaean women. The battle scene from the same site (Fig. 3.19) presents something new and unexpected: a battle between Mycenaeans with helmets and leggings and men dressed only in skins, dubbed Tarzans by the excavators. We have no idea who these people are, but the subject fits well with what we think we know of Mycenaean life and society.

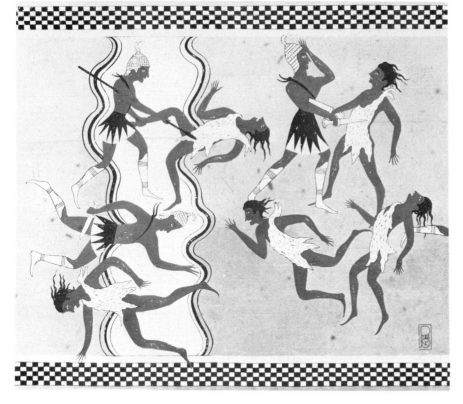

3.19 Reconstruction of the Tarzan fresco, Pylos. Reprinted by permission of Princeton University Press and the University of Cincinnati.

POTTERY

The decoration of Mycenaean pottery and many of its forms were dependent on Crete in their early stages and then developed with a progressive stylization of Cretan motifs, as we have already seen in the Cretan pottery of the Palace period.[19] Mycenaean pottery, widespread throughout the Mediterranean world, is well made if rather repetitious and dull in its decoration, and stands directly in the line of development from its Middle Helladic predecessors, especially in regard to the fabric. Designs in dull black-to-brown glaze show the progressive stylization of the original Minoan Floral and Marine designs into a Pattern style of decoration. Figure 3.20 shows the progressive simplification of designs while Figure 3.21 shows typical shapes in use in the Late Helladic IIIB period, including the tall-stemmed kylix, developed from a rounder and shorter form from the beginning of the Late Helladic, and the stirrup jar, developed from the form invented on Crete and extremely popular throughout the Mycenaean world. Further examples of these typical Mycenaean shapes are shown in Figures 3.22 and 3.23.

A rather debased Pictorial style existed at the same time as the Pattern style. The painted scenes give the impression that the subjects of wall paintings were being reproduced on pottery by poor artists. A number of large kraters decorated with scenes of chariots belong to this style.

[19] The basic study on this subject is Arne Furumark, *Mycenaean Pottery*, 2 vols. (Stockholm, 1972). The basic handbook is Penelope A. Mountjoy, *Mycenaean Pottery: An Introduction* (Oxford, 1993).

3.20 Simplification of motifs in Mycenaean pottery. From A. D. Lacy, *Greek Pottery in the Bronze Age* (London: Methuen, 1967), p. 206, Fig. 80. Reproduced by permission.

Rockwork and seaweed   through   becomes

A 'bivalve shell'   through   becomes

A double-axe   through   becomes

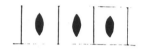

A murex shell   through   becomes

An argonaut   through   becomes

As has been mentioned, during the LH IIIC period, after the destructions at the end of IIIB (c. 1190), pottery styles varied from place to place. Most shapes continued in use but the decoration varied. Simple linear patterns, such as running spirals, could be the only ornamentation (Fig. 3.24, left). In the Close style, in contrast, the whole surface is covered with a close-fitting net of conventional designs, often elaborated with rosettes, fish, and birds (Fig. 3.24, right). The east coast of Attica and the islands developed a variant of the Close style that featured marine creatures, especially the octopus (Fig. 3.25). A comparison of the LH IIIC octopus with its parent LM IB octopus is instructive (see Fig. 2.32).

The Pictorial style continued into the IIIC period; the Warrior Vase from Mycenae (Fig. 3.26), dating to this period, is well known. A file of warriors wearing horned helmets, body armor, and leggings moves to the right, away from a mourning woman. Over their shoulders the warriors carry spears, from which hang pennons or bags. On the reverse a file of warriors identically dressed except for their helmets, which appear to be covered with spikes, also advances to the right, with raised spears and shields held out in front of them.

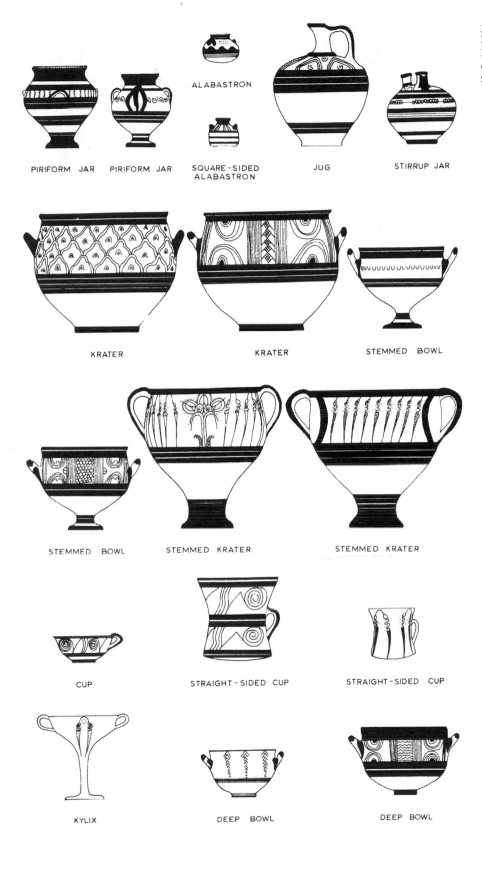

ALABASTRON

PIRIFORM JAR   PIRIFORM JAR   SQUARE-SIDED   JUG   STIRRUP JAR
ALABASTRON

KRATER   KRATER   STEMMED BOWL

STEMMED BOWL   STEMMED KRATER   STEMMED KRATER

CUP   STRAIGHT-SIDED CUP   STRAIGHT-SIDED CUP

KYLIX   DEEP BOWL   DEEP BOWL

3.21 Typical pottery shapes of the Late Helladic IIIB period. Adapted from a chart by Elizabeth French, K. A. Wardle, and Diana Wardle. Courtesy of E. B. French. Drawing by John Huffstot. Scale 1:8.

3.22 (right) Typical undecorated kylikes from the pantries of the palace at Pylos. Pylos Museum. Reprinted by permission of Princeton University Press and the University of Cincinnati.

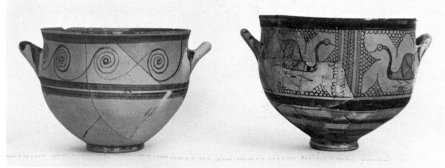

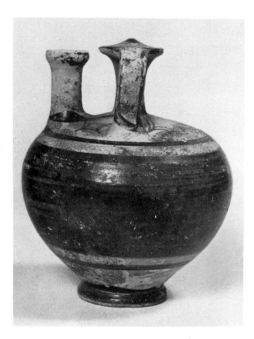

3.23 (above) Mycenaean stirrup jar. Photo: Museum of Art and Archaeology, University of Missouri–Columbia.

3.24 (right) Late Helladic IIIC bowls with simple decoration (left) and the Close style (right). Photo: American School of Classical Studies at Athens: Corinth Excavations.

3.25 Typical Late Helladic IIIC octopus stirrup jar, from Athens. National Archaeological Museum, Athens. Photo: Deutsches Archäologisches Institut, Athens.

3.26 (far right) Warrior Vase from Mycenae. National Archaeological Museum, Athens. Photo: Alison Frantz.

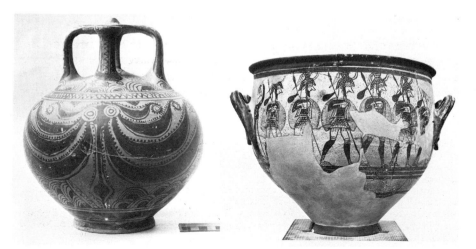

Similar in style are the paintings on coffins or larnakes, often showing funeral scenes or marching figures.[20]

TERRA COTTA FIGURINES

Mycenaean terra cotta figurines are unique and are found in great numbers.[21] The most common type is a female figure ultimately derived from Crete at the beginning of LH III. The figurines seem to have been subjected to the same ruthless stylization as were designs on pottery. The three basic types (shown in Fig. 3.27) are named after the letters of the Greek alphabet which they resemble, Phi, Psi, and Tau, with a number of variations. Phi figurines are the earliest type and Tau the latest. Found both in cemeteries and in settlements, the figurines represent standing women dressed conservatively in an overall garment, either disc-shaped and armless (Phi type) or with their arms extended in a crescent (Psi type). Simply modeled and covered with usually vertical stripes, they have been variously interpreted. Some may represent divine beings while others were perhaps simple dedications. Other types of figurines are also known, including bovine animals, horses and riders, oxen and riders, chariots, and groups, including paired female figures similar to the miniature group from Mycenae (see below, "Ivory").

A number of large figurines, considered to be idols by their excavator, Lord William Taylour, were found in Mycenae's cult area. They vary considerably in size, clothing, position of arms, painting, and attitude, from a delicately painted fourteenth-century female figurine about 29 centimeters in height (Fig. 3.28) to larger, cruder, and fiercer figures some 60 centimeters high. The idols were made on a potter's wheel, with the arms and sometimes the facial features added separately. Most of the larger figures are painted in simple slashes of black glaze, with areas reserved to emphasize the face. A bust of one of the female figures, 30 centimeters high (Fig. 3.29), shows clearly the power and individuality such idols could attain. The holes in the figure are considered by the excavator to be firing holes, but may also have served to secure decoration to the figure.[22]

Various other objects in terra cotta are of course known from Late Bronze Age contexts throughout the Mediterranean, including buttons or spindle whorls, loom weights for use in weaving, and the like.

STONEWORK

The carving of scenes on stone vessels does not seem to have been to Mycenaean taste, although a number of plain stone vases have been found. Stone seals continued to be carved, but it is difficult to distinguish Minoan seals from Mycenaean. Battle and hunt scenes are Mycenaean in conception, but religious

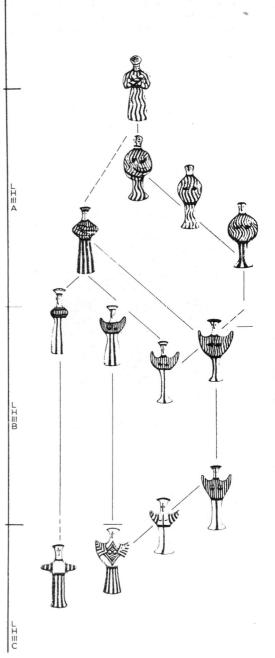

3.27 Development of Mycenaean female terra cotta figurines. Courtesy of E. B. French. Drawing by Tamarra McNicoll.

20 See Emily T. Vermeule, "Painted Mycenaean Larnakes," *JHS* (1965): 123–148, and her *Aspects of Death in Early Greek Art and Poetry* (Berkeley, 1979), pp. 42–82.
21 For Mycenaean figurines see Elizabeth French, "The Development of Mycenaean Terracotta Figurines," *BSA* 66 (1971): 101–187.
22 The figures are discussed in Lord William Taylour, "Mycenae, 1968," *Antiquity* 43 (1969): 91–97, and "New Light on Mycenaean Religion," *Antiquity* 44 (1970): 270–280. For differing interpretations, see Andrew Moore, "The Large Monochrome Terracotta Figures from Mycenae: the Problem of Interpretation," in *Problems in Greek Prehistory*, ed. Elizabeth French and Kenneth A. Wardle (Bristol, 1988), pp. 219–228.

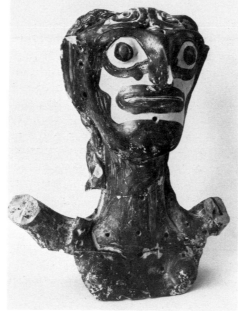

3.29 Upper half of a large idol from Mycenae. Archaeological Museum, Nauplia. Photo: Lord William Taylour.

3.28 Small female idol from Mycenae. Archaeological Museum, Nauplia. Courtesy of Lord William Taylour.

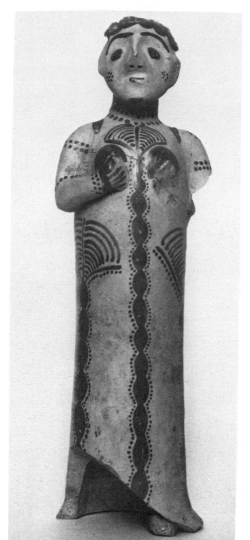

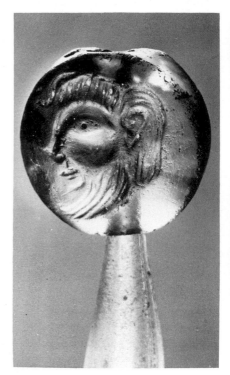

3.30 Amethyst seal from Mycenae. National Archaeological Museum, Athens. Photo: Deutsches Archäologisches Institut, Athens.

scenes are open to various interpretations. At this stage in our knowledge we are uncertain whether the Minoan religion was completely adopted by the mainlanders or whether the religious scenes depicted on the gems had become merely decorative by the time they were reproduced by the Mycenaeans. A possible Minoan product is the amethyst gem with a bearded head cut into it from Grave Circle B at Mycenae (Fig. 3.30). It appears to contrast with the smooth-cheeked and long-haired Minoans we know from their frescoes, but Minoan representations of bearded priests are not unknown.

Stone was used also for the ubiquitous small whorls or buttons known from many Late Bronze Age sites both in Crete and on the mainland. Some were also made of clay. The development from a simple cone (the most common stone shape) to a more elaborate shanked form is shown in Figure 3.31.[23] Stone was used also for numerous tools and for arrowheads, weights, grinders, polishers, beads, pommels, and a multiplicity of other objects, as might be expected even in the Bronze Age.

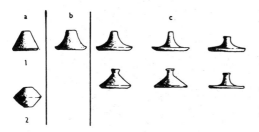

3.31 Shape development of spindle whorls or buttons. From Arne Furumark, *Mycenaean Pottery,* vol. 2, *Chronology* (Gothenburg: Svenska Instituten i Rom och Athen, 1941; reprinted Stockholm, 1972), p. 89, Fig. 2. Reproduced by permission.

[23] A suggestion is that these common objects are actually weights for clothing. See Spyros Iakovidis, "On the Use of Mycenaean 'Buttons,'" *BSA* 72 (1977): 113–119.

IVORY

Ivory carving was a Mycenaean specialty, probably derived once again from Crete. Typically Mycenaean are ivory relief plaques used to adorn furniture and various objects of wood. Since ivory was an imported material, its presence indicates foreign trade. A large amount of carved ivory is known in the eastern Mediterranean from this time, and the art may have been international.

An ivory pyxis, or toilet box, from Athens, carved from a section of elephant tusk, is decorated with scenes of winged griffons attacking deer (Fig. 3.32). The flat, elongated bodies and twisted poses of the attacked animals express the savagery of the battle. Flat plaques used as inlays, such as the head of a warrior wearing a boar's-tusk helmet from Mycenae (Fig. 3.33), were made with consummate skill. The discovery of an ivory workshop at Mycenae suggests that this site may have been a center of the industry.

Although the ivory carvers primarily produced plaques and inlays, a small sculpture in ivory from Mycenae indicates that they were also capable of figures in the round (Fig. 3.34). Two female figures in close contact and sharing a common stole are shown seated. They wear the Minoan court costume. Leaning against the knee of one is a small child. This group, of exquisite

3.32 Ivory pyxis from Athens. Agora Museum, Athens. Photo: American School of Classical Studies at Athens: Agora Excavations.

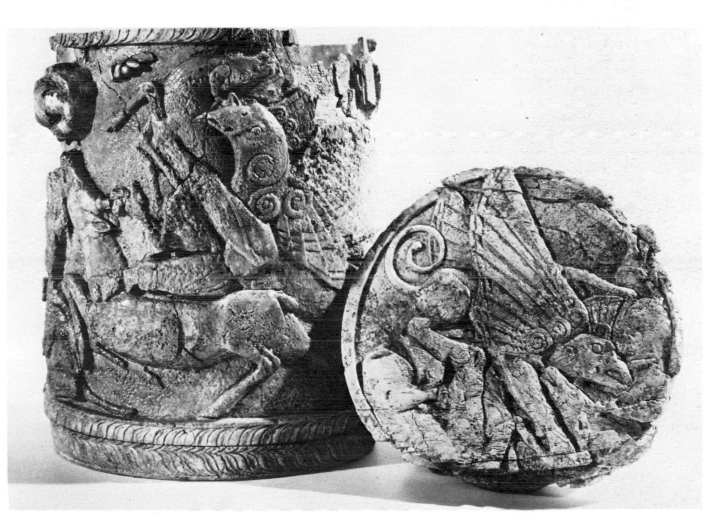

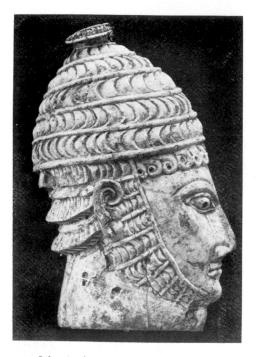

3.33 Inlay in form of helmeted head from Mycenae. National Archaeological Museum, Athens. Photo: Deutsches Archäologisches Institut, Athens.

3.34 (right) Ivory triad from Mycenae. National Archaeological Museum, Athens. Photo: Hirmer Fotoarchiv, Munich.

3.35 Ivory head from Mycenae. Archaeological Museum, Nauplia. Photo: Lord William Taylour.

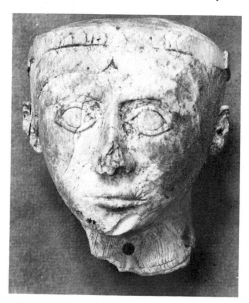

workmanship, brings to mind the cruder terra cotta group figurines that include a child. Although they are generally interpreted as two goddesses with a divine offspring, the true identity of these figures still eludes us.

In the same area at Mycenae that yielded the idols, a small (6 centimeters in diameter) ivory head of a man was also found (Fig. 3.35). The presence of attachment holes indicates that the head was attached originally to a body of some other material, but no trace of it has been found. The face is the same long visage with big eyes we have come to expect, but the workmanship is of superior quality. Note the carefully engraved hair; the excavator suggests it may represent a wig.

The ivory inlay of the warrior's head shows another industry, more utilitarian than artistic, the preparing of boars' tusks to be sewn onto leather caps to form helmets. These helmets must have been luxury items because of the great

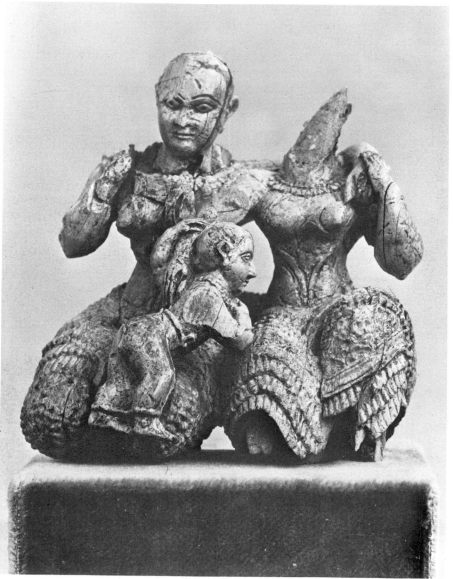

number of boars that had to be killed to make one, but they are well represented in art, and specimens of split tusks with holes bored into them for attachment have been found in graves. Homer actually describes such a helmet (*Iliad* X, 265–266), which must have been an outlandish anachronism in his day.

Ivory and bone were also used for such objects as combs and carved handles for bronze mirrors, as well as for a variety of small tools and implements, as throughout antiquity.

METALWORK

From the contents of the shaft graves through to the end of LH IIIB, Mycenaean metalwork, especially in precious metals, is of high quality. A combination of metals on a single object, as in the inlaid daggers found in the shaft graves (Fig. 3.36), is characteristic. The technique involved the laying of a sheet of darker bronze into a shallow bed cut on the bronze blade. Cutouts of figures and landscape elements in silver or gold were set into this sheet. The surface was then polished to remove the hammer marks and oxidized to darken the silver sections. Details of clothing, faces, skins of animals, and so on were then engraved upon the cutouts. Finally the incisions from the engraving were filled

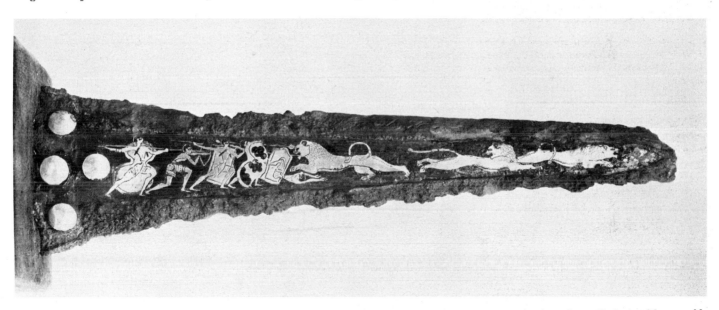

3.36 Dagger from Grave Circle A at Mycenae. National Archaeological Museum, Athens. Photo: Alison Frantz.

with black niello, a substance composed of copper, lead, sulfur, and borax, which was burned in by the application of heat. The niello technique can be seen in the lion-hunt scene on the dagger blade from Grave Circle A in Figure 3.36. The scene, featuring tower and figure-eight shields that we have seen before, is pure Mycenaean.

Gold was worked into vases both alone and in combination with other metals, and a number of gold vessels and cups are known. Two gold cups dating to about 1500 were found in a tholos tomb on the mainland, at Vapheio in Laconia. They are decorated with scenes of the capture of wild bulls worked in repoussé technique, in which the design is raised by hammering on the reverse of the gold sheet. In Figure 3.37 a bull is being tied by one leg; in Figure 3.38 another is being caught in a net. A glance at the male figure in Figure 3.37

3.37 Gold cup from Vapheio, showing the capture of a wild bull. National Archaeological Museum, Athens. Photo: Alison Frantz.

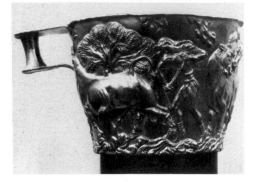

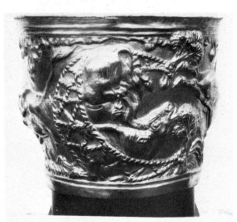

3.38 Gold cup from Vapheio, showing a netted bull. National Archaeological Museum, Athens. Photo: Alison Frantz.

3.39 Gold mask from the shaft graves at Mycenae. National Archaeological Museum, Athens. Photo: Alison Frantz.

and at the distortion of the bull in Figure 3.38 reveals clearly that the scenes are Minoan in style.[24]

The unique and famous gold masks from Grave Circle A at Mycenae are probably the most well-known gold objects from this civilization. The one shown here (Fig. 3.39) is the best preserved and most individualistic of the group found by Schliemann. Hammered over a presumably wooden form, the mask has conventional eyes and ears and was found, according to Schliemann, still over the face of the deceased. Gold was fashioned also into jewelry, which may be seen reproduced in the frescoes. Magnificent gold rings with scenes of the hunt and war cut into their surfaces are masterpieces of engraving on a small scale (Fig. 3.40). Religious scenes also appear, with female figures, sacred trees, and so on, but as in the case of gems, their significance is uncertain. Gold ornaments were probably used in everyday life as well as in the funeral contexts in which we find them. Some of the bodies in the shaft graves were literally covered with mounds of gold ornaments, most very thin beaten gold in the form of rosettes, butterflies, and the like.

Silver was also used for vessels, but as it has a tendency to corrode, fewer examples are known. A battered rhyton from Grave Circle A preserves a siege or battle scene (Fig. 3.41). The warlike subject is appropriate for Mycenaean art,

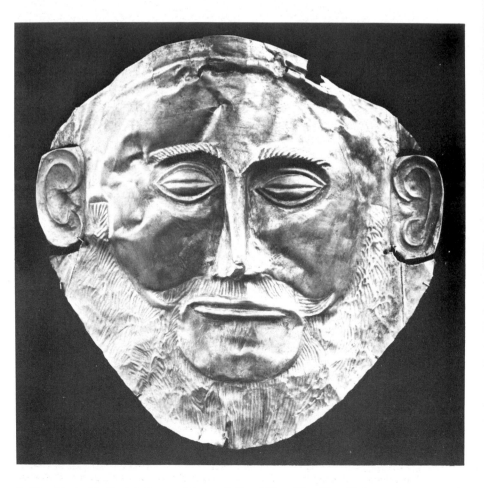

[24] Ellen Davis, *The Vapheio Cups and Aegean Gold and Silver Ware* (New York, 1977).

although the object it decorates is Minoan in form. The buildings remind one of those in the Thera fresco.

Many bronze vessels of various shapes, produced by hammering, riveting, soldering, and so on, have survived from the Late Bronze Age. Bronze found its greatest use in the production of implements of war and tools, and quantities of arrowheads, spearheads, daggers, knives, and swords are known.

Bronze was also used for jewelry and dress fasteners.[25] Straight pins of bone, ivory, and bronze are found occasionally in Late Bronze Age contexts but can

3.40 Gold rings from the shaft graves at Mycenae. National Archaeological Museum, Athens. Photo: Deutsches Archäologisches Institut, Athens.

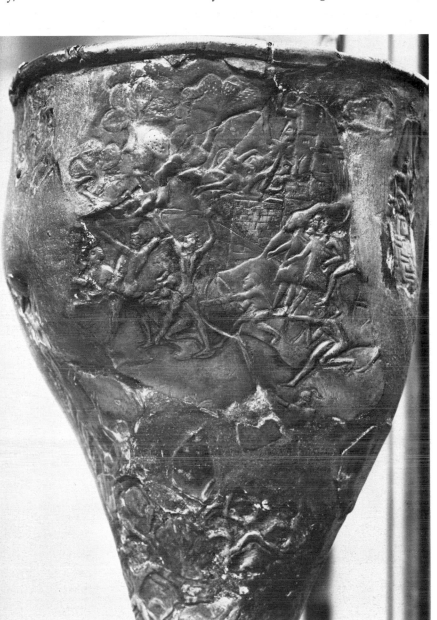

3.41 Silver Siege Rhyton from the shaft graves at Mycenae. National Archaeological Museum, Athens. Photo: Hirmer Fotoarchiv, Munich.

[25] The basic study of the straight pin in English is Paul Jacobsthal, *Greek Pins* (Oxford, 1956). Bronze Age straight pins have received little attention beyond scattered references in excavation reports. A typological scheme for the fibula, however, is given in Arne Furumark, *Mycenaean Pottery*, vol. 2, *Chronology*, pp. 91–93.

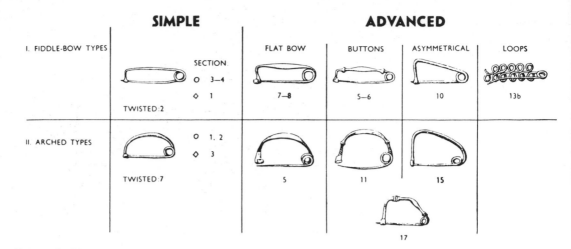

	SIMPLE		**ADVANCED**			
I. FIDDLE-BOW TYPES			FLAT BOW	BUTTONS	ASYMMETRICAL	LOOPS
		SECTION				
		○ 3—4				
		◇ 1	7—8	5—6	10	13b
	TWISTED:2					
II. ARCHED TYPES						
		○ 1, 2				
		◇ 3				
	TWISTED:7		5	11	15	
					17	

3.42 Fibula shapes. From Arne Furumark, *Mycenaean Pottery*, vol. 2, *Chronology* (Gothenburg: Svenska Instituten i Rom och Athen, 1941; reprinted Stockholm, 1972), p. 91, Fig. 3. Reproduced by permission.

hardly be considered typical of the period. Long, ornamented pins with rock-crystal heads were found in the shaft graves and examples with disc heads are known from Pylos in graves of the same period. A number of types are known from the very end of Mycenaean times and into the Dark Ages, often with a swelling on the upper part of the shank and moldings above and below it. (Examples from Crete and the mainland are shown in Figure 4.11.) In Argos, bronze pins with a globe on the shaft are recorded in Late Helladic IIIC contexts.

Pins bent into oval or circular shapes with clasps are known as fibulae (Fig. 3.42). The simple fiddle-bow type is the earliest, with more elaborate versions popular in LH IIIB and IIIC. The arched type arrives toward the end of the period and continues into Protogeometric times (see Chapter 4). Fiddle-bow pins, the most representative Mycenaean type, were widely distributed. Safety pins of this type were usually used in conjunction with thick garments, and the fibula is often considered to have originated in a colder area to the north.

1. (facing page) Fresco from Thera. National Archaeological Museum, Athens. Photo: Ekdotike Athenon, S. A.

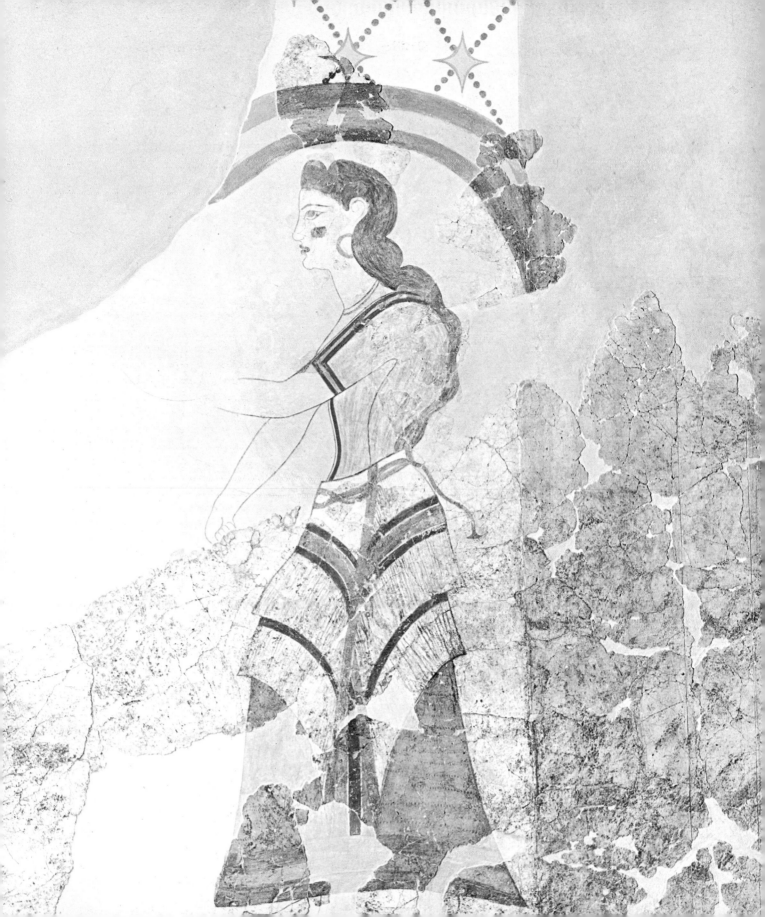

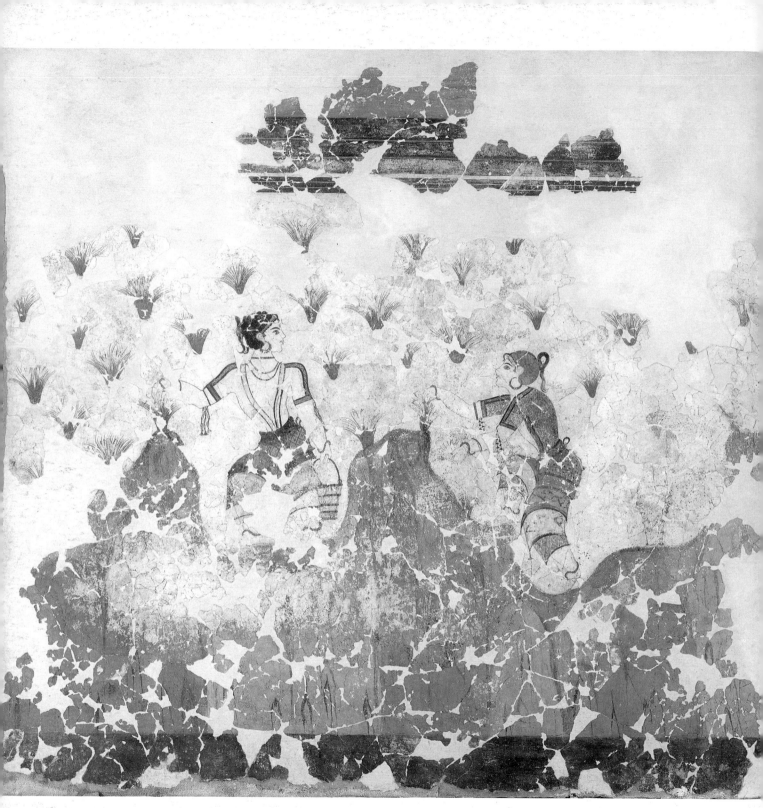

2. Women gather crocuses in a fresco at Xeste 3, Thera. Courtesy of The Thera Foundation.

3. (*facing page*) Phrasikleia and kouros as found. Photo: Nikos Kontos.

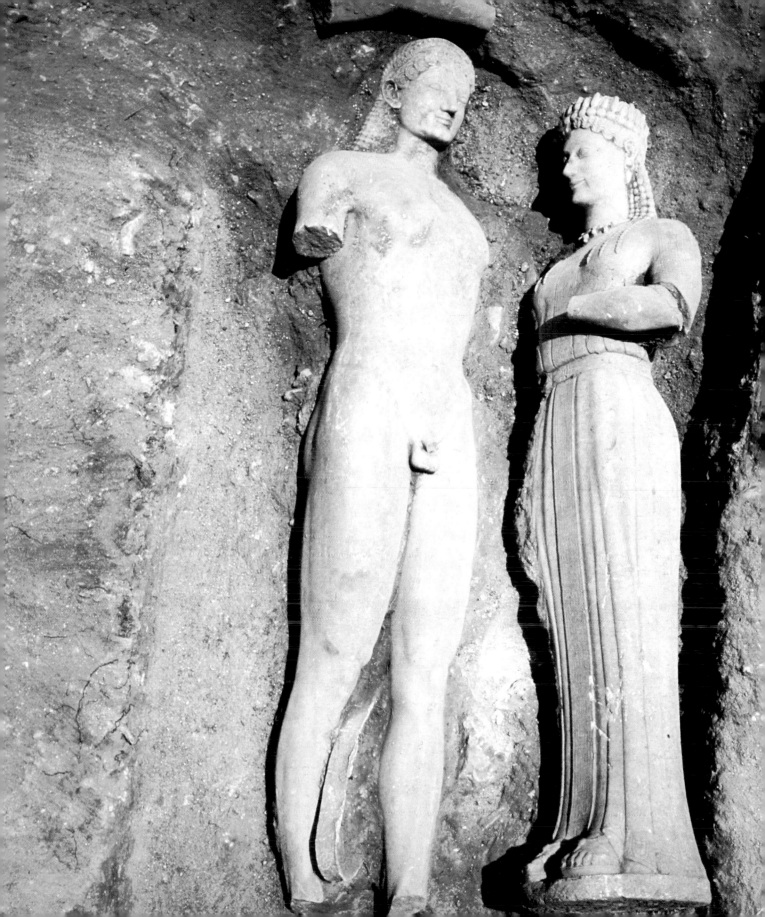

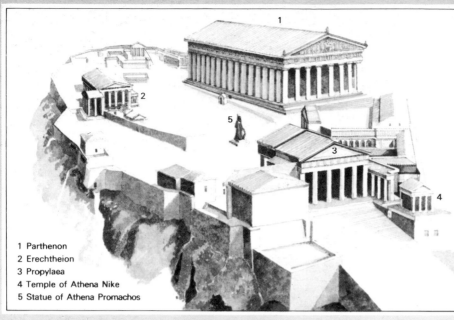

1 Parthenon
2 Erechtheion
3 Propylaea
4 Temple of Athena Nike
5 Statue of Athena Promachos

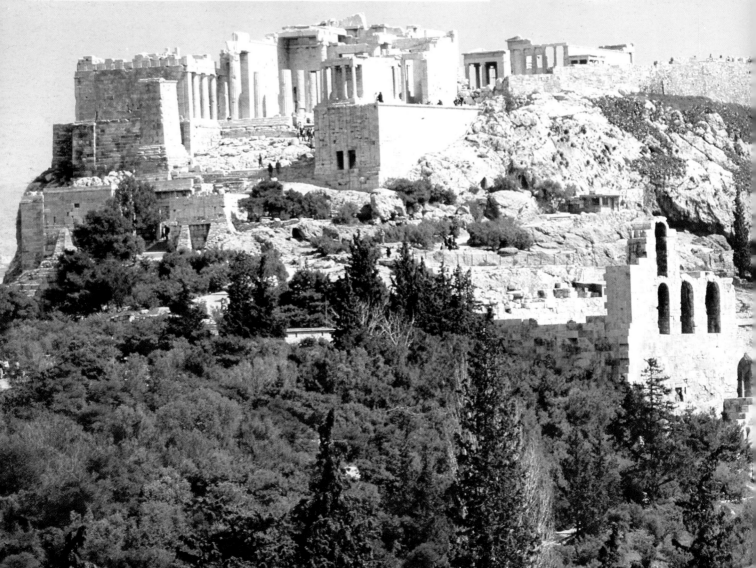

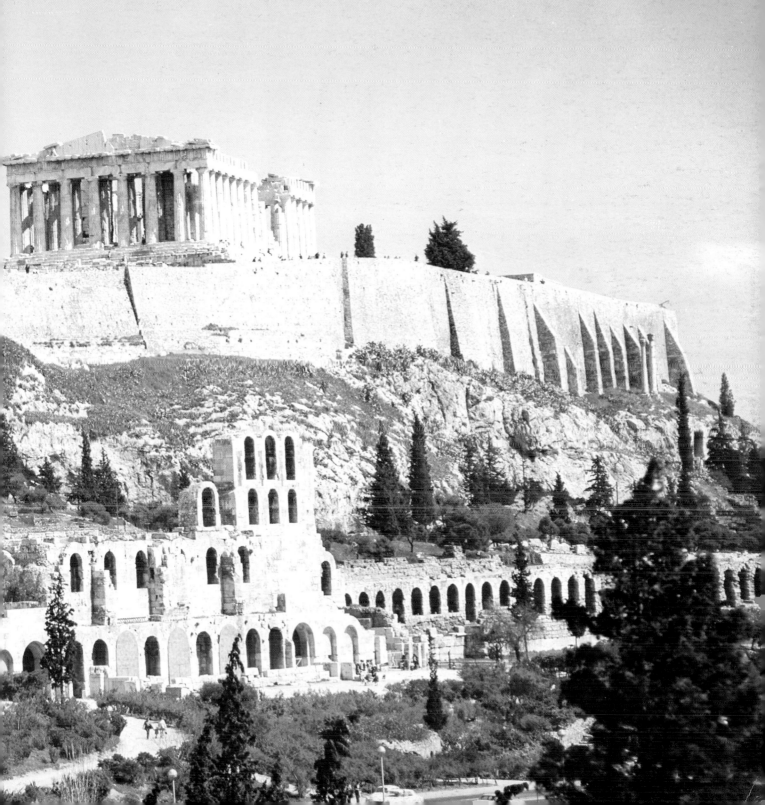

4. The Acropolis^p from the southwest. Photo: Ekdotike Athenon, S.A.

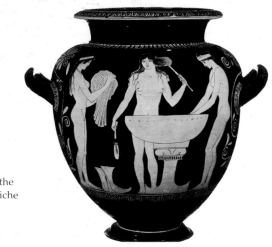

5. Stamnos by follower of the painter Polygnotus.[P] Staatliche Antikensammlungen und Glyptothek, Munich.

6. Gold bowl from Olympia. Museum of Fine Arts, Boston. Photo: Raymond V. Schoder, S.J.

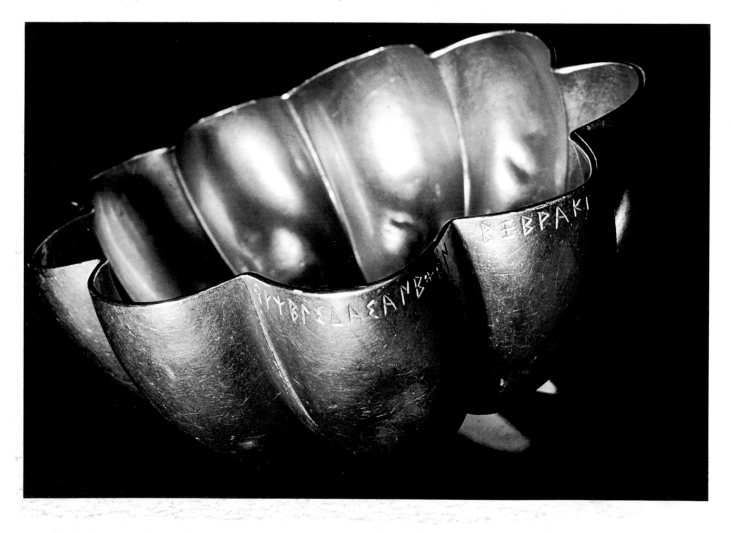

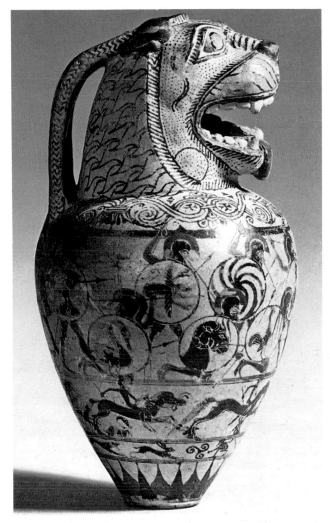

7. The Macmillan aryballos[P]. Reproduced by permission of the Trustees of the British Museum.

8. Wooden plaque from Pitsa, near Corinth. National Archaeological Museum, Athens. Photo: Ekdotike Athenon, S.A.

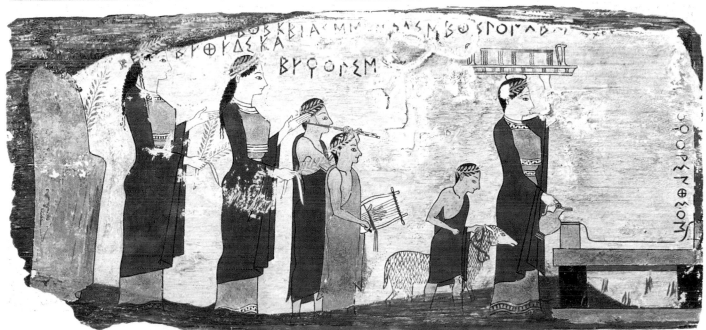

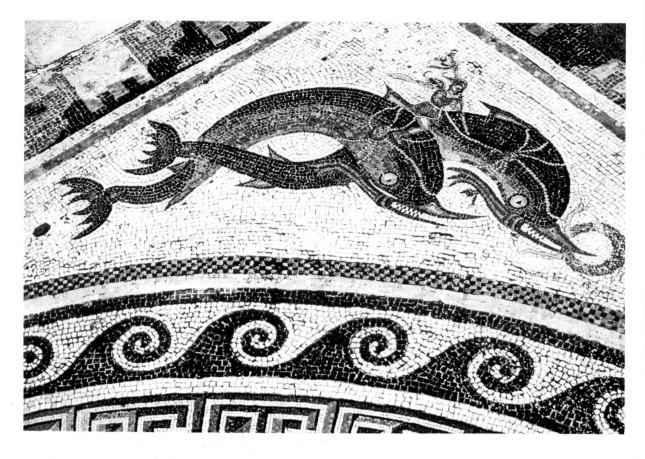

9. Floor mosaic from the House of the
Dolphins, Delos. Photo: Raymond V.
Schoder, S.J.

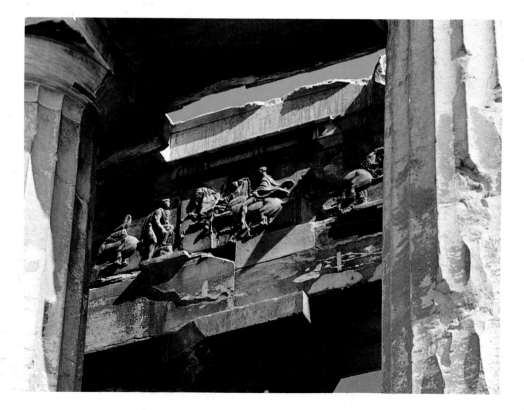

10. The west frieze of the Parthenon,
viewed from below. Photo: Elsevier
Publishing Projects, S.A.

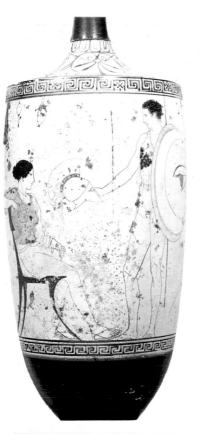

11. Lekythos by the Achilles Painter. National Archaeological Museum, Athens, Photo: Ekdotike Athenon, S.A.

12. Dinos by the Gorgon Painter.ᴾ Musée du Louvre, Paris. Photo: Chuzeville.

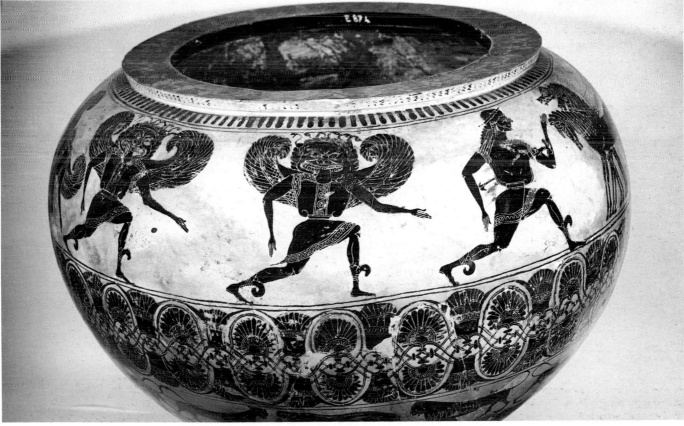

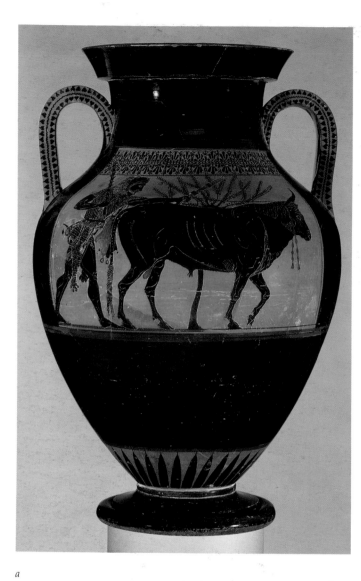

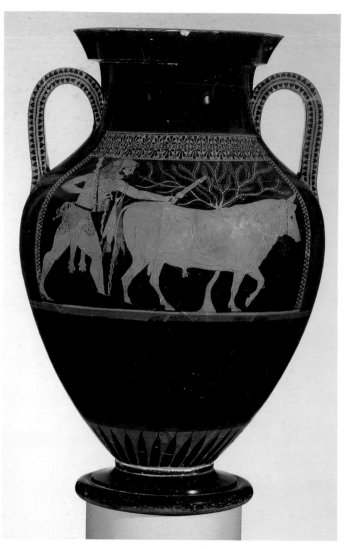

a   *b*

13. Attic bilingual amphora by the Andokides Painter.ᴾ (*a*) Black Figure side; (*b*) Red Figure side. Photo: Museum of Fine Arts, Boston, H. L. Pierce Fund.

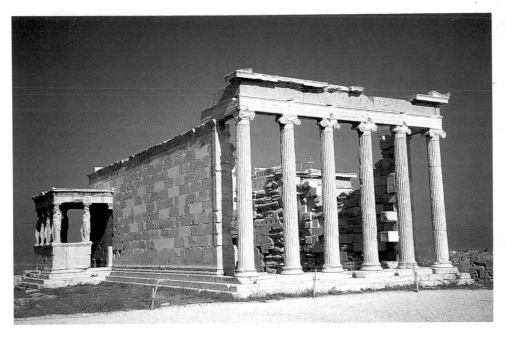

14. The Erechtheion from the southeast. Photo: William R. Biers.

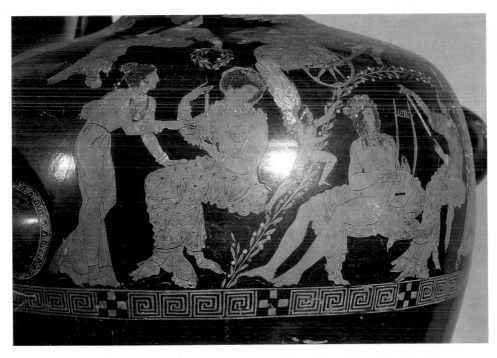

15. Detail of a hydria by Meidias Painter, now in Florence. Photo: Hirmer Fotoarchiv, Munich.

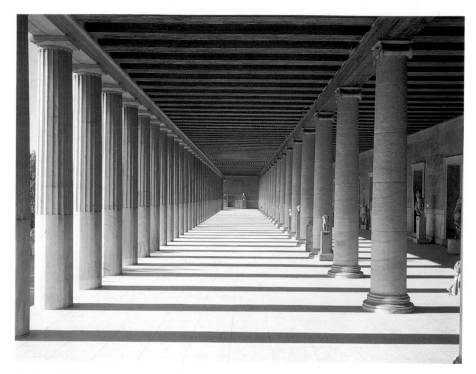

16. Ground floor of the Stoa of Attalos. Photo: American School of Classical Studies at Athens: Agora Excavations.

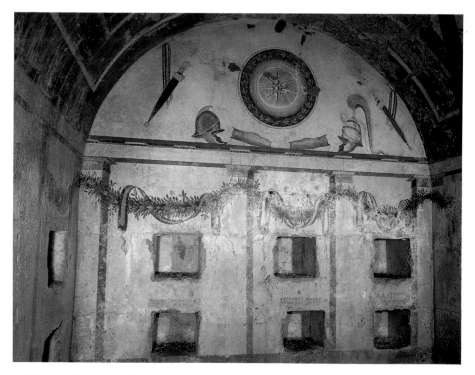

17. North wall of the tomb of Lyson and Kallikles. Photo courtesy of Stella Miller-Collett.

4

The Dark Ages

BY THE END OF the Sub-Mycenaean period, or about 1020, the Mycenaean civilization had more or less faded away, sometimes accompanied by evidence of destruction, as at the settlement at Miletos, in present-day Turkey, but more characteristically in abandonment and decay. LH IIIC had opened with large-scale destructions and population movements and had been a sort of sunset for the Mycenaean Empire; the succeeding years mark the total collapse of the civilization. This chapter is concerned with the approximately 150 years that have been termed the Dark Ages of Greece, a period that has yielded few finds and of which we therefore know little.

A civilization can perhaps be said to have fallen when the characteristics that are peculiar to it either no longer exist or have been altered so radically as to be all but unrecognizable. In the case of the Mycenaean civilization, this process of collapse and dispersal can be seen to have begun with the destructions at the end of LH IIIB and to have continued throughout the next hundred years. Archaeology has shown that numbers of Mycenaeans moved to other parts of the Mediterranean—Asia Minor, Cyprus, Crete—probably as a result of the upheavals on the mainland. It seems clear that the mainland palaces represented the heart of the Mycenaean system, and when that system ceased to exist, society changed. When the palaces fell, their bureaucracy disappeared, and with them the need for and eventually the knowledge of writing. The same thing happened to large-scale architecture and representational art.

The Dark Ages were years of poverty and recession throughout Greece, marked by depopulation, a decline in the standard of living (reflected in the finds, or rather in the lack of finds), isolation, stagnation, and perhaps an increase in pastoralism. It was only at the end of the period that things began to change, with the rise of the Protogeometric style of pottery in Athens and the beginning of a general upswing of civilization, which is clearly seen in the succeeding period. In this period of poverty momentous changes took place, many of which served as foundations of later Greek society. In the present state of our knowledge it is extremely difficult to date these changes, to see where they came from, and to judge their significance. Many of them are visible only in later times, and the date and manner of their introduction are usually disputed by scholars. The gradual adoption of cremation is a case in point. All that can be said about it is that it was an innovative feature of the early Dark Ages that was accepted in the eleventh century by Athens and partially elsewhere. Its significance as a possible indication of intrusive elements in the population has been endlessly discussed and disputed.[1] To the eleventh century is also

---

[1] The works listed in the Suggestions for Further Reading for this chapter are the basic studies that deal with this period; they treat this particular problem at great length.

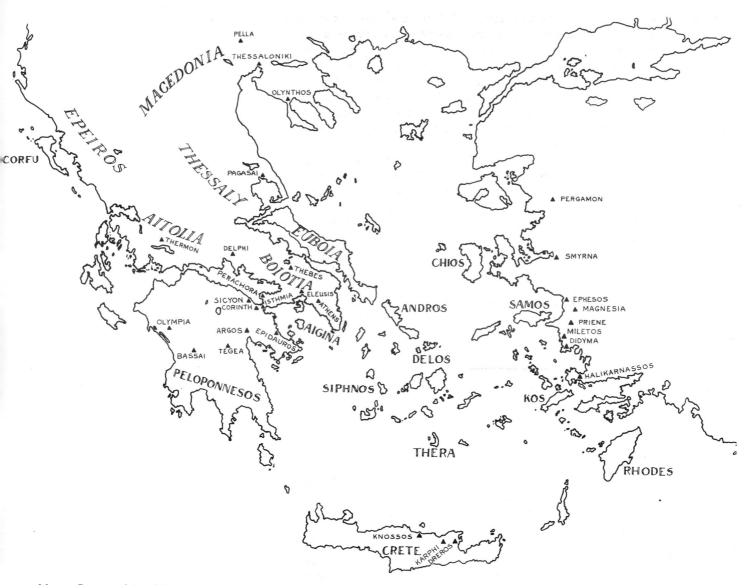

Map 3. Greece and Asia Minor in the Iron
Age. Map by John Huffstot.

assigned the introduction of the technique of ironworking from Cyprus. With
the recognition of iron in Greece itself and its regular use for weapons and
tools, the area can be said to pass into the Iron Age. The principal Iron Age
cities and sites referred to in this book are shown in Map 3. It was also in the
eleventh century that a migration of settlers to the east took place, consisting
not only of Ionian speakers but also of Aeolic and Dorian peoples. This east-
ward movement lasted throughout the Dark Ages. The initial wave settled the
coast of Asia Minor in the area later called Ionia, thus founding Greek presence
in that area which continued without interruption into the twentieth century of
the Christian era.

Despite the innovations and changes accepted by archaeologists, the evidence, which is confined mainly to graves, shows an impoverished society that
at the beginning of the period was clearly living poorly off the past. Something

new is seen with the introduction at Athens of Protogeometric pottery, but although the pulse begins to quicken toward the end of the period, it is not until the ninth or even the eighth century that a major recovery can be seen. Archaeology has begun to illuminate these "dark ages," at least in some corners. Remarkable finds from Lefkandi, on the island of Euboea, have shown us that life may have attained a higher level of civilization than we had thought, at least in that area. Evidence for foreign contacts is appearing, and many features of the succeeding period of "recovery" are beginning to be seen as perhaps beginning in the so-called Dark Ages.

The general lack of remains from the Dark Ages, attributable to the low level of civilization, the use of ephemeral materials in construction, and later re-buildings that eradicated traces of earlier construction on the same sites, has thoroughly obscured the answer to another of the great problems of Greek archaeology: the question of the continuity of Iron Age Greece with Bronze Age Greece. Only on Crete is there demonstrable continuity, in such things as cult, from Minoan-Mycenaean religion into the Dark Ages. The evidence from the mainland consists of only a few Protogeometric sherds in later sanctuaries, and there is almost always a time lapse between the last Mycenaean finds and the first Iron Age ones, even when later shrines have been established on or near Bronze Age settlements. This problem will be considered again later, in the context of the new beginnings of art and architecture. Although it seems certain that a number of Bronze Age buildings were still standing, if in ruin, during the Dark Ages, no fully documented case of physical continuity of remains has been found on the mainland with the possible exception of Athens, shown by a continuous series of graves in the Kerameikos cemetery from Sub-Mycenaean times. Continuity in art, or rather crafts, however, can be seen.

Direct evidence of the political and social structure of Greece in the twelfth and eleventh centuries is lacking. It would appear that the large Mycenaean kingdoms gave place to smaller groups ruled by basileis, or petty kings. Small agricultural villages existing at a low level of cultural development, ruled by kings of greater or lesser power, seem to have been the rule. They appear to have had little or no contact with the outside world. This is perhaps all one can say with conviction, although a certain number of shadowy figures could be called up from myth or legend to populate the bleak landscape. It does seem clear that kingship, essentially a holdover from the Bronze Age, waned during this period, to be replaced by the rule of the nobles.

ART

It is perhaps not quite accurate to say that there is no art to be found in the Dark Ages, but that is close to the truth. It is generally only in vase painting that any artistic sense is manifested, and then only on a craft level. Representational art is almost nonexistent, being confined to a few figurines and an occasional horse painted on a vase. If art is a leisure activity, it would appear that the people of the Dark Ages were generally too busy surviving to produce artistic works. Facile explanations are likely to be contradicted by the spade, however, and the centaur from Lefkandi, perhaps the earliest certain mythological representation (see Fig. 4.9), is a warning of the difficulties inherent in sweeping generalizations.

ARCHITECTURE

As we have seen, both the need and the ability to build well with large blocks vanished with the previous age, and it is difficult to find any architectural remains assignable to the Dark Ages, especially their earlier years. A unique site does preserve the flavor of the times, however, although it must perhaps be approached with care because of its cultural isolation. It is its physical isolation that probably preserved such fragile remains from destruction. Located on a high and almost inaccessible peak more than 300 meters above the Lasithi Plain in east-central Crete, the little city of Karphi was excavated by the British School of Archaeology shortly before World War II.[2] Although the earliest pottery cannot be dated with certainty, the character and isolation of the site give strong indications that it was a refugee city. Sometime in the late twelfth century a group of people of a mixed Minoan-Mycenaean culture made the long and difficult climb, presumably to escape unfavorable conditions on the plain below. They established a sprawling town of some 3,500 people. A plan of the town is shown in Figure 4.1. The houses were crudely made of fieldstones split lengthwise. No foundations, bonding, or interior plastering were used. Well-cut thresholds and doorjambs have been found, however. Here and in the roughly built tholos tombs that accompany the site some lingering connection with earlier building practices can be discerned. Within the village itself there are carefully paved roads and a broad open area near the largest house, which is called the Great House by the excavators. This building, consisting of a large square room to which another room was subsequently added at the front, originally had two columns along its axis (evidence of their bases has been found) and a stone jar stand against one wall. Associated with this room were storerooms and open courtyards. One may see in this complex a sort of vestigial palatial megaron. This fact, together with the location of the house in one of the most sheltered areas in the city, led the excavators to postulate that it was the residence of the ruler of Karphi. The most northern building of the town served as a cult center, entered from the east, with a number of subsidiary rooms. In one of these rooms terra cotta idols were found; one is reminded of similar arrangements in the cult areas of Kea and Mycenae. The main room, according to the excavators, was probably open to the sky. A ledge against its south wall probably held the idols.

Karphi, then, exhibits a fusion of Minoan and Mycenaean characteristics in straitened circumstances. Whatever the conditions that caused this small settlement to be established, they apparently moderated and it was abandoned, probably at the beginning of the tenth century. Other Cretan refugee settlements existed, but apparently at an even lower level of development than Karphi, and their sites are not so well preserved.

While the Creto-Mycenaean refugees were huddling together up in the mountains, other victims of the upheavals of the period took to sea and founded colonies on the coast of Asia Minor. Investigations have revealed that settlements existed there by the tenth century; the initial arrival is usually placed somewhat earlier. The earlier levels have been destroyed in most areas or are covered by later buildings, but at the site of Old Smyrna, on the coast of modern Turkey, a small (3-by-5-meter) oval house datable to the end of the

---

[2] The basic excavation report by J. D. S. Pendlebury and others can be found in "Karphi: A City of Refuge of the Early Iron Age in Crete," *BSA* 38 (1937–1938): 57–145.

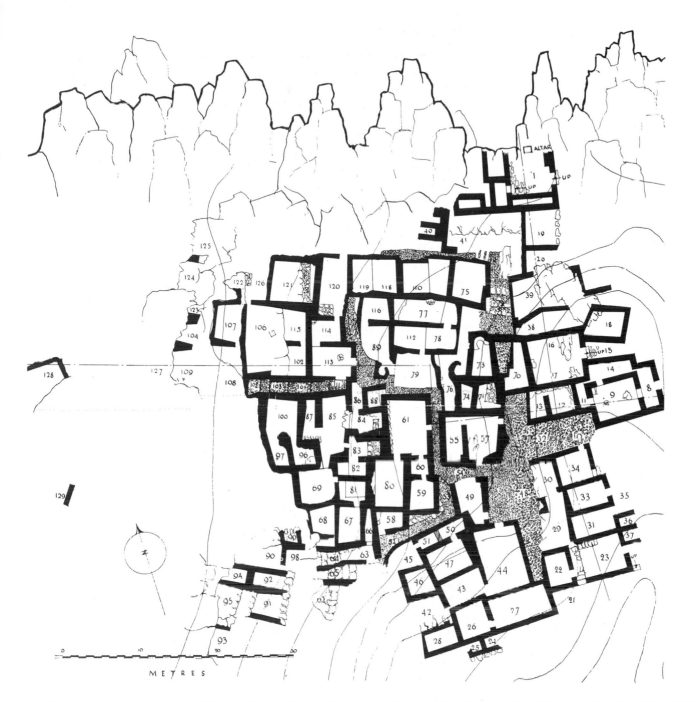

tenth century was recovered.[3] It consisted of a single room with mud-brick walls set on a low course of stones to keep them out of puddles, and enough was preserved to allow a reconstruction (Fig. 4.2). This primitive little house is a good example of the kind of architecture current in this period and is in fact one of the earliest Greek buildings known in any detail. The oval plan can be seen as a break with previous Bronze Age practice, which favored apsidal or

4.1 Plan of the central portion of Karphi[P]. Nos. 8 and 9, great house; no. 1, cult center. From J. D. S. Pendlebury et al., "Excavations in the Plain of Lasithi, III. Karphi: A City of Refuge of the Early Iron Age in Crete," *Annual of the British School at Athens* 38 (1939): 57–145, Plate 1. By permission of the British School at Athens.

[3] The principal excavation report for Smyrna is J. M. Cook and others, "Old Smyrna," *BSA* 53/54 (1958–1959): 1–152.

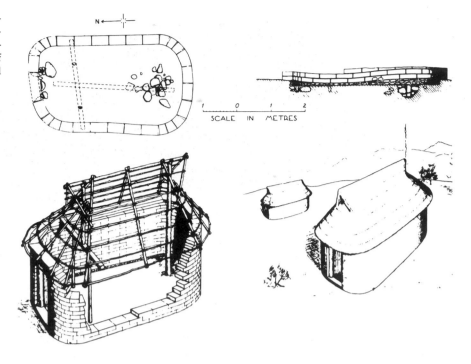

4.2 Plan and reconstruction of oval house at Smyrna.[P] Drawing by R. V. Nicholls, from A. M. Snodgrass, *The Dark Age of Greece* (Edinburgh: Edinburgh University Press, 1971). By permission of Edinburgh University Press and the British School at Athens.

N ←

SCALE IN METRES

rectangular plans. A similar but larger building found in the excavations at Nichoria in the southwestern Peloponnesos, on the Greek mainland, indicates that relatively simple constructions were to be found all over the Greek world at this time. An artist's reconstruction (Fig. 4.3) shows the apsidal building in its final phase in the ninth century. Measuring 15.90 meters in length by 8.0 meters in width and constructed apparently of mud brick reinforced with wooden posts, this building must have had some importance in the village in which it was built.[4]

The remains of a remarkable early building (Fig. 4.4) were excavated between A.D. 1981 and 1983 at Lefkandi, on Euboia, a large island off the east coast of Greece. Measuring almost 13.80 meters wide and about 50 meters long, it is bigger and more carefully built than any other remains we know. It was constructed of mud brick on a stone socle, like smaller houses already mentioned, but here a line of pits dug for rectangular pillars around the building led the excavators to restore a veranda some 1.80 meters deep around the sides and back (Fig. 4.5.). The building contained the cremated remains of a warrior in a bronze amphora made in Cyprus in the late thirteenth or twelfth century, the skeleton of a woman, and the bones of four horses. The building, located very close to a cemetery already in use, apparently was intentionally demolished and filled with earth, which formed a mound soon after the interments, and a burial area was begun in front of it. It may then have been a funeral monument in itself, either the house of the deceased or one made as a final resting place for him. The richness of the burials (which included objects in precious metals),

---

[4] The Dark Age remains at Nichoria are described in William A. McDonald, William D. E. Coulson, and John Rosser, eds., *Excavations at Nichoria in Southwest Greece*, vol. 3: *Dark Age and Byzantine Occupation* (Minneapolis, 1983). A differing interpretation of the excavation evidence is provided by A. Mazarakis Ainian, "Nichoria in the South-West Peloponnese: Units IV-1 and IV-5 Reconsidered," *Opuscula Atheniensia* (annual of the Swedish Institute in Athens) 19 (1992): 75–84.

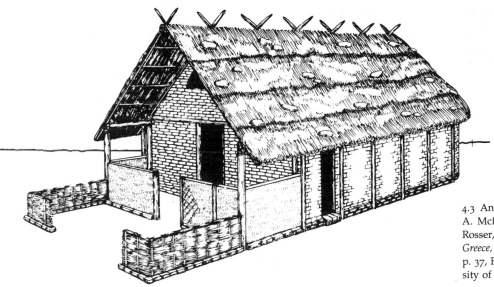

4.3 An apsidal building at Nichoria. From William A. McDonald, William D. E. Coulson, and John Rosser, eds., *Excavations at Nichoria in Southwest Greece*, vol. 3: *Dark Age and Byzantine Occupation*, p. 37, Fig. 2–23. Copyright © 1983 by the University of Minnesota. Reproduced by permission.

the sophistication of the building (particularly the evidence for what appears to be an early colonnade around a building), and its early date (the construction, use, and conversion to a mound all took place between 1000 and 950 B.C., according to the excavators) indicate that there is still much to learn about the so-called Dark Ages.[5]

POTTERY

Pottery provides us with almost our sole evidence of artistic change and development in the Dark Ages. Many of the basic shapes of Greek pottery had already been established; Figure 4.6 shows the outlines of their developed forms of the sixth and fifth centuries. Greek pottery was made to be used, and

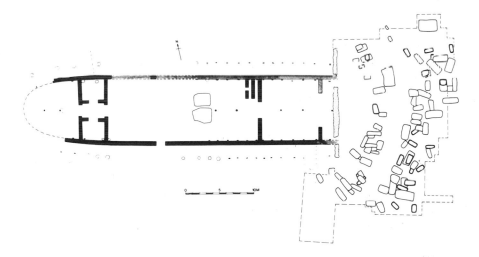

4.4 Plan of an apsidal building at Lefkandi.[P] From *Archaeological Reports* 35 (1988–89): 129, Fig. 28. Reproduced by permission.

[5] Two of the three final excavation reports on the building have appeared, edited by M. R. Popham, P. G. Kalligas, and L. H. Sackett: *Lefkandi II: The Protogeometric Building at Toumba*, pt. 1: *The Pottery*, by R. W. V. Catling and I. S. Lemos (Athens, 1990), and pt. 2: *The Excavation, Architecture, and Finds*, by J. Coulton and H. W. Catling (Athens, 1993).

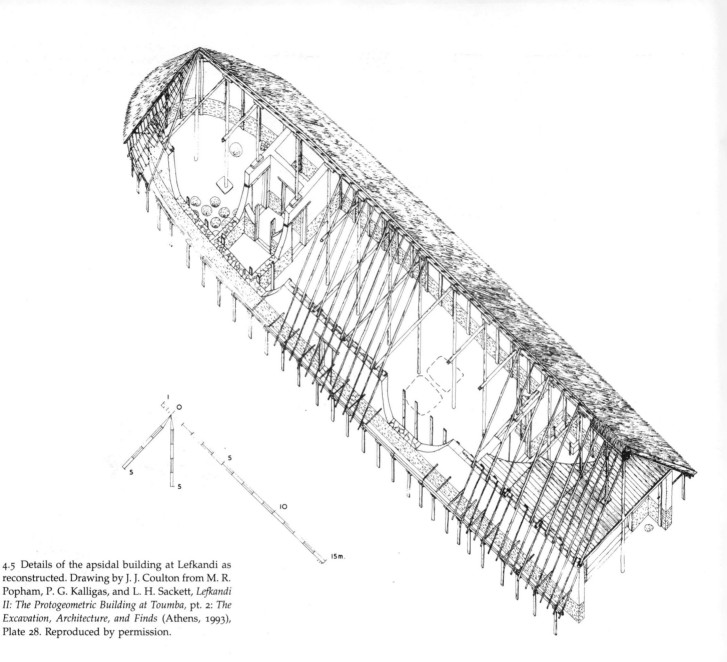

4.5 Details of the apsidal building at Lefkandi as reconstructed. Drawing by J. J. Coulton from M. R. Popham, P. G. Kalligas, and L. H. Sackett, *Lefkandi II: The Protogeometric Building at Toumba,* pt. 2: *The Excavation, Architecture, and Finds* (Athens, 1993), Plate 28. Reproduced by permission.

each shape is associated with a specific function: the amphora, pelike, and stamnos were used for storage; the krater and lebes for the storage and mixing of wine and water; the hydria for carrying water; the oinochoe for pouring; the kantharos, kylix, skyphos for drinking; and the lekythos, aryballos, and alabastron for holding oil. Specialty vases include the psykter, a wine cooler that floats in a krater full of cold water; the lebes gamikos, the marriage bowl; and the loutrophoros, used to hold water for a ritual bath before marriage and often as a funeral monument for unmarried women.[6]

The earliest part of the period is characterized by a declining Mycenaean

---

[6] The shapes of Greek pottery have been well discussed most recently in Brian A. Sparkes, *Greek Pottery: An Introduction* (Manchester, 1991), pp. 60–92.

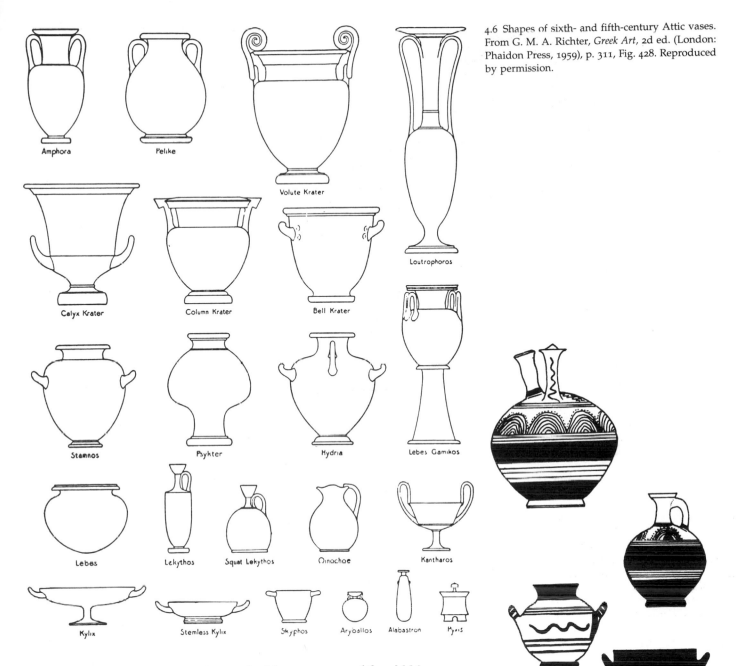

4.6 Shapes of sixth- and fifth-century Attic vases. From G. M. A. Richter, *Greek Art*, 2d ed. (London: Phaidon Press, 1959), p. 311, Fig. 428. Reproduced by permission.

Amphora

Pelike

Volute Krater

Loutrophoros

Calyx Krater

Column Krater

Bell Krater

Stamnos

Psykter

Hydria

Lebes Gamikos

Lebes

Lekythos

Squat Lekythos

Oinochoe

Kantharos

Kylix

Stemless Kylix

Skyphos

Aryballos

Alabastron

Pyxis

style, rooted in Bronze Age traditions. In this stage many of the old Mycenaean shapes, such as the stirrup jar, the small amphora, and the lekythos, are still used, but their shapes are clumsy and the few motifs with which they are decorated, mainly half circles and wavy lines, have lost their precision (Fig. 4.7). The style in Attica is known as Sub-Mycenaean, a term that captures its basic nature as the Mycenaean style in decline. Sub-Mycenaean in Attica may overlap with the style called late LH IIIC elsewhere, but everywhere this early Dark Ages pottery is the lingering end of an earlier tradition.

About the middle of the eleventh century a new style started in Athens and rapidly swept through Greece, beginning almost simultaneously in Thessaly and other places as well. Growing out of Sub-Mycenaean, the style is called

4.7 Common Sub-Mycenaean pottery shapes. Top to bottom: stirrup jar, lekythos, small amphora, cup. After Wilhelm Kraiker and Karl Kubler, *Die Nekropolen des 12 bis 10 Jahrhunderts*, Kerameikos, vol. 1 (Berlin: Walter de Gruyter, 1939), Plates 10, 12, 16, and 22. By permission of the Deutsches Archäologisches Institut, Berlin. Drawing by John Huffstot. Scale 1:5.

Protogeometric, a name that indicates its relationship to the succeeding style.[7] Although most of the fourteen shapes current in this style are continuations of Mycenaean forms, important changes occur. A few of the older shapes disappear, such as the stirrup jar and the remaining ones, such as the amphoras shown in Figure 4.8, are often taller and more slender in their Protogeometric manifestations, perhaps as a result of the adoption of a faster wheel. Four types of amphora are known, all derived from Mycenaean prototypes and classified on the basis of the placement of the handles: from shoulder to neck, from shoulder to lip, on the shoulder, on the belly. They were used to hold ashes in graves, for cremation had taken over in Attica by this time. A comparison of the belly-handled amphora, the most common form, with the small Sub-Mycenaean amphora in Figure 4.7 reveals the thinning of the contour. Next in popularity among the closed shapes were the trefoil-mouthed oinochoai, lekythoi, and hydriai. Among the open shapes, deep bowls and drinking cups on high feet were popular. The cups are unique to the Protogeometric period. Figure 4.8 shows some of the most common shapes of this period.

Along with the adoption of the fast wheel came the use of the compass and a multiple brush, a combination that produced more even semicircles and gave a more organized look to the decoration. Two overall systems of decoration were used on Protogeometric pots: a clay-ground technique, in which dark designs were painted on a light clay body, and a dark-ground technique, in which the vase was covered with black glaze paint with the painted designs in reserved bands. The latter technique was more popular toward the end of the period and is easily distinguishable in Figure 4.8. The motifs used, generally on the shoulder or belly of clay-ground vases, were commonly circles, semicircles, and wavy lines derived from the earlier period. A few simple rectilinear motifs were also introduced, almost in anticipation of the succeeding style. The Protogeometric is a sober style showing a close relationship between the potter and the painter: the painter always strove to emphasize the shape of the pot. Quite simple in form and content, it evolved easily and quickly into the somewhat harsher and stiffer Geometric style about 900.

TERRA COTTA FIGURINES

Except in Crete, very few figurines survive from the period between the end of the Mycenaean age and the ninth century.[8] Exceptions of particular importance are partially wheel-made animal figures, such as a late-tenth-century deer from the Kerameikos cemetery in Athens, which has been thought to bear a relationship to similar examples from the Late Bronze Age. A recent find from the cemetery at Lefkandi is the earliest representation of a centaur and is more or less contemporary with the Athenian deer (Fig. 4.9). Standing some 36 centimeters in length and 26 in height, it has a wheel-made body and is truly a remarkable work of art from the tenth century.

Continuity from the Bronze Age can be seen in "household goddess" idols of a late Minoan type which were found at Karphi (Fig. 4.10) and elsewhere. With

---

[7] This style has been exhaustively studied by V. R. d'A. Desborough. See his *Protogeometric Pottery* (Oxford, 1952).

[8] Some mysterious handmade dolls with flaring skirts and detachable legs are exceptions and are not included here. They are discussed in R. A. Higgins's basic handbook, *Greek Terracottas* (London, 1967), pp. 20–21.

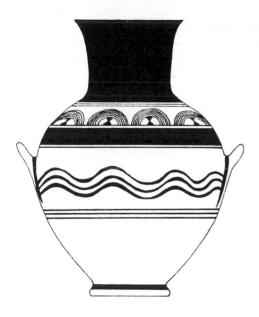

BELLY-HANDLED AMPHORA

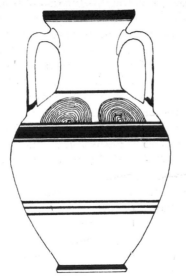

NECK-HANDLED AMPHORA

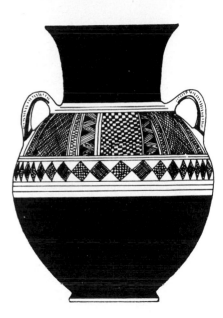

SHOULDER-HANDLED AMPHORA

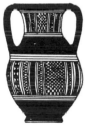

LIP-HANDLED
AMPHORA

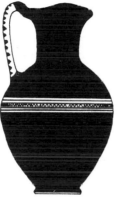

TREFOIL-MOUTHED
OINOCHOE

LEKYTHOS

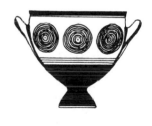

FOOTED CUP

their wheel-made bell skirts, upraised hands, and elaborate headdresses, they bear a strong resemblance to earlier Minoan figures. An unusual feature is their prominently displayed feet, which were made separately and attached. John Pendlebury has remarked that these Karphi goddesses certainly needed their feet to get up to their remote shrine.

METALWORK

Although the working of iron became common during the Dark Ages, bronze was still used for minor objects, as it was throughout antiquity, and is actually more common in all types of objects from the earlier part of the period.

Straight pins of various types were known in the earlier years of the Dark

4.8 Common Protogeometric shapes. After Wilhelm Kraiker and Karl Kubler, *Die Nekropolen des 12 bis 10 Jahrhunderts*, Kerameikos, vol. 1 (Berlin: Walter de Gruyter, 1939), Plates 43 and 57; Karl Kubler, *Neu Funde aus der Nekropole des 11 und 10 Jahrunderts*, Kerameikos, vol. 4 (Berlin: Walter de Gruyter, 1943), Plates 8, 12, 15, 18, and 23. By permission of the Deutsches Archäologisches Institut, Berlin. Drawing by John Huffstot. Scale 1:6.

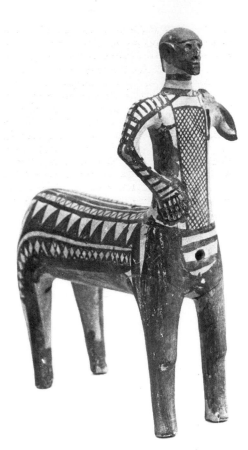

Ages, including short pins with simple roll tops and a few with only flattened and widened upper shafts.[9] A simple version of another type, with a bulbous swelling near the top of the shaft and a nail-like head, was found at Karphi. More elaborate types with various moldings both above and below the swelling on the shaft are known from both Crete and the mainland (Fig. 4.11*a–c*). In general these pins did not last into the later years of the period; they were either holdovers from the end of the Bronze Age or short-lived imports from elsewhere.

The most common type, one that is characteristic of Protogeometric times although it appeared earlier, in Attic Sub-Mycenaean and Argive LH IIIC (which may overlap, as we have seen), is distinguished by a globe on the shaft instead of a mere swelling, and is generally quite long (Fig. 4.11*d* and *e*). Above the globe the shaft continues, sometimes bearing engraved rings and with a small head. As time goes on, the head becomes a flat circular disk. With further elaboration, this shape continues on into the ninth century. Many of these pins have been found in graves. Their use generally coincides with the introduction of the peplos, a piece of cloth wound around the body and secured at the

4.9 Terra cotta centaur from Lefkandi, Euboia. Courtesy of L. H. Sackett. By permission of the British School at Athens.

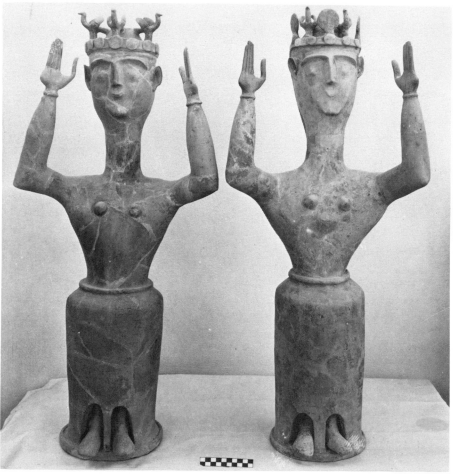

4.10 Terra cotta idols from Karphi. Heraklion Museum, Crete. Photo: British School at Athens.

[9] The standard work in English on pins is Paul Jacobsthal, *Greek Pins* (Oxford, 1956).

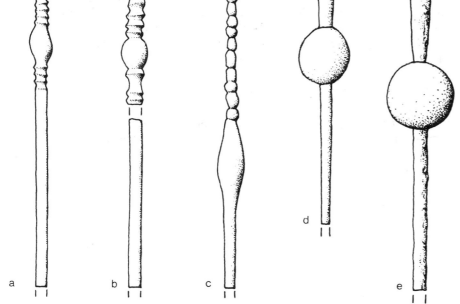

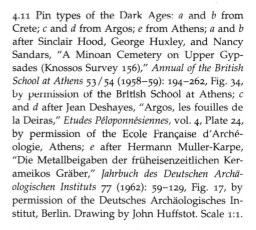

shoulders with these straight pins. Often they are found made of iron, occasionally with a separately cast globe of bronze.

FIBULAE

By the end of the eleventh century the fiddle-bow fibula, the principal Mycenaean form, had virtually disappeared and the arched fibula (a development of the fiddle-bow type) had taken its place (see Fig. 3.42). Several varieties were used and were occasionally made of iron, as were the straight pins. In Athens the form regularly had a thickened bow with a bulb on either side flanked by two rings and a double spiral hinge. This type continued into the Geometric period.

Metal was used for other articles as well: rings for the fingers and for the hair, household utensils, weapons. The earliest graves contain a few poorly made metal objects, giving the impression of a scrap-metal industry, but gradually the quantity of metal finds increases and their quality improves.

5

The Geometric Period

THE YEARS FROM approximately 900 to approximately 700 do not really constitute a historical period except in the sense that during these centuries the Geometric style of art was predominant; and at that, the beginning and ending dates have been chosen more or less as a convenience. The ninth century can with some justice be considered a continuation of the Dark Ages, yet a change can be noted with the birth of Geometric art in Athens at the beginning of the century. In the second half of the century, as foreign communications improved and the standard of living rose, the style developed and stabilized. It is an interesting coincidence that one of the diagnostic features of the previous period, cremation, ceased to be the most common method of burial in Attica in the Geometric period. During the course of the period inhumation was reintroduced, and both cremation and inhumation were then practiced side by side. It was in the eighth century that the most obvious changes were made; most of the examples used in this chapter are from that time.

Evidence for the internal history of the Geometric period is almost as scarce as for that of the Dark Ages. Much of what we know has been discovered by the process of working back from institutions or happenings in later periods. For instance, the process of deemphasis of the kingship accelerated, so that we find that by the eighth century almost everywhere the nobles had superseded the king and held power in aristocracies based on families organized in tribes. As the kingship weakened, the society moved toward the establishment of the *polis*, that peculiar Greek institution which is known, not very satisfactorily, as "city-state," though it was in fact more than a city and less than a state. Although most cities simply grew larger, Sparta and Athens slowly gained control of the villages in their immediate vicinity. Thus the story of Athens, at the beginning of recorded history, is already the story of Attica. Traditionally, the legendary king Theseus was responsible for the unification of Attica into a single state, though the process was probably gradual, completed only as late as the seventh century with the incorporation of Eleusis. Whenever these events occurred—and dates from Mycenaean times to the ninth century have been suggested for the primary amalgamation—the early political unification of such a large and rich area certainly is one of the reasons for Athens' preeminence in later years.

By the early years of the eighth century the development of Greek society was accelerating, with an increase in population, the beginning of industry, and an increase in foreign contacts and trade, advanced by the establishment of trading colonies on the coast of Asia Minor. This period also saw the beginning of the great colonizing movement from mainland Greece, primarily to the West but also, somewhat later, into the area of the Black Sea. In fact, so many settlements were founded in southern Italy that the area became known as Magna Graecia, or Great Greece. From about 750 down even into the sixth century, official colonies sent out by mother cities established themselves on foreign shores, often in turn sending out further colonies of their own. The reasons for the colonizing movement were many and varied, and specific and unique factors probably figured prominently in occasional cases. Certain underlying causes, however, seem to have been at least partially responsible in a great majority of cases: the need for additional land to accommodate an increasing population, political discontent with the ruling aristocracies, the desire for expansion of trade, and the search for metals.

A number of innovations can be seen during the eighth century, many of them linked to the newly reopened contacts with the outside world. Particularly striking is the presence of objects of foreign origin in places where they had previously appeared only sporadically. The introduction of alphabetic writing, the rebirth of representational art, the rise of sanctuaries and hero cults, the increase in quantity and quality of architectural remains, the beginnings of literature with the diffusion of the Homeric poems and the works of Hesiod and his followers, the growth of trade—all these can be attributed to the eighth century. At this time also comes the first full awareness of the Greeks as Greeks, an awareness that can be seen in the founding of the Olympic games, traditionally in 776, and which must have been fostered by increased contact with other peoples. It is this contact that allows Eastern influence to be seen in the arts of the leading Greek states, first in a trickle in the eighth century and then in a flood as the next century approaches.

ART

Developing out of the Protogeometric style, Geometric art obeyed specific rules that differed from those of earlier times but were obviously rooted in the past. Its basic characteristics are discussed in the context of Geometric pottery decoration later on in this chapter. Athens clearly leads in the development of the Geometric style. The increasingly frequent use of figures and complex figure scenes begins in Attic art as early as the middle of the eighth century. Once introduced, a strong school of representational painting is established. Geometric figures are soon found elsewhere than on pottery, specifically in metalwork and probably also in wood though most wood has now of course perished. Toward the end of the century mythological scenes and episodes from the Trojan cycle were portrayed on Geometric pots and elsewhere, but the extent of the influence of such things as the Homeric poems is difficult to judge. Figure 5.1 illustrates the problem in the reconstruction of a scene from a sherd found in the Athenian agora. Each drawing preserves the central portion of the composition. The scene can be reconstructed in such a way as to show the death of Astyanax at Troy (a) or simply as a musical program or celebration (b)—a common activity having nothing to do with myth or epic. Such are the difficulties involved in reconstruction and interpretation.

Geometric art was largely a homegrown art, the product of a society growing from its own roots.[1] It was simple and conservative, in danger of stagnation

---

[1] A major problem, which has already been touched upon, is that of the possible influence of the Bronze Age on Geometric art, particularly the figure style. Opinions differ, ranging from recognition of only slight influence to the view that Geometric art was so heavily influenced by Mycenaean art that it amounted almost to a revival of the earlier style. The latter view is expressed in J. L. Benson, *Horse, Bird, and Man* (Amherst, Mass., 1970).

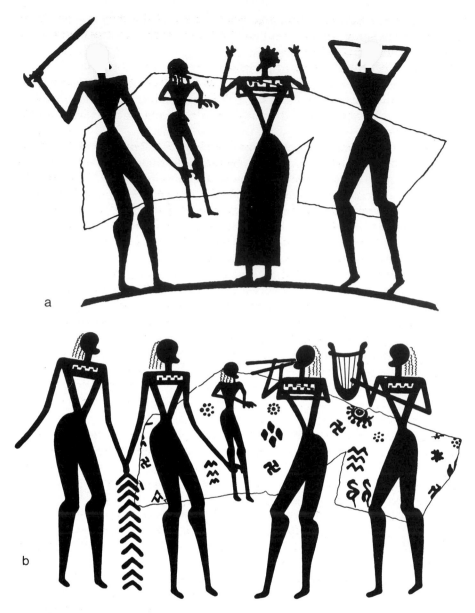

a

b

5.1 Reconstructions of a scene on a Geometric sherd from the Athenian agora: *a*, from Eva Brann, "A Figured Geometric Fragment from the Athenian Agora," *Antike Kunst* 2 (1959): 35, by permission of Karl Schefold; *b*, courtesy of Klaus Fittschen.

unless something happened to change it. Change it did, as we shall see in the next chapter.

ARCHITECTURE

Despite the increase in population and the improvement in living standards in the eighth century, surprisingly little evidence of large-scale architecture has been found. There are two basic reasons for this state of affairs. For one thing, the art of building was still in an early stage of development after the poverty of the previous centuries, and construction was still carried out in such ephemeral materials as mud brick, wood, and thatch. Second, the developing cities of the period went through periodic rebuildings, during which any traces of the fragile early constructions were eradicated. Many of the remains that have survived are in remote and perhaps architecturally backward areas. Such sites often pose problems of chronology.

Cult practices crystalized in the Geometric period, and a house for the representation of the god became necessary; earlier a simple enclosure, or temenos, around a sacred spot or an altar was sufficient. The ruins of the earliest sacred buildings have little to distinguish them from those of ordinary houses, unless votive offerings survive.

The growth of sanctuaries produced quantities of votive objects, but often not clearly enough associated with architectural remains to allow the structures that housed them to be identified as religious buildings. Small models of buildings of various shapes have been found in votive deposits and have been interpreted as representing either a cult building or the dedicator's own dwelling. Fragments of three models from a deposit at Perachora, on the Corinthian Gulf opposite Corinth, show that at least one of them had a horseshoe-shaped ground plan with a tall roof, thought to represent thatch, and with pairs of posts at the front forming a shallow porch before the door (Fig. 5.2). A wall at the same sanctuary, connected to a votive deposit and belonging to the ninth century, indicates an apsidal temple to Hera, and this building has been claimed as the inspiration for the apsidal model. A rectilinear plan with a high pointed roof and a separately roofed porch supported by posts is indicated by another model from the Argive Heraion in the Argolid (Fig. 5.3) of the later eighth century. Although details of the reconstructed model may be incorrect, it has also been interpreted as a representation of the first temple of Hera on the site. It has often been used—perhaps overused—in attempts at restorations of the elevations of other early buildings.

Thus these two models illustrate two traditions, one of buildings with curved or apsidal rear walls and one with a more or less rectangular ground plan. Examples of both forms are known from the late Bronze Age. It is of course the rectilinear plan—essentially a continuation of the megaron form— that eventually predominated in sacred architecture.

Actual remains from the Geometric period are controversial and difficult to date. Crete, with its conservative ways, has preserved several early rectangular cult buildings. One of the best preserved is the temple of Apollo at Dreros, in which a sacrificial hearth (often found in these early buildings) is flanked by bases for posts to hold up the ridge beam. Figure 5.4 shows an actual state plan of the building when it was excavated and Figure 5.5 is a restored plan based on recent research. Figure 5.6 is a model of the building with the roof and side walls broken away to show how the interior was arranged. Behind the hearth and against the back wall is a construction in which horns of sacrificed goats were found; a bench next to it probably held bronze cult figures (Fig. 5.14). This small cult building (about 10.8 by 7.2 meters) of relatively well laid masonry obviously relates to Bronze Age traditions but probably dates toward the end of the eighth century. Similar rectangular buildings with internal sacrificial hearths are known from other sites on Crete and on the mainland.

The first of the many temples of Hera at Samos is also dated to the eighth century, although the chronology is tentative because of the loss of most of the stratigraphic evidence in World War II. The building was very long and narrow (32.86 by 6.50 meters) with three posts between the thickened ends of the walls at the east. No traces of a door have been found here, so this end must have been left open. The plan (Fig. 5.7) shows an alternate possibility for the

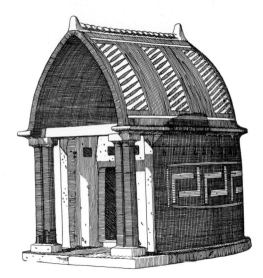

5.2 Reconstruction of a model building found at Perachora.[P] Photo: British School at Athens.

5.3 Building model from the Argive Heraion.[P] National Archaeological Museum, Athens. Photo: Deutsches Archäologisches Institut, Athens.

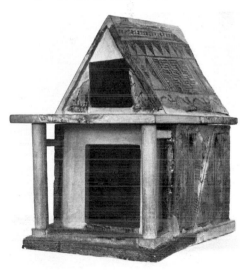

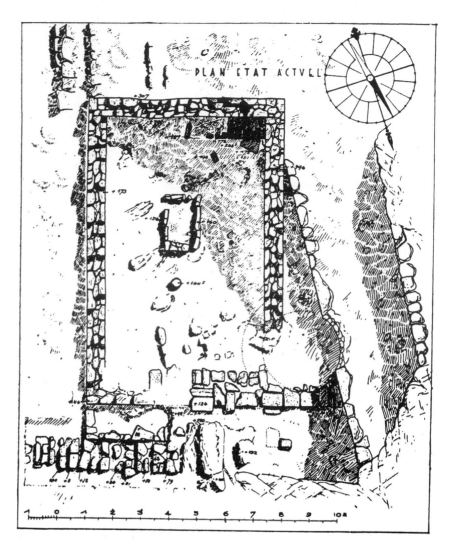

east end of the building, with only one post in the door opening. A row of twelve posts or columns ran down the center of the building to support the ridge beams of the roof. The base for the cult statue was placed slightly off center to the north, so that it would not be obscured by the line of supports for the roof or ceiling. There was no hearth in this temple; it faced a preexisting altar that was originally the only cult construction at the site. It was originally thought that a peristyle was added to this long, narrow building still in the eighth century, but recent research has indicated that columnar supports for the roof first surrounded the cella of the second Heraion, which succeeded this simple building around the middle of the seventh century (see Chapter 6). Just when a line of columns was first introduced around a largely stone building to support an overhanging roof has been debated. It appears at this point that with the possible exception of the early building under the later temple of Artemis at Ephesos, it may have been generally a phenomenon of the seventh century.[2]

2 The new evidence on the early buildings at Ephesos is discussed in Anton Bammer, "A *Peripteros* of the Geometric Period in the Artemision of Ephesus," *Anatolian Studies* 40 (1990): 137–160.

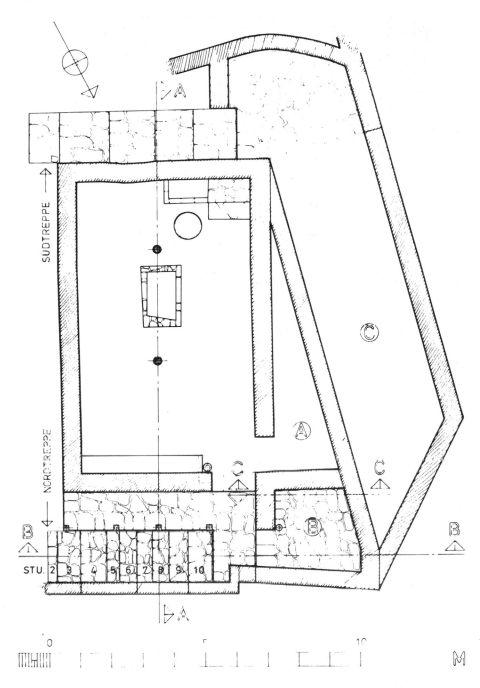

A unique find allows us to visualize what one of these primitive religious buildings looked like in elevation. At the site of Eretria on the island of Euboia and beneath a later temple to Apollo Daphnephoros, the well-preserved remains of a small (8.25 by 5.40 meters) horseshoe-shaped building, built probably in the mid-eighth century, was recovered by Swiss excavators. Low stone walls protected the inside of the building and lent strength to vertical wooden posts, whose sunken bases were found both inside and outside the walls. Evidently the entire superstructure was of wood and was covered with some

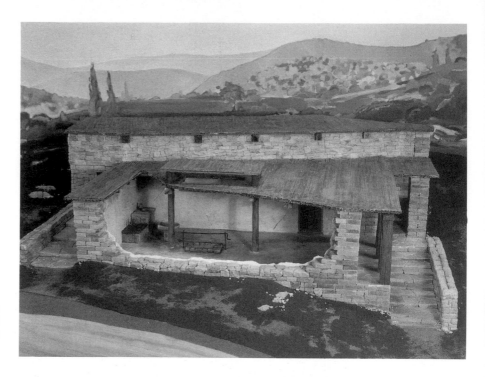

5.6 Model of the Temple of Apollo at Dreros in the Museum of Art and Archaeology, University of Missouri-Columbia. Model and photo by Barbara Smith. Reproduced by permission.

sort of perishable material, perhaps brushwood or branches. By means of a study of the carpentry involved and with some reference to other evidence, such as building models, a 1:20 facsimile has been constructed (Fig. 5.8). This building is unique, not only because the remains have been well enough preserved to allow a reconstruction but also because it belongs to Apollo, whose earliest temple in Delphi is traditionally said to have been made of laurel boughs. This reconstruction of the little building may give us an impression of the way such primitive buildings could have looked.

The excavations at the sanctuary of Athena Alea at Tegea have recovered evidence for two small apsidal cult buildings, one following the other in the Geometric period, beneath the later temples. Numerous postholes indicate walls of reed-reinforced clay between wooden posts that supported the roof. The apses of both buildings were located under the place where the cult statue

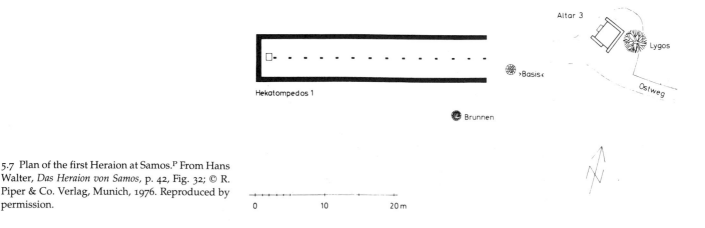

5.7 Plan of the first Heraion at Samos.ᵖ From Hans Walter, *Das Heraion von Samos*, p. 42, Fig. 32; © R. Piper & Co. Verlag, Munich, 1976. Reproduced by permission.

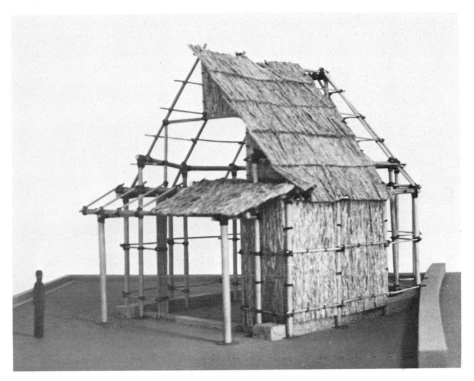

5.8 Model of the early temple of Apollo Daphnephoros in Eretria.ᴾ Photo: Paul Auberson.

would have been in the later temples. Although the remains are very poorly preserved within the foundations of the later temples (Fig. 1.5), we know that the later building (destroyed in the early decades of the seventh century) measured some 12 meters in length and 4 meters in interior width, and had walls covered with white stucco.[3]

SECULAR ARCHITECTURE

Examples of early dwellings show a variety of forms, including apsidal, oval, square, and rectangular. Single-room plans are most common, although occasionally rambling multiroom houses are also found. Simply built of ephemeral materials, these houses do not seem much different from the oval cottage from Old Smyrna mentioned in Chapter 4. Larger structures for the wealthy or members of ruling families must have been built, but no examples definitely dated to our period are known.[4]

The increase in foreign contacts during the eighth century appears to have been associated with renewed colonization. A number of small town sites have been found on the islands, with small rectilinear houses grouped together and often surrounded by fortification walls. The houses are often of the megaron type, with an internal hearth flanked by two posts and a porch with two piers or

[3] Gullög C. Nordquist, "Evidence for Pre-Classical Cult Activity beneath the Temple of Athena Alea at Tegea," in *Peloponnesian Sanctuaries and Cults* (Athens, forthcoming).
[4] Probably the long, rectangular Megaron Hall at Emporio on Chios, with a central row of inner supports and two supports for the porch on one end, represents one of these large buildings. No direct evidence exists for its date, but it should belong at least to the beginning of the seventh century, perhaps to the end of the eighth. See John Boardman, "Excavations in Chios, 1952–1955: Greek Emporio," *JHS*, supplementary vol. 6 (Oxford, 1967).

columns. Also common is a square house, often with raised stone benches, probably for sleeping, across one end. One of the largest of these settlements, at Zagora on Andros, belongs to the late eighth century.[5] It was later abandoned, although a temple was constructed near the old settlement in the sixth century (Fig. 5.9). The main area excavated occupies the flat top of a hill on which a mass of square bench houses and a few megaron houses were built. A reconstruction of a house from this site is shown in Figure 5.10. All of them are built of local stone by techniques peculiar to the islands; a number of similar simple settlements have been found on Chios, Siphnos, Tenos, and Rhodes. More elaborate architecture can be found farther to the east, at Old Smyrna, where an impressive stone-faced fortification wall was built as early as the ninth century.[6]

In general, architecture of the Geometric period was still simple and old-fashioned; it was not until later that the Doric and Ionic orders were fully developed.

5.9 Plan of houses and later temple at Zagora, Andros. Plan by J. J. Coulton. Photo: Ray Scobe. Courtesy of the director of the excavations, Alexander Cambitoglou, and the Athens Archaeological Society.

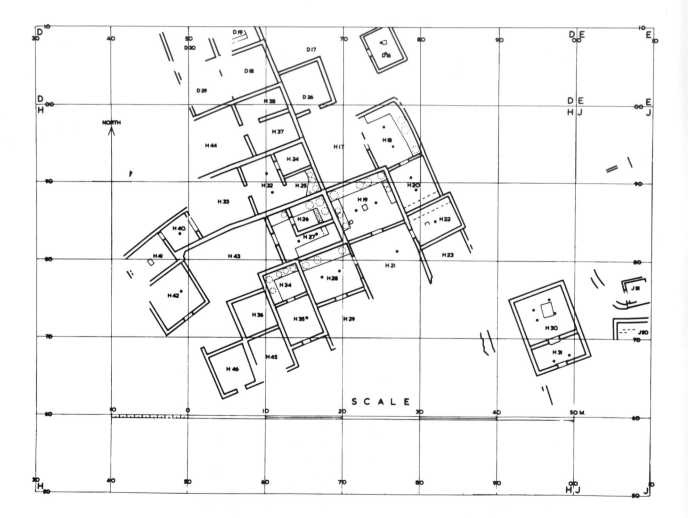

[5] Alexander Cambitoglou and others, *Zagora I*, Australian Academy of Humanities Monograph 2 (Sydney, 1971).
[6] See Chapter 4, note 3.

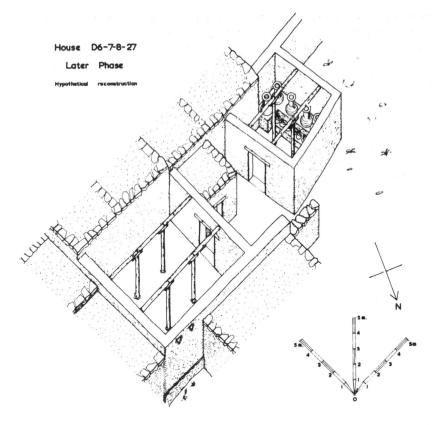

House D6-7-8-27

Later Phase

Hypothetical reconstruction

5.10 Hypothetical reconstruction of a house at Zagora. Plan by J. J. Coulton. Photo: Ray Scobe. Courtesy of the director of the excavations, Alexander Cambitoglou, and the Athens Archaeological Society.

SCULPTURE

Large-scale sculpture as such does not exist in the Geometric period. We hear of early cult statues made of wood, the so-called Xoana, which were kept into later times as venerated objects of great antiquity, but we have no idea what they looked like; they may have been extremely primitive. Sanctuary deposits have produced relatively large numbers of bronze figurines representing gods and worshipers as well as animals, often horses, of varying degrees of sophistication, which must represent the art of sculpture for this period (Fig. 5.11). These small bronze figurines were cast in molds. Their size was limited by the weight of the metal. Some quite large bronze figures are known, however. Many types exist, their characteristics varying from region to region. A primitive-looking human figure, which may not be the earliest, is shown in Figure 5.12. The stance with the raised arms reminds one of Mycenaean predecessors. Somewhat more sophisticated are naked male figures with pointed helmets; they may be either gods or mortal warriors (Fig. 5.13). The Geometric style is most at home, however, with animal figures. Horses with thick necks, long bodies, and relatively thin, sticklike legs lend themselves to the flat "geometricized" treatment common to this art (see below). Such figurines were dedicated in sanctuaries and often were used as parts of the bronze tripod caldrons that came into prominence in this period. These caldrons are discussed below.

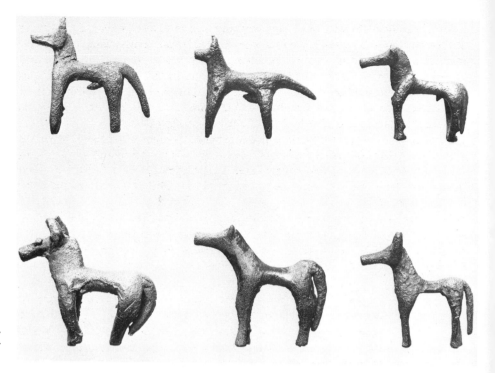

5.11 Typical horse figurines found at Olympia. Olympia Museum. Photo: Deutsches Archäologisches Institut, Athens.

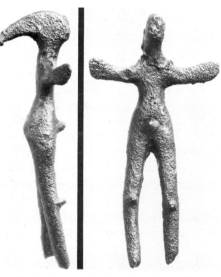

5.12 Early bronze figurine found at Olympia. Olympia Museum. Photo: Deutsches Archäologisches Institut, Athens.

5.13 Helmeted male figurine. National Archaeological Museum, Athens. Photo: Deutsches Archäologisches Institut, Athens.

An alternate technique of bronze working is seen in a large male figure from Dreros that may represent the god Apollo (Fig. 5.14). It was found with two smaller, stiffly standing draped female figures, perhaps representing Leto and Artemis. The male figure stands with one leg slightly in front of the other and with arms separated from the body. There is a strong division of the body at the waist, as well as strict frontality, but some attempt has been made to represent musculature. The body has a rounded appearance, perhaps at least partly because the technique of its manufacture influenced its form. The figure is made of thin plates of bronze hammered over a core and nailed to a wooden form. This technique, called sphyrelaton (hammered) work, is known to have been used for early statues of large scale, but the Dreros Apollo is the only example extant.

Here also should be mentioned the ivory female figurine found with four other statuettes in a grave in the Athenian Kerameikos cemetery (Fig. 5.15). It is datable to the third quarter of the eighth century and in the rendering of the human body is vastly superior to the average figurines of the Geometric period. It wears a round cap, or polos, which is ornamented with a meander. Although it is made of a foreign material and imitates known eastern types of naked figurines, it is considered by most scholars to have been carved by a Greek. Although the rigid geometric simplicity can still be seen, the natural curves of the female body are treated in a naturalistic way that is surprising for such an early date. Perhaps our surprise only proves how limited our knowledge still is.

POTTERY

It is in Athens that one can see most clearly the evolution of the Geometric style of pottery painting in the ninth century.[7] Several of the changes characteristic of the Geometric style can be traced to the very end of the Protogeometric period, but when they reach their full development they result in a style quite different from that of the earlier period. The shapes of the pots dispense with the swelling volumetric curves inherited from the past and become taller and slimmer. The amphora, for example, seems to pull itself up, becoming tauter as it grows in height. Most shapes are continuations of those known in Protogeometric times, with some additions. The high conical feet so characteristic of Protogeometric cups disappear and so does the ovoid oinochoe, which is replaced by a broad bottomed type. A shallow cup, a high-handled kantharos, a high rimmed bowl, and innovations on standard shapes are introduced throughout the period (Fig. 5.16).

The changes in decoration are more radical than those in shape. Decoration leaves the shoulder and moves to the neck and to the handle zone, emphasizing the shape. Design panels first float in a sea of black glaze that covers the entire pot, thus forming a light-on-dark color scheme. As time goes on, the areas of black glaze are broken up by bands of decoration that widen to cover almost the entire surface, eventually forming a light ground. Figures 5.17 and 5.18 show the extremes in decoration and shape on earlier and later Geometric neck amphoras. The decorative motifs of the Geometric style are almost exclusively linear, and there are more of them than in the Protogeometric repertoire.

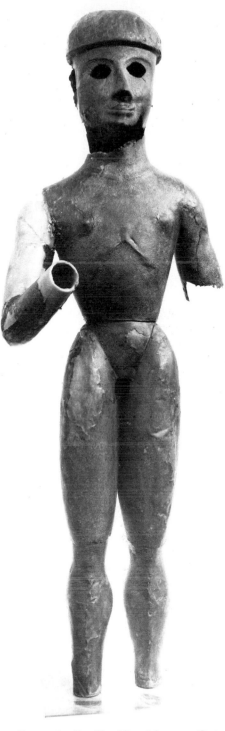

5.14 Dreros Apollo. Heraklion Museum, Crete. Photo: Alison Frantz.

[7] The basic work for the pottery of our period is J. N. Coldstream, *Greek Geometric Pottery* (London, 1968).

121

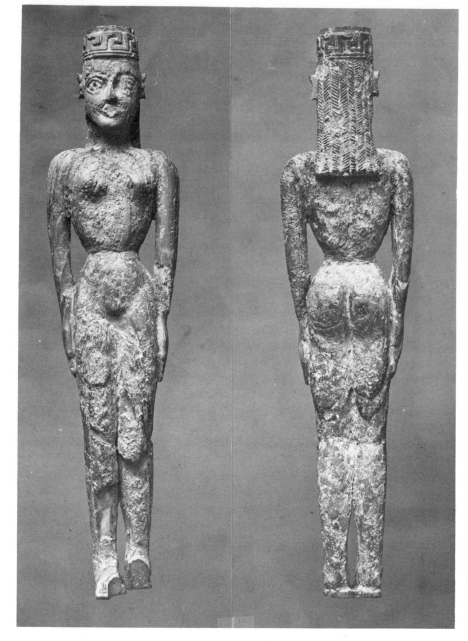

5.15 Ivory figurine from the Kerameikos cemetery. National Archaeological Museum, Athens. Photo: Deutsches Archäologisches Institut, Athens.

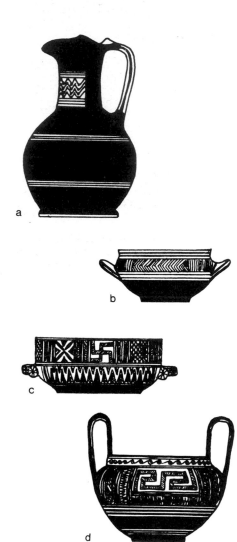

a

b

c

d

5.16 New Geometric shapes: *a*, oinochoe; *b*, shallow cup; *c*, bowl; *d*, kantharos. After J. N. Coldstream, *Greek Geometric Pottery* (London: Methuen, 1968). By permission of the Deutsches Archäologisches Institut, Berlin. Drawing by John Huffstot. Scale 1:5.

Except for a few lingering circles, the painter relied almost exclusively on dots and lines formed into angles, squares, triangles, lozenges, oblique strokes, and the like. Battlements, zigzags, and meanders, usually cross-hatched, are common motifs. The meander is used so often that it can perhaps be considered the symbol of the style. This style of decoration, which depends on a few basic forms repeated and combined in various ways, sometimes covering the whole surface with a rich tapestry of design, reinforces the articulation of the pot it decorates by emphasizing its parts.

After about 800, figures from nature began to appear regularly in Geometric painting, first usually as bands of grazing deer or marsh birds repeated endlessly around the vase. Horses were popular from the beginning, as they no doubt were in life for those who could afford them; they probably carried social distinction as well as riders. These animals and birds were pressed into geometric shapes in the overall ornament. Human figures soon appeared in the most conspicuous place, the handle zone. By the middle of the eighth century a figured style had evolved, though the animal files still formed part of the decoration.

The use of these figured drawings was probably stimulated by a small group of artists who developed gigantic vases to be used as grave markers. These Dipylon vases, named after the part of the Kerameikos cemetery in Athens where they were first found, are often as big as a man (1.75 meters) and are as close to monumental art as can be found in the eighth century (Fig. 5.19). These great amphoras and kraters usually bore a principal decorative zone at the handle level depicting a funeral scene and occasionally other zones as well. Subjects include the lying in state of the corpse (*prothesis*), or processions of mourners or warriors on foot or in chariots or carts following the body to the cemetery (*ekphora*), and battle scenes both on land and on sea. These scenes are bordered by bands of geometric ornament, which have begun to lose their prominence. The figures themselves are crowded by the filling ornament that takes up all available space in the figured panels.

A detail of one of the mourning scenes shows the main points of the Geometric painting style (Fig. 5.20). It is almost as if the artist had been more concerned to convey what he was aware of intellectually than what he saw. Within the framework of Geometric decoration human figures are defined rather than pictured, and their most significant parts are characteristically cobbled together to form an almost solid silhouette. A man is defined as having a triangular frontal torso with a blob for a profile head and only slightly curving thighs and calves. Female figures are defined as having long hair—at first rendered by individual lines sticking out of the head and later by a mass of lines—and breasts, which appear first as strokes one above the other under the armpit. Female figures are also later given hatched skirts. It may be that the conflict between geometric principles and human curves promoted the development of the representation of the body as artists tried to work out the problem. Objects are shown tipped up so that the viewer can understand them, as in Figure 5.20, in which the corpse is shown on its side and the webbing of the bed is depicted as a zigzag pattern between the sides of the bedframe. Above the corpse is placed a checkered shroud, or perhaps a canopy. Mourners tearing their hair flank the central scene. Notice that nearly all of the space between the objects is crowded with filling ornaments—a logical development for an artist who had grown up in the Geometric tradition.

As the period wore on, the solid black geometricized figures are occasionally seen in contexts other than funerals, war, or processions. A problem of interpretation confronts us here. It is thought that the Homeric poems had become known throughout Greece by the second half of the eighth century and scholars are often quick to identify scenes with episodes from, for instance, the Trojan War. The famous Late Geometric scene of a male and female figure and a warship (Fig. 5.21) can be interpreted as Paris taken Helen away from Sparta. It could also be interpreted as a biographical scene, however, or simply one

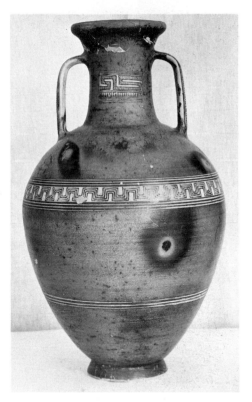

5.17 Ninth-century Geometric neck-handled amphora from Athens (h. 72.5 cm). Kerameikos Museum, Athens. Photo: Deutsches Archäologisches Institut, Athens.

from everyday life.[8] Similar problems arise when reconstruction is necessary, as we saw at the beginning of this chapter.

As an essentially indigenous style, the Geometric style in Attica had its roots in the previous period and of course ultimately in Mycenaean pottery. It was a relatively simple art, depending on the combination and repetition of a limited

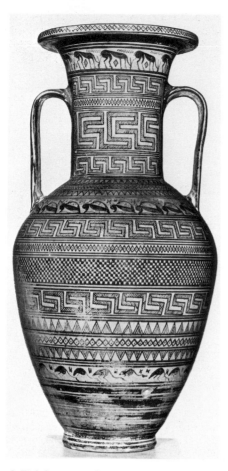

5.18 Eighth-century Geometric neck-handled amphora from Attica (h. 51 cm). Staatliche Antikensammlungen und Glyptothek, Munich. Photo: Hartwig Koppermann.

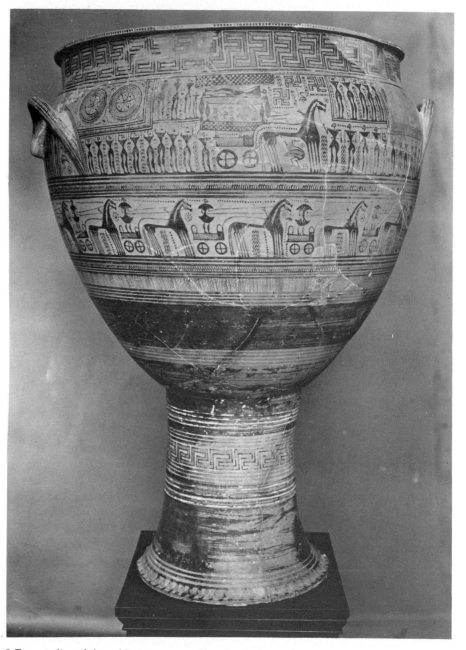

5.19 Krater from Dipylon cemetery, Athens. National Archaeological Museum, Athens. Photo: Deutsches Archäologisches Institut, Athens.

[8] Two studies of the subjects represented on Geometric pots give insight into the society that commissioned them, but some of the author's conclusions should be treated with care: Gudrun Ahlberg, *Prothesis and Ekphora in Greek Geometric Art* (Gothenburg, 1971), and *Fighting on Land and Sea in Greek Geometric Art* (Stockholm, 1971).

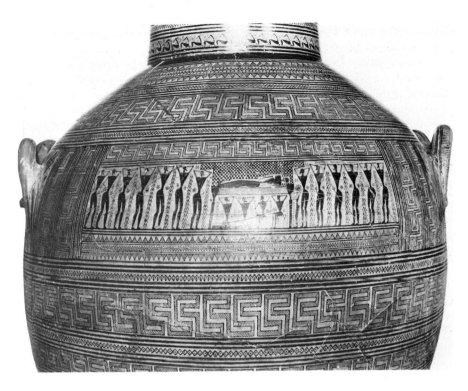

5.20 Detail of a mourning scene from a Dipylon amphora. National Archaeological Museum, Athens. Photo: Deutsches Archäologisches Institut, Athens.

number of forms. The introduction of the human figure and the possibilities thus opened up obviously attracted the artists, and it is in that direction that attention was focused. Late Geometric painting in Attica was a strong local style with interesting and unique figured scenes. The number of motifs and of filling ornaments generally dwindled while the human figures tended to fill out in shape and occasionally to have parts of the silhouette left in reserve, that is, not painted over. Change was in the air. It came first not in Attica but in the city of Corinth, to the west.

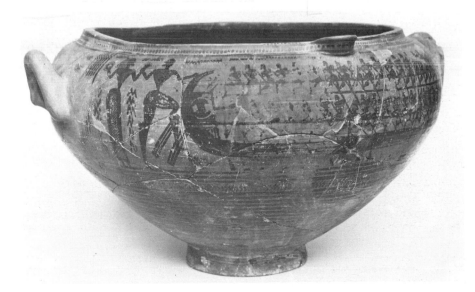

5.21 Departure scene on a Geometric krater from Thebes.[P] Reproduced by courtesy of the Trustees of the British Museum, London.

125

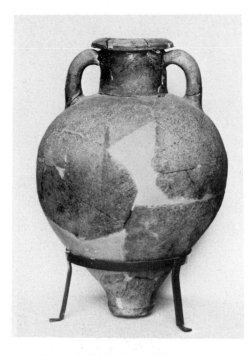

5.22 Corinthian transport amphora found at Gela. Scale 1:10. Photo: Carolyn Koehler.

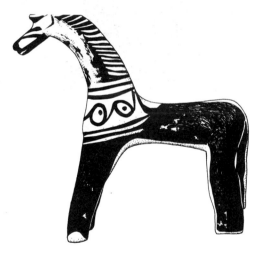

5.23 Typical Geometric terra cotta horse from Athens. Composite drawing after Karl Kübler, *Die Nekropole des 10 bis 8 Jahrhunderts*, Kerameikos, vol. 5 (Berlin: Walter de Gruyter, 1954), Plate 143. By permission of the Deutsches Archäologisches Institut, Berlin. Drawing by John Huffstot. Scale 1:2.

TRANSPORT AMPHORAS

Among the most common finds in excavations are the handles, toes, and body fragments of transport amphoras. These large, two-handled vases were designed to move large amounts (seven gallons or so) of liquid or semiliquid produce; they were most commonly used to transport wine. Each city shipped its product in a distinctively shaped vessel so that it would be instantly recognizable. Further ease of identification was provided by the use of stamps, which were pressed into the fabric of the pot while it was still soft, usually on the handles. They identified the origin of the wine, guaranteed the quantity and quality, and sometimes even gave the date of manufacture. Although most amphoras have the same basic shape—large, swelling body, small mouth, two vertical handles, and a pointed toe that could be used as a third handle in carrying and lifting—the shape, fabric, and stamps change enough over the years to give the archaeologist valuable aid in chronology and to provide clues to trade patterns and distribution of produce in the ancient world.[9]

Although large jars for the transport of produce were common in earlier times in the Near East, the city of Corinth provides examples of the first known Greek transport amphoras. The earliest series, known as Corinthian A, begins in the late eighth century; an example found in ancient Gela in Sicily is shown in Figure 5.22. Standing 74 centimeters high, this early example already shows the basic characteristics of shape that were further refined in the following centuries. The general progression was toward taller and slimmer proportions.

TERRA COTTA FIGURINES

As has been said, few terra cotta figurines survive from the Dark Ages, but numerous handmade figures of horses appeared in Athens in the ninth century and a whole new range of figures was introduced in the eighth. The earliest horses (Fig. 5.23) are covered with black glaze, with portions (usually the head or mane) reserved and painted with geometric patterns. These figures are often attached to lids of pyxides (small boxes), and so were made by the potter. They are in general quite crude and more or less geometricized, the eighth-century examples perhaps more so than the earlier ones. In the eighth century, in addition to horses, seated female figures (goddesses?) and mourning and standing women are occasionally found (Fig. 5.24). Several children's toys have been identified, including chariot groups and wheel-made figurines of cocks and pomegranates. A few clay mules on wheels carrying amphoras were also found, and pull toys of various types are well represented.

METALWORK

Although tools, weapons, and everyday utensils were made of iron in this period, bronze was still widely used for all sorts of objects. The Geometric period marks the beginning of a series of one-piece tripod caldrons of beaten bronze whose legs and high circular handles were separately cast and then attached by rivets. The caldron illustrated in Figure 5.25 stands to a total height of some 65 centimeters and is a typical example of the early form. Solid cast

[9] An excellent short introduction to this subject is to be found in Virginia Grace, *Amphoras and the Ancient Wine Trade*, Agora Picture Book no. 6 (Princeton, 1961). See also Elizabeth Lyding Will, "The Ancient Commercial Amphora," *Archaeology* 30 (1977): 264–270.

figures, usually horses, were often attached to the handles as decoration, and in fact it is from caldron handles that many of our Geometric horse figurines come. The legs of these caldrons were often decorated with incised designs and occasionally with figured scenes. The discovery in Lefkandi of molds for the manufacture of caldron legs indicates that bronze tripod caldrons were being produced by about 900 or earlier.[10] These caldrons served as prizes in funerary or festival games and were common dedications in sanctuaries, where the greatest number of them have been found.

The increasing prosperity of the Geometric period can be seen in the number of luxury goods that now turn up in graves. Imports are also found again, and precious metals reappear. Thin bands of gold foil shaped by being hammered in stone molds appear in Athens in the ninth century. These narrow strips, 30 to 40 centimeters long, with holes at each end, were evidently used to decorate graveclothes. The earliest ones have zigzag or tongue designs. By the second

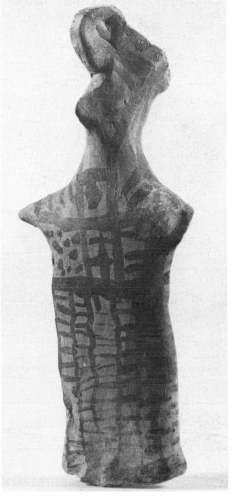

5.24 Typical female Geometric figurine. Courtesy, Museum of Fine Arts, Boston. Gift of the National Museum, Athens.

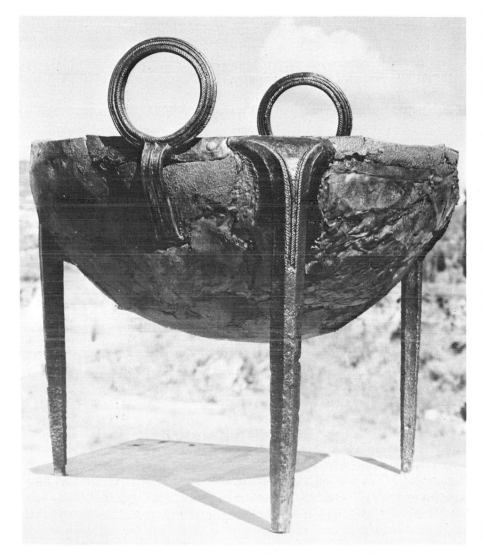

5.25 Bronze tripod caldron from Olympia. Olympia Museum. Photo: Deutsches Archäologisches Institut, Athens.

[10] The molds discovered at Lefkandi are discussed in Mervyn Popham, *Excavations at Lefkandi, Euboea, 1964–66* (London, 1968).

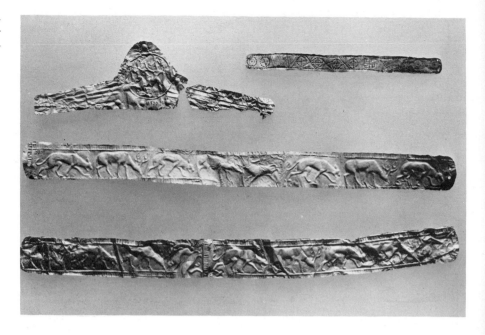

5.26 Gold bands from the Kerameikos cemetery, Athens. National Archaeological Museum, Athens. Photo: Deutsches Archäologisches Institut, Athens.

half of the eighth century they were being decorated with animal friezes, which are generally considered to indicate Eastern influence (Fig. 5.26). Human figures are also shown—fighting animals, in processions, mourning, and so on; in fact, the general repertoire of funeral scenes. Thin gold plates decorated in identical fashion adorned boxes and other wooden objects.

The presence in Athens of goldsmiths of considerable ability is further indicated by occasional finds of jewelry made of precious metal. Gold jewelry from a grave dated about 850 found in the Athenian agora in A.D. 1967 provides a further example of the skill of these workmen (Fig. 5.27). Broad and narrow finger rings and a pair of magnificent earrings, decorated with fine granules and gold wires in simple patterns and fringed by tiny pomegranates, make up this group. The earrings are only some 6.4 centimeters long.

PINS

Pins are somewhat less numerous than in the previous period and tend toward an elaboration of the earlier shape of globe and disc, but now appear mostly in bronze. They tend to get shorter after the beginning of the period and differ from their Protogeometric predecessors in several other ways, too. The shank is generally rectangular in cross section between the globe and the head and gradually becomes circular as it nears the point. The shank often bears incised decoration—zigzags, lines, and so on. The globe is now more distinct than before, a round object rather than a simple circle, thickening in shape, and is often set off from the shank by two small collars above and below it. Occasionally more than one globe is found. In Geometric pins the projection of the shaft beyond the disk is now elaborated into a finial, often taking the form of a vase or other object (Fig. 5.28a–c). More elaboration is to be seen in a second group of pins of a later date in the period (Fig. 5.28d and e), their shafts decorated with cubes, prisms, truncated pyramids, and other geometric shapes. The disk is lower on the shaft than before and is either a thin plaque separately made or small, thick, and cast with the pin. The decorated shaft now

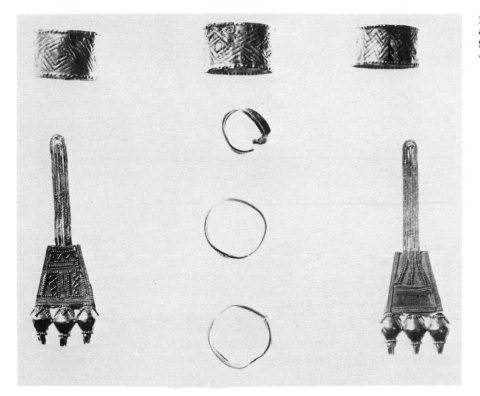

5.27 Gold jewelry from a grave in the Athenian agora. Agora Museum, Athens. Photo: American School of Classical Studies at Athens, Agora Excavations.

continued for some distance above it and the head either is a point or ends in a series of decorative moldings. In a group of pins classed as Sub Geometric, the upper shank is formed by a row of beads varying in number and shape (Fig. 5.28*f*). These pins are generally shorter than the previous examples and the molded portion often terminates with a cube or truncated pyramid. The finial is usually simple, either a plain plaque or disk.

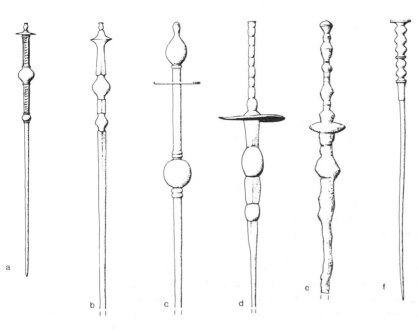

5.28 Typical Geometric pins. From *Greek Pins* by Paul Jacobstahl, published by Oxford University Press, 1956. *a, b, c,* and *e* by permission of Oxford University Press; *d* by permission of the Ecole Française d'Archéologie, Athens; *f* by permission of the American School of Classical Studies. Drawing by John Huffstot. Scale 1:2.

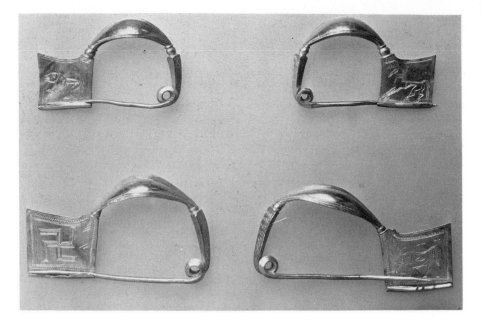

A great variety of geometric fibulae survive but examples of each type are so few that relationships among them are difficult to discern. The type with the thickened bow, common in the tenth century, continues into the ninth with a number of variations. A new type, the plate fibula, appears shortly after the middle of the century and continues well into the seventh century. The fibula is now more rectangular, with a curved bow that appears in various shapes—high, low, in sections, and so on—and is decorated with knobs, disks, balls, moldings, and the like. Most characteristic is the catch plate, which has grown greatly and now dominates. The shape varies but is generally square. Abstract or figural designs are often incised on the plate. The figural designs are often composed of simple geometric motifs but sometimes represent scenes from nature, war, and occasionally mythology. Some fibulae were made of precious metals; four gold examples, with simple designs on the catch plates and relatively plain bows, are shown in Figure 5.29. This so-called Attico-Boiotian type is at home in these regions, and cognate types are known throughout the Greek world. Both fibulae and pins seem to have disappeared from Athens by the end

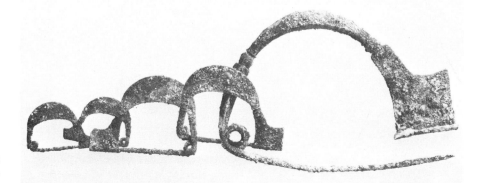

5.30 Plate and bow fibulae found together in the Kerameikos cemetery, Athens. Kerameikos Museum, Athens. Photo: Deutsches Archäologisches Institut, Athens.

of the eighth century, but in Boiotia, at least, the type continued into the seventh century, with increasingly elaborate incised decoration.[11]

An alternate shape, less common than the plate fibula, has a large decorated bow and a relatively small catch plate. Figure 5.30 shows a find of fibulae from a grave in the Kerameikos cemetery in Athens, consisting of a large plate fibula to which are attached four smaller fibulae with large bows.

Although the fibula continues throughout ancient times in simple forms, it becomes less important as a diagnostic feature after the Geometric period.

[11] The best summary in English of the Attico-Boiotian fibula is to be found in Keith De Vries, "Incised Fibulae from Boeotia," *Forschungen und Berichte* (Staatliche Museen zu Berlin) 14 (1972): 111–127.

6

The Orientalizing Period

THE SEVENTH CENTURY developed the trends that emerged in the eighth. The first contacts with the East took place in the eighth century; in the seventh they were developed and probably even regularized on a commercial and perhaps even a personal level. Colonization continued and Eastern goods flooded the Greek world, causing something approaching a revolution in the arts.

The city-state now grew more rapidly but also developed a sense of parochialism and rivalry with its fellows. It was quite common to be hostile toward one's neighbor while entering into an alliance with a state that bordered that neighbor on its other side. The political geography of Greece thus took on a characteristic checkerboard quality. At the same time came a heightened awareness of common speech, background, religion, and traditions. The development of the *polis,* fostered by increases in population, wealth, industry, and commerce, led to political strains that seem to have been only partially offset by the colonization movement. By the middle of the century the reins of power in many states had been seized by one person who set himself up as a "tyrant," an Oriental word used by the Greeks with no disparaging connotation to designate someone who ruled arbitrarily, without constitutional or other restrictions. Many of the tyrannies must have more or less copied Eastern models; some lasted well into the sixth century. The tyrants' courts provided some stimulation for the arts, particularly in the sixth century. So did the general rise in the standard of living in the seventh century, stimulated by foreign contacts and trade.

Athens took no great part in the colonization movement, probably because it already controlled a large amount of land. This factor may also be cited to help explain the fact that Athens escaped a tyranny until the sixth century and was able to suppress one attempt to seize the government. The resulting unrest led to some changes, such as the codification of the laws traditionally undertaken by Draco, but no comprehensive effort to solve the twin problems of political power and a changing society was made until the reforms of Solon, in the following century.

ART

Goods from the Near East reached Greece in an increasing stream, particularly from northern Syria and Phoenicia, which was rapidly coming under Assyrian domination, and even from such inland areas as Phrygia, whose king Midas is known in Greek folktales, and remote Urartu, on Lake Van in present-day eastern Turkey. Metalware, ivory carvings, trinkets of one sort or another, and probably textiles made up the major items of import. It may be that people as well as objects arrived from the East; resident foreign craftsmen have been postulated for some of the famous Cretan metalwork of the seventh century.

Greeks seem to have traveled more, too, many as mercenaries; we hear of them deep in Egypt in the next century.

However foreign influence may have arrived, whether by way of imported goods, migrating craftsmen, or observation in foreign lands, it was immediately felt in the visual arts. Geometric art, conservative and ingrown, was swiftly swept away by the new styles and new motifs from nature. New subjects and new methods were rapidly absorbed. The change is first seen in the scenes painted on pottery—and, strangely enough, not at Athens, which was the leader in the previous century, but at the Dorian city of Corinth. Athens had a strong geometric figured style while Corinth did not, and the latter's early and strong commercial ties promoted the new influence. So it is in the pottery of Corinth in the last quarter of the eighth century and perhaps a generation later in Athens that the Geometric style is seen to break up. Oriental influences are also visible in sculpture, with the so-called Daedalic style, and even in the minor finds.

In all cases the Oriental prototypes, even if at first adopted more or less entire, were quickly transformed into Greek objects. In a sense, the Greek characteristics of balance, symmetry, and line blended with the new Oriental motifs and subjects to form a new style, which found its greatest expression in the Archaic period of the sixth century.

ARCHITECTURE

The seventh century is also the time of the development of the two major styles of Greek architecture, the Doric order and the Ionic order. The extent of outside influence involved is difficult to determine. In development and final forms these two orders are uniquely Greek and are among the major gifts of that civilization to Western art.

The best known symbol of Greek civilization is the temple. It was during the seventh century that its form was defined and the first examples appeared, built mostly of stone. The stages by which the Doric and Ionic orders of architecture were created are obscure, as indeed is their origin, and it is probable that development did not proceed evenly in all centers. Recent work has shown that Corinth may have been a leader here, as it was in other fields in the Orientalizing period. Certain details of decoration and probably the techniques of masonry probably came from the East. Before we look at examples of these early stone buildings, it is necessary to say something about the developed forms.

The first tentative steps toward the standard ground plan, shown in Figure 6.1, had already been taken in the Geometric period with the adoption of the rectangular plan for a temple, with a colonnade or peristyle around the rectangular structure (cella) that housed the cult statue. Front and back porches (pronaos, opisthodomos) were formed by the extension and thickening of the cella walls (antae; singular, anta). When two columns stand between the wall ends, they are said, in Latin, to be *in antis.* Such porches were already in evidence in eighth-century buildings and became standard in the developed form of the plan. Once the standard form had been reached in the fifth century, it was destined to be constantly repeated with endless variations, not only in Greek architecture but to the end of antiquity and beyond. A series of rules and proportions gradually developed, which, when they were finally standardized in the fifth century, dictated the general proportions, placement, and use of the

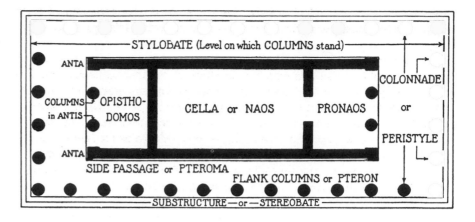

6.1 Typical temple ground plan. From Isabel Hoopes Grinnell, *Greek Temples* (New York: Metropolitan Museum of Art, 1943), p. xv. By permission of Isabel Hoopes Grinnell.

various decorative and functional members of the building. The flank columns, for instance, ideally numbered two times the number of front columns plus one; six by thirteen became the most common arrangement in the full developed Doric temple, with a colonnade that ran all the way around the cella (a peripteral temple).

The strict body of rules and relationships among the parts of the building also extended to the elevations of the buildings in the two major styles, Doric and Ionic (Figs. 6.2 and 6.3). Both orders rely on the post-and-lintel system, familiar from Bronze Age architecture. The Doric order grew up on the mainland in Dorian areas and probably in Corinthian territory; Ionic probably began in the East, perhaps in the Greek cities on the coast of Asia Minor. The Doric order is much the plainer of the two and may have developed somewhat earlier than the Ionic. Their origins are debated. The arguments turn on whether the individual features of each order, which are purely ornamental in stone construction, originally had structural functions when buildings were constructed of ephemeral materials, or were derived from earlier decorative designs.

The principal characteristics of the Doric order can be seen in Figure 6.2. The simple shaft bearing twenty channels or flutes with sharp divisions (arrises) between them tapers slightly from bottom to top. A capital consisting of a swelling member, the echinus, is topped by a block-shaped slab, the abacus, as a transition from the vertical column shaft to the mainly horizontal upper entablature. Above the columns and supported by them is the epistyle, formed of lines of blocks that extend from column to column. The epistyle blocks are plain except for a molding along the top, which is decorated at intervals with raised panels (regulae) from which circular projections called guttae project downward. Above the epistyle is the frieze course, consisting of grooved slabs, or triglyphs, ("three glyphs," so called because each groove is called a glyph and there are two whole and two half glyphs to each unit) are separated by blank panels called metopes, which in the more elaborately decorated temples are adorned with painting or sculpture. Above the frieze comes a horizontal course and above that the roof, double pitched, with open triangular spaces, the pediments, at both ends. The pediments were often filled with sculpture. The roof is usually adorned with architectural devices, sometimes sculptured figures on the ridge or at the corners and usually with brightly painted upright palmettes and lion-head waterspouts along the eaves. The undersurface of the

DORIC ORDER

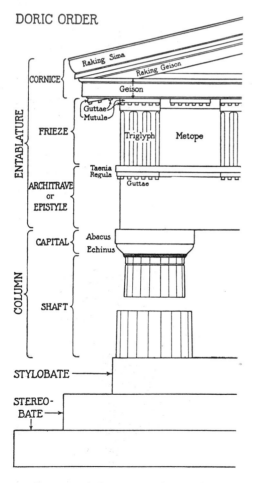

6.2 Elevation of the Doric order. From Isabel Hoopes Grinnell, *Greek Temples* (New York: Metropolitan Museum of Art, 1943), p. xviii. By permission of Isabel Hoopes Grinnell.

134

horizontal course (geison) above the frieze course is also ornamented with slabs (mutules) bearing guttae and placed over every triglyph and every metope.

The Doric frieze, with its triglyphs and its regula-guttae and mutule-guttae constructions, looks like a translation in stone of wooden construction. The theory of a "petrification" of previously wooden forms suggests that the triglyphs were boards secured by wooden pegs (guttae) protecting the faces of the roof beams from the weather, with the open spaces between them covered with plain slabs (metopes). Unfortunately, such evidence as we have from the earliest buildings suggests that the roof beams were probably entirely independent of the frieze course. An alternate theory sees the triglyph-metope frieze as primarily a decorative design with no structural function.[1]

The Doric order apparently had a major drawback: the difficulty of placing a triglyph over the exact center of each column and over the exact center of the space between each column. A moment's thought will show that such a scheme, if rigidly applied, would leave an empty slab at each corner of the building—an outcome that was considered unacceptable. Greek architects apparently wrestled with this problem by moving the corner column or adjusting the elements of the frieze but never arrived at a solution that pleased everyone. A Roman writer claimed that the triglyph-metope problem led to the decline of the Doric order. Evidently observation was more accute then than it is now.

The Ionic order is lighter and more slender than the Doric, and more highly decorated. The earliest manifestations have been found in Ionia but its specific origins are as obscure as those of the Doric. The Ionic column has an elaborately carved base—unlike the Doric, which sits directly on the stylobate—and twenty-four flutes separated by broad, flattened arrises rather than the pointed ones of the Doric column. The capital consists of two hanging volutes. Beneath them is an ornamental area; above is a small abacus. The volute may owe its origin to natural forms; some early Aeolic or Proto-Ionic capitals show a close association with vegetal motifs (Fig. 6.4). The epistyle is generally carved, with three flat undecorated projecting bands, and the frieze is either continuously sculptured or decorated with a row of toothlike projections, known appropriately enough as dentils. As Figures 6.1, 6.2, and 6.3 indicate, the vocabulary of Greek architecture is complex, with a specific name applied to each individual part. Moldings and all other minor components obey specific rules as to placement, shape, and ornament. As mentioned in Chapter 2, parts of Greek buildings changed in shape over time. Figure 6.5 shows the many variations in the profile of the Ionic base between the sixth and the second centuries.

Some paint was used for details above the columns of Greek temples and as backgrounds for sculpture. The backgrounds of metopes, friezes, and pediments were generally painted solid red or blue to help the sculpture stand out. The same colors were used for the mutules, triglyphs, regulae, and many of the moldings. The alternation of these two colors against the bright white of the building must have had a striking effect in the bright Mediterranean sunlight.

The establishment of the Doric order in permanent materials can be traced to

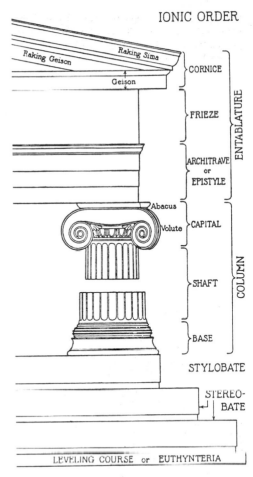

IONIC ORDER

6.3 Elevation of the Ionic order. From Isabel Hoopes Grinnell, *Greek Temples* (New York: Metropolitan Museum of Art, 1943), p. xix. By permission of Isabel Hoopes Grinnell.

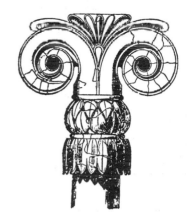

6.4 Aeolic or Proto-Ionic capital. From W. B. Dinsmoor, *The Architecture of Ancient Greece,* 3d ed. rev. (New York: W. W. Norton, 1975), p. 61, Fig. 21. Reproduced by permission.

---

[1] A statement of this theory can be found in R. M. Cook, "The Archetypal Doric Temple," *BSA* 65 (1970): 17–19. J. J. Coulton, *Ancient Greek Architects at Work: Problems of Structure and Design* (Ithaca, N.Y., 1977), pp. 37–41, suggests that the Doric order was invented at one time and in one place to create a monumental style. The theory that the Doric order derives from wooden prototypes is more generally held.

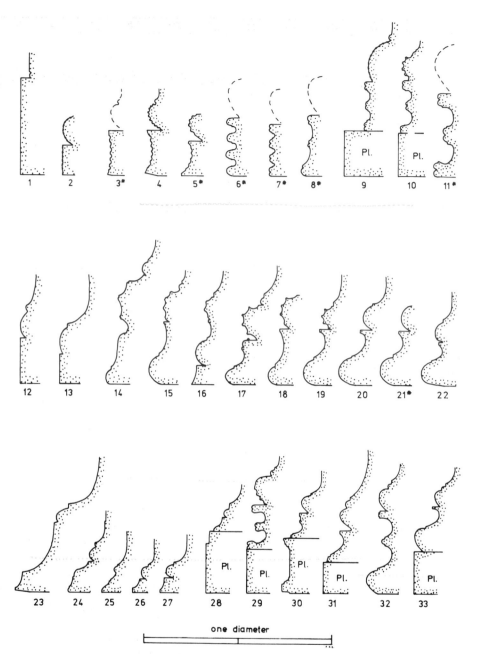

6.5 Ionic base profiles. From J. J. Coulton, *Ancient Greek Architects at Work* (Ithaca, N.Y.: Cornell University Press, 1977), published in England as *Greek Architects at Work* (London: Paul Elek Ltd., 1977), p. 100, Fig. 40. Drawing by J. J. Coulton, based on various sources, including L. T. Shoe, *The Profiles of Greek Mouldings* (1936). Reproduced by permission.

Corinth. Recent excavations both at Corinth itself and at the nearby sanctuary of Poseidon on the Isthmus of Corinth, at a site known as Isthmia, have recovered the remains of large stone temples beneath the later temples. Both sites were destroyed by fire, the latter in the fifth century, the one at Corinth in the sixth. The Corinthian building is known so far only as scattered remains of wall blocks and tiles that belong to a primitive form of roofing known from some other sites. The invention of terra cotta tiles, again probably at Corinth, must have been an important step in the development of the stone temple, as their weight necessitated more support than could be given by the generally flimsy construction of earlier buildings. Investigations of the Corinthian building give

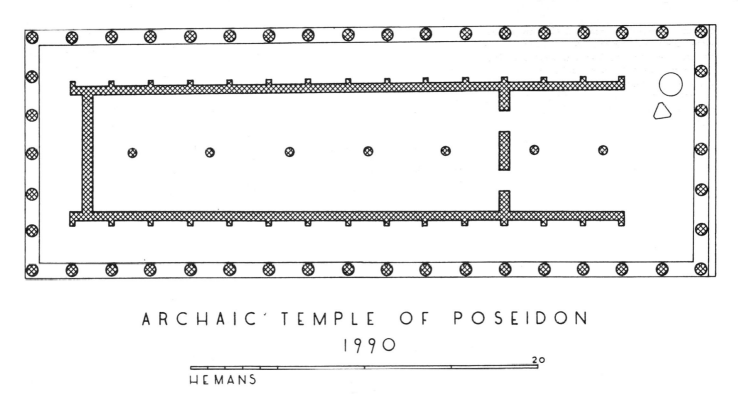

ARCHAIC' TEMPLE OF POSEIDON
1990

20

HEMANS

6.6 Restored plan of the seventh century temple of Poseidon at Isthmia,[P] drawn by Frederick P. Hemans. Plan courtesy of the University of Chicago Excavations at Isthmia.

it the early date of about 680 or a little later and suggest that the temple consisted only of a masonry cella. Unfortunately, nothing of this interesting building has yet been found in position.[2]

More information has been recovered from the excavations at Isthmia, which completely cleared the area of the earlier and later temples of Poseidon. The ground plan can be recovered with some assurance. Figure 6.6 shows an extremely long building, over 39 meters in length by more than 14 meters in width, with a central row of five columns in the cella and two in the pronaos. Seven columns stood at each end and eighteen on each flank. The building was constructed of stone blocks with a roof similar to that at Corinth but with a peristyle and a relatively well-developed Doric elevation containing elements of both wood and stone, according to the reconstruction of the excavator.[3] An interesting detail is the fragmentary evidence of painted panels containing figured scenes on the outer walls of the cella. The date of construction of this early temple is put in the first half of the seventh century, perhaps in the second quarter, slightly later than the one at Corinth, which seems, at least on present evidence, earlier and cruder.

Terra cotta decorations apparently developed over the course of the century. Some have been associated with a temple of Apollo that was erected about 630 at Thermon, in northwest Greece (Fig. 6.7). Its ground plan is similar to the

[2] For a survey of what is known about early Corinth, including the early temple, see J. B. Salmon, *Wealthy Corinth: A History of the City to 338 B.C.* (Oxford, 1984).
[3] Much of the evidence for the early temple of Poseidon on the Isthmus of Corinth can be found in Oscar Broneer, *Temple of Poseidon*, Isthmia series, vol. 1 (Princeton, 1971). The latest investigations that added to the earlier information concerning the temple and the whole site are discussed in Elizabeth R. Gebhard and Frederick P. Hemans, "The University of Chicago Excavations at Isthmia, 1989: I," *Hesperia* 61 (1992): 1–77.

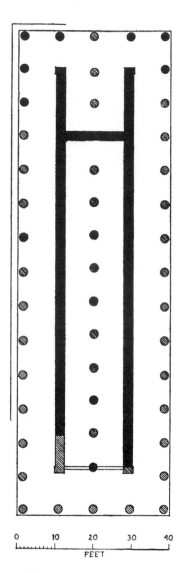

restored ground plan of the early temple at Isthmia, with five columns across the ends, fifteen on the flanks, and an interior row to hold up the roof. The building measured 38.23 by 12.13 meters. The peristyle, probably originally of wood, was replaced in stone at a later date. The upper parts of the walls were of perishable material, mud brick and wood. A wooden entablature is conjectured on the basis of the lack of stone remains and the existence of large painted terra cotta metope slabs that evidently belong to the temple, as well as a series of molded terra cotta heads that lined the building's gutter and belonged to several reroofings. The style of the earliest of these heads dates the original building. A conjectural reconstruction of the wood and terra cotta entablature is shown in Figure 6.8; the architectural decorations probably belonged to a later roof or a repair to the original, seventh-century building.

To the seventh century also belongs the second temple of Hera on Samos, which replaced the earlier temple after the middle of the century (Fig. 6.9). Still very long (37.88 by 11.65 meters), this building had six columns on each end and eighteen on each flank. New here is the deepening of the colonnade on the east end, which became a typical feature of large temples in Ionia, emphasizing the front of the building. It also reflects a typical Eastern preference for a forest of columns in a large building. The interior represents a great improvement,

6.7 Plan of the seventh-century temple of Apollo at Thermon.[P] From W. B. Dinsmoor, *The Architecture of Ancient Greece,* 3d ed. rev. (New York: W. W. Norton, 1975), p. 52, Fig. 18. Reproduced by permission.

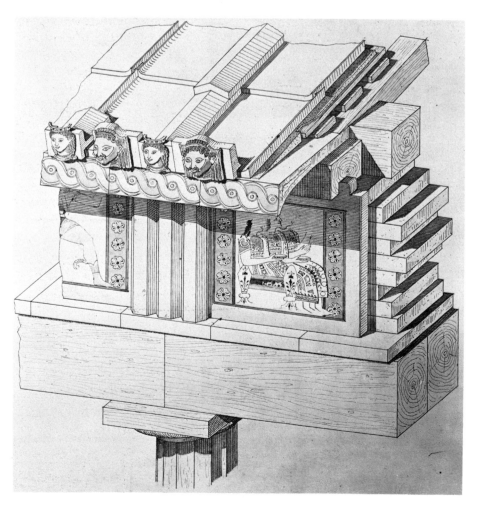

6.8 An early reconstruction of the entablature of the temple of Apollo at Thermon. Photo: Deutsches Archäologisches Institut, Athens.

with the supports for the roof now next to the walls on either side rather than down the middle of the building like a spine. The temple was built of stone and wood and doubtless was Ionic, although little except a fragment of a sculptured frieze is preserved.

On the mainland, the Doric order developed rapidly, and by the end of the century the ground plan more closely approached the proportions that became standard in the fifth century. The new investigations at Tegea have revealed the remains of a large temple, probably with a peristyle of six by eighteen columns, that preceded the fourth-century temple (fig. 1.5). The double row of columns on the interior allows an unobstructed view, which was not possible with earlier arrangements, such as that of the Temple of Poseidon at Isthmia (Fig. 6.6). The building's walls were of mud brick in a framework of wooden beams, with slabs of local marble to reinforce the lower portions, at least in one place. The external colonnade was probably of wood, as was the entablature; it has been partially restored on analogy with the slightly later and more advanced temple of Hera at Olympia. Burned in 394, this early temple probably belongs to the last quarter of the seventh century.[4] At Olympia the better-preserved temple of Hera was one of the last of the large temples to have major portions constructed of ephemeral materials. The temple, built around 600, was constructed of limestone to a height of a little over a meter, then continued up in mud brick. All the rest of the structure was originally of wood, except for the tiled roof and its terra cotta ornaments. Two large terra cotta disks (about 2.13 meters in diameter) stood at the peak of the roof, one at each end. The original wooden columns were replaced as they wore out; one is recorded to have been still standing in the second century of the Christian era. The remaining capitals are of all styles, the echinus varying from flat to upright. In plan (Fig. 6.10) the temple now has all the necessary components of cella, pronaos, and opisthodomos with two columns *in antis* but is still somewhat long in relation to width, with six columns on each end and sixteen on each flank, measuring 50.01 by 18.76 meters on the stylobate. On the interior, spur walls originally extended from the sides, dividing the cella into a series of eight bays. They are unusual features and may have been intended in the beginning to help support the roof; perhaps the architect was nervous without a central row of columns and did not trust the new system of two rows of interior supports.

SECULAR ARCHITECTURE

Private housing in this period differed little from the small, unpretentious dwellings known from the eighth century, and the extensive use of perishable materials has left little trace of other nonreligious construction. The seventh-century sanctuary of Hera on Samos, however, contained one of the earliest examples of a stoa (Figs. 6.9, 6.11). This type of building consists basically of a back wall from which a roof slopes to a line of columns or posts along the front. In its simple form, as here, the stoa is little more than an open shed with wooden posts on stone bases supporting a wooden entablature, which in the reconstruction shows a possible wooden origin for Ionic dentils. Later stoas are more enclosed, with back rooms and second stories, and served as shelters and commercial centers.[5]

---

[4] The identification of the remains of the early temple can be found in Erik Østby, "The Archaic Temple of Athena Alea at Tegea," *Opuscula Atheniensia* 16 (1986): 75–102.

[5] A study of the stoa form in Greek architecture is J. J. Coulton, *The Architectural Development of the Greek Stoa* (Oxford, 1976).

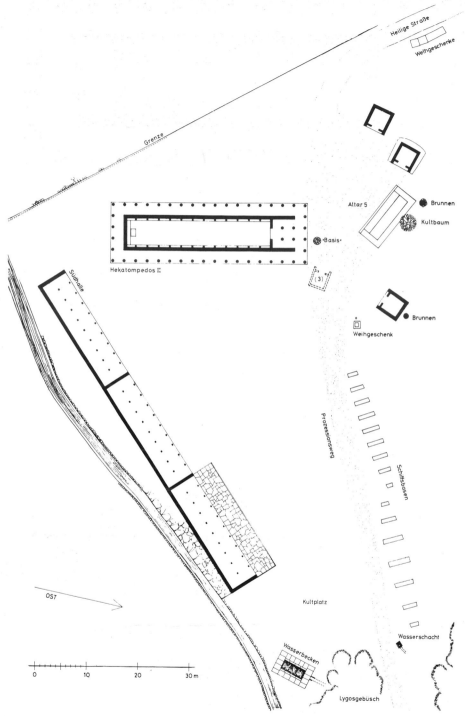

Heilige Straße

Weihgeschenke

Grenze

Brunnen

Altar 5

Kultbaum

· Basis ·

Hekatompedos II

(3)

Brunnen

Weihgeschenk

Südhalle

Prozessionsweg

Schiffsbasen

OST

Kultplatz

Wasserschacht

Wasserbecken

0   10   20   30 m

Lygosgebüsch

6.9 Plan of the Heraion on Samos, between 650 and 570. From Hans Walter, *Das griechische Heiligtum dargestellt am Heraion von Samos* (Stuttgart: Urachhaus, 1990), p. 83, Fig. 92. Reproduced by permission.

SCULPTURE

In the seventh century the first relatively large stone sculptures appear. With numerous terra cotta figurines that survive from about the same time, they have certain specific stylistic characteristics that recall the Eastern prototypes

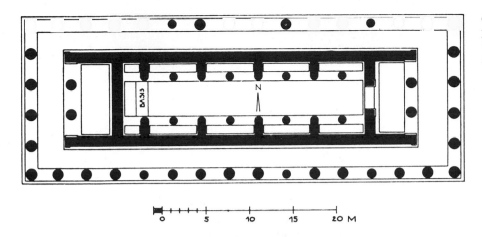

6.10 Ground plan of the temple of Hera at Olympia.[P] From Gottfried Gruben, *Die Tempel der Griechen* (Munich: Hirmer Verlag, 1966), p. 49, Fig. 38. Reproduced by permission.

from which they both descend. This style, which has received the conventional name of Daedalic after a legendary Cretan artist, emanated from several centers on the mainland, Crete, and the islands.[6] It is known from a number of sites in Greece but seems not to have been popular in Attica, which was somewhat less influenced by foreign styles at this period than other regions of Greece.

Almost all the figures are draped women or youths, often wearing broad belts. The musculature is quite schematized. Each figure is conceived frontally, that is, meant to be seen from the front. The bodies are rendered in a flat,

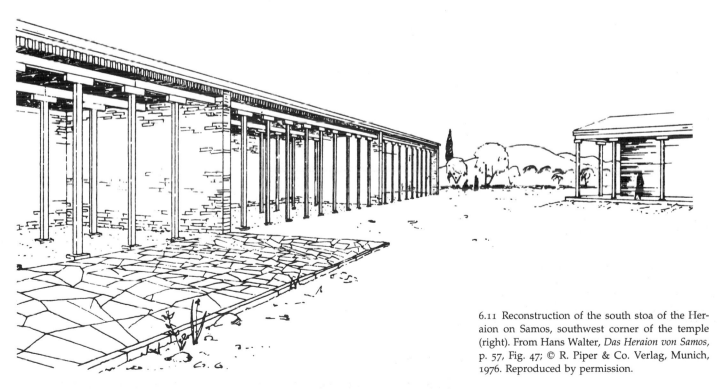

6.11 Reconstruction of the south stoa of the Heraion on Samos, southwest corner of the temple (right). From Hans Walter, *Das Heraion von Samos*, p. 57, Fig. 47; © R. Piper & Co. Verlag, Munich, 1976. Reproduced by permission.

6 The basic study in English on the Daedalic style is still Romilly Jenkins, *Dedalica* (Cambridge, 1936), though it is now generally believed to overemphasize the Dorian character of the style. See John Boardman, *Greek Sculpture: The Archaic Period* (New York and Toronto, 1978), pp. 11–17.

planklike fashion with a flat, often unworked back. The characteristic flat head has a low forehead and large eyes set in a triangular face. The hair, represented as horizontal tresses, has the appearance of a wig, and is thought to derive from one.

This style, although clear enough in its characteristics, can perhaps be seen developing. At the end of the Geometric period the characteristic angularity of the human body tended to break down into a more rounded treatment, as can be seen in a small statuette, now in Boston, dedicated by a certain Mantiklos to Apollo about 700 (Fig. 6.12). Here the geometric rigidity and the triangular

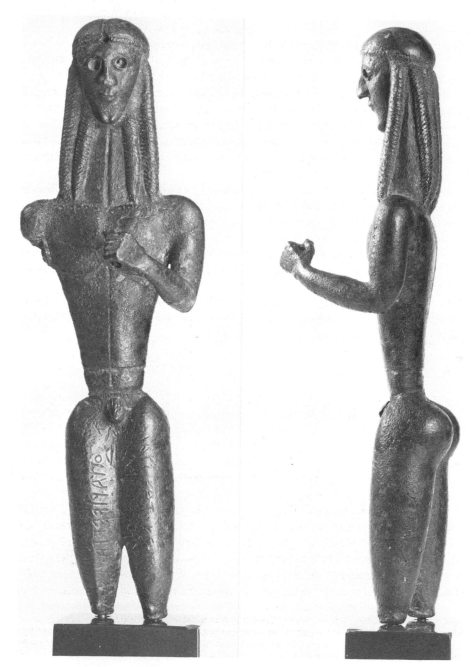

6.12 Mantiklos figurine (h. 20 cm), front and side views. Courtesy, Museum of Fine Arts, Boston. Francis Bartlett Collection.

chest can be seen, but the figure has become rounder and more corporeal in the shoulders, chest, thighs, and buttocks. At the same time, however, the triangular face, large eyes, heavy strand of hair, and belt indicate that a third element of stiffening and formalization has begun to appear.[7] In a sense the impulse toward natural, more rounded forms is stopped by Daedalic schematization.

The earliest stone sculpture in Daedalic style is a life-sized marble standing female figure from Delos. An inscription indicates that the figure was dedicated by one Nikandre to Artemis. It is so badly worn that the features are obliterated but its primitive form indicates a date in the first half of the century. Better preserved and more advanced anatomically and technically is a smaller limestone figure once in Auxerre and now in the Louvre (Fig. 6.13). Only about one-third life-size (65 centimeters high), the Lady from Auxerre shows quite clearly the typical Daedalic style in the flat body, long triangular face, large eyes, and wiglike hair. She wears a simple straight garment, as did the Nikandre dedication, but it is elaborated by a shawl and enlivened by incised decorations on the skirt, which were once brightly painted. She holds her right hand up to her breast while the left hangs down stiffly at her side. Her body is indicated under the drapery and the thick belt emphasizes the division of the body into upper and lower portions. In its general outlines this figure has Assyrian parallels, and, as has been noted, it is in this part of the world that the initial stimulus for the style originated.

By the last quarter of the century the Daedalic style was softening, the sharp angles and divisions becoming more rounded, as can be seen in the so-called Mycenae Metope, dated 640–620 (Fig. 6.14). This small piece of sculpture, only 40.6 centimeters high, preserves the head of a woman wrapped in a heavy garment. It perhaps belonged to an altar or other small construction. Here the strictures of the style are loosening: the face appears fuller, more rounded, and less triangular than previously.

The Daedalic style was abandoned toward the end of the century and larger, bolder, more monumental figures suddenly appeared, probably influenced from Egypt.

POTTERY

It is in the painted pottery of the great mercantile city of Corinth that the new Oriental motifs first appear. Corinth had had a modest Geometric school, almost purely decorative, with very few figured scenes. In the last third of the eighth century new figures appeared and the Corinthian Geometric style was rapidly discarded. Along with this change came some new shapes: a form of deep skyphos, or drinking cup, and the aryballos, a small round vessel with a narrow mouth, for perfume or precious oils. The aryballos in particular is a typical Corinthian product. The rapid development of its shape and of the figures that adorn it can be seen in Figure 6.15. Animals appear, at first those of the barnyard and later exotic creatures, whose ultimate home is in the East but which appear almost immediately in their Greek form. Such creatures as Pegasos and the Chimaira make their appearance now, as presumably also do their stories. Other new formalized motifs borrowed from vegetal decoration of the

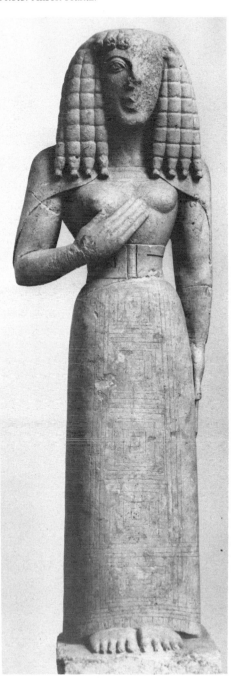

6.13 Auxerre statuette.[P] Musée du Louvre, Paris. Photo: Alison Frantz.

---

[7] An inscription on the figurine, "Mantiklos dedicated me to the Far-Darter of the silver bow, as part of his tithe, do thou, Phoebos, grant him gracious recompense," indicates a cheerful reciprocal relationship between man and god. In the great Eastern civilizations, in contrast, humans were simply small and insignificant cogs in nature, far removed from the gods.

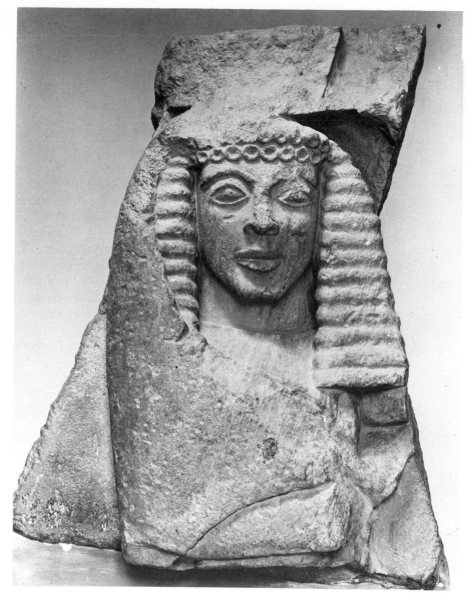

6.14 Mycenae Metope. National Archaeological Museum, Athens. Photo: Deutsches Archäologisches Institut, Athens.

East are used as secondary or even primary subjects. A common motif, and one characteristic of seventh-century design, is the dot rosette, consisting of a circle of dots around a central dot, to which they are often connected by strokes (Fig. 6.15*b* and *c*).

The technique of painting changed at the end of the eighth century also. Two differing techniques were developed. In one, the outline technique, the face and figure are drawn in outline, with inner details indicated by black lines. The spaces within the outlines are sometimes reserved—that is, left the natural color of the surface—but female flesh is usually white, male white or brown. The inner markings on the figures are sometimes white or red rather than black. The outline technique found a home in East Greek painting but it was rejected quickly in Corinthian and, after some experimentation, in Attic painting. the Black Figure technique found readier acceptance on the mainland.[8] This method of vase painting retained the silhouette figure but achieved the inner markings, and sometimes the outlines, by deep incisions that penetrated the light-colored clay beneath. Color was sometimes added to the figures—red, white, purple. Geometric painting had been essentially monochromatic, but now with the brighter colors, the precision of the incision, and the new and exciting subject matter, Corinthian painters proceeded to produce the finest painted pottery of their day. The straight line gave way to the curve, while the figures were filled out more convincingly than in the past.

The style of Corinth is very disciplined and controlled almost from its first appearance. The Black Figure technique, which is considered a Corinthian invention and probably derives partially from metalworking skills, lent itself to work on a small scale and appears mostly on small vases. In the seventh century Corinthian pottery was clearly the best being made and included occasional polychrome masterpieces such as the Chigi Vase (Fig. 6.16). Here in Black Figure are lively scenes, including clashing warriors and huntsmen. The men's flesh is painted a warm brown and other features of the scene are painted in various colors. A battle is depicted on an unusual lion-headed aryballos of the same style that is only 6.8 centimeters high (Color Plate 7, following p. 96). The use of many colors is a rare occurrence and is not seen again for some time.

After the middle of the century, however, with a few exceptions Corinthian painters settled down to an uninspired style consisting of files of animals running around the vase in procession. The olpe, a Corinthian shape, illustrated in Figure 6.17, is an early example of this style, produced at a time when the animals were still taut, full of life, and carefully drawn. From that time on, however, although some good paintings were still produced, in general the animal style degenerated badly into endless repetition of stock types. By the middle of the sixth century, generally speaking, Attic wares had ousted the Corinthian from the international market.

Attica, with its strong local tradition, accepted Oriental influences less readily than did Corinth and never adopted them wholeheartedly. Although Oriental features can be seen in the Geometric period, it was not until about a generation after Oriental motifs began to appear at Corinth that the strong Attic Geometric style started to break up. The geometric silhouette had begun to bend and to enclose reserved areas in the late Geometric period and the change accelerated in the seventh century. The amphora shown in Figure 6.18 has been attributed to the Analatos Painter, one of the first Athenian painters whose style we can identify. His real name is not known, and he is therefore named after the place where one of the pots painted by him was found. In its slimness and elongation the amphora follows a general seventh-century trend. A number of geometric shapes, including various krater and oinochoe variants, were discarded at the beginning of the century and a few were added, such as the skyphos, borrowed from Corinth but given a characteristic Attic shape. The filling in of the handles of the Analatos Painter's amphora is also typical of the period. The painting of this period as it appears on the vases is known as Proto-Attic.

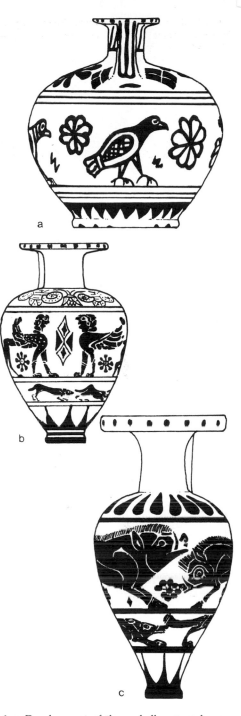

6.15 Development of the aryballos: *a*, early seventh century; *b*, first half of the seventh century; *c*, mid-seventh century; *a* and *c* after Humfry Payne, *Necrocorinthia* (Oxford: Oxford University Press, 1931), Plates 1 and 9, by permission of Dilys Russell; *b* after R. M. Cook, *Greek Painted Pottery*, 2d ed. (London: Methuen, 1972), Plate 9. Drawing by John Huffstot. Scale 1:1.

[8] The black color in both the Black Figure and the Red Figure techniques was obtained by chemical reaction in a three-stage firing process; it is not a paint in the modern sense, but a clay solution. The technical aspects of Greek pottery, including the Greek black glaze, are discussed in Joseph Veach Noble, *The Techniques of Painted Attic Pottery*, rev. ed. (London, 1988).

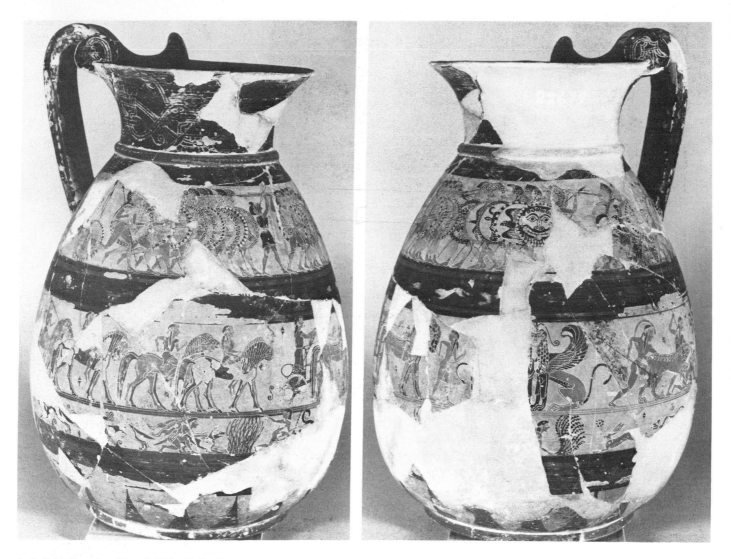

6.16 Chigi Vase (h. 26.2 cm). Villa Giulia, Rome.
Photos: Deutsches Archäologisches Institut, Rome.

Although at first sight the Analatos Painter's amphora appears Geometric in style, a closer examination shows that the strict geometric scheme is breaking up and Orientalizing features are beginning to appear. There are three zones of decoration: the upper one, containing individualized sphinxes drawn partially in outline; below it, a dance scene in the same technique; then the principal zone, containing a standard Geometric scene, a chariot parade, painted in silhouette. A new spirit is at work here, however: the men and the horses are more organic and less stylized than Geometric examples. The horses are rendered in silhouette but with some incision, while the human figures are in silhouette, in outline, and in combination of the two. This mixture of techniques betrays the experimental nature of the painting. All the empty spaces of the figured scenes are packed with filling ornaments, a Geometric characteristic. These ornaments consist mostly of wavy lines, but an occasional stylized plant intrudes. Subsidiary zones include cable patterns, rosettes, spirals, leaves, and the like—elements that are foreign to the Geometric repertoire but at home in the seventh century.

146

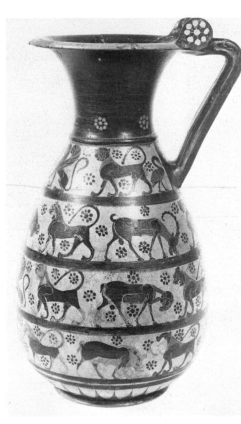

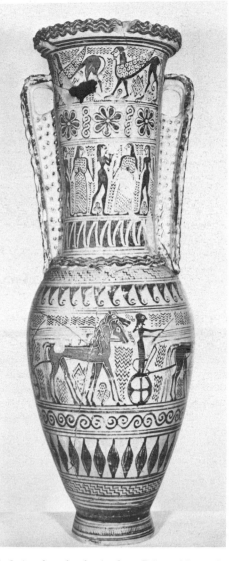

6.17 Olpe in animal style. Photo: Museum of Art and Archaeology, University of Missouri–Columbia.

The seventh century was a period of experimentation in Attic painting as the Geometric style was replaced. Incision appeared early but outline drawing, a more natural development from the Geometric style, was also employed, and the two techniques were often used on the same vase. The monumental Attic tradition produced large figures, at first crude but always alive and interesting, if undisciplined. Scenes from myth were prominent features from the beginning.

The amphora from Eleusis (Fig. 6.19) typifies this experimental phase. Only one side carries figure decoration. The reverse is decorated with a design of entwined plants. On the neck is pictured Odysseus and his companions driving a stake into the eye of the Cyclops. In this scene the geometric background is clearly seen in the figures, painted mainly in silhouette, but the face of the Cyclops is reserved and the faces of the Greeks and the body of Odysseus are painted white. A scene of animal combat is shown on the shoulder of the vase, with the lion's head in outline. The large zone on the body of the vase bears Gorgons, Perseus, and Athena, the last two badly preserved. Medusa is shown headless under one of the handles while her sister Gorgons advance to the right, to be stopped by Athena as Perseus flees with Medusa's head. The Gorgons, their outlines partially filled with white, are quite extraordinary. Their heads have been compared with the monumental bronze caldrons with griffin-head attachments, so common in this century (see below). Clearly the standard Gorgon type established in Corinth (see Fig. 7.1) had not yet reached this artist; he was thus free to experiment. In all three scenes appear minor and weak filling ornaments, including rosettes, modified dot rosettes, and occa-

6.18 Amphora by the Analatos Painter. Musée du Louvre, Paris. Photo: Chuzeville.

147

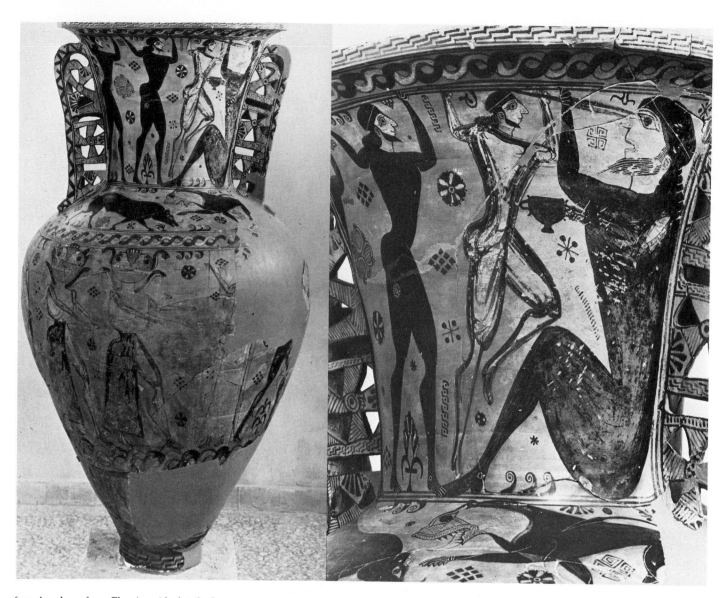

6.19 Amphora from Eleusis, with detail of scene on neck. Eleusis Museum. Photos: Deutsches Archäologisches Institut, Athens.

sional plant designs (between the legs of the figure behind Odysseus) which show some slight Oriental influence.

The large, highly decorated, crude figures and the robust representations of mythical scenes emphasize the difference between this style and that of Corinth in the same century. The Proto-Attic style soon received a strong wave of Corinthian influence that organized and disciplined the wild excesses of the seventh century to a more sober but no less vivid and alive Black Figure style, which contrasts strongly with the repetitious Corinthian competition.

TRANSPORT AMPHORAS

A late-seventh-century example of a transport amphora, almost 64 centimeters high, is shown in Figure 6.20. The change in shape from the first amphora in the series (see Fig. 5.22) is subtle. The process of refinement and elongation had hardly begun and became obvious only in succeeding centuries.

TERRA COTTA FIGURINES

The seventh century was marked by the introduction of the mold for figurines, an event that can probably be linked with the development of the Daedalic style and traced to Eastern origins. In fact, a common type of Eastern terra cotta, the Astarte plaque, along with more or less direct imitations, has been found in Greece. The centers of the seventh-century molded figurines, particularly Crete and Corinth, have some claim as originators of the sculptural style presumably derived from the terra cotta figurines. Molded and painted terra cotta plaques in Daedalic style are most common on Crete, but the concept of using a mold for a full, rounded figure apparently did not find immediate acceptance even there. Some of the earliest examples are nude, as are their Astarte models, but this was evidently not to Greek taste and the draped female figure rapidly became the rule. Figure 6.21 shows one of these figurines, molded on the front but flat at the back.

Molds were commonly used for the heads, which were then attached to handmade or sometimes wheel-made bodies. The bodies are often female, perhaps representing goddesses, and are sometimes extremely crude.

Attica again shows its relative independence from the Daedalic style in its terra cotta figurines. A number of more or less Daedalic heads that probably were once attached to wheel-made or handmade bodies—a practice still followed in the sixth century—and a plaque with a Daedalic-featured woman are the only known manifestations of the style. Although more Daedalic examples from the seventh century probably exist, either unexcavated or unreported, the major figurine production seems to have been a development from the Geometric human and animal figures. Most of the figures are handmade with rudimentary bodies and tubular extremities, and are decorated with glaze or matt paint occasionally laid over a white slip. Found mainly in graves, these Attic terra cottas are obviously funerary in conception. They were often used as appendages to funeral vases. Groups still occur; an outstanding example from Vari in Attica consists of a funeral wagon carrying a corpse under a coverlet, four female mourners, and an accompanying horseman (Fig. 6.22). This composition reminds one of the scenes on the Dipylon vases.

Molds were also used for some of the decoration on great clay storage vessels that were manufactured in a number of centers, including Sparta, Boiotia, Crete, and the islands. Standing sometimes as high as a man, they were built up of coils of clay, their surfaces adorned with scenes and decorative designs in relief, which were variously cast in molds or handmade, impressed with stamps or engraved by hand. The figures were generally roughly made by hand, attached with a thin slip of clay for binding, and then modeled and tooled. Mythological scenes adorn some of the larger examples, with Orientalizing animals as subsidiary ornaments (Fig. 6.23).[9]

METALWORK

The metalwork of the seventh century shows unmistakable Oriental influences. Crete was one of the centers of metalworkings, as it was of stone sculpture, and metal objects found in a cave sacred to Zeus on Mount Ida have been

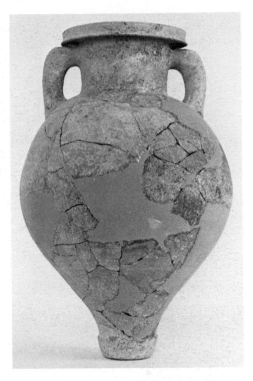

6.20 Transport amphora from Corinth. Corinth Museum. Photo: American School of Classical Studies at Athens: Corinth Excavations.

[9] For a short, general treatment of these relief vessels, see Martin Robertson, *A History of Greek Art* (Cambridge, 1975), 1:28–29.

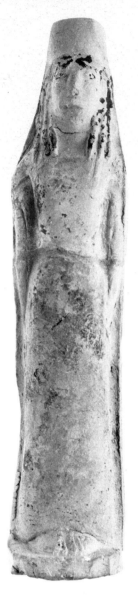

6.21 Seventh-century figurine from Corinth. Corinth Museum. Photo: American School of Classical Studies at Athens: Corinth Excavations.

interpreted as early imitations of Eastern metalwork or perhaps actually made by Eastern craftsmen. Most of the objects are shields bearing rows of animals and humans running around a central boss in the form of an animal's head (Fig. 6.24). They differ from Geometric examples both in technique and in style, but their dating has been disputed; some scholars are willing to put them as far back as the end of the ninth century. Whatever their date, their similarity to Eastern examples indicates one source of Oriental influence. The actual existence on Crete of Oriental craftsmen has in fact been postulated for a number of sites, as a means of explaining these and similar Oriental-looking objects.[10]

The problem of distinguishing direct imports from the East, objects made by Oriental craftsmen in Greece, Greek copies of imports, and original Greek creations in an Eastern style is more pronounced in connection with the sev-

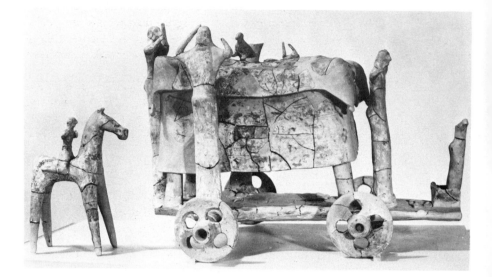

6.22 Terra cotta funeral wagon and horseman from Vari in Attica. Photo: National Archaeological Museum, Athens.

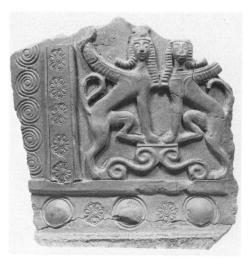

6.23 Fragment of a relief vessel with two sphinxes. Photo: Museum of Art and Archaeology, University of Missouri–Columbia.

[10] The close relationship of early Crete with the lands to the east is emphasized in Sarah Morris, *Daidalos and the Origins of Greek Art* (Princeton, 1992), pp. 150–194.

enth century than with the eighth. A case in point is the great caldrons, now separated from their stands, which are found throughout the Greek world as dedications in sanctuaries. The type seems to have originated in the eastern kingdom of Urartu, around present-day Lake Van in Turkey. Separately made figures set around the opening take various forms, including human-headed birds that look over the rim and serve as attachments for ring handles. Many caldrons also have long-necked griffins, lions, or other creatures attached to them, looking in or out. These protomes, especially the griffins, are considered by some scholars to be clearly Greek creations, which were added to caldrons in addition to the handle attachments that are seen as Oriental in origin. Figure 6.25 shows a reconstruction of a caldron found in Olympia which had both lion and griffin protomes and must have had a diameter of approximately 65 centimeters. These protomes are made of hammered bronze, but others, perhaps generally of later date, were made of cast bronze. When the protome was particularly large, the head was sometimes cast alone and then attached to a hammered neck. In the cast griffin protome in Figure 6.26 we see an exotic creature with a bird's beak and upright horses' ears, a fabulous Oriental animal that has been turned into a decorative Greek object, with the topknot stylized into a knob.

The opulent life-style of the early tyrants and the skill of workers in precious metals are seen in the hammered gold bowl shown in Color Plate 6 (following p. 96). It was found at Olympia, and the inscription, in the Corinthian alphabet, indicates that it was dedicated by the sons of Kypselos, who was tyrant of Corinth toward the end of the century.

PINS

Pins continued to be made in the seventh century, especially in Dorian areas and particularly in the Peloponnesos. Those attributed to the seventh century have short heads set off from round shanks (Fig. 6.27). The number of decora-

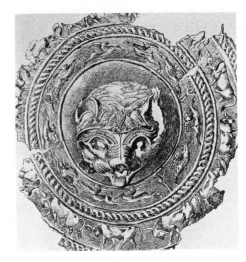

6.24 Shield from the Idaean Cave. From Georges Perrot, *Histoire de l'art dans l'antiquité*, vol. 3 (Paris: Hachette, 1898), p. 131, Fig. 19.

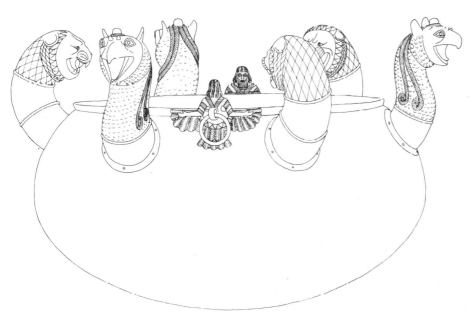

6.25 Reconstruction of a bronze caldron from Olympia. From H.-V. Hermann, *Die Kessel der orientalisierenden Teil*, Olympische Forschungen, vol. 4 (Berlin: Walter de Gruyter, 1966), Plate 4. By permission of the Deutsches Archäologisches Institut, Berlin.

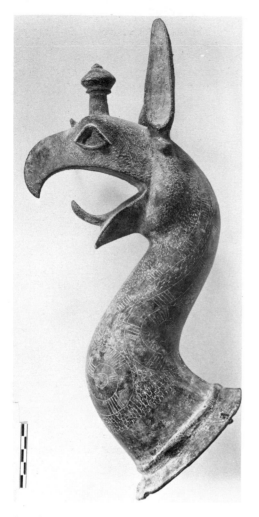

6.26 Cast griffin head from Olympia. Olympia Museum. Photo: Deutsches Archäologisches Institut, Athens.

tions on the shank was reduced and new elements appeared. The disk was at first thin and relatively long; later it became smaller and thicker. The decorations on the shaft started simply but became more elaborate and highly decorated as the century progressed. New motifs were added to the Geometric repertoire and numerous combinations led to pins that appear topheavy and overdecorated in comparison with Geometric examples (Fig. 6.27b and c). Some had heads in the form of knobs, in some cases resembling fruit (Fig. 6.27b).

The more elaborately decorated examples of the seventh century appear to extend well into the following century. Except for isolated pins used as jewelry, however, pins as decorative fasteners of clothing became uncommon by the fifth century in Greece and thus will not be discussed further.

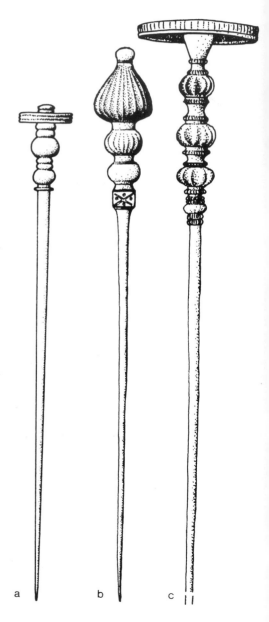

6.27 Pins showing Oriental influence: a, from Perachora; b, from Ithaka; c, from Trebenište. After *Greek Pins* by Paul Jacobstahl, published by Oxford University Press, 1956. Drawing by John Huffstot. Scale 1:1.

a   b   c

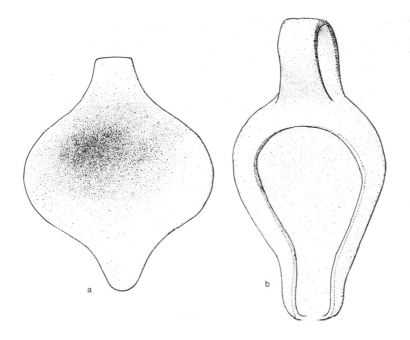

6.28 Typical seventh-century lamps. After Richard Hubbard Howland, *Greek Lamps and Their Survivals*, Athenian Agora Series, vol. 4 (Princeton: American School of Classical Studies, 1958), Plate 29. By permission of the American School of Classical Studies. Drawing by John Huffstot. Scale 1:2.

a

b

LAMPS

A common find in strata of the Greek period are fragments of terra cotta lamps. The production of oil lamps began in the seventh century and ran without interruption throughout antiquity in classical lands. As common archaeological finds they are a great help in chronology, for their types changed with some regularity. They have therefore been more intensively studied than other classes of minor objects. The types that will be discussed here are mainly those found at the Athenian agora, which has yielded numbers of lamps adequately stratified for study.[11]

The earliest seventh-century lamp was a simple shallow saucer with the rim pinched out at one point to form a nozzle, providing a place for a wick. This "cocked hat shape" is clearly seen in Figure 6.28a. Handmade and undecorated, such lamps generally have a flat handle attached opposite the wide nozzle. The earliest lamps actually had no rims as such, but late in the century the side walls were curved over to form a flat rim and the nozzle was elongated. The later lamps are bigger than the earlier examples and the inward-curved rim provided a more or less flat space on which simple incised decoration is sometimes found. The lamp has more form to it now and is no longer a simple open saucer (Fig. 6.28b), though it is still handmade and unglazed. By the end of the century wheel-made lamps of similar shape were being made, with a dull brown glaze in the interior and around the rim. These simple lamps continued to be used in the sixth century, along with more sophisticated types developed at that time.

11 The basic study on which the following presentation of lamps is based is Richard Hubbard Howland, *Greek Lamps and Their Survivals*, Athenian Agora series, vol. 4 (Princeton, 1958).

7

The Archaic Period

THE SIXTH CENTURY was a momentous one for Greece, during which its very existence was threatened by outside forces and its stability tested by internal unrest. In general, the city-states continued to grow and prosper under their various forms of government. The historical development of Athens is the best documented, and the Athenian culture and physical remains are the best known.

The social and political problems that had plagued the city in earlier times were evidently still troublesome, for a number of constitutional and political reforms attributed to the sage Solon were instituted in the early 500s. Essentially these reforms laid the basis for Athenian democracy by changing the criterion for office from status based on birth to status based on wealth. A council of four hundred chosen from four tribes prepared legislation for a popular assembly in which all citizens could participate. All classes were eligible to avail themselves of a court system that allowed appeals from the acts of city officials. Solon's reforms were sweeping but unfortunately they are not completely clear to us. His aim seems to have been to extend the government to the lowest classes while maintaining some of the privileges of the upper class.

According to tradition, Solon left the country after having instituted his reforms. In time strife broke out again, to end about mid-century in one of the things Solon had hoped to avoid, tyranny.

The Peisistratid tyranny, named after its instigator, Peisistratos, and carried on after his death by his sons, Hippias and Hipparchos, did not affect the changes Solon had instigated; it simply laid a heavy hand on the nobles and made certain that friends of the tyrants filled key positions. The tyranny appears not to have been burdensome at first. The tyrant's court encouraged the arts, and a certain amount of building was undertaken in the city. It changed for the worse with the assassination of Hipparchos in 514. The embittered Hippias then began to act like a tyrant in the modern sense. He was finally driven out by the exiled nobles, with help from Sparta, in 510.

Once the restraining hand of the tyranny was gone, factional strife broke out again. Probably about 508 another and more radical set of reforms, attributed to Kleisthenes, was pushed through. These reforms combated the problem of sectionalism by establishing ten new tribes, each made up of equal numbers of citizens from the three main geographical divisions of Attica—the city, the coast, and the inland areas. Thus each tribe consisted of a cross section of the population and theoretically no one group could gain control, although generally the city element, being more cohesive, was likely to get the upper hand. A new council of five hundred, chosen annually by lot from each of the ten tribes, was established with a standing committee of fifty, chosen by lot in turn from each tribe, to carry on the daily business of the city. The peculiar practice of ostracism, which was mentioned in Chapter 1, is also attributed to Kleisthenes, but it and other practices of the government may have come after the main body of his reforms. The Athenians were well on the way to self-government.

While the Athenians and other Greeks were caught up in political and social strife, the great Persian Empire was developing to the east. By the last quarter of the century it had absorbed the Greek cities on the coast of Asia Minor and had even undertaken an expedition to European Thrace, to the north of Greece proper. In 499 the Greeks of Asia Minor revolted, with some help from the mainland Greek states Eretria and Athens. The revolt was eventually stamped out, but the involvement of the Greek cities of the mainland in what the Persians must have considered their own affairs led to retribution. A raid in 490 resulted in the destruction of Eretria, but ended in the repulse of the Persians by the Athenians and their Plataian allies at the Battle of Marathon, in Attica. This battle, in which the outnumbered Athenian hoplites met and mastered the feared Persians in battle, electrified the Greek world and added considerably to the average Athenian's faith in his fledgling democracy.

A more massive invasion designed to conquer Greece was mounted by the Persian king Xerxes ten years later. The Persians smashed through a heroic Spartan resistance at the Pass of Thermopylai and invaded Attica. Under the influence of Themistokles, one of Athens' leading statesmen, most Athenians abandoned their city to the invaders, putting their trust in the fleet. The Persians captured the city, stormed the Acropolis, slaughtered the defenders, and burned the buildings. A major sea engagement took place, the Battle of Salamis, in which the Greeks were victorious. The next year the army defeated the invading Persians at Plataiai and once and for all removed the Persian threat from the country. The Athenians returned to their ruined city to begin again, filled with the pride of victory and belief in the justice and superiority of their civilization. The defeat of the Persians in 479 stands as an arbitrary end of the Archaic period, but stylistically there is no such clear cut-off point.

ART

The sixth century was as momentous a period for the development of Greek art as it was for Greek history. In an astonishingly short period a "national" art was forged from what had gone before. The conservative, locally developed Geometric style with its Bronze Age roots combined with the Oriental influences of the seventh century to form a unique style in the sixth. The sixth century, particularly in its early years, was a time of experiment. Form and style developed together until the fifth century, when a new concept of style gained ascendancy.

Artistic and architectural developments of the sixth century can be seen in hindsight as attempts at solving problems. In sculpture, for instance, the problem was to reproduce the human body in stone. Greek sculptors eventually solved the problem so well that by the beginning of the next century they could quite realistically reproduce the curves and muscles of the male body. The representation of the world as it is appears to us to have been the artists' goal, and their ability constantly improved throughout the century. Whether or not artists in this period consciously tried to attain absolute realism is debatable. There is, however, something demonstrably different between a statue from the beginning of the century and one from the end, and it is clearly an advance in realistic representation.

A specific date for the end of the period is difficult to determine on artistic grounds. Archaic characteristics continue well into the fifth century in sculpture and painting before a recognizably different style, called the Severe style, becomes manifest. The chronological point at which the new style emerged is hard to determine but appears to have fallen somewhere in the period of the Persian Wars. Stylistic change was not uniform, however, appearing first in one place, then at another. The year 480 is used here as a convenient end point for the Archaic period, but it should be understood that it has been arbitrarily selected.

ARCHITECTURE

Progress was fairly rapid in the development of the temple plan and elevation in the sixth century. Increasing prosperity permitted the use of costly and more permanent building materials. The first large all-stone temple erected was the temple of Artemis on Corfu, the ancient Kerkyra, a large island off the west coast of Greece. Although very little of this building is preserved, the remains indicate an overall measurement of 49.00 by 23.46 meters, making it one of the most ambitious buildings built to this time. Eight burly columns extended across the front and seventeen along each side, giving a dense and heavy impression to the elevation (Fig. 7.1). The scanty evidence appears to indicate two rows of ten columns each in the long and narrow cella, with pronaos and opisthodomos with two columns *in antis.* The space between the cella wall and the colonnade was wide enough to have allowed a second row of columns all the way around but was not so utilized, thus forming a pseudo-dipteral plan, the earliest known.

The temple of Artemis, also known as the Gorgon temple because of the central figure on its west pediment, is important not only for its structural character but also for its sculptural decoration. Both pediments seem to have contained the same scene; that on the east front is preserved only in fragments but the west pediment is almost completely preserved (Fig. 7.1). The style of

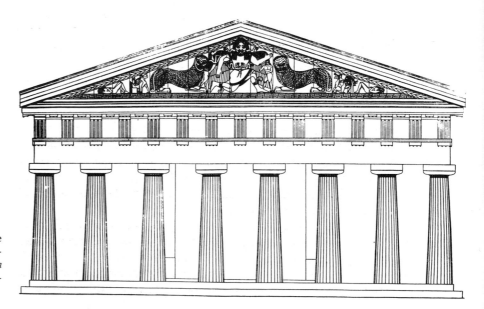

7.1 West front of the temple of Artemis (the Gorgon temple) on Corfu.[P] From Gerhart Rodenwaldt, *Die Bildwerke des Artemistempels von Korkyra* (Berlin: Gebr. Mann Verlag, 1939), Plate 1. Reproduced by permission.

the sculpture, an early attempt to fill the triangular pedimental space (see below), indicates that the temple was built about 580.

The middle of the century witnessed the replacement of the seventh-century temple at Corinth by a new building, probably dedicated to Apollo and erected perhaps between 560 and 540. There were now six columns across the front and fifteen on each flank, the columns considerably less squat than those of the Gorgon temple and their abaci less swelling and more upright in contour (Fig. 7.2). The columns, of which seven are still standing, are monoliths, or cut from one block of stone rather than being made up of drums.

Although the building is almost completely destroyed, cuttings in the bed-rock of the hill for the lowest courses of the foundations allow a plan to be made out with some certainty (Fig. 7.3). An approximate overall measurement of 53.84 by 21.48 meters can be derived from these cuttings, as well as the existence of the now usual pronaos and opisthodomos with two columns *in antis*. The building had an abbreviated cella with two rows of four columns each and behind it another room facing west with four interior columns to hold up the ceiling. The apparent existence of two cellas has never been satisfactorily explained. Apollo was an oracular god and his temples often show some peculiarity of ground plan.

The temple of Apollo in Corinth shows some architectural refinements that became common in the next century and were carried out with great precision in the Parthenon. Here there is indication of a slight but measurable convex curve to the columns, called "entasis," a horizontal curvature of the stylobate and of the columns to the level of the capitals, and a slight inward inclination of the corner column. These refinements are generally considered to have been undertaken to overcome optical illusions that would have been engendered by strict adherence to right angles and straight lines. This subject will be discussed further in Chapter 8, when we consider the Parthenon.

By the end of the Archaic period the Doric canon had been established in its main outlines in the temple of Aphaia at Aigina, some of whose pediment sculptures survive (see below). Built of limestone, originally stuccoed, the tem-ple was dedicated to a local goddess and is quite small, with a stylobate measuring 28.8 by 13.7 meters (Fig. 7.4). The columns represent a further elongation of proportions, their height being 5.33 times their lower diameters as against 4.15 times on the front at Corinth. This thinness, together with a higher entablature, gave the building a lightness not seen in earlier temples. Six columns extended across the short ends but only twelve lined each side, giving a thickset appearance that contrasted with the increased lightness of the eleva-tion. The interior had superimposed rows of Doric columns on each side, forming a two-storied colonnade, which was converted after the initial con-struction to support a floor or walkway between the columns and the walls of the cella at the level of the epistyle. From this time on, the two-storied interior colonnade became a part of the Doric canon. An unusual feature is the door that at a later time was cut into the opisthodomos, which was closed off by grilles on the outside, thus forming a small subsidiary room behind the cella; it may have been connected with the cult.

Gigantic temples were erected in the East during the sixth century; those on Samos and at Ephesos were famous. In these buildings the decorative quality of the Ionic order was fully exploited. The influence of the East is to be seen in the complicated ground plans, with the doubling and sometimes tripling of the rows of columns to give the effect of a dense forest of supports. On Samos the

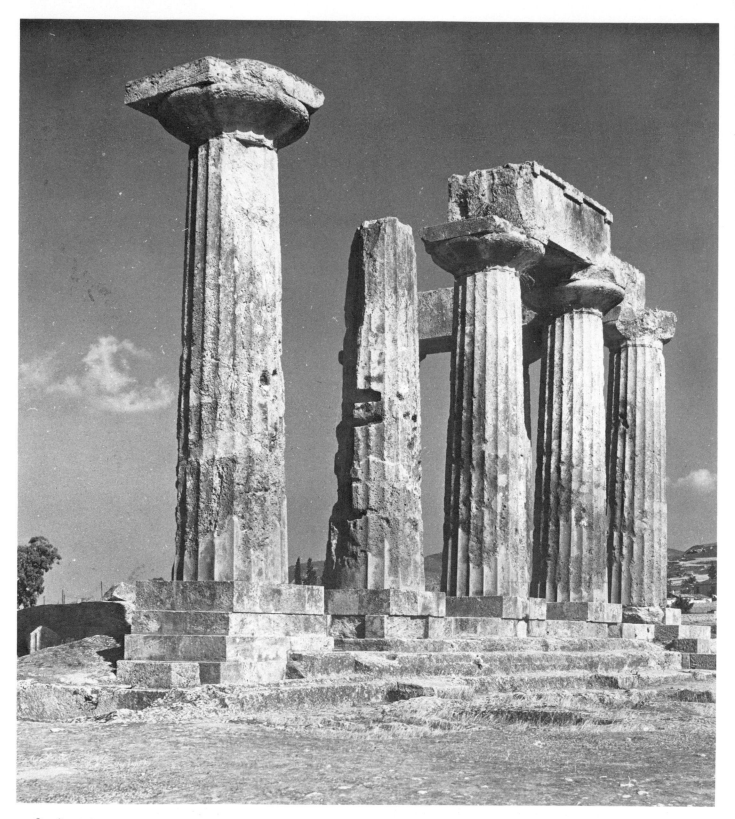

7.2 Standing columns of the temple of Apollo at Corinth,ᵖ viewed from the northwest. Photo: Alison Frantz.

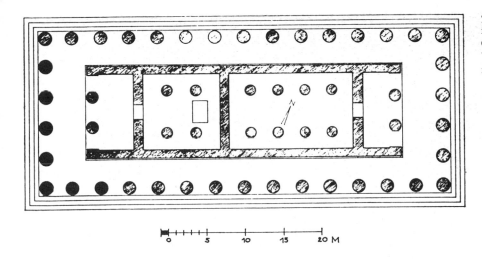

7.3 Plan of the temple of Apollo at Corinth (standing columns shown in black). From Gottfried Gruben, *Die Tempel der Griechen* (Munich: Hirmer Verlag, 1966), p. 95, Fig. 90. Reproduced by permission.

sanctuary of Hera continued to expand with the addition of new buildings and a monumental gateway or propylon (Fig. 7.5). At the same time a great new temple (105.00 by 52.50 meters) was begun about 570 by the local architects Rhoikos and Theodoros. With twenty-one columns on each side, eight on the front, and ten at the rear arranged in two rows (dipteral columniation), the building was one of the largest of the Archaic period. It had a deep pronaos and a long cella with two rows of interior supports. The same essential plan was elaborated in an even longer (112.20 by 55.16 meters) and more heavily decorated building built by the tyrant Polykrates (538–522). Twenty-four columns now stood on each flank, with eight at the front and nine at the rear. Work continued on the building well into the third century, but it was never completed.

More famous and even longer than the Heraion on Samos was the temple of Artemis at Ephesos, which was constructed in the middle of the century and measured some 115 meters in length and 50 in width (Fig. 7.6). Some of the columns of this great building were erected at the expense of King Kroisos of

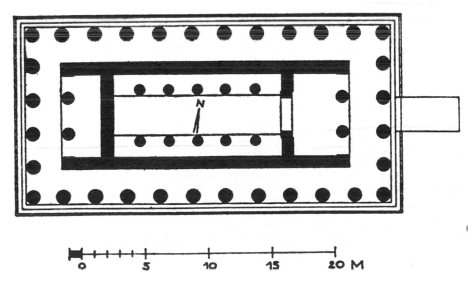

7.4 Ground plan of the temple of Aphaia at Aigina.[P] From Gottfried Gruben, *Die Tempel der Griechen* (Munich: Hirmer Verlag, 1966), p. 112, Fig. 102. Reproduced by permission.

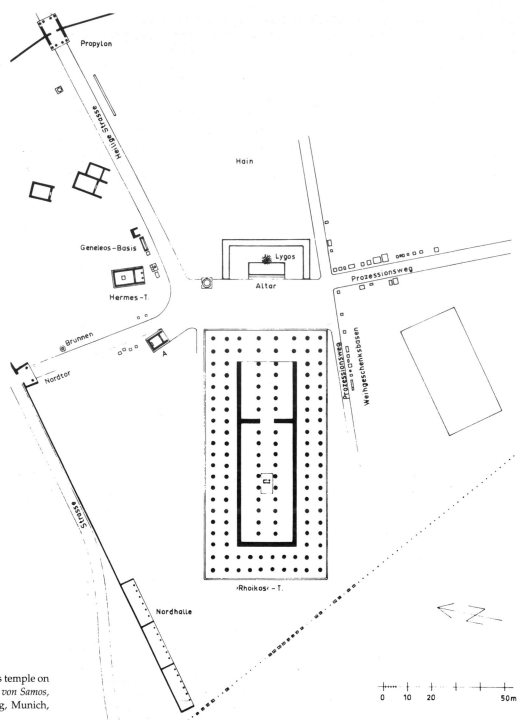

Labels on plan: Propylon · Heilige Strasse · Hain · Geneleos-Basis · Lygos · Prozessionsweg · Hermes-T. · Altar · Brunnen · Prozessionsweg · Weihgeschenksbasen · A · Nordtor · Strasse · >Rhoikos< - T. · Nordhalle

Scale: 0 · 10 · 20 · 50m

7.5 Plan of the Heraion and the Rhoikos temple on Samos. From Hans Walter, *Das Heraion von Samos*, p. 71, Fig. 66; © R. Piper & Co. Verlag, Munich, 1976. Reproduced by permission.

Lydia. A number of them, following the Eastern practice of placing sculpture near eye level, carried sculptural decoration on their lowest drums (Fig. 7.7). The building had eight columns at the front and nine at the rear, with twenty-one on each flank. It was burned down in 356, traditionally at the time of the birth of Alexander the Great. Rebuilt on the same plan, it was classed as one of the wonders of the ancient world in Hellenistic and later times, along with the Pyramids of Egypt and other monuments of artistic ingenuity.

The sixth century was also a period of tremendous activity in the western Greek cities. A great number of stone temples are known from southern Italy and Sicily, some of which are very well preserved. One example, the first temple of Hera at Paestum in southern Italy, is shown in Figure 7.8. Western architecture followed the architecture of mainland Greece but, being separated from the mainstream of architectural tradition, was free to experiment, and sometimes surprising and unique variations on the Doric theme are to be found. These buildings are difficult to date and must remain beyond our major interest, as they stand outside the main lines of development of the Doric order as it unfolded on the mainland.[1]

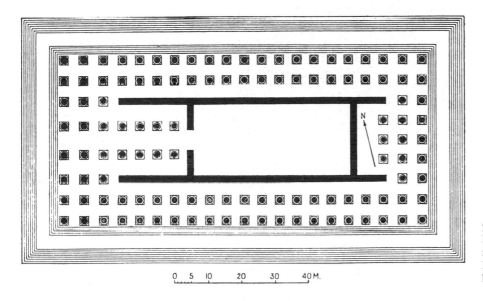

0 5 10   20   30   40 M.

7.6 Plan of the later temple of Artemis at Ephesos,[P] as rebuilt on the old plan. From Gottfried Gruben, *Die Tempel der Griechen* (Munich: Hirmer Verlag, 1966), p. 334, Fig. 268. Reproduced by permission.

SECULAR ARCHITECTURE

The rapidly developing city-states had an increased need for buildings of all types, as did the newly expanding sanctuaries. At the latter, states often erected treasuries to hold dedications. These structures were build in the form of small temples, since the buildings themselves were conceived as dedications to the god. A number of these buildings have survived (Fig. 7.9). In general, however, the constant rebuilding and replacement of utilitarian buildings throughout antiquity leaves us with few examples of secular constructions from the sixth century. An exception is the marketplace, or Agora, in Athens (Fig. 7.10), where excavations by the American School of Classical Studies have revealed the remains of the city's administrative center in the sixth century. It lay at the foot of a low hill, Kolonos Agoraios, destined in the next century to bear the temple of Hephaistos. Here were placed from south to north the committee chambers (Prytanikon), council house (Bouleuterion), small temples

[1] Western Greek architecture in the Archaic period is conveniently summarized by R. Ross Holloway in his *A View of Greek Art* (Providence, 1973), pp. 56–68.

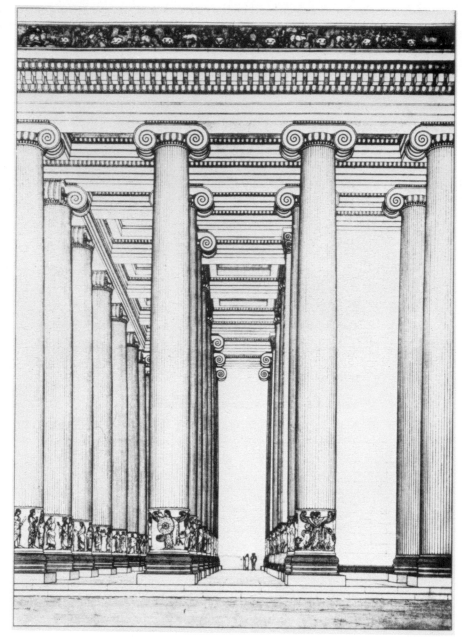

and shrines, and even at the beginning of the next century an area for one of the law courts, the Heliaia. The north end of the line was closed, at least in the fifth century, by the little Royal Stoa, the seat of one of the principal magistrates, the "king archon." This simple building, first erected possibly as early as the middle years of the sixth century, according to the excavator, remained in use throughout much of antiquity. Serving as a law court and repository for the city laws, the building was one of the most famous in the city and is well known from literary references. Of extremely simple construction, with plain benches on the inside and two columns to support the roof, it well represents

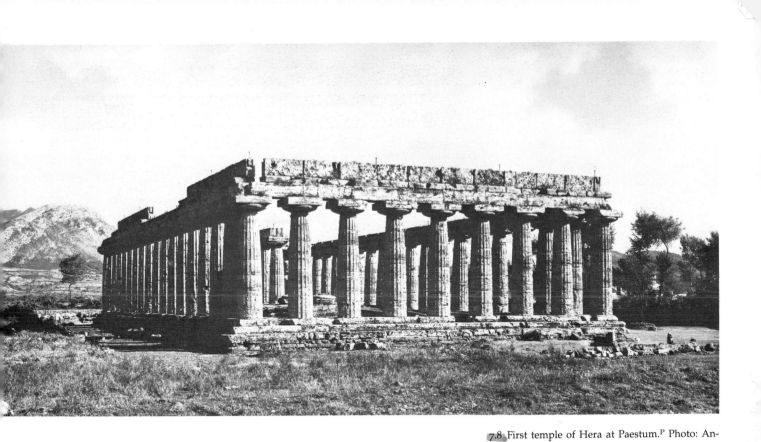

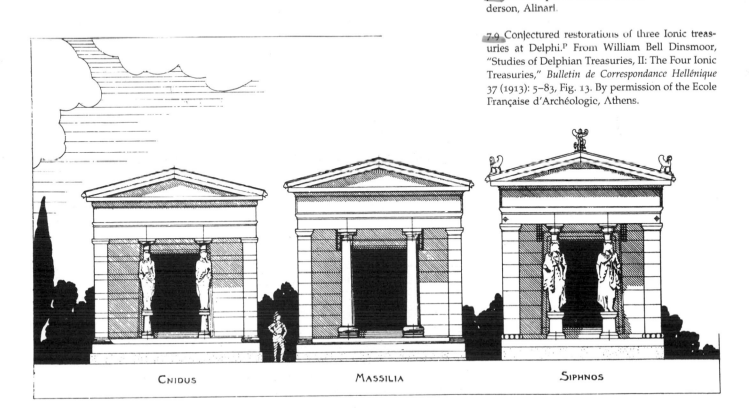

7.8 First temple of Hera at Paestum.[P] Photo: Anderson, Alinari.

7.9 Conjectured restorations of three Ionic treasuries at Delphi.[P] From William Bell Dinsmoor, "Studies of Delphian Treasuries, II: The Four Ionic Treasuries," *Bulletin de Correspondance Hellénique* 37 (1913): 5–83, Fig. 13. By permission of the Ecole Française d'Archéologie, Athens.

CNIDUS   MASSILIA   SIPHNOS

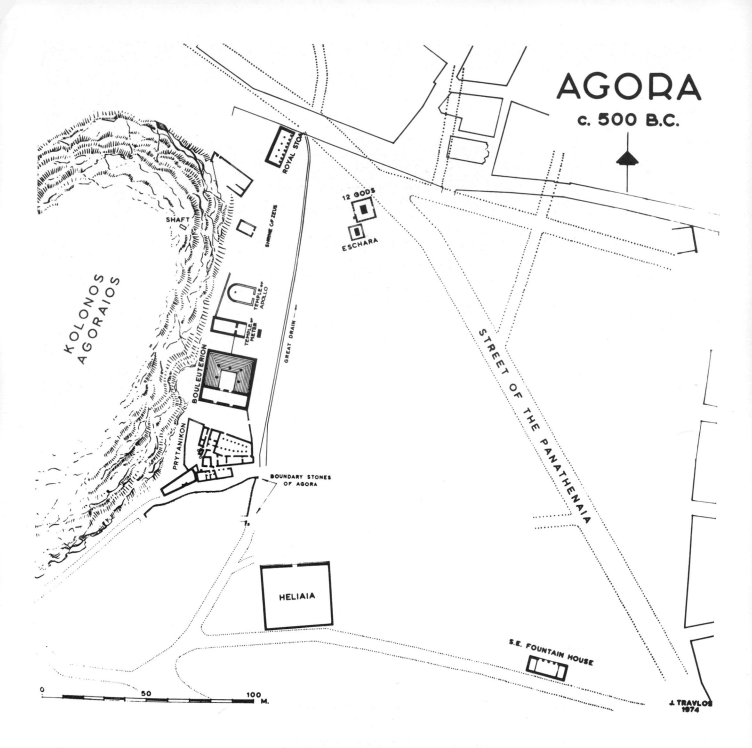

AGORA
c. 500 B.C.

KOLONOS AGORAIOS

SHAFT

ROYAL STOA

SHRINE OF ZEUS

12 GODS

ESCHARA

TEMPLE OF APOLLO

TEMPLE OF METER

BOULEUTERION

PRYTANIKON

GREAT DRAIN

BOUNDARY STONES OF AGORA

HELIAIA

STREET OF THE PANATHENAIA

S.E. FOUNTAIN HOUSE

J. TRAVLOS
1974

0   50   100 M.

7.10 Plan of the Agora at Athens[P] at the end of the sixth century. Photo: American School of Classical Studies at Athens: Agora Excavations.

the kinds of utilitarian uses to which the stoa form could be put. Similar buildings must have been erected in cities throughout the Greek world. A drawing of the Royal Stoa as it appeared in the middle of the fifth century is shown in Figure 7.11.[2]

[2] A survey and guide to the Agora excavations is John Camp, *The Athenian Agora: Excavations in the Heart of Classical Athens* (London, 1986).

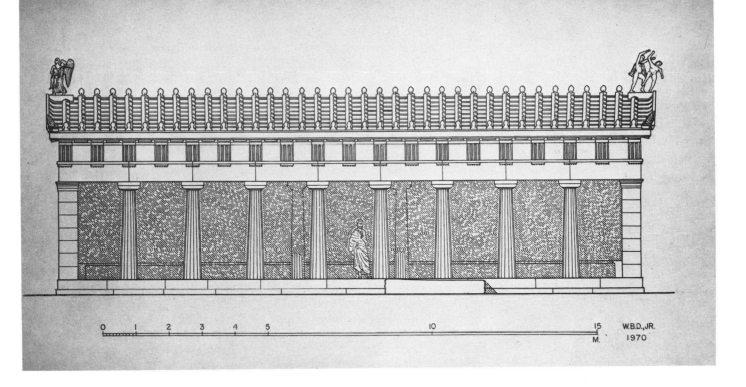

7.11 The Royal Stoa in the Agora at Athens as it appeared in the fifth century. Photo: American School of Classical Studies at Athens, Agora Excavations.

SCULPTURE

At the very end of the seventh century large-scale standing marble statues appeared as dedications in sanctuaries and as funeral monuments.[3] In these works one can clearly see stylistic change as sculptors worked out the realistic representation of the human body standing at rest. These figures are given conventional names: kouroi for the nude males (singular, kouros) and korai (singular, kore) for the draped females.

These sculptural forms are generally believed to have been derived from Eastern prototypes, the kouros from Egyptian sources and the kore from elsewhere in the Near East. An alternate theory sees them as developments from Daedalic tradition. Although the extent and even the existence of the debt of early Greek sculptors to Egypt is debated, it is hard to deny it completely when one looks at a contemporary Egyptian standing male.[4] The basic form, a stiff,

[3] Two works that deal specifically with the sculpture of the Archaic period are Brunilde Sismondo Ridgway, *The Archaic Style in Greek Sculpture*, 2d ed. (Chicago, 1993), and John Boardman, *Greek Sculpture: The Archaic Period* (New York and Toronto, 1978). They attack the material from different angles and are complementary to each other. Boardman's book is intended as a handbook and has a great many illustrations.

[4] The question of the extent and quality of contact between Greece and Egypt and the problem of the origin of large-scale stone sculpture in Greece have long fascinated scholars. A sensible treatment is found in Jeffrey M. Hurwit, *The Art and Culture of Early Greece, 1100–480 B.C.* (Ithaca, N.Y., 1985), pp. 179–202. The amount and significance of the influence of Afro-Asiatic civilizations on Greece have been matters of spirited controversy since the publication of Martin Bernal's *Black Athena: The Afroasiatic Roots of Classical Civilization*, 2 vols. (New Brunswick, N.J., 1987, 1992). Opposing views are expressed by John Coleman and Bernal in *Archaeology* 45 (1992): 48–55, 77–79, and 53–55, 82–86. Also useful are two review articles: Molly Levine, "The Use and Abuse of *Black Athena*," and Robert Pounder, "*Black Athena 2*: History without Rules," both in *American Historical Review* 97 (1992): 440–460, 461–464.

upright figure with one extended leg and fixed frontal glare, remains the same throughout the century while the details of musculature and the rendition of the human body become increasingly realistic.[5]

One of the earliest of these figures, which must date close to 600, is the 1.843-meter kouros in New York (Fig. 7.12). The general stance of the figure certainly looks Egyptian at first glance, but the differences are important. The most obvious is the fact that it is nude. Nudity would have been impossible in any formal Egyptian context but was taken for granted in Greece, where men regularly exercised nude in the gymnasiums. The figure is also more liberated from the block of stone than similar Egyptian statues: although the hands are still attached to the thighs in Egyptian fashion, the arms are separate from the body and the figure stands without a back support. Similarly, in a typical Egyptian sculpture the weight of the figure rests on the back leg, with the other thrust artificially out in front; the kouros stands firmly on both feet, with the weight evenly distributed. Although the figure is not yet moving, the potential for movement is there, giving a much more realistic pose to the body.

The figure is rigidly composed, with the divisions of the body clearly marked, and is abnormally proportioned, maintaining the foursquare character of the block, from which each side appears to have been separately cut. The anatomy is summary, muscles and bones indicated by grooves and bumps. Pattern still plays an important part, and such natural features as the knees and ears are rendered as designs. The head is cubic, with an exceedingly long jawline and unrealistic metallic-looking ears. The eyes are large and flat, with no tear ducts; the mouth runs straight across the face, giving it a somber cast. The hair is rendered in a series of connected globules, secured with a band knotted at the rear and descending in a symmetrical fan over the back. This kouros wears a neckband as his only decoration.

From the time of the New York kouros to the end of the century, an unbroken development in the rendering of the human body can be seen within the framework of the kouros pose. The kouros from Anavysos (Fig. 7.13), dating to the third quarter of the century, is much more rounded and naturalistic than the earlier kouros. An inscription on the base of this statue indicates that it was a funeral monument to a certain Kroisos, who died in battle. The foreign name, recalling the Lydian king Kroisos, perhaps reflects the close connections that we surmise were maintained between Athens and Ionia and the East in the sixth century. The head of this kouros demonstrates an increased ability to render anatomy realistically. It has taken on a much more natural shape, with greatly improved detail. The tear ducts, for instance are now represented. The lips are formed into a shallow smile, the so-called Archaic smile, which probably derives from attempts to indicate the structure of the lower face rather than any particular state of mind.

Although the kouros from Anavysos shows a great development from earlier examples, it is still executed in the old frontal stance. Sometime, probably just before or just after the Persian invasions, sculptors took the momentous step that finally produced a pose more in harmony with the increasing realism of the anatomical renderings. The Kritios boy (Fig. 7.14), named for its likeness to another statue by a sculptor named Kritios, shows by the elevation of the left buttock that the weight has been transferred to the left leg. The head is slightly

---

[5] The basic work in English on the kouros type is G. M. A. Richter, *Kouroi,* 3d ed. (London and New York, 1970).

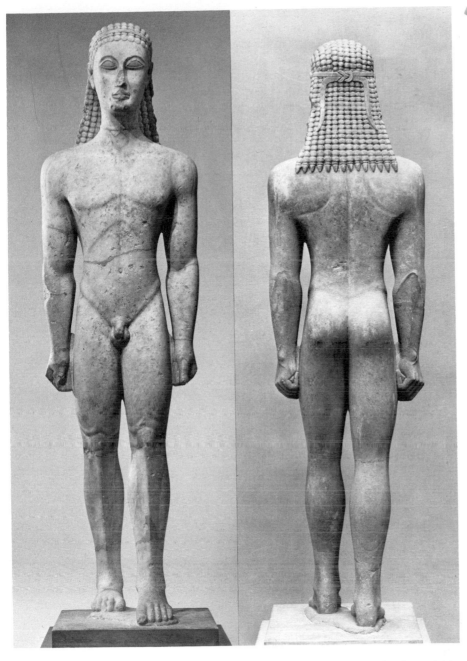

7.12 Front and rear views of the New York kouros. the Metropolitan Museum of Art, Fletcher Fund, 1932.

turned toward the flexed leg, thus setting up the beginning of a rhythm within the figure. The structure of the body and of the head now shows a more developed mastery of anatomy, although a certain simplification is to be seen in the Archaic smile and the relatively plain treatment of the hair. This simplification is a trait of the so-called Severe style of the following century, and this statue may in fact be a post-Persian monument, erected in the early fifth century.[6]

[6] See Jeffrey M. Hurwit, "The Kritios Boy: Discovery, Reconstruction, and Date," *AJA* 93 (1989): 41–80.

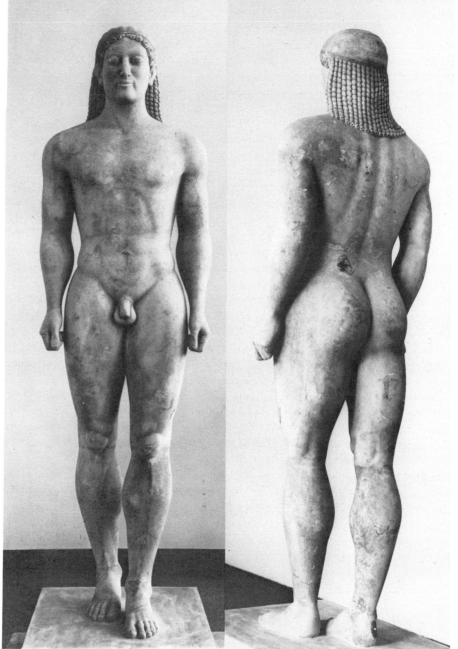

7.13 Front and rear views of the Anavysos kouros. National Archaeological Museum, Athens. Photos: Alison Frantz.

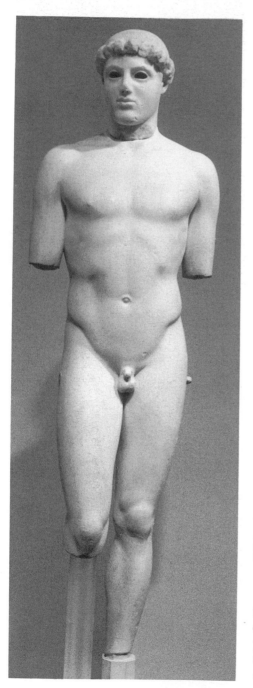

7.14 The Kritios boy.ᴾ Acropolis Museum, Athens. Photo courtesy of Jeffrey M. Hurwit.

A parallel development can be seen in the korai, the standing female figures.[7] Frontal standing figures in Daedalic style are known from the seventh century, as has been noted, and are considered by some experts to be direct predecessors of the later korai. Since Greek society and artistic convention did not accept a nude female figure in this period, the korai are shown fully draped, the contrasting patterns and fabrics of their garments providing a rich

[7] G. M. A. Richter, *Korai* (London and New York, 1968).

field for the sculptors to mine. The earliest garment, the peplos, was a heavy one-piece tunic, generally of wool, which was frequently worn with an over-fold and a shawl in the seventh century. Considered a typically Dorian or mainland dress, it hung from neck to feet and was fastened at the shoulder by a pin or fibula. Often a lighter garment of linen, called the chiton, was worn beneath it.

Then, as now, fashions underwent periodic changes. During the sixth century the peplos was discarded and a sleeved chiton was worn alone or with a mantle. The mantle, or himation, became the standard dress of the korai, draped obliquely from the right shoulder to below the left armpit. The folds and decoration of this garment and its contrast with the lighter chiton beneath encouraged decorative renderings, and the korai of the latter part of the century reach great heights of elaborate ornamentation. This change in dress, apparently originating in Ionia, has been attributed to the influences of the tyrant's court, with its close connections to the East and its presumed luxurious tastes.

One of the earliest of the sixth century korai is now in Berlin (Fig. 7.15). She wears a sleeved chiton and a shawl, which hangs down in front on both sides. The face with its large eyes and prominent nose indicates an anatomical development that places this kore about 570–560. It was found in Attica and is said to have been wrapped in a sheet of lead, a circumstance that may account for its splendid preservation. Highly decorative yet simple in her straight-hanging garment, she wears a necklace with pendants, earrings, and a spiral bracelet on her left arm. On her head is a polos (headdress) decorated with an incised meander and lotus pattern. Traces of paint indicate that the edges of the shawl as well as the chiton were brightly patterned in red, yellow, and blue.

Another discovery from Attica vies with the Berlin kore in preservation.[8] This kore, which was found buried together with a kouros (Color Plate 3, following p. 96), wears a long-sleeved garment secured with a belt at the waist. One hand holds the drapery slightly away from her leg in a gesture common to later korai, while the other hand holds a flower bud in front of her. She wears bracelets and an elaborate diadem decorated with alternate lotus blossoms and buds; a similar necklace circles her neck. The decoration of the garment consists of painted and incised ornaments in black, yellow, and red, and the use of incision to form the designs is reminiscent of the Black Figure technique of vase painting. The base on which the kore stood bears an inscription indicating that the figure is a monument to one Phrasikleia, who died unmarried. The name of the artist is also given: one Aristion of Paros—an island artist. The statue of Phrasikleia is probably to be dated not much later than about 540, and we await the definitive publication of this important find.

The well-known Peplos kore of about 530 from the Athenian acropolis is one of the last korai to be shown wearing the heavy woolen peplos (Figs. 7.16 and 7.17). The garment is belted and worn over a chiton, whose crinkly fabric can be seen below the hem of the heavier outer garment. The figure still stands in a rather stiff frontal attitude with her right hand, which originally held a tubular object, against her leg and her left hand extended outward. The left arm and hand were made of a separate piece of marble and are now missing. The kore was richly painted; numerous traces of colored designs survive on the drapery.

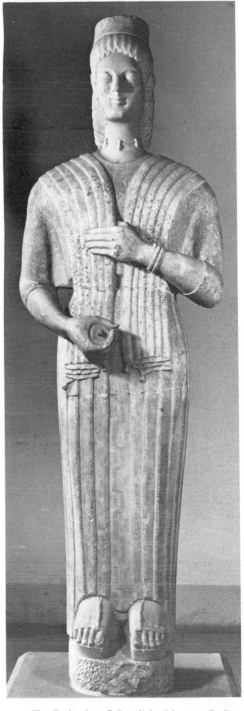

7.15 The Berlin kore.^P Staatliche Museen, Berlin. Photo: Alison Frantz.

[8] Only a preliminary report in Greek with some illustrations has appeared: E. I. Mastrokostas, "The Kore Phrasikleia, a Work of Aristion of Paros, and a Marble Kouros Discovered in Myrrhinous," *AAA* 5 (1972): 298–314.

The hair was painted, as were such details as the eyes, lips, and eyebrows. The Peplos kore was further decorated with metal additions—a wreath in her hair and apparently earrings and pins for the peplos, to judge from the surviving holes. The anatomy shows great advancement from the Berlin kore, with better proportions and softer, rounder features.

The Peplos kore was discovered on the Acropolis at Athens with a large number of other statues and dedications that had been knocked down by the Persian invaders and then intentionally buried by the Athenians after the Persians had withdrawn. This deliberate burial would account for its relatively good state of preservation; several other statues from this deposit show similar traces of color.

The kore of Acropolis 675 exhibits the full Ionic style in her dress (Fig. 7.18). The copious remains of color and the elaborate decorative quality of the work

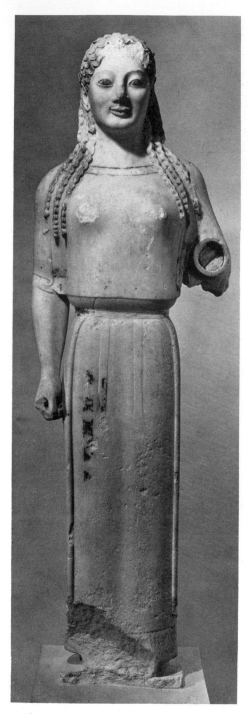

7.16 The Peplos kore.ᴾ Acropolis Museum, Athens. Photo: Alison Frantz.

7.17 Detail of the Peplos kore. Acropolis Museum, Athens. Photo: Alison Frantz.

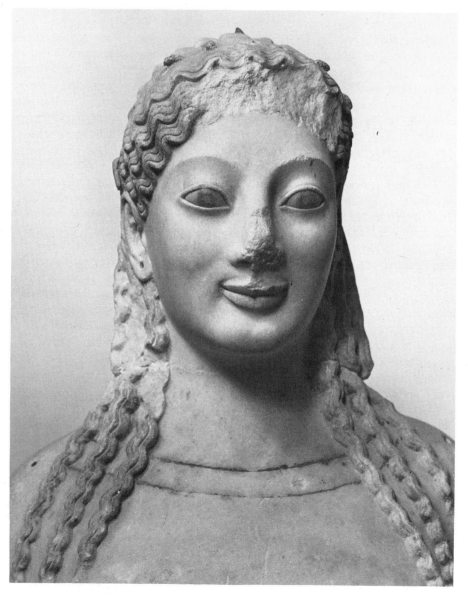

shows how far the love of contrasting surface textures could go. Preserved now only to a height of some 92 centimeters, she wears a chiton with a short himation over it. Both garments were once richly painted. She originally grasped the skirt of the chiton in her left hand; her right hand and arm, which had been made separately and inserted, extended outward. It is interesting to note that the skirt of the chiton bears painted designs similar to those on the himation, while the portion of the chiton over the shoulder is a solid color. This confusing use of color must result from the artist's sensibilities rather than direct observation of actual garments. The figure stands in a slightly more realistic way than the Peplos kore, with one leg advanced and the right arm breaking out of the strictly frontal figure. She is usually dated in the last quarter of the century.

Both korai and kouroi underwent simplification in the early years of the next century. When one compares the Euthydikos kore (Fig. 7.19), named after its dedicator and also found in the Acropolis, with the earlier no. 675, one is struck by the appearance of intentional simplification and at the same time by an increasing feeling for the swelling forms of the body beneath the garment. The kore stands in the usual pose, with one leg advanced and both feet still flat on the ground, and she faces forward—unlike her counterpart, the Kritios boy, who looks to one side. The simplification appears in the hair, which looks almost as if it had been cut against the rim of a bowl, the loss of the Archaic smile, and the severe treatment of the himation and the chiton. In many ways the Euthydikos kore, in the simplification of surface forms and the increase of volume of the body, belongs to the Early Classical period and marks the beginning of the break with the Archaic.

The Greek temple was regularly enlivened by sculpture, and its method of placement in the spaces provided by pediments, metopes, and friezes follows a clear line of development throughout the sixth and fifth centuries. Specific problems were involved in trying to fill these spaces—the triangle of the pediment, the square of the metope, the elongated rectangle of the frieze. In the case of the pediment, we can see clearly that various placements were tried until the problem can be said to have been brilliantly solved in the Parthenon. The pediment presented peculiar problems: the vertical height available decreased to nothing at the corners; any sculpture placed in this triangular space would be at a great height above the eyes of viewers on the ground, yet should be not only visible but interesting; and the subject matter should be unified and appropriate to the building it adorned.

The temple of Artemis at Corfu (see Fig. 7.1) provides an early example of pedimental composition. The central space is dominated by the great Medusa, almost 2.8 meters high, in a conventional running pose. She is flanked by her offspring, the winged horse Pegasos and the human Chrysaor. Perhaps her image was intended here to avert evil. Two long feline creatures adapt well to the decreasing vertical space available beneath the slope of the pediment. Next come two groups of smaller figures, Zeus attacking a giant and a seated figure about to be speared, which bear no relationship to the central theme. Extending into the corners are two men lying on their backs and looking outwards, with their feet pointing toward the center of the action. Obviously the sculptor has failed to provide unity of subject matter or scale, which the Greeks believed necessary for a successful composition. But the figures, almost in relief, were highly painted and must at least have been visible from below.

The use of figures with long bodies that fitted into the pediment corners

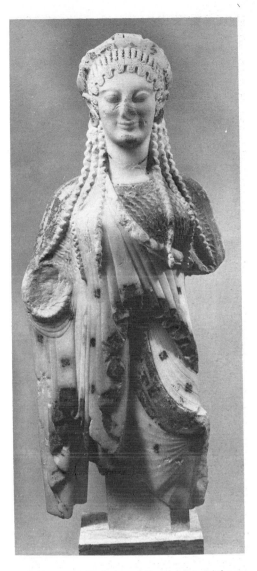

7.18 Kore no. 675. Acropolis Museum, Athens. Photo: Alison Frantz.

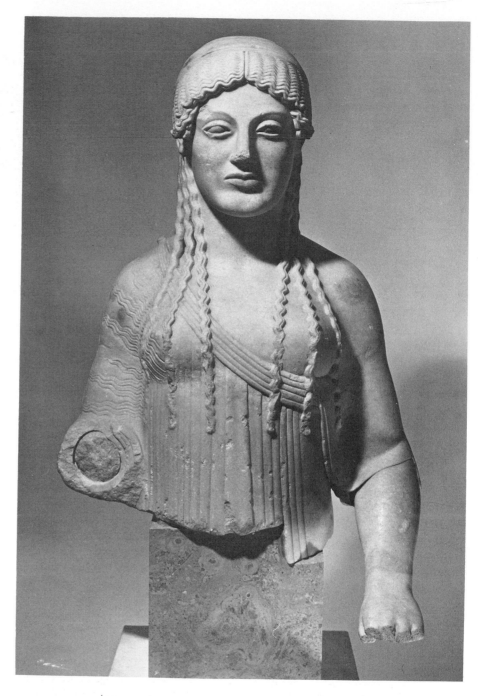

7.19 The Euthydikos kore.^P Acropolis Museum, Athens. Photo: Alison Frantz.

continued for some time in the sixth century. A series of poros pediments from pre-Persian buildings on the Athenian acropolis contained various snaky-tailed creatures.

Another interesting attempt to solve the compositional problems of the pediment came to light in A.D. 1973 in Corfu. The find consists of a portion of one side of a sculptured pediment (Fig. 7.20). Composed of two joining slabs, the pediment when complete was much smaller than that of the Gorgon temple,

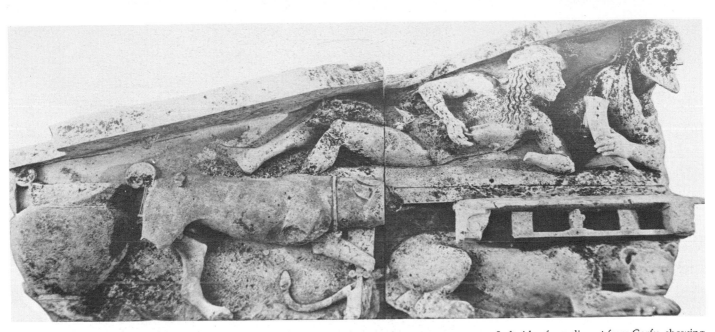

7.20 Left side of a pediment from Corfu, showing a banquet scene. Corfu Museum. Photo: Angelos Choremis.

for its present measurements are only 2.73 meters in preserved length and 1.19 meters in maximum height. It must also be later in date, but still in the first half of the century. The unique scene shows the god Dionysos and a boy, perhaps his son, reclining on couches and gazing intently toward the now missing center of the composition. The god holds a drinking horn in his left hand and the boy a drinking cup of relatively datable shape (see Fig. 1.2) in his right. Beneath the couch and the table in front of it is a feline creature, while a dog with a collar paces in from the left. A large volute krater closes the scene on the left.

The reclining figures serve the same purpose as snaky-tailed monsters in dealing with the pediment slope, and the tall krater is useful in filling the corner and has a place in the scene as a necessary adjunct to a banquet. The scale here obviously presents no problem to the artist, although the animals may seem a little large in this two-tier composition. The section that has been preserved is clearly part of a single scene. Unfortunately, we have no idea what the central action or the general subject may have been, though one is reminded of banquet scenes on Corinthian vases, with pet animals tethered under the couches. Corfu was originally settled by Corinthians and the Corinthian influence is strong here.

An extremely important building is the little treasury dedicated by the island of Siphnos at Delphi, since literary evidence permits us to assign a date to its erection with relative certainty: c. 530.[9] Much of the lavish sculptural decoration has been preserved, including most of the pediment, which depicts the struggle between Herakles and Apollo for the Delphic tripod (Fig. 7.21). In the

[9] Ancient writers give a date for a blow that struck the island and ruined its finances, after which it could not have built such a building. This date is connected with an incident in Near Eastern history which we know to have occurred in 525. Since the treasury shows no signs of being unfinished, it must have been completed by this time. Most scholars thus place its completion about 530.

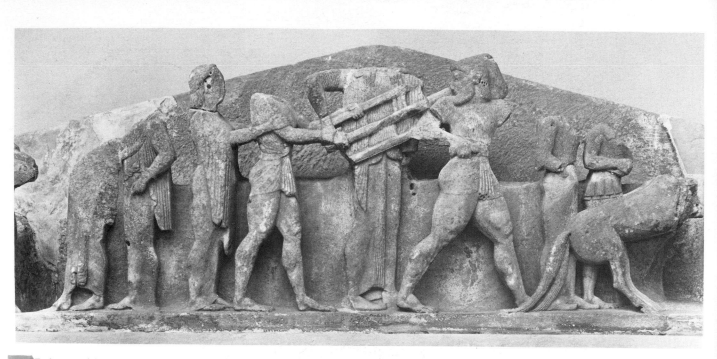

7.21 Pediment of the Siphnian treasury at Delphi.ᴾ
Delphi Museum. Photo: Alison Frantz.

center stands Zeus, the arbiter in the dispute and appropriately the tallest figure in the scene. The supporters of the contestants flank the central figures. The central scene is closed by chariots facing toward the corners. It is uncertain just how the corners were treated, but fragmentary remains indicate that they may have held kneeling figures. This pediment presumably exhibited unity of scale with a more or less successful composition of human figures, but the isolation of the central group and their general stiffness and flatness are still primitive features.

A sculptured frieze circled the treasury above the epistyle (Fig. 7.22). Such relief sculpture presented its own set of problems, particularly in the means of indicating depth and in the avoidance of monotony in a series of usually upright human figures. The sculptor drew the figures on the block, then cut away the surrounding stone to make a background, thus establishing a uniform frontal plane that was never violated, at least not until much later times. Depth could be indicated in the carved scene only by the introduction of intermediary planes between the front and back surfaces of the relief. In a shallow relief the sculptor could partially overcome the difficulty by overlapping the figures, as was done in the best executed portion of the treasury frieze, depicting the battle of the gods and giants (Fig. 7.22), one of the most popular mythological themes in Greek art. The gods, identified by their attributes and originally by names written above them, attack from the left against the giants, who are depicted as fully armed foot soldiers. In a detail of the battle (Fig. 7.23) Artemis and Apollo stride forward, overlapping a giant, who is rendered in somewhat lower relief and thus physically as well as visually behind them. As he flees he looks back at a companion who is being mauled by the lions of Hekate's chariot. The gods stride forward realistically on heavily muscled legs. The positions of their arms, up and forward as they draw their bows, serve to mask the division between chest and waist. The giant, however, is in an impos-

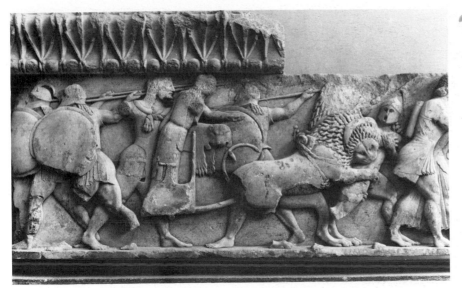

7.22 Portion of the sculptured frieze from the Siphnian treasury, depicting the battle of the gods and giants. Delphi Museum. Photo: Alison Frantz.

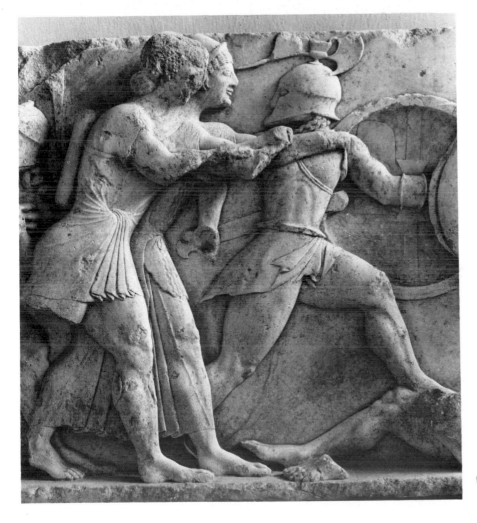

7.23 A detail of the Siphnian treasury frieze: Artemis, Apollo, and giant. Photo: Alison Frantz.

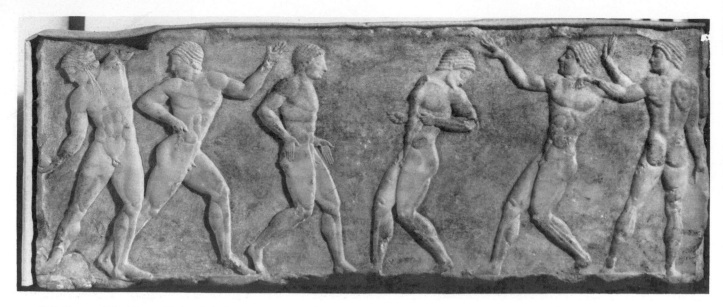

7.24 Ball Game relief, Athens. National Archaeological Museum, Athens. Photo: Alison Frantz.

sible pose, full frontal chest awkwardly attached to profile legs, an old-fashioned rendition going back to the kneeling-running convention of Medusa on the pediment of the Artemis temple on Corfu (see Fig. 7.1). The musculature of his legs and the manner in which his drapery blows backward to emphasize his forward motion are advanced renderings, however, illustrative of the transitional stage of this frieze. The representation of the human body in torsion was a major problem in two-dimensional art. It must have been closely studied toward the end of the century by both sculptors and painters, for attempts to improve on the old renderings of the body in a twisted pose can be seen.

A series of statue bases at Athens, built into the fortification wall that Themistokles had hastily built around the city following the Persian withdrawal, illustrate this preoccupation. The artist tried to discard the old convention of frontal chest with legs in profile in favor of a more realistic twist in the torso, sometimes successfully and sometimes not. One of the bases, showing a ball game in progress, can almost serve as a compendium of representations of the human body in various positions (Fig. 7.24).

On the pediment of the temple of Aphaia on Aigina, unity of scale, subject matter, and composition is finally attained. Unfortunately, this temple presents unique problems, for evidence of at least three sets of pedimental sculpture has been found, including two sets for the east end, one stylistically later than the other. It is generally assumed that the surviving fragments of the earlier east pediment represent either a rejected design or one that was damaged or simply replaced for one reason or another some years after the west pediment had been put in position. The dating of the two pediment groups is difficult and disputed, but the earlier (west) pediment is usually thought to coincide with the erection of the buildings, at the end of the sixth century. The east pediment must then be put in the fifth century, perhaps even after the Persian invasion, if the replacement of the earlier pediment was occasioned by damage inflicted by an unrecorded enemy raid.

The two best preserved pediments, the west and the later east pediment,

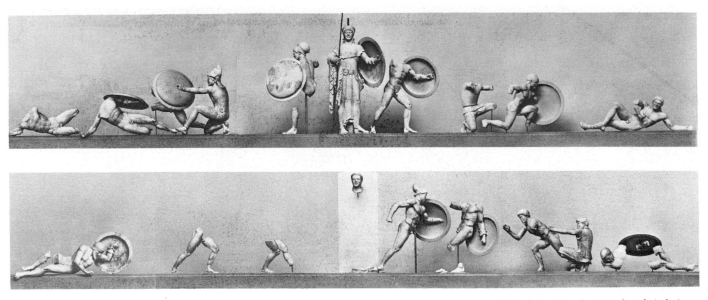

7.25 Pediments from the temple of Aphaia on Aigina:P top, west pediment; bottom, east pediment. Staatliche Antikensammlungen und Glyptothek, Munich. Photos: Hartwig Koppermann.

both depicting battle scenes, exhibit enough differences in style and composition to represent the difference between the Late Archaic and the Early Classical. A glance at these two pediments as they are to be seen in Munich (Fig. 7.25) shows how the composition has changed. Each has a large central Athena figure presiding over a battle scene, which may represent Aiginetan heroes in combat at Troy. She is flanked by groups of fighting figures that fill the decreasing triangular space in kneeling, falling, and supine poses.

In the Archaic west pediment the decorative Athena faces front while combatants are grouped on either side of her. Beyond, archers shoot into the corners, while fallen warriors look out with their feet pointing to the center, very much like the figures in the corners of the pediment of the Gorgon temple on Corfu. The contrast in composition on the east pediment is striking, even though less of this pediment is preserved. Here Athena takes part in the action, although somewhat awkwardly, and the fighting figures more completely form one scene, with the archers uniting the composition by shooting inward toward the center. The individual figures, too, show a great change: the Archaic love of decorative pattern, still lingering in the west pediment in the treatment of musculature and clean silhouette, gives way to a more rounded and lifelike conception that suggests the figures' weight and muscle. The Archaic smile, seemingly so out of place in the warriors of the west pediment, is replaced by primitive attempts to show expression, a characteristic of the succeeding period. A definite change in outlook and in representation had taken place between the time of the west pediment and that of the east.

One can see these differences clearly by comparing two corner figures from the east and west pediments (Figs. 7.26 and 7.27). Although they are in similar positions to accommodate the decreased space at the corners, the fallen warrior on the east pediment clearly appears in a more developed pose than that on the west. Details of the heads of the warriors (Figs. 7.28 and 7.29) reveal the same contrast: on the west figure, the incongruous Archaic smile; on the east, a hint of the pain and despair of death.

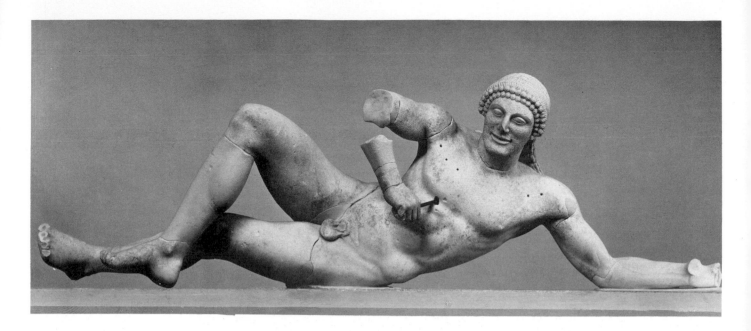

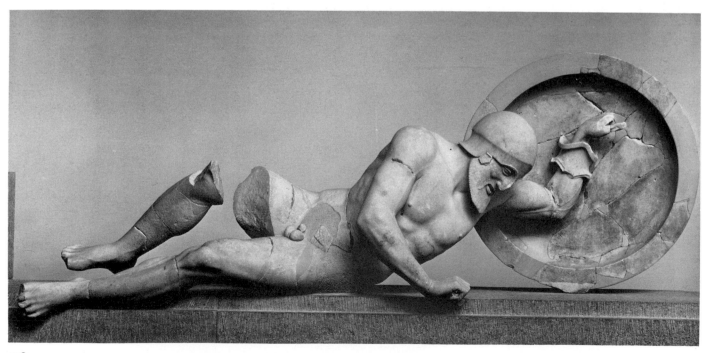

7.26 Fallen warrior from the west pediment of the temple of Aphaia, Aigina. Staatliche Antikensammlungen und Glyptothek, Munich. Photo: Hartwig Koppermann.

7.27 Fallen warrior from the east pediment of the temple of Aphaia, Aigina. Staatliche Antikensammlungen und Glyptothek, Munich. Photo: Hartwig Koppermann.

PAINTING AND POTTERY

Although painting other than that found on pots is known from this period, only a few examples have come down to us on terra cotta and wooden plaques. The example shown in Color Plate 8 (following p. 96), dedicated to the nymphs, depicts a votive procession. This particular painting does not differ significantly from contemporary Black Figure painting except for the lack of incision, the light background, and the bright polychromy. Whether one can

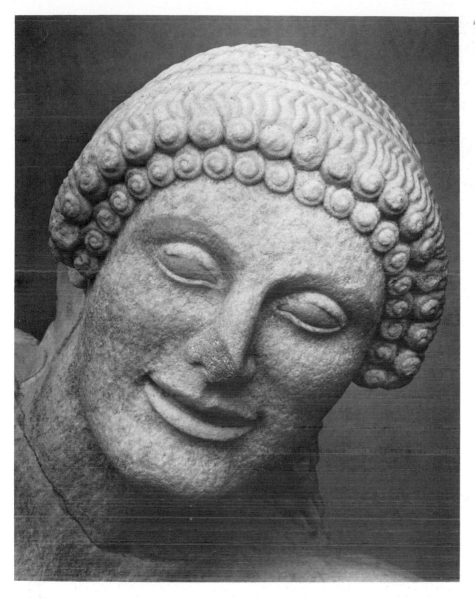

7.28 Detail of a head of a fallen warrior from the west pediment of the temple of Aphaia, Aigina. Staatliche Antikensammlungen und Glyptothek, Munich. Photo: Hartwig Koppermann.

conjecture what major painting may have looked like from this plaque and a few similar examples cannot be known.[10] No major wall painting from this period has been preserved. By the sixth century the major shapes of Greek pottery, both the fine decorated ware and the more common black glaze and coarse household pottery, were well on the way to being established.[11]

The Black Figure style developed quickly at Athens under the sobering

[10] Although these examples do not differ significantly from contemporary Black Figure painting, the figures are often painted in brighter colors. An assessment of these paintings can be found, together with illustrations, in Martin Robertson, *A History of Greek Art* (Cambridge, 1975), 1:120–121, 123.

[11] For plain, undecorated pottery, see Brian A. Sparkes and Lucy Talcott, *Black and Plain Pottery of the Sixth, Fifth, and Fourth Centuries,* Athenian Agora series, vol. 12 (Princeton, 1970). For Black Figure pottery, see J. D. Beazley, *The Development of Attic Black Figure,* rev. ed., ed. Dietrich von Bothmer and Mary Moore (Berkeley and Los Angeles, 1986); and John Boardman, *Athenian Black Figure Vases* (New York, 1974).

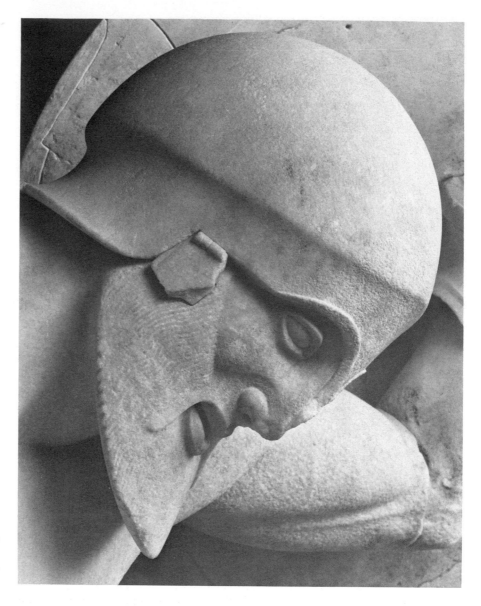

7.29 Detail of a head of a fallen warrior from the east pediment of the temple of Aphaia, Aigina. Staatliche Antikensammlungen und Glyptothek, Munich. Photo: Hartwig Koppermann.

influence of Corinthian painting. This development can be seen in the reduced size of the figures on a large bowl, or dinos, by the Gorgon Painter, from the early years of the century (Color Plate 12, following p. 96). The gorgons here are now of Corinthian type, which has become standard, and the vegetal ornament below the main figured zone also ultimately derives from Corinthian examples. Minature painting enjoyed a vogue in the first half of the century; one of the latest examples is found on the famous François Vase (Fig. 7.30), made about 570, slightly later than the Gorgon painter's dinos. Now standing a full 66 centimeters, it was found smashed to pieces in a tomb in Italy in the nineteenth century, was broken again in 1900, and is now in Florence. The shape of this Attic volute krater—the first preserved—is adapted from Corinthian models. It is decorated with concentric bands of figured scenes contain-

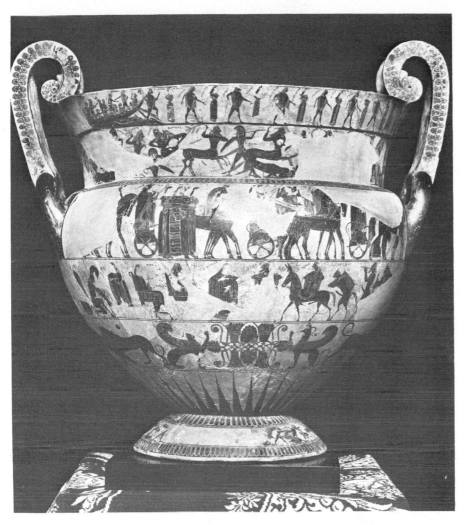

ing more than 250 figures. The vase is signed by Kleitias as painter and Ergotimos as potter.

The principal scene occupies the handle zone and runs all the way around the vase. It shows a procession of mythological characters on their way to the wedding of Peleus and the nymph Thetis—a famous social event that led to the Judgment of Paris, starting the chain of events that culminated in the Trojan War and the eventual death of Achilles, the son of Peleus and Thetis. In Figure 7.31 we see the head of the procession approaching the house of Peleus, where Thetis is to be seen through the door holding her veil aside in the traditional bridal gesture. Before the building Peleus welcomes Chiron, the civilized centaur, and Iris, the messenger of the gods. At the left comes Dionysos, carrying his own wine, staggering slightly and looking out at the viewer. Unfortunately the surface of the vase has been badly damaged and many scenes can be appreciated only through reproductions made at the turn of the century, as in our Figure 7.31. Such details as the features of the female figures, which were added in brown, have disappeared, and portions of the vase itself are missing. Still, the liveliness of subject and skill of the painter can

7.31 A portion of the François Vase, showing Peleus greeting his guests; from a drawing. Photo: Deutsches Archäologisches Institut, Rome.

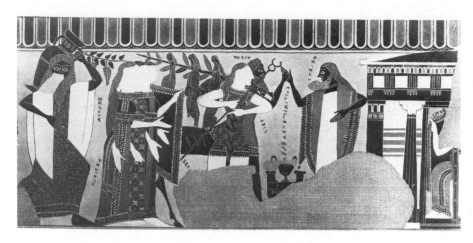

be appreciated. Note the writing with which both people and objects are labeled.

In Figure 7.32 we see a part of another scene from a particularly well-preserved portion of the same vase. Hephaistos, accompanied by Dionysos' satyrs (called "silenoi" here) and maenads (female followers of Dionysos), is being taken to Olympos on a mule led by the wine god. The comic nature of the scene is emphasized by the rendering of the figures. Hephaistos' lameness is indicated by the position of his feet below the mule's belly. The extreme delicacy of incision and overall quality of drawing in these small figures can be appreciated.

Scenes from the life of Achilles, including his death, and the adventures of Theseus and other mythological stories make up the remainder of the figured areas on the François Vase. It is thus not only a masterpiece of the potter and the painter but also a contemporary source of mythology.[12]

The Black Figure style reached its fullest development in the works of a number of artists who were painting around the middle and into the third quarter of the century. A vase by one of these artists, the Amasis Painter, is shown in Figure 7.33. This belly amphora, so called because of its shape, has a continuous curve from the lip to the foot. Such vases are also called Type B amphoras. Characteristic are the straight lip, rounded foot, and cylindrical handles.

The Amasis Painter, so named because he painted a number of vases signed by the potter or workshop owner Amasis, was an artist of great refinement and delicacy.[13] In this painting the god of wine, Dionysos, stands watching the antics of satyrs, his favorite companions, and maenads. The group has gathered to make wine. One of the satyrs treads the grapes while the others dance and drink to the sounds of pipes played by the satyr standing behind the wine god. Amasis' satyrs are distinctive shaggy creatures with long noses and elegant tails. To the right a maenad and a satyr come dancing up wrapped in each

---

[12] An excellent short description of the vase is to be found in J. D. Beazley, *The Development of Attic Black-Figure,* rev. ed. (Berkeley and Los Angeles, 1986), chap. 3.
[13] For this painter see Dietrich von Bothmer, *The Amasis Painter and His World* (Malibu, Calif., 1985). It is interesting to note that the name Amasis is a Hellenized form of Ahmosis, a common Egyptian name. Another painter of this period signed himself "Lydos," the Lydian. These names, whose significance is difficult to interpret, at least indicate a certain international aspect, which has also been noted in sculpture.

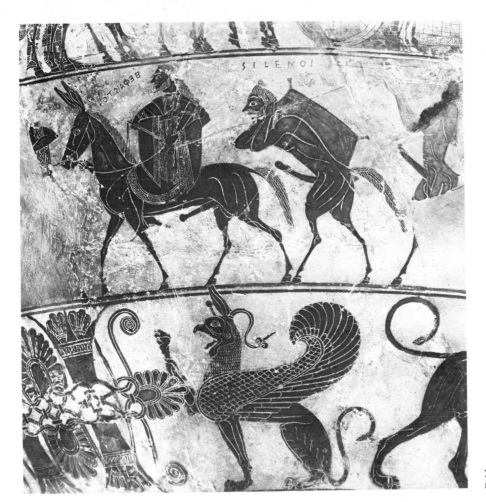

7.32 A portion of the François Vase, showing the return of Hephaistos. Photo: Alinari.

other's arms. In a departure from the Black Figure technique, the female figure is painted in outline and reserved in the color of the clay rather than painted white. Although outlining was often used in the early days of vase painting and is usual elsewhere in the sixth century, its appearance in Athens at this date perhaps heralds the new Red Figure style. This vase, with its large black figures standing out against the light clay background, its decorative design above the central scene, and its general high quality of draftsmanship, shows the Black Figure style at its most attractive. At the same time, however, the drawbacks of the technique are obvious in the dancing figures. The difficulty of clearly showing two overlapping figures can be appreciated when differentiation can be indicated only by incisions. In this case the figures are quite clearly defined by the use of contrasting colors; differentiating them would be much more difficult if they were wholly black.

The amphora in Figure 7.34 represents the work of a competent painter, the Antimenes Painter, who worked in the last thirty years of the century, at a time when the new Red Figure style was coming into use. Known as a neck amphora, it displays a shape that goes back to Protogeometric times. The neck is clearly set off from the rest of the vase, providing artists with two distinct zones for decoration. The subject is an olive harvest, a scene from everyday life, and the small neat figures are carefully drawn in a satisfying composition. The

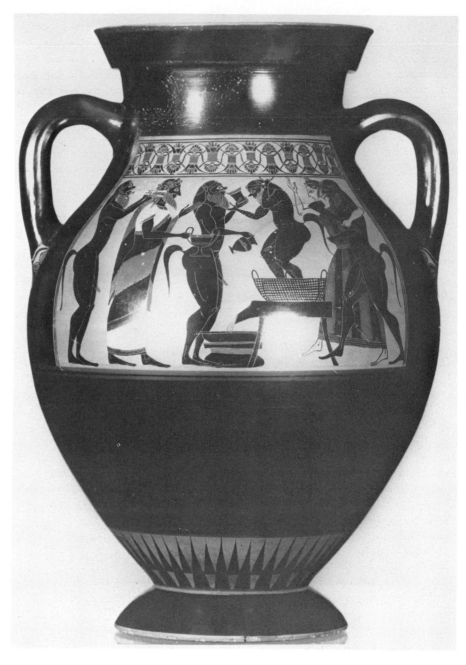

7.33 Amphora by the Amasis Painter. Photo: Antikenmuseum, Basel.

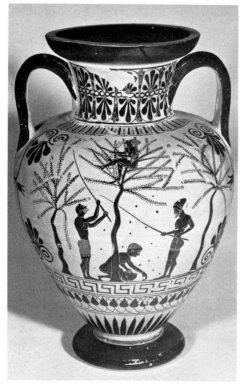

7.34 Neck amphora by the Antimenes Painter. Reproduced by courtesy of the Trustees of the British Museum, London.

artist has not tried anything beyond his ability and the decorative quality of the somewhat unusual scene is well adapted to the shape. Good work was thus still being done in the Black Figure style toward the end of the century, but the new style rapidly became more popular.

The Red Figure style of painting arose at Athens shortly after 530, and by the end of the century the most original painters had switched to the new technique. In Red Figure technique the figures were reserved and the background was fired black—just the reverse of the Black Figure style. As if to advertise the differences between the two techniques, so-called bilingual vases were produced by some of the first artists to try out the new style. Color Plate 13 shows one of these works by the Andokides Painter, named by convention after the presumed potter who signed some of the vases he painted. Here we find Herakles holding spits and leading a bull to sacrifice painted in Black Figure style on one side and an almost identical scene painted in the new Red Figure style on the other. Some investigators believe the Andokides Painter was the inventor of the new painting technique, but this vase is not among the earliest attempts at Red Figure and may have functioned as a display piece to illustrate the new invention. The shape itself, known as a Type A amphora, identified by its flanged handles with decorated edges and stepped foot, was introduced around the middle of the century and became a favorite of some of the outstanding painters of the Red Figure style.

In Red Figure painting, musculature and other details were painted in a dilute glaze, which varied in hue with the thickness of application. Contours and specific details were often indicated by relief lines. The relief line, restricted to Red Figure painting, was achieved by use of a thick glaze that actually formed a raised line on the surface. Sometimes additional colors, especially red, were also used. The advantages of Red Figure technique were many, not the least being the realism of light-colored bodies against dark background. Relief lines gave great precision, and the use of dilute glaze for details gave the artist increased freedom to depict the musculature of twisted bodies.[14] The first painters to try their hands at the new technique were slow to realize the potential of the style, but by the time of the painter Euthymides, just before the end of the century, experimentation was in the air, as is shown by the relief bases from the Themistoklean wall (see Figure 7.24). The Type A amphora shown in Figure 7.35, painted by Euthymides, bears a scene of three men dancing. Particular attention has been paid to the central figure, which presents a reasonably correct three-quarter back view. The artist has written in dilute glaze a phrase that may be rendered in English "as never Euphronios." Euthymides seems to have been in friendly competition with Euphronios, another painter whose work we know, to overcome one of the artistic problems of their time, the presentation of the human body in a twisted pose. Evidently vase painters as well as sculptors were concerned with the problem.

Under the successors of Euthymides and Euphronios, Attic Red Figure settled into a mature and less experimental stage after the turn of the century. The tendency, already to be seen in the waning days of the Black Figure style, toward scenes of everyday life rather than myth also continues and expands under the more realistic Red Figure technique. These Late Archaic painters worked well into the fifth century and are generally regarded as representing the high period of the Red Figure style, a time in which the subtleties of the technique were fully explored. The painters of the period have been the subjects of numerous studies.[15]

---

[14] A variety of works are devoted primarily to the Red Figure style. G. M. A. Richter's *Attic Red-Figured Vases*, rev. ed. (New Haven, 1958), is an early handbook. More recent are John Boardman's *Athenian Red Figure Vases: The Archaic Period* (London, 1975) and *Athenian Red Figure Vases: The Classical Period* (London, 1989); and Martin Robertson, *The Art of Vase-Painting in Classical Athens* (Cambridge, 1992).

[15] Scholarship has begun to move away from strictly stylistic studies toward attempts to understand more clearly the seemingly complicated world of interlocking painter-potter workshop relationships. A pioneering study along these lines is T. B. L. Webster, *Potter and Patron in Classical Athens* (London, 1972). See also the works cited in Chapter 1, note 5.

7.35 Amphora by Euthymides.P Staatliche Antikensammlungen und Glyptothek, Munich. Photo: Hartwig Koppermann.

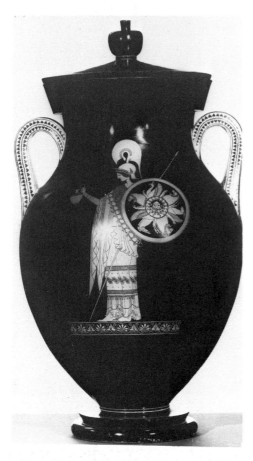

7.36 Amphora by the Berlin Painter: Athena. Photo: Antikenmuseum, Basel.

7.37 Detail of amphora by the Berlin Painter: Herakles. Photo: Antikenmuseum, Basel.

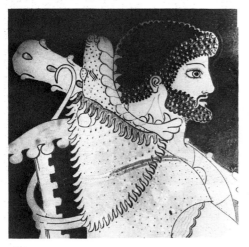

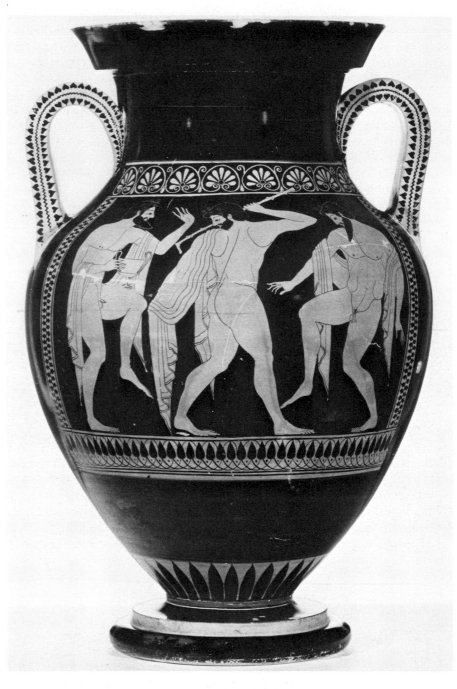

One of the preeminent painters of the time, an artist who specialized in large vases, is known as the Berlin Painter, after the present location of one of his outstanding amphoras, on which Hermes and satyrs are depicted. The example of his work seen in Figures 7.36 and 7.37 shows his most characteristic composition, single figures with a minimum of subsidiary decoration posed on each side of an almost completely black vase. Here we have graceful Athena offering to pour wine for Herakles, who, on the other side of the amphora, extends his cup to her. The tall, elegant figures with small heads and the sure draftsmanship are typical of this painter. Here all the details of Red Figure painting—dilute glaze, relief line, added red, and so on—are used with precision to produce highly decorative figures. Note that Athena's garment falls in heavy folds similar to those to be seen on the korai from the Acropolis.

A number of artists specialized in the decoration of cups, particularly the kylix, which had evolved into a delicate shape with a shallow bowl that presented the painter with problems of composition in the curving outer surfaces interrupted by handles and the interior circular area at the bottom of the cup. The kylix in Figure 7.38, by the Brygos Painter, shows how one of the leading cup painters tried to overcome these problems. The exterior is decorated with a line of revelers moving to the right. Beneath each handle is a palmette, with the feet of the celebrants extending beneath them to give continuity to the line of movement. The large figures move confidently, holding large kylikes in their hands. The drapery, although rich, is rendered less elaborately than that of the

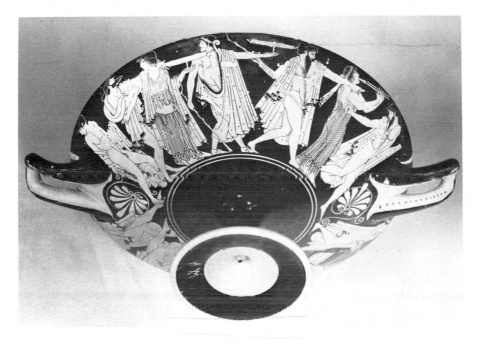

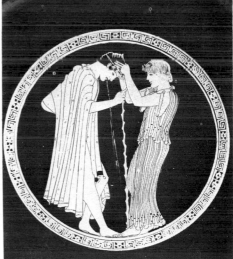

7.38 Kylix by the Brygos Painter.[P] Photo: Martin v. Wagner-Museum, Würzburg.

Berlin Painter's Athena. The tondo (circular painting) on the interior (Fig. 7.39) was perhaps intended as a joke on the drinker, who, upon emptying the cup, comes face to face with his possible future. The somewhat unattractive subject is rendered with some restraint, the two figures standing on the curve as if on a ground line. Although it is difficult to fill the circular space with two vertical figures, the man's pose deviates sufficiently from the vertical to fill the space satisfactorily. The subject matter of the painting on this cup strays from the world of myth. Mythical subjects were still popular, but scenes from everyday life had become much more common than they had been earlier and increased in popularity as time went on.

Close to these paintings in style is a unique tomb painting. Apparently dating to about 480, if we may judge by parallels in vase painting, the Tomb of

7.39 Tondo on the interior of the kylix by the Brygos Painter. Photo: Martin v. Wagner-Museum, Würzburg.

7.40 Tomb of the Diver, Paestum. Drawing of the tomb as found. From Mario Napoli, *La Tomba del Tuffatore* (Bari: De Donato Editore, 1970), p. 97, Fig. 30.

7.41 Detail of a banqueter from the Tomb of the Diver, Paestum. From Mario Napoli, *La Tomba del Tuffatore* (Bari: De Donato Editore, 1970), Plate 18.

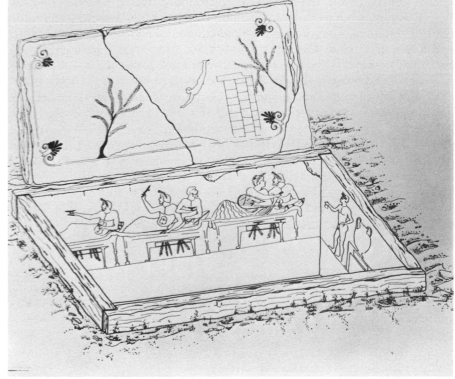

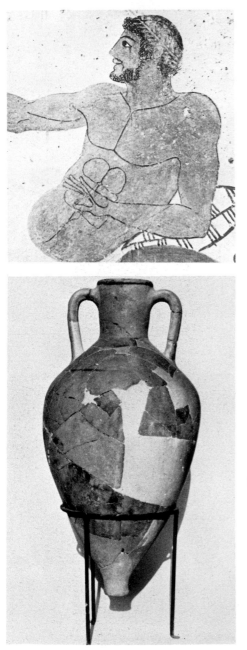

7.42 Amphora from Chios. Photo: American School of Classical Studies at Athens: Agora Excavations.

the Diver (Figs. 7.40 and 7.41) was found in A.D. 1969 in Paestum, in southern Italy. It was constructed of five slabs of local stone. The walls were decorated with a funeral banquet and the lid with a diver, hence its modern name. Differing from local painting of this period in composition, draftsmanship, and treatment, these paintings are clearly Greek. A detail of one of the banqueters shows the similarity, especially in the representation of the musculture, to Late Archaic vase painting styles. The figures stand out against a white background in dark flesh tones, but exhibit little shading or much advancement beyond the stage that had been reached by vase painting at this time.

TRANSPORT AMPHORAS

The sixth century saw the beginning of a series of transport amphoras from the island of Chios which can be traced through changes in shape all the way down into Roman times. The shape of the amphora, as we have seen, followed a general line of development from round and capacious to tall and angular, with accompanying changes in neck, handles, and toe. The sixth-century amphora from Chios shown in Figure 7.42 displays the typical swelling form of the earlier types together with a short neck and sloping shoulder. Later on, in the early years of the fifth century, the neck developed a curious swelling that was represented on coins of Chios even after the type had gone out of use.

TERRA COTTA FIGURINES

The terra cotta figurines of the sixth century are similar to those of the seventh century. Both entirely handmade and partially wheel-made figurines were

188

popular. At the end of the century mass-produced figurines made in molds became common, but in the early years of the century much variety and individuality were still preserved in the production of the various centers.

A typical product of Boiotia is the handmade flat-bodied standing goddess shown in Figure 7.43. Crudely decorated with black glaze, she wears a headdress and costume suggestive of Demeter or Persephone.

Distinctive vases modeled in various animal and human forms are known from the islands and Ionia (Fig. 7.44) and were widely exported in the latter half of the century. Similar production centers have been identified in Corinth and Etruria. Standing female figurines, painted with polychrome matt paint and conventionally identified as Aphrodite (Fig. 7.45), are representative of the soft and fleshy East Greek style of the second half of the century.

Figure 7.46 illustrates the range of figurines recovered from Archaic levels in a sanctuary of Demeter at Corinth. Among them are entirely handmade figures and some with molded heads.

METALWORK

The knowledge of bronze working increased rapidly in the Archaic period, as the increasing number of finds indicate. Although bronze is less likely to survive than stone or pottery because of its scrap value, quite a number of Archaic bronzes are known.

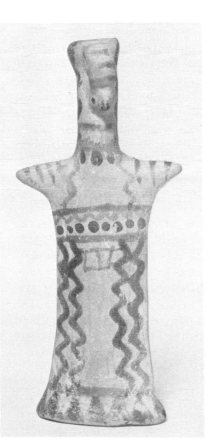

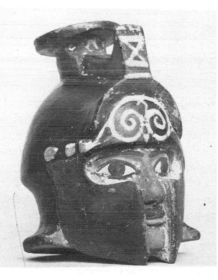

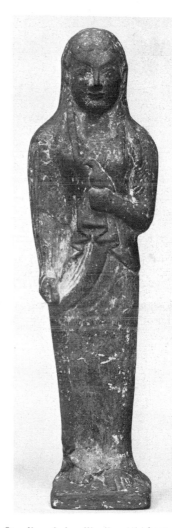

7.43 Terra cotta figurine from Boiotia. Photo: Museum of Art and Archaeology, University of Missouri–Columbia.

7.44 Vase in the form of a helmeted head. Reproduced by courtesy of the Trustees of the British Museum, London.

7.45 Standing Aphrodite figurine from Rhodes. Reproduced by courtesy of the Trustees of the British Museum, London.

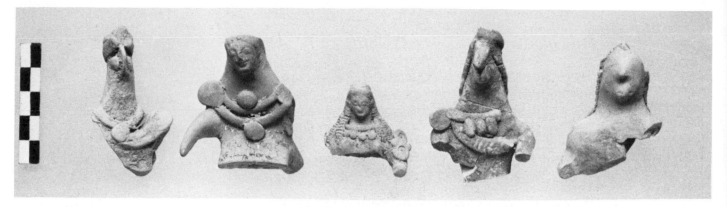

7.46 Typical Archaic figurines from Corinth. Corinth Museum. Photo: American School of Classical Studies at Athens: Corinth Excavations.

A large volute krater found in the grave of a Celtic princess near Vix in northeastern France and thus called the Vix Vase (Fig. 7.47) is a prime example of Archaic metalwork as well as of export activity. Standing to a height of 1.64 meters, the krater has a capacity of 262 gallons. The body of the vase was made of sheet bronze; the handles and the relief figures of warriors and chariots on the neck were separately cast and attached.

The German Archaeological Institute's excavations at Olympia have brought to light a great number of metal objects that luckily escaped the melting pot. Many of them belong to the sixth century, including an important series of shield bands decorated with mythological scenes in low relief (Fig. 7.48). These bands, used to secure the round hoplite shield to the arm, are divided into panels, each containing an individual scene. The drawings shown here, reproducing two such scenes in the straightforward manner of Archaic art, represent the death of Priam from the story of the sack of Troy and the miraculous birth of Athena from the head of Zeus. Dating to the first half of the century, these crude but lively representations find parallels in the mythical scenes popular in vase paintings.

COINS

The sixth century saw the rise of another category of minor finds whose stylistic evolution is significant for chronology. Coinage—the process of shaping a lump of metal and stamping it with a symbol of some authority that guarantees its weight and purity—began in the Greek cities on the coast of Asia Minor or in Lydia at the end of the seventh century and spread quickly throughout the Aegean.[16] The early coins bore on one side a symbol or badge of the issuing city and on the reverse a deep punch mark, probably designed originally to show that the coin was made of the same metal all the way through (Figs. 7.49 and 7.50). The earliest mainland coins were issued by Aigina in the early sixth century with a sea turtle as a symbol (Fig. 7.50). In Athens it was not until late in the sixth century that the famous series with the head of Athena first ap-

[16] The best general account of Greek coins is G. K. Jenkins, *Ancient Greek Coins,* 2d ed. (London, 1990). As the subject is too large and complex to be covered here, only a few of the most typical examples will be presented throughout the text to illustrate the types and no detailed descriptions or explanations will be attempted.

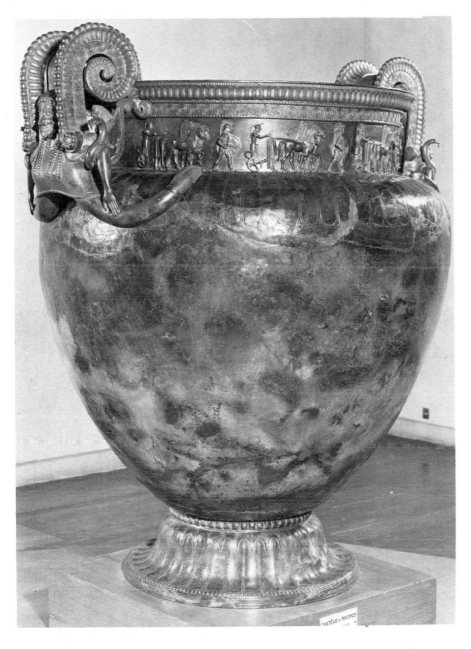

7.47 Vix Vase. Musée de Châtillon-sur-Seine. Photo: Giraudon.

7.48 Typical shield band designs from Olympia. From Emil Kunze, *Archaische Schildbänder*, Olympische Forschungen, vol. 2 (Berlin: Walter de Gruyter, 1950), Plate 31. By permission of the Deutsches Archäologisches Institut, Berlin.

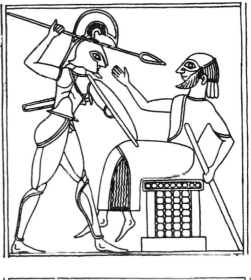

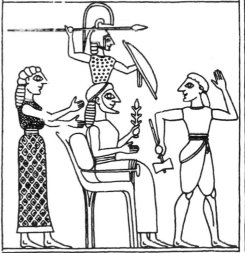

peared, replacing an earlier series of diverse designs or "types." Now the reverse bears her favorite companion, the owl, and an olive branch together with the first letters of the city's name (Fig. 7.51). Other cities established their coin types by late in the century. The great city of Corinth adopted the winged horse, Pegasos, as the most important obverse design and a helmeted Athena on the reverse (Fig. 7.52).

Once established, two-sided coins bearing specific types generally continued throughout the life of a city, although they sometimes changed to reflect contemporary styles. Coins of various denominations and sizes were made of gold, silver, and base metals.

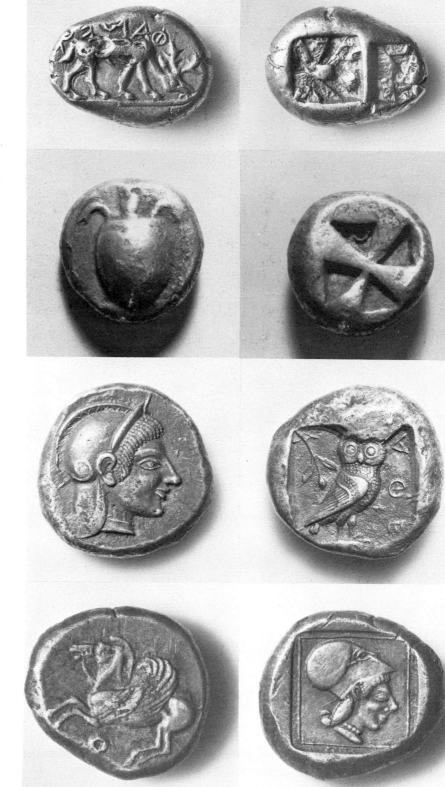

7.49 Sixth-century coin from Ionia: obverse, stag; reverse, punch mark. Photos: Hirmer Fotoarchiv, Munich. Scale c. 3:1.

7.50 Sixth-century coin from Aigina: obverse, sea turtle; reverse, punch mark. Photos: Museum of Art and Archaeology, University of Missouri–Columbia. Scale 2:1.

7.51 Sixth-century coin from Athens: obverse, Athena; reverse, owl. Photos: Hirmer Fotoarchiv, Munich. Scale 2:1.

7.52 Sixth-century coin from Corinth: obverse, Pegasos; reverse, Athena Chalinitis. Photos: Hirmer Fotoarchiv, Munich. Scale 3:1.

LAMPS

The typical Athenian oil lamp of the sixth century is a further development of the types current in the last century. Made on a wheel with an incurved rim, such a lamp invariably has an oval nozzle added to the body at a point where a section of the rim is broken away (Fig. 7.53a and b). Some examples have horizontal handles. Generally the interior of these lamps has been glazed to reduce the porosity of the fabric. In later types of the sixth century the outside also received a coat of glaze. Imported lamps from Asia Minor and the Peloponnesos have rims that continue all the way around, over the nozzle (Fig. 7.53c). Such "bridge nozzle" lamps eventually became the predominant type used in Attica.

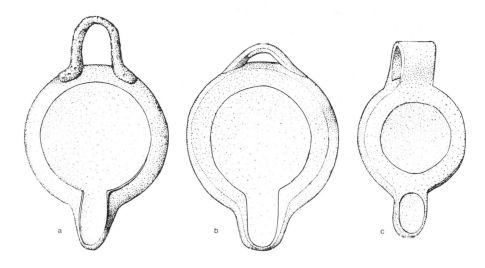

7.53 Typical sixth-century lamps. After Richard Hubbard Howland, *Greek Lamps and Their Survivals*, Athenian Agora series, vol. 4 (Princeton: American School of Classical Studies, 1958), Plates 30 and 31. By permission of the American School of Classical Studies. Drawing by John Huffstot. Scale 1:2.2.

8

The Fifth Century

IN THE FIFTH CENTURY Athens knew both the heights of glory and the depths of defeat. A tremendous flowering of civilization under the leadership of Perikles was destined to influence the Western world for ages to come. But while Athens was producing abiding masterpieces in art, philosophy, and drama and maintaining the world's first democracy, it was ruthlessly pursuing an imperialistic foreign policy.

Following the final defeat of the Persians at the Battle of Plataiai and their withdrawal from Greece, the alliances among the Greek powers began to deteriorate. Sparta, primarily a land power, showed little interest in further prosecution of the war with Persia, but the Athenians did. They had some notable successes and in 477 established the Delian League, based on the island of Delos, to carry on the war with Persia and to protect Greek cities of Asia Minor from the Great King. The member states paid money or contributed ships to the cause. Athens was the driving force in the confederacy, its primary power, and was easily able to convert it into an empire. By encouraging states to give money rather than ships, by ruthlessly suppressing those that wished to leave the confederacy, and by annexing others, it was able to draw all the powers into its own hands. Following an abortive expedition to Egypt, the league treasury was moved to Athens in 454. From this time on, the city took one-sixtieth of the tribute money paid by its "allies" for its own treasury, and the empire can be said to have been well established. By 456, at the height of its power, Athens even had a considerable land empire. It was short-lived, however, for Athens' strength was in its navy.

The principal proponent of Athens' imperial ambitions was the famous Perikles, who was the leading statesman from about 460 until his death in 429. During this period, while the city was waging intermittent war abroad and ruthlessly promoting the empire, democracy at home was further developed and Athens was adorned with some of the greatest works ever known—paid for by the tribute from its empire. It is important to note that Perikles' influence rested on constitutional grounds and that he was elected by the assembly to a board of ten generals. In fact, during the period of his influence there were only one or two years when he was not in office. He ruled the state, in effect, but by his own powers of persuasion rather than by nonconstitutional means. During this period the assembly was made more powerful and the law courts were further democratized by the payment of jurors, so that even some of the poorer citizens could serve. Most public offices were filled annually by lot on the theory that all citizens above the lower classes were capable of administering the business of the state and were entitled to serve. It must be remembered that Athenian democracy omitted women and slaves from the assembly, but the principle was liberal for its time.

It was one of those extraordinary periods when circumstances combine to produce outstanding geniuses in a number of fields. Athens' incomparable artistic productions can only be touched upon in this book; nothing can be said about the many advances in such fields as literature, philosophy, science, and medicine.

The Athenian Empire, essentially running counter to the pervasive parochialism of the city-state system, was bound to be seen as a challenge by the other major power, Sparta. The methods by which Athens chose to maintain and administer its empire led directly to the Peloponnesian War, in which Athens and its allies were pitted against Sparta and its allies. The Peloponnesian War, recorded by the first contemporary historian, Thucydides, broke out in 431. In two years Perikles was dead, a victim of a plague that attacked Athens. Successes were won by both sides, and a truce was declared in 421. After a period of "cold war," open hostilities were renewed in 415, when Athens attacked Syracuse. The final blow came in 405, when Athens' fleet was destroyed in a battle at Aigospotami, on the Hellespont. The next year Athens surrendered; the fortification walls connecting the city to the port were demolished and a Spartan garrison was admitted.

Domestic strife followed at Athens under an oligarchic government known as the Thirty, which had been set up with Spartan support. The Thirty, after a short rule characterized by political suppression and murder, were ousted by democratic forces in 403. Sparta, called in to settle what was in effect a civil war, forced a reconciliation, and ultimately the Athenian democracy was restored. The upheavals of the long war, however, had changed the Greek world for victor and vanquished alike. Henceforth things were to be very different.

ART

The fifth century, known as the Classical period of Greece, has been considered the height of Greek and Roman civilization, after which everything inevitably declined.[1] Today it is generally recognized that the art of the fifth century is part of the general development of Greek art and not to be extravagantly praised at the expense of any other period; most modern scholars, at least, manage to suppress any old-fashioned enthusiasm. Nor is the art of the fifth century now considered as homogeneous as that of the sixth; three more or less distinct phases are recognized.

The art of the first half of the century is somewhat less uniform stylistically than that of the second half and has been interpreted less uniformly as well. For some it is a transitional period in which lingering Archaic forms exist beside more advanced Classical renderings. For others it is an experimental period or an early stage of the High Classical style of the second half of the century. The period has all of these characteristics. For convenience the term "Severe style" has been applied to the art of this period, encompassing the meanings of both transitional and Early Classical. The style is characterized by (1) a simplification of forms, (2) a return to the plain Doric garments with a resulting simplification in the treatment of drapery, and (3) new subjects often shown in motion or expressing emotion, with varying degrees of success.

---

[1] The fifth and fourth centuries are often lumped together as the Classical period, but for our purposes only the fifth century will be so designated, with the art of the period of Perikles called High Classical to denote its special stylistic character. For general works dealing with the fifth century, usually together with the fourth, see the Suggestions for Further Reading.

Often the moment just before or after an event or a moment of rest within a complex movement will be shown rather than the action itself. These last two characteristics are typical of Classical art in general, but they were new in the first half of the century.[2]

In the second half of the century, or more specifically in the period of Periklean supremacy (460–429), a very strong and potent style developed. In this High Classical style, which had its roots in much of the sculpture of the earlier part of the century, the human form was idealized. Individual traits were suppressed, as were extremes of youth and old age; almost the only subjects were perfect men and women in their prime. A certain homogeneity was achieved; it has been said that all High Classical statues look alike, with their straight noses, down-turned mouths, vacant stares, and simplified musculature. This powerful style has been seen as a creation of Perikles' circle, especially of his chief artist, Phidias, and as a reflection of their confidence and outlook on life. According to this theory, Phidias' style, supported by the artistic and political dominance of Athens at this time, actually suppressed the tentative movement toward naturalism and the display of emotion that can be seen in the works of the Severe style.[3] Suppressed too was the natural tendency toward the development of a variety of styles under individual masters, which appeared again in the fourth century.

The last quarter of the century saw a loosening of the Phidian style in the direction of elaboration and sophistication of treatment of details, especially drapery. This change can be clearly seen in the sculptures of the Nike Parapet and in late fifth-century vase painting. The change is obvious, but greater changes were to come in the next century.[4]

ARCHITECTURE

The most famous and at the same time the most important of the religious buildings of the first half of the fifth century is the great temple of Zeus at Olympia, which was erected between 470 and 456 (Fig. 8.1). Here the canonical number of columns is to be found, six across the front and thirteen on each side. The building was one of the largest on the mainland, however, measuring 64.12 meters in length and 27.68 meters in width on the stylobate. The building was decorated with pedimental sculptures at both ends and by sculptured metopes illustrating the twelve labors of Herakles and placed not on the exterior but in the pronaos and opisthodomos, above the columns *in antis.*

In comparison with those on Aigina, the Doric columns of the exterior have grown taller and slimmer. The temple is constructed of local shelly limestone, which originally was stuccoed to give the appearance of marble. The ground plan shows few peculiarities. The cella had two double-tiered rows of Doric columns flanking a great seated gold-and-ivory (chryselephantine) cult statue of Zeus, constructed by Phidias toward the end of his career (Fig. 8.2). The two-storied cella supported a balcony from which the statue might be viewed. This

[2] The foregoing is based entirely on the best treatment of the Severe style: Brunilde Sismondo Ridgway, *The Severe Style in Greek Sculpture* (Princeton, 1970), pp. 3–11. The following discussion of Severe-style sculpture is also heavily dependent on this excellent source.

[3] This view of the art of the second half of the fifth century is outlined in G. M. A. Richter, *Three Critical Periods in Greek Sculpture* (Oxford, 1951), pp. 7–14.

[4] An interesting question to ponder is whether art reacts directly to history and politics. Does late fifth-century Attic art, for instance, reflect the crises of the time? See J. J. Pollitt, *Art and Experience in Classical Greece* (Cambridge, 1972).

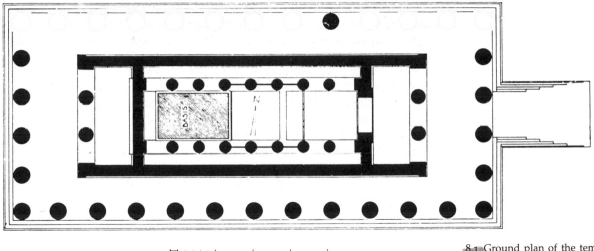

8.1 Ground plan of the temple of Zeus at Olympia.[P] From Gottfried Gruben, *Die Tempel der Griechen* (Munich: Hirmer Verlag, 1966), p. 53, Fig. 41. Reproduced by permission.

building, which expressed the Doric canon in its developed form, was built by a local architect, Libon of Elis.

An excellently preserved example of the Doric canon of the middle years of the century is the temple of Hephaistos on Kolonos Agoraios, overlooking the Athenian agora (Figs. 8.3 and 8.4). Almost completely intact as a result of its conversion into a church by the Christians, the Hephaisteion is much smaller than the temple of Zeus (31.77 by 13.71 meters on the stylobate) and is representative of the Attic Doric temple of the fifth century. That the building was designed to be seen primarily from the east and below is evident from the fact that sculptured metopes adorn only the east end and the four most easterly intercolumniations on the north and south. This building shows a number of specific characteristics derived from fifth-century Attic architecture and from

8.2 Section of the temple of Zeus at Olympia, with cult statue, as it appeared in the fifth century. Photo: Deutsches Archäologisches Institut, Athens.

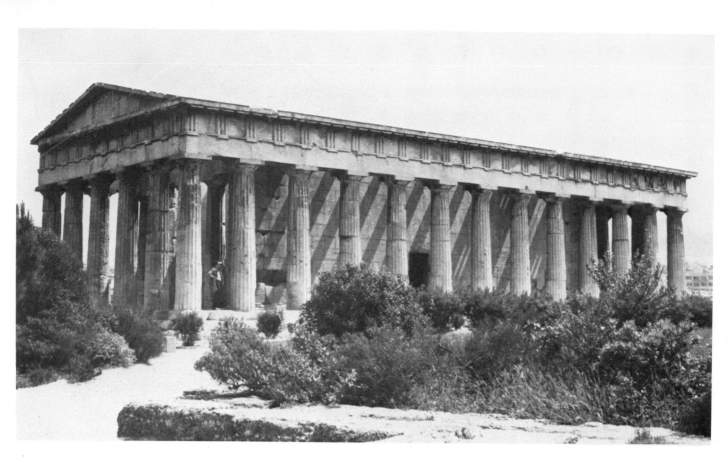

8.3 The Hephaisteion at Athens, viewed from the southwest. Photo: William R. Biers.

the architect whose hand has been identified in a number of other temples.[5] One of these fifth-century characteristics is the use of Ionic features to enliven the severity of the Doric order. One such feature used here, a base molding around the cella wall, was first used in the predecessor of the Parthenon, destroyed by the Persians in 480. The alignment of the pronaos columns and antae with the exterior colonnade and the use of a continuous figured Ionic frieze in the pronaos and opisthodomos are characteristic contributions of the architect. In the opisthodomos the frieze runs from anta to anta above the columns, while in the pronaos it runs to the outer colonnades on the north and south. The subject of the frieze at the east end is the combats of Theseus, at the west the battle of centaurs and Lapiths. The metopes depict the labors of Herakles and the adventures of Theseus. The interior of the building shows evidence of a change in plan in the arrangement of the cella, which was shortened and given an interior two-tiered Doric colonnade. It is usually said that this change reflects influence on the architect by plans for the Parthenon, on which construction began only a few years later. The dates given for the building of the Hephaisteion are 449–420s.

As a result of the almost complete destruction of the Archaic monuments on

[5] A study of the buildings assigned to this unknown architect is to be found in W. H. Plommer, "Three Attic Temples," *BSA* 45 (1950): 66–112.

Although the temple of Kolonos Agoraios is now considered by most scholars to be the Hephaisteion, its sculptures record the deeds of Theseus, and it was earlier identified as the Theseion. For a short summary of the building, see John M. Camp, *The Athenian Agora* (London and New York, 1992), pp. 82–87.

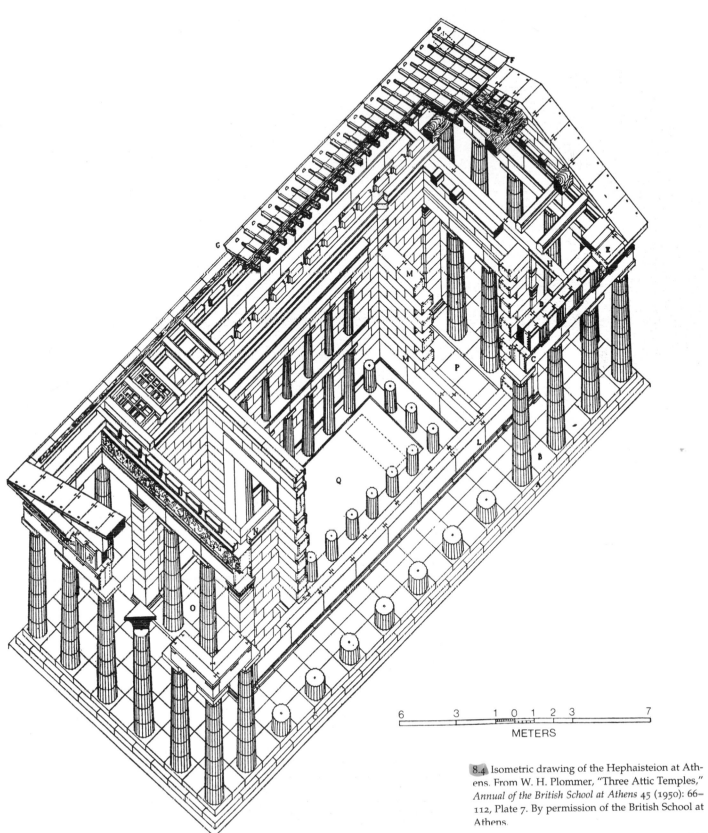

6   3   1 0 1 2 3   7

METERS

8.4 Isometric drawing of the Hephaisteion at Athens. From W. H. Plommer, "Three Attic Temples," *Annual of the British School at Athens* 45 (1950): 66–112, Plate 7. By permission of the British School at Athens.

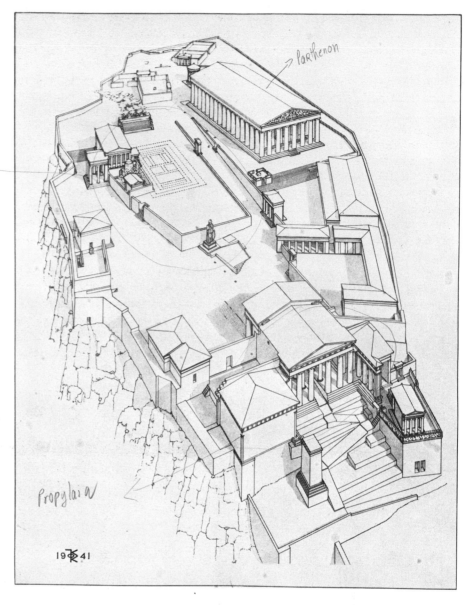

8.5 The Acropolis, Athens,[P] as restored by Gorham Phillips Stevens. Photo: American School of Classical Studies at Athens: Agora Excavations.

the Athenian acropolis by the invading Persians, the returning Greeks had an opportunity to construct new buildings once hostilities had been concluded. Here on a low hill rising out of the Attic plain the architects and artists of the second half of the fifth century erected a number of fascinating buildings of exquisite workmanship (see Color Plate 4, following p. 96). Hampered occasionally by the needs and boundaries of the numerous ancient shrines and cult places that covered the hilltop, they nevertheless managed to complete the main outlines of their plans, although portions were destined to remain unfinished or truncated (Fig. 8.5).

Reused and pillaged throughout the centuries, these buildings have suffered greatly from pollution in modern times and even from earlier attempts at repair and rebuilding. A current massive effort to restore and preserve them has provided an opportunity for scholars to restudy each building as a preliminary step in its restoration. The information gained from this project has greatly enhanced our knowledge of the monuments of the Acropolis and has served to correct some misconceptions. The restoration project has also brought up a problem commonly encountered in efforts to preserve historic building sites throughout the world. If one wants to restore a building that has been used and changed for almost two and a half thousand years, how much does one restore and to what period should it be restored? What should be kept and what should be discarded? Should a partially destroyed building be kept as a ruin or rebuilt as it looked in antiquity? Both approaches have been taken. The Stoa of Attalos in the Agora, for instance, has been completely rebuilt (see Chapter 10); on the Acropolis the east facade of the Erechtheion has been partially reconstructed (Color Plate 14).[6]

Of the various buildings that adorned the top of the hill, we shall deal with the Parthenon (447–438), the Erechtheion (421–414, 409–406), and the monumental entranceway, the Propylaia (437–432). The Parthenon and the Propylaia were surely planned at the same time as part of the Periklean plan for the Acropolis.

The Parthenon is justly regarded as the high point of Doric architecture as conceived by the Periklean architects.[7] Built between 447 and 438 by the architects Iktinos and Kallikrates, it is a Doric peripteral temple built on remains of a pre-Periklean temple but much bigger, measuring 69.50 by 30.88 meters on the stylobate, with eight columns across the front and seventeen on each flank (Figs. 8.6–8.10). The restored ground plan, Figure 8.6, reflects the most recent

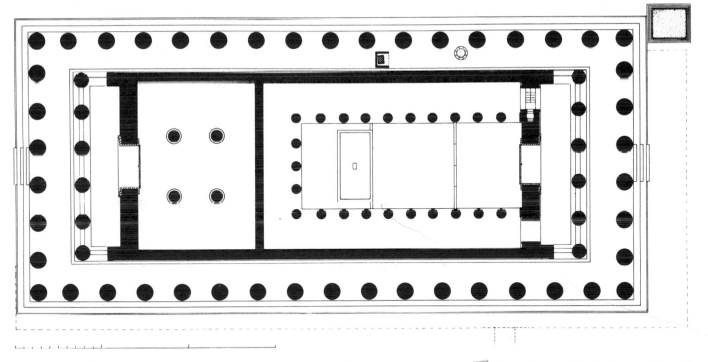

8.6 Ground plan of the Parthenon, Athens,[P] reflecting recent research. From Manolis Korres, *From Pentelikon to the Parthenon* (Athens, 1995), p. 112, Fig. 35.2. Reproduced by permission.

[6] The history of the various attempts at restoration as well as the modern debate and action concerning the Acropolis buildings is set forth in Richard Economakis, ed., *Acropolis Restorations: The CCAM Interventions* (London, 1994).

[7] Much has been written about the Parthenon but apparently much still remains to be said, to judge from the continual flow of studies concerning it. A collection of articles on various aspects of the building can be found in Vincent J. Bruno, *The Parthenon* (New York, 1974). A broader view of the building and its entire history can be found in Panayotis Tournikiotis, ed., *The Parthenon and Its Impact in Modern Times* (Athens, 1994).

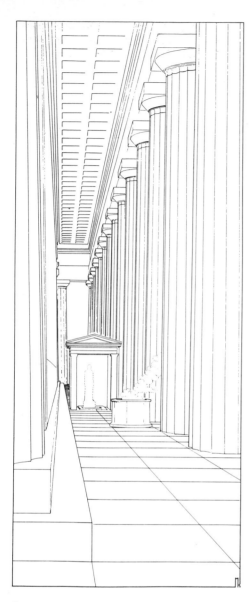

information about the building that the restoration program has yielded. A significant discovery is that the great east door was originally flanked by windows, which increased the visibility of the cult statue of Athena in the cella. Somewhat surprising is the discovery that the space between the cella wall and the north colonnade was not completely open, as one would expect it to be in a Greek peripteral temple, but partially blocked by a little shrine and altar (reconstructed in Fig. 8.7), apparently representing an earlier holy place that had been covered over by the fifth-century temple. The interior plan offers several unusual features. Instead of having columns *in antis*, the pronaos and opisthodomos had porticoes, each consisting of six columns standing well in front of the short antae. The scheme was evidently inherited from the predecessor on the site, as were many of the details. The Parthenon actually reused portions of the earlier building. The number of portico columns, however, was increased from four to six. The cella contained two rooms separated by a solid

8.7 Reconstruction of the shrine and altar in the north peristyle of the Parthenon. From *Bulletin de correspondance hellénique* 12 (1988): 614, Fig. 3. Reproduced by permission.

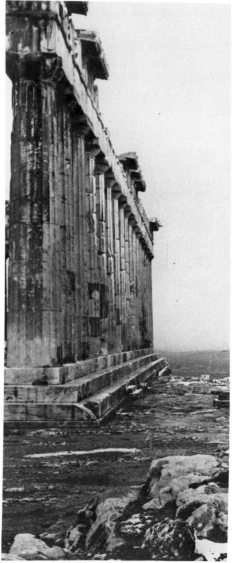

8.8 The Parthenon viewed from the east. Note the doming of the stylobate and steps. Photo: Alison Frantz.

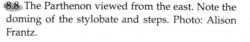

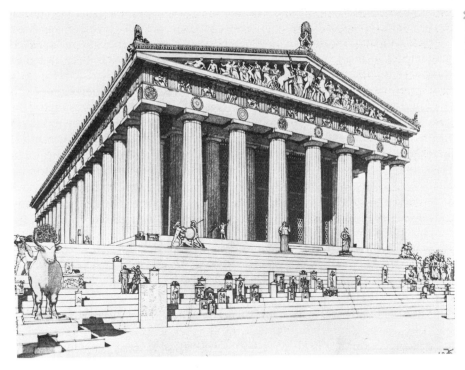

8.9 The west facade of the Parthenon as restored by Gorham Phillips Stevens. Photo: American School of Classical Studies at Athens: Agora Excavations.

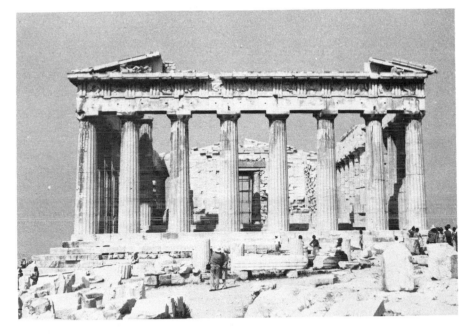

8.10 The east facade of the Parthenon today. Photo: William R. Biers.

wall. The rear chamber contained four Ionic columns to hold up the ceiling and was entered from the opisthodomos. Literary evidence indicates it was used as a treasury. The main room—indeed, the whole building—was designed to hold the great gold-and-ivory statue of Athena Parthenos. The statue was framed by a two-storied Doric colonnade, already familiar from Aigina and Olympia; here, however, the colonnade continued behind the statue, thus visually framing it and allowing visitors to walk all the way around it (see

Fig. 8.50). Interest in the arrangement of interior space is not generally considered a characteristic of Greek architecture but appears in a tentative way here.

The Parthenon, more than any other temple, shows the use of so-called refinements in the fabric of the building. Their existence has been noted in some earlier buildings but nowhere else have they been applied so rigorously and with such exquisite workmanship. The architectural refinements of this one building form a separate study in themselves. Suffice it to say here that the building intentionally contains a great number of deviations from the norm and from mathematical regularity: lines that are usually straight are curved, members that are usually vertical are inclined, dimensions vary from the norm. The stylobate, for instance, is domed (Fig. 8.8), and this upward inclination is carried on into the entablature, whose various parts incline inward or outward, depending on their positions. The columns of the peristyle have a slightly convex curve (entasis) and lean inward. In view of the fact that these marble columns were constructed of a number of separately cut drums, the quality of the workmanship that produced these refinements is staggering.

It is the interpretation and the meaning of these refinements that are difficult to discover. The most widely held view is that many of them were introduced to overcome the optical illusions that the planners felt would be produced when straight lines and right angles were viewed from a distance against the sky. Thus the columns would appear too thin without an outward curve, and the stylobate would appear to be hollowed unless it were given an upward curve. Another suggestion is that the irregularities were introduced for the specific purpose of deviating from a rigid mathematical plan in order to give life to the building in the same way that a human body is alive.[8] This concept will be further discussed when we deal with the famous canon of Polykleitos.

Construction on the Erechtheion, on the north side of the hill, was begun in 421 but was suspended in 414, to be taken up again in 409. The building was completed in 406.[9] As Figures 8.11 and 8.12 indicate, the temple was strangely shaped, containing four sets of columnar supports, four levels, and three structural units, each with its own roof. The reason for this complexity lies in the configuration of the rock in the area and in the necessity of building around various cult spots in one of the most sacred places on the hill. This area contained many signs and remains of Athens' mythical past, such as the olive tree of Athena and the marks of Poseidon's trident. The peculiarities of plan are equaled by our uncertainties as to the arrangement of the interior, which was thoroughly destroyed in later times. We do know, however, that the most sacred and venerated image of Athens, the wooden Athena Polias, had its home in the building, thus perhaps continuing an old tradition. This place had long been sacred to the goddess, perhaps as far back as the Bronze Age, when the Mycenaean palace stood in the vicinity. Many other Attic deities also crowded in, including Erechtheus, after whom the building is named.

Despite the problems of reconstruction, the Erechtheion stands as an example of Ionic elaboration and elegance. The building is highly decorative and must have appeared even more elegant when its details were painted. The highly elaborate north porch and the unusual south porch, its roof supported

---

[8] Several suggestions as to the reasons for the refinements are discussed in Pollitt, *Art and Experience*, pp. 74–78. Pollitt makes it clear that all the explanations may have some validity. See also J. J. Coulton, *Ancient Greek Architects at Work* (Ithaca, N.Y., 1977), pp. 108–112.

[9] The basic study of this building is James Paton, ed., *The Erechtheum* (Cambridge, Mass., 1927).

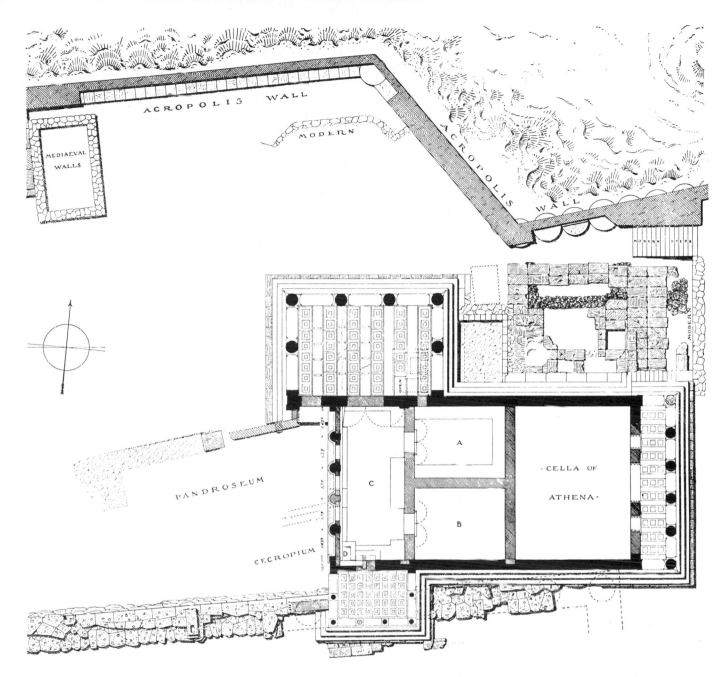

8.11 Plan of the Erechtheion.[P] From James M. Paton, ed., *The Erechtheum* (Cambridge: Harvard University Press, 1927), Plate 1. By permission of the American School of Classical Studies at Athens.

by female figures, or karyatids, added to the impression of elegance. We can appreciate the results of the modern restoration program by comparing the view of the east end of the building as restored today (Color Plate 14) with the restored elevation in Figure 8.12. The whiter marble marks what was restored; note particularly the north corner column and the partially restored entablature above it.

The Acropolis was approached through a great entranceway, the Propylaia, whose construction, on the remains of an earlier entrance, was another project of the Periklean building program. The architect was one Mnesikles. The work

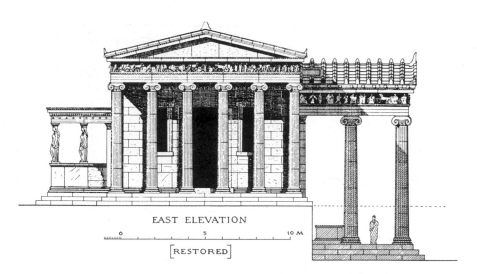

EAST ELEVATION

0   5   10 M

[RESTORED]

of building began in 437 and was abandoned, unfinished, in 432 because of the Peloponnesian War. The architect had a serious problem to overcome in the steep slope in this area, the only point that is at all suitable for entry to the Acropolis. Mnesikles obviously conceived of a grandiose plan that far overshadowed the simpler, smaller, pre-Persian gate over which he built, but a combination of factors frustrated the scheme. The plan of the building, as we have it today (Fig. 8.13), consists of a T-shaped design with the stem of the T projecting into the Acropolis. Six Doric columns stand at both the east and west ends in pairs of three on either side of a central ramp, up which sacrificial animals presumably were led. A wall pierced by four doors, two on each side, stands at the head of a flight of five steps that mark the transition between the eastern and western porticoes. The steps are approached by a fairly long rectangular hallway, edged on one side by a solid wall and on the other by three tall Ionic columns, which border the ramp. Mnesikles had intended to erect two large buildings to the right and left of the portico, within the Acropolis, but they were never built.

He also envisioned two smaller rooms on the outside to the west, but only one was completed, with three columns *in antis* and a window on either side of the central door. We know from literary sources that this room was known as the Pinakotheke (picture gallery) and was adorned with movable paintings on wooden boards. We have no idea what the other room would have held, for it stopped at the Mycenaean wall on the east. This wall was probably considered sacred, for the upper courses of the Propylaia were actually beveled to go around it. The gate building was also truncated on the west in order to leave space for the sanctuary of Athena Nike, which was located on a narrow bastion, later to be crowned by a little Ionic temple. It was felt, however, that the facades on both sides of the entranceway had to match, so the architect erected three columns framed by two antae, although the west anta was free-standing, with no wall behind it. The visitor would see a tristyle *in antis* facade to both left and right, not immediately realizing that the one to the south was in fact false.

The concern for the viewer shown by the plan of the Propylaia, with its two large wings sweeping out to enfold the visitor and the false facade, was unusu-

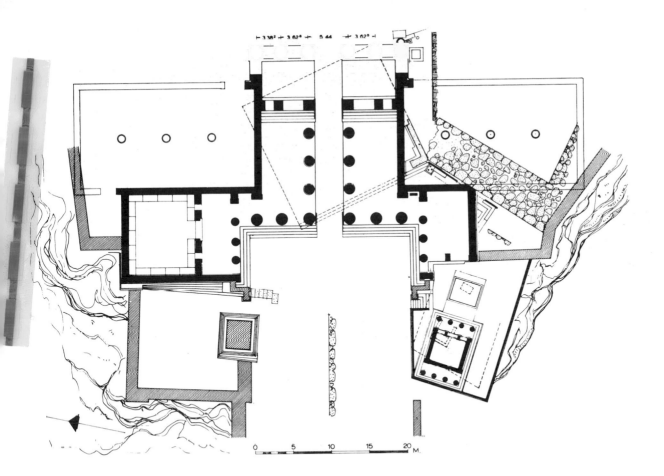

8.13 Plan of the Propylaia;[P] broken lines indicate pre-Persian buildings. From John Travlos, *Pictorial Dictionary of Ancient Athens* (New York: Praeger Publishers, 1971), p. 487, Fig. 613. By permission of John Travlos and Verlag Ernst Wasmuth, Tübingen.

al, perhaps unique for its time, but became increasingly manifest in Greek architecture in later years. The Propylaia and the Parthenon, with their parallel axes, were obviously part of the same general plan. The space around the Parthenon was cleared so that the first view of it from the Propylaia would be impressive (see Fig. 8.9). Such formal relationships of buildings were another feature that became more common in later times.

The Propylaia was built entirely of marble except for the dark Eleusinian limestone used for certain details, such as doorsills, where a contrasting color enhanced visibility and safety. This use of a darker accenting stone in marble buildings is another Periklean characteristic. The Doric order above the central entrance on the west carries three metopes rather than the customary two, to allow space for the ramp. This three-metope system is known to have been used in the early fifth century for short spans and by the end of the century was in use for long stretches, especially in stoas. The ceilings of the interior vestibules spanned some 5.48 meters, and the weight of solid marble beams and coffers has been estimated to deliver loads of over six tons on the epistyle below. In a rare and in fact unnecessary measure, the architect inserted iron beams in the tops of the epistyles to deflect the weight from the center of each marble epistyle and conduct it to the columns. The ceilings of the central halls remained intact into the Middle Ages.

The later years of the fifth century also witnessed the birth of a new order of architecture, the Corinthian order, which differed from the Ionic mainly in the vegetal shape of its capital. The Corinthian capital consists of a bell-shaped echinus decorated with spirals and vegetal motifs. Acanthus leaves reach up the bell from the base of the capital, and as time goes on more and more of the bell is covered by the advancing foliage. The first example of this type of capital that is known to us was used on the interior of the enigmatic but well-preserved temple of Apollo at Bassai, in the highlands of Arcadia (Fig. 8.14). This temple, which is unusual in its orientation (it runs north-south) and its interior arrangement (a sort of adyton, or shrine, lies behind the cella proper), was attributed to Iktinos in antiquity and presents more problems of chronol-

8.14 Temple of Apollo at Bassai.ᴾ Photo: Alison Frantz.

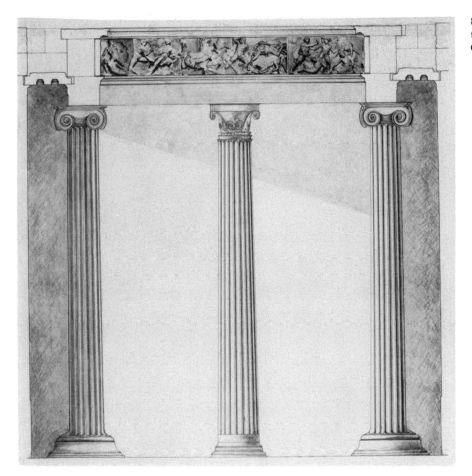

8.15 Reconstruction of the south end of the cella of the temple of Apollo, Bassai. Photo: Frederick A. Cooper.

ogy and interpretation than can be conveniently detailed here.[10] The interior has attached Ionic columns with large, spreading bases and a single free-standing Corinthian column opposite the entrance at the end (Fig. 8.15). Above the epistyle, where it would be difficult to see, runs a continuous sculptured frieze that stylistically dates toward the end of the century, although work on the building probably began somewhat earlier. The frieze is discussed further below.

SECULAR ARCHITECTURE

In the Agora, a great amount of rebuilding was undertaken to repair the considerable damage inflicted by the Persian invasion. The city offices along the foot of Kolonas Agoraios were rebuilt (Fig. 8.16). A round building (the Tholos) was constructed for the working committee of the council, probably in the decade 470–460, and a building with orchestra-shaped seating arrange-

[10] A number of studies have attempted to explain Bassai's peculiarities. Frederick A. Cooper, *The Temple of Apollo at Bassai: A Preliminary Study* (New York and London, 1978), gives tentative explanations. The completion of the building may have extended into the first decade of the fourth century. The definitive study of the temple continues in the series *The Temple of Apollo Bassitas*, edited by Frederick A. Cooper under the auspices of the American School of Classical Studies. So far vol. 2, *The Sculpture*, by Brian C. Madigan (Princeton, 1992), and vol. 4, a collection of plans and drawings by Cooper (Princeton, 1992), have appeared.

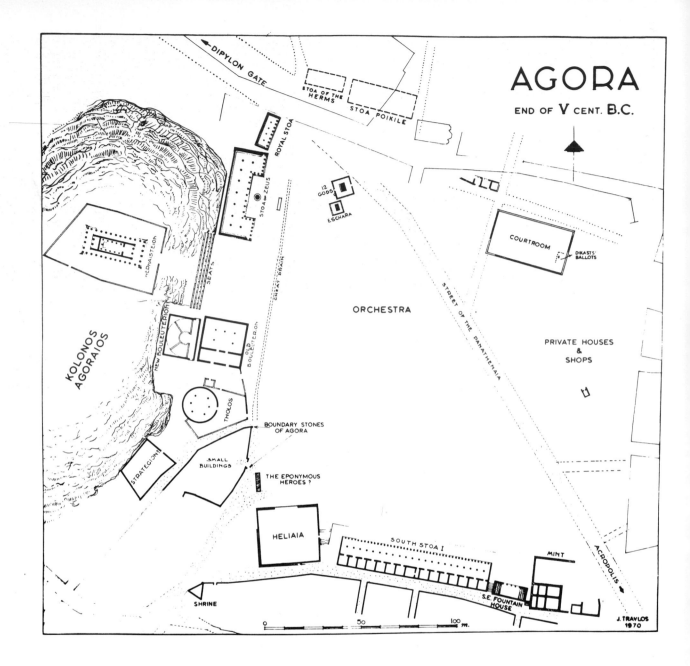

AGORA

END OF V CENT. B.C.

8.16 Plan of the Agora at Athens at the end of the fifth century. Photo: American School of Classical Studies at Athens: Agora Excavations.

ments was built for the council meetings. This new construction was placed behind the old Bouleuterion, which was probably restored to serve as an annex and place to store records.

Several stoas were built in the Agora in the fifth century, and a new type was erected just south of the old Royal Stoa. This stoa, sacred to Zeus, contained a number of features that were introduced in the last third of the fifth century and later became standard. Its two projecting wings, each bearing six columns, were treated like temple facades. The central portion of the building employed a three-metope system that recalls the central span of the Propylaia. Unfluted Ionic columns stood inside—a feature that became common in later stoas.

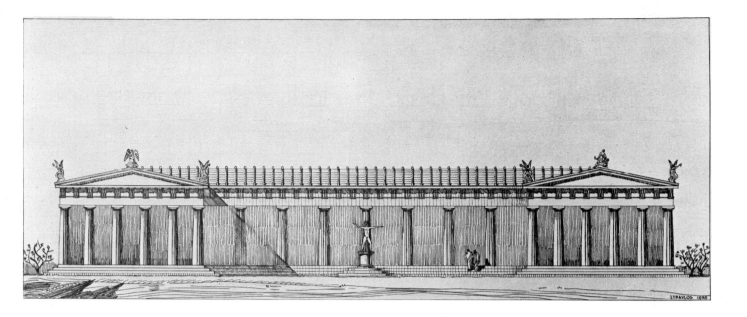

8.17 The Stoa of Zeus,[P] Athens, as it appeared in the fifth century. Photo: American School of Classical Studies at Athens: Agora Excavations.

There were no rooms behind the interior colonnade, however, such as appeared in other contemporary stoas in the Agora and elsewhere. A statue of Zeus may have stood on a round base between the two wings (Fig. 8.17). The Stoa of Zeus may have been begun about 430 and completed after the peace of 421.

The rebuilding of the Agora was a piecemeal affair, with little attention apparently being given to planned effect. By the end of the century the classical Agora was more or less complete; only minor additions and rebuildings were undertaken during the next two centuries. The planning of architectural units in a fixed scheme was in the air, however.

The ancient sources credit the inception of formal city planning to Hippodamos of Miletos.[11] It is unlikely that this shadowy figure actually invented the concept of streets crossing at right angles, the gridiron approach, for earlier examples are known, but he took part in a number of projects and must have been the leading proponent of city planning. He planned the layout of Athens' port, Peiraeus, in the second quarter of the century. Although the ancient remains are hidden under modern buildings, boundary stones have been found to attest to the division of the city into recognized quarters. Excavations in Miletos have found evidence of a grid town plan, and other cities from this time on adopted similarly regular layouts.

About 432 at Olynthos, in northern Greece, a new quarter was established which provides a good example of grid planning (Fig. 8.18). Several broad avenues ran north and south, intersected at regular intervals by east–west streets. The blocks thus formed were rigidly filled with houses, five on the north and five on the south of each block with a narrow alley separating their

[11] The basic work in English on Greek city planning and urban development is R. E. Wycherley, *How the Greeks Built Cities*, 2d ed. (paperback) (New York, 1969). A good, short discussion of Hippodamos is to be found in the excellent volume by J. B. Ward-Perkins, *Cities of Ancient Greece and Italy: Planning in Classical Antiquity* (New York, 1974). See also E. J. Owens, *The City in the Greek and Roman World* (London and New York, 1991), chaps. 2–5.

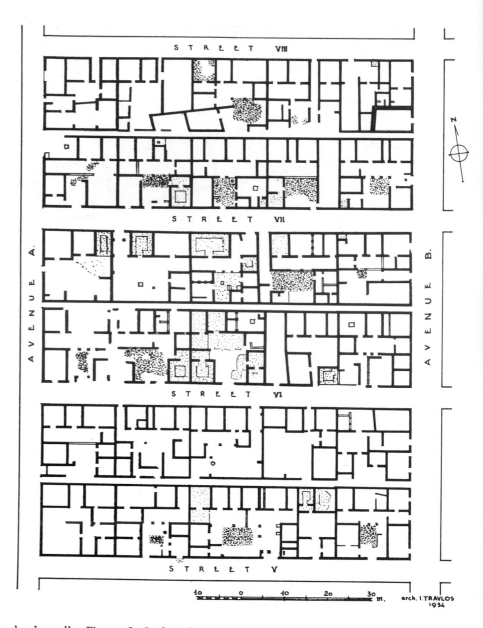

8.18 Plan of house blocks at Olynthos.P From David M. Robinson and J. Walter Graham, *The Hellenic House,* Excavations at Olynthus series, vol. 8, Plate 94. Copyright 1938, The Johns Hopkins Press.

back walls. Figure 8.18 also shows the typical house plan in this section of Olynthos during the period between 432 and the destruction of the city by philip of Macedon in 348.

The typical Olynthian house faced inward, as most Mediterranean houses still do, with an unobtrusive entrance from the street. Beyond an inner courtyard, often cobbled, lay a long rectangular room, called the pastas by the excavators. The remaining rooms on the ground floor opened off the pastas or the court. Their purposes cannot usually be determined, although the dining or entertainment room, the andron, can often be identified by its internal arrangement to accommodate dining couches. An upper floor that probably contained sleeping rooms and storage areas completed the typical Olynthian house.[12]

[12] Olynthian houses are discussed in D. M. Robinson and J. W. Graham, *The Hellenic House,* Excavations at Olynthus, pt. 8 (Baltimore, 1938).

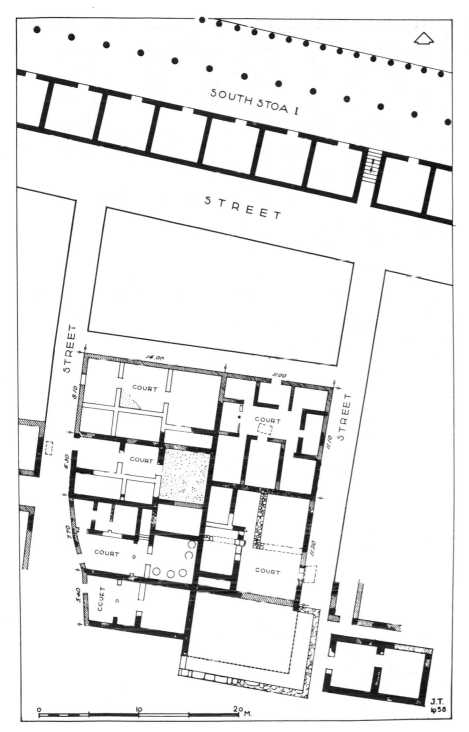

8.19 Plan of houses south of the Agora in Athens. Photo: American School of Classical Studies at Athens: Agora Excavations.

The usual housing in old cities was probably less formal than that found in the new area of Olynthos; sprawling ramshackle constructions took up all available space. The plan of a block of houses found at Athens is shown in Fig. 8.19. A courtyard is perhaps the only recurring feature; around it are grouped a few rooms of no regular plan, as in simple dwellings of almost all

8.20 Reconstruction of the Dema house, Attica: *A*, plan; *B*, front elevation with court wall removed. From J. E. Jones, L. H. Sackett, and A. J. Graham, "The Dema House in Attica," *Annual of the British School at Athens* 57 (1962): 75–114, Fig. 13. By permission of the British School at Athens.

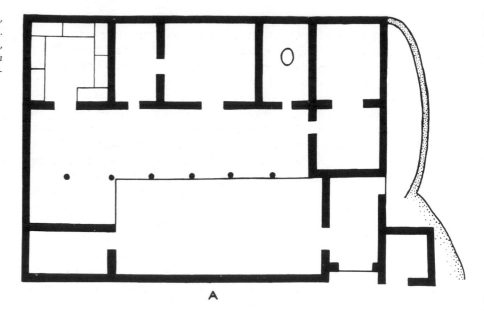

A

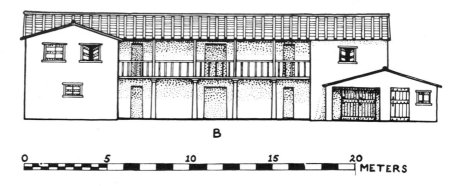

B

periods in Greece. The construction was simple, consisting of mud brick and wood on a stone foundation.

An interesting country farmhouse of the late fifth century has been found in western Attica (Fig. 8.20). This relatively large pastas-style house (22 by 16 meters overall), probably with two stories and courtyard, gives us some indication of what the country establishments of the relatively prosperous looked like.[13]

SCULPTURE

The increased roundness and three-dimensionality apparent in the individual figures of the east pediment at Aigina are apparent also in such free-standing statues as the so-called Omphalos Apollo, found in Athens (Fig. 8.21). This is a much more lifelike figure than the Kritios boy, displaying a more fully developed representation of anatomy. It is but a step from this figure to Polykleitos' famous Spear Bearer (see Fig. 8.35). The Omphalos Apollo, however, is a Ro-

[13] This and other buildings are discussed in J. E. Jones, L. H. Sackett, and A. J. Graham, "The Dema House in Attica," *BSA* 57 (1962): 75–114.

man copy of a Greek original bronze, and this fact brings up a problem in identification and interpretation which is unique to Greek sculpture.

The Romans were great collectors, and works of what was for them already ancient Greek art were especially prized. Statues were carried off by the shipload from Greek lands both as war loot and as "collectibles." The source was soon exhausted, however, so the practice of making copies of works of famous artists of the past became a thriving business. With the loss of the original statues, we must depend mainly on Roman copies for an idea of the style of the famous artists of Greece. Unfortunately, there are serious drawbacks to our enforced reliance on copies made for the Roman market. Copies of Greek originals were made in many ways by artists of widely varying abilities. A statue could be copied more or less freehand or by means of a "pointing machine" that gave almost exact reproductions.[14] Further problems arise in the ease with which a given type—for instance, a young athlete—could be changed into another type, such as Hermes, by the simple addition of an attribute by the copyist. Depending as we do on ancient authors' relatively vague references to particular works, we are often reduced to trying to pick out a likely reproduction of a famous statue from among a host of copies of varying quality. Further, once it is thought that a known work of a famous artist can be identified, one can never be certain how faithful the copy is to the original, or, when faced with varying treatments of such details as hair, which example is likely to have belonged to the original statue. These problems make the definite identification of the works of a particular sculptor and analysis of his style tricky at best, though this difficulty has not deterred the publication of numerous learned studies of individual artists. The knowledge that can be gained from meager evidence is incredible, but it is as well to remember the problems involved.

A few original works remain to us from the first half of the century, but none that can be definitely attributed to a known artist. A large bronze statue of a god, probably Zeus, found in the sea shows the characteristics of the new style (Fig. 8.22).[15] The Zeus is larger than life-size, standing some 2.09 meters tall. He is shown just as he is about to throw his weapon, a thunderbolt. His right arm is pulled back and his left extends toward the target. He stands firmly on one foot while the other only lightly touches the ground. The resulting extended pose expresses the momentary action, but there is no differentiation between expanded and contracted muscles. The figure is not really as three-dimensional as it may look. It is in fact rather flat, extending outward in only one plane, and is meant to be viewed from one angle, from which the triangularity of the extended pose can be appreciated. The head, with the elaborate hair treatment and great beard, captures the majesty and power of the traditional gods, superior beings in human form (Fig. 8.23). The loss of the eyes, which must have been inlaid in another material, now gives even greater power to the face. One

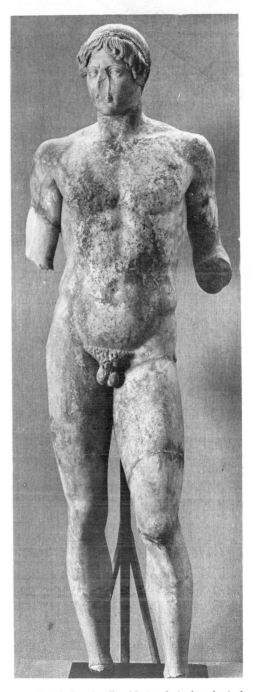

8.21 Omphalos Apollo. National Archaeological Museum, Athens. Photo: Deutsches Archäologisches Institut, Athens.

[14] The pointing process and the various methods of copying are discussed in G. M. A. Richter, *The Portraits of the Greeks*, 3 vols. (London, 1965), vol. 1, pp. 24–28. Studies of the subject and the problems are Margarete Bieber, *Ancient Copies: Contributions to the History of Greek and Roman Art* (New York, 1977), and Brunhilde Sismondo Ridgway, *Roman Copies of Greek Sculpture: The Problem of the Originals* (Ann Arbor, 1984).
[15] The bronze found in the sea off Cape Artemision is not unanimously accepted as Zeus. The alternate candidate is Poseidon. Since the two were brothers, perhaps the difference is not of great significance. The best argument in English for the identification as Zeus is given in G. E. Mylonas, "The Bronze Statue from Artemision," *AJA* 48 (1944): 143–160.

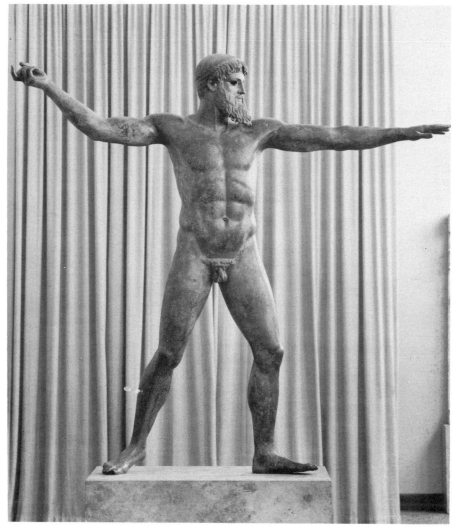

8.22 Zeus from the Sea.ᴾ National Archaeological Museum, Athens. Photo: Hirmer Fotoarchiv, Munich.

8.23 Detail of the head of the Zeus from the Sea. National Archaeological Museum, Athens. Photo: Alison Frantz.

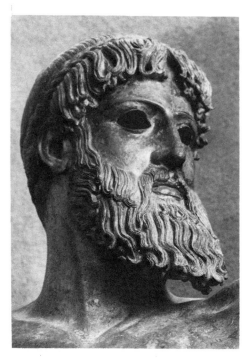

must imagine the sanctuaries of Greece crowded by forests of bronze statues such as the Zeus—now practically all vanished into the melting pot.[16]

The extended pose seen in the Zeus can be found also in one of the most famous statues of antiquity, the Diskobolos (Discus Thrower) of Myron (Fig. 8.24). The works of Myron, who worked in the middle years of the fifth century, display Severe as well as High Classical characteristics. His innovations in pose and composition were not paralleled until Hellenistic times. Unfortunately, his work is known only through Roman copies, and only one or two statues are securely attributed to him.

[16] Weight alone would have precluded the casting of a statue the size of the Zeus in solid bronze. Large bronze statues were generally made in pieces, which were later joined by rivets, dowels, or solder. Portions of large statues were often made by the lost-wax method, in which a wax model is molded over a core and encased in a clay mantle. The entire object is then heated. The wax melts and runs out, leaving a space between the core and the mantle, which is filled with molten bronze. When it has cooled, the mantle is broken away, leaving the bronze. The core may or may not be removed. For the techniques of bronze casting and a survey of bronze statuary see Denys Haynes, *The Technique of Greek Bronze Statuary* (Mainz am Rhein, 1992); Carol C. Mattusch, *Greek Bronze Statuary* (Ithaca, N.Y., 1984) and *Classical Bronzes* (Ithaca, N.Y., 1996).

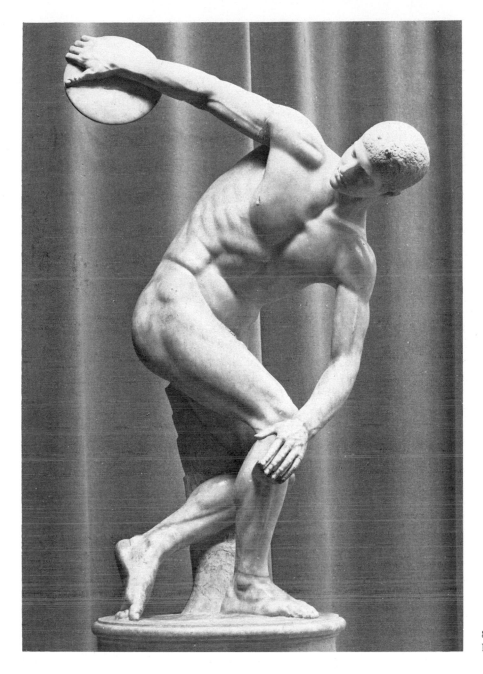

8.24 Diskobolos. Museo Nazionale, Rome. Photo: Deutsches Archäologisches Institut, Rome.

The Diskobolos, originally in bronze, shares with the Zeus an openness of form and a static anatomy in which the tension of the various parts of the body are hardly reflected. This figure, too, is meant to be viewed from only one angle; from the rear it appears impossibly balanced, and it is extremely flat. The human body cannot flatten itself to the extent shown here, as numerous athletes can attest. The simplification of features, here idealized without individuality or emotion, is particularly striking. The head could easily be taken from the body and set up as a bust, so divorced is it from the action of the body below it. In general, the figure forms a beautiful, clear pattern—a legacy of earlier times but with idealized musculature and features.

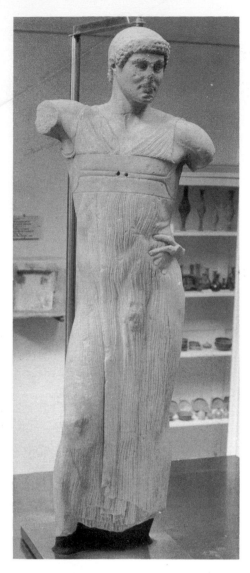

8.25 The Charioteer of Motya. Motya, Whitaker Museum. Photo courtesy of Malcolm Bell.

Despite scholars' confidence in their ability to discern artistic movements such as the Severe style, archaeologists occasionally produce something to remind them of the depth of their ignorance. The discovery of a larger-than-life-size marble statue (Fig. 8.25) in A.D. 1979 at the Carthaginian site of Motya in western Sicily is a case in point. The Severe-looking head in combination with the curving pose confuses the viewer. The wide belt, if that is what it is, over the semitransparent garment is also unusual. The figure has been dubbed the Charioteer because of that long, clinging garment, but the placement of the arms makes it unlikely that it represents a charioteer. Many alternative identifications have been suggested—a hero, a historical personage, a local worthy, a priest for a Phoenician god. Most authorities assign the statue to the first half of the century.[17]

The sculptures of the temple of Zeus at Olympia sum up the nature of the Severe style of the first half of the fifth century. The two pediments, particularly in composition, show the familiar combination of characteristics.[18] In the east pediment the subject is the preparation for a chariot race—not any chariot race, but that in which the hero Pelops by a trick defeats and kills King Oinomaos, winning the princess Hippodameia and the kingdom (Fig. 8.26). The subject must have been well known to the visitors to the temple, for Pelops had been worshiped at Olympia since early times. The moment just before the action is represented here. Zeus, the arbiter, stands between the two contestants, inclining his head toward Pelops, to his right.[19] The central group of figures is closed by two horsedrawn chariots. The use of long-bodied animals is an old-fashioned device, but the horses are a legitimate part of this story. Behind are kneeling and reclining figures that fill up the pediment space.

The west pediment contains a scene of action (Fig. 8.27). Again a large central figure dominates, this time Apollo. The subject is the battle between the human Lapiths and the bestial centaurs at the wedding feast of the Lapith king. From the great central figure of Apollo, one of the most imposing figures to come down to us (Fig. 8.28), who stretches out his hand to calm the uproar, great two- and three-figure groups of struggling bodies sink down toward each angle of the pediment. Again the corners are closed by reclining spectators. The equine bodies of the centaurs again perform the useful function of filling the reduced space, aided by the very carefully arranged composition. The action seems to roll right and left from the central figure only to bound

[17] A short statement and bibliography are provided in Brian Sparkes, *Greek Art* (Oxford, 1991), p. 14.

[18] The best discussion of the sculptures from Olympia is to be found in Bernard Ashmole and Nicholas Yalouris, *The Sculptures of the Temple of Zeus* (London, 1967). Ashmole's later thoughts on the temple and the sculpture are presented in his *Architect and Sculptor in Classical Greece* (New York, 1972), pp. 1–89.

[19] The exact arrangement of the figures in the east pediment is uncertain. The problem well illustrates the difficulties encountered in one of our major sources of knowledge about the monuments of ancient Greece. In the second century of our era a traveler, Pausanias, wrote a sort of guidebook on mainland Greece, in which he described many of the monuments and works of art that he saw on his travels. The vagueness of his descriptions and his apparent errors, however, have given rise to scholarly controversies. In writing of the east pediment at Olympia, Pausanias said that Oinomaos stood at the right of the central figure, without making it clear whether the point of view was that of the central figure or of the spectator. For Pausanias' work, see the old but still basic study and translation by J. G. Frazer, *Pausanias's Description of Greece* (reprinted New York, 1965). For a recent statement on the problem, with bibliography, see Andrew Stewart, *Greek Sculpture: An Exploration* (New Haven, 1990), pp. 142–146.

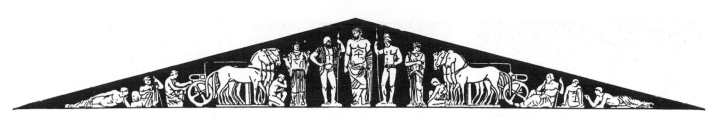

8.26 Temple of Zeus at Olympia:[P] reconstruction of the east pediment, after Franz Studniczka. From Reinhard Lullies and Max Hirmer, *Greek Sculpture* (New York: Harry N. Abrams, 1960), p. 73. Fig. 5. By permission of Hirmer Verlag, Munich.

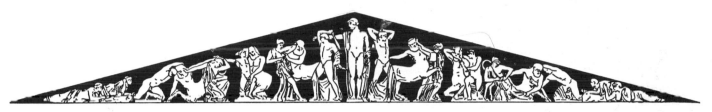

8.27 Temple of Zeus at Olympia: reconstruction of the west pediment, after Georg Treu. From Reinhard Lullies and Max Hirmer, *Greek Sculpture* (New York: Harry N. Abrams, 1960), p. 73, Fig. 6. By permission of Hirmer Verlag, Munich.

back from the corners, through the interlocked yet clearly distinguishable figures.

A closer look at some of the individual figures from these great compositions reveals the style. The figure that originally was placed third from the right on the east pediment, directly behind the chariot, is generally identified as an old seer (Fig. 8.29). Supporting himself on a now missing staff, he peers toward the central group with a hand-to-mouth gesture that is interpreted as one of horror and anxiety at the event and what it entails for the future. (A whole history of misfortunes had its origin in the Pelops story, a fact evidently known to the seer and presumably to the viewer.) The attempt at realism in the depiction of the old man is extraordinary: the flabby musculature, the receding hairline, the wrinkled forehead. The expression is all on the surface, like a mask, but such an impulse toward realism was to disappear in the second half of the century under the idealism of Phidian sculpture. Idealism is of course dominant in the superhuman Apollo and even in the all-too-human Lapiths who struggle with the centaurs. The third figure to the left of Apollo in the west pediment, being attacked by a grimacing centaur, whom she elbows in the head, maintains a calm expression in the midst of the battle (Fig. 8.30). Most of the humans, in fact, appear calm; only the centaurs snarl and rage, contorting their features. Such idealization probably symbolizes here the superiority of civilized beings, in contrast to the uncivilized forces of nature; yet some of the humans, too, display natural emotions in occasional open mouths, pinched features, and lined foreheads. This contrast between what may be called the real and the ideal can also be seen in such details as a centaur's hand closing on the leg of a woman who is trying to flee (Fig. 8.31). The hand and the woman's foot are rendered in extreme detail, even to the veins in the hand, and the pressure on the material is well shown—yet the drapery subsides into a highly decorative fold.

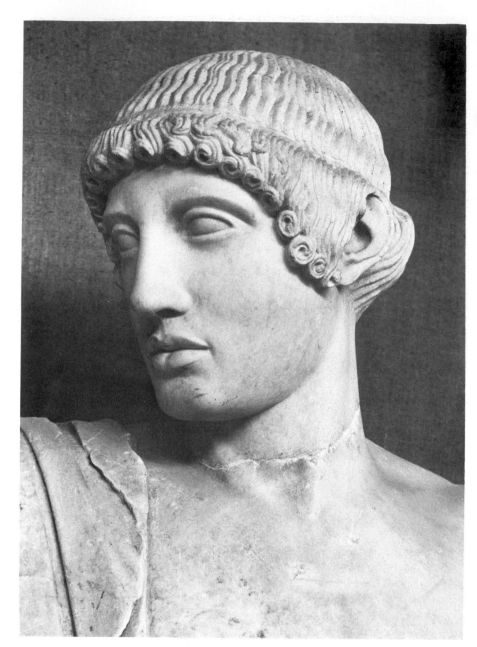

8.28 Detail of the head of Apollo from the west pediment of the temple of Zeus at Olympia. Archaeological Museum, Olympia. Photo: Alison Frantz.

The metopes of the temple of Zeus represent for the first time the twelve canonical labors of Herakles, six at each end of the building, over the pronaos and opisthodomos porches. The compositions tend to be patterned on geometrical shapes—crosses, verticals, triangles—to fit into the square space available. In the scene with the Cretan Bull (Fig. 8.32) some ingenuity was used in a crossing pattern to squeeze the great animal and the hero into the small space. Quieter scenes were also shown. A simple composition of three verticals makes up the scene of the labor of the Apples of the Hesperides (Fig. 8.33). Atlas has returned with the apples in his hand, and Herakles, who earlier took the world from the giant's shoulders, considers how to reverse their positions. Athena is

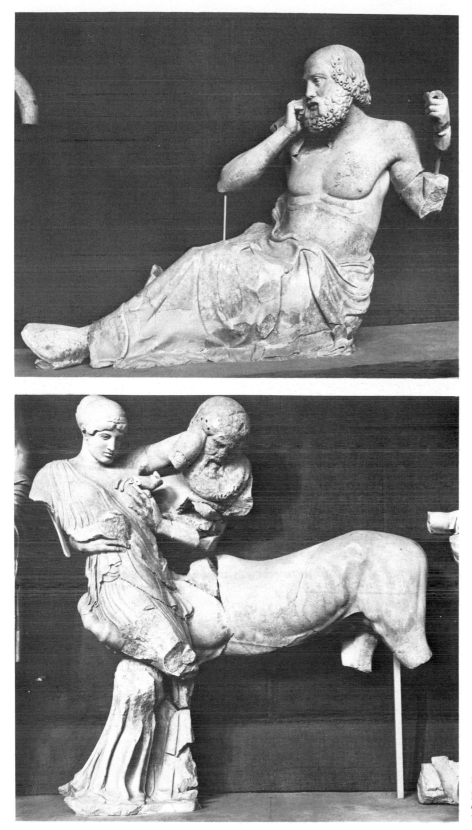

8.29 Old seer from the east pediment of the temple of Zeus at Olympia. Archaeological Museum, Olympia. Photo: Alison Frantz.

8.30 Lapith woman and centaur from the west pediment of the temple of Zeus at Olympia. Archaeological Museum, Olympia. Photo: Alison Frantz.

221

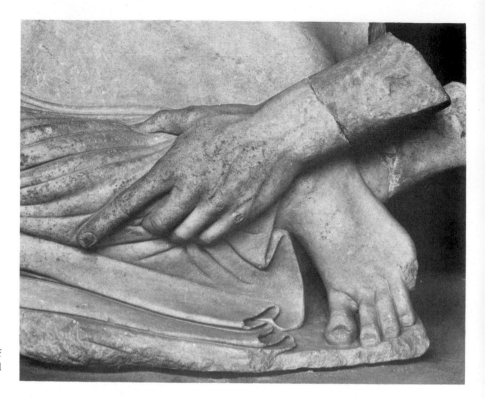

8.31 Detail of a group from the west pediment of the temple of Zeus at Olympia. Archaeological Museum, Olympia. Photo: Alison Frantz.

present, helping to support the burden with one hand, and Herakles has arranged a cushion to help ease the weight. These three dignified figures are shown in monumental simplicity. The Athena is especially handsome, wearing a plain peplos that falls in straight vertical folds broken slightly by the right leg to suggest the body beneath. As the daughter of Zeus, she is able to support the world with one hand. This is again an old-fashioned composition, with its three vertical figures, but the unusual character of the scene and the monumentality of the figures go well beyond earlier conceptions.

The second half of the century was dominated by the High Classical style of Phidias and his circle. Phidias was famous for his colossal chryselephantine (gold and ivory) cult statues, particularly the Zeus in Olympia (see Fig. 8.2) and the Athena in the Parthenon, to be discussed later. Attributions to him of various Roman copies are disputed. Two bronze statues, recovered from the sea at Riace in Italy, appear to date from Phidias' time and have even been attributed to him (Fig. 8.34). There are so few original large bronzes that these figures assume great importance. Their identification (heroes? gods? warriors? generals? athletes?) is still under discussion.[20]

Polykleitos was a Peloponnesian sculptor who was known for his idealized humans.[21] The most famous of his works, the Doryphoros or Spear Bearer, known from a number of copies, was highly praised in antiquity and has exercised great influence ever since (Fig. 8.35). The figure is shown striding forward, holding a spear, now missing, over his shoulder. The original, doubt-

---

[20] See Mattusch, *Greek Bronze Statuary*, pp. 200–208.
[21] Stewart, *Greek Sculpture*, pp. 160–163. A well-illustrated short study of this sculptor is Cornelius Vermeule, *Polykleitos* (Boston, 1969).

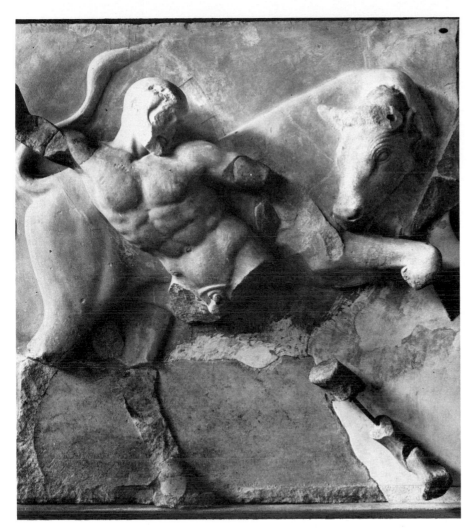

8.32 Metope of the Cretan Bull from the temple of Zeus at Olympia. Archaeological Museum, Olympia. Photo: Alison Frantz.

less made of bronze, would have had no need for the supporting tree trunk that has necessarily been included in the marble copy. The close-knit musculature, with the major divisions of the body clearly marked, and the idealized head with close-cropped hair are typical, as is the stance. The man rests his weight on his right leg while the left is pulled back and to one side, with the foot resting lightly on its toes. This suggestion of shifted weight is reflected in the makeup of the whole, in which a rhythm of tension and relaxation is achieved. Thus the right arm hangs straight and free while the opposite left leg is bent without tension. The left arm and the right leg similarly oppose each other. The head is inclined slightly toward the engaged leg. The whole composition produces a freedom and sense of movement not achieved before. The stance is often described by the Italian word *contrapposto* (counterpoise) and is from this time on a constantly recurring pose in art.

Figures 8.36 and 8.37 show a Roman copy generally thought to reproduce another of Polykleitos' bronzes. This, the Diadoumenos, or Fillet Binder, is considered to be a somewhat later work than the Doryphoros because of the

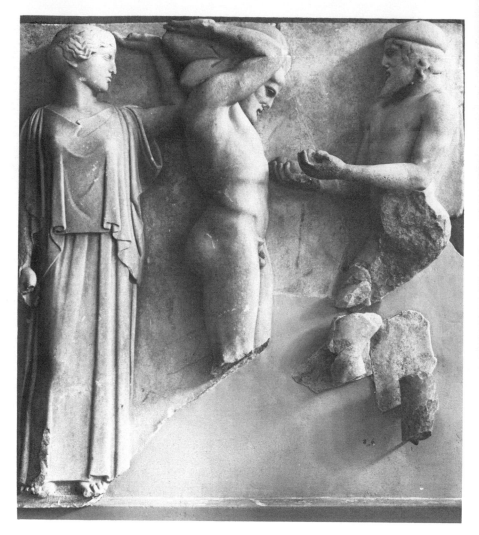

8.33 Metope of the Apples of the Hesperides from the temple of Zeus at Olympia. Archaeological Museum, Olympia. Photo: Alison Frantz.

more open form and advanced composition. The musculature and features, however, indicate the same artist.

The Doryphoros is said to embody "the canon of Polykleitos," the sculptor's ideal of human proportions, and attempts to explain this canon by observations and theories have been a favorite pursuit of scholars. The lack of any originals and the ambiguous nature of the literary evidence has made the problem fiendishly complicated. Most scholars feel that the canon rests on mathematical or geometrical relationships of proportions. Others, noting the lack of success in deriving any system from a study of the various copies, have suggested that the sculptor willfully deviated from an ideally proportioned body in order to give the figure the illusion of life; the parts of the human body, after all, bear no precise mathematical relationship to each other. This line of reasoning might be extended to explain the refinements of the Parthenon.[22]

[22] The best expression of this theory in relation to the famous canon is to be found in Rhys Carpenter, *The Esthetic Basis of Greek Art* (Bloomington, Ind., 1959), pp. 124–126. This whole problem revolves around the interpretation of the literary references. See the treatment of this and similar problems in J. J. Pollitt, *The Ancient View of Greek Art* (New Haven, 1974). See also Stewart, *Greek Sculpture*.

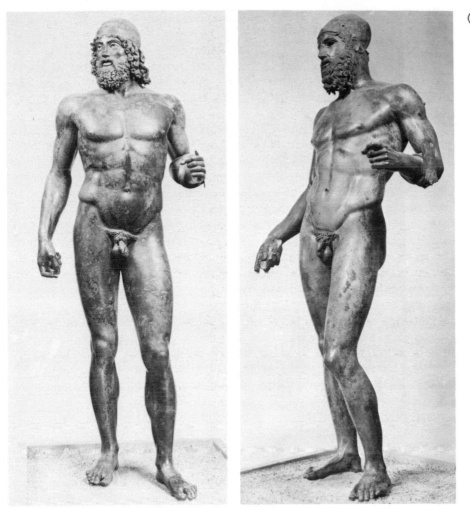

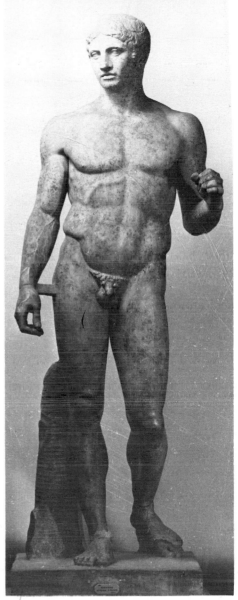

8.34 Bronze statues from Riace. Photo: Alinari/ Art Resource, New York.

The sculptures of the Parthenon hold the same high place as representatives of their age as do the sculptures of the temple of Zeus at Olympia.[23] The great building, exceedingly elaborate in its decoration and constructed largely with money collected from tributaries, not only had sculpture in all the metopes and both pediments (see Fig. 8.9) but also had a sculptured frieze on the outside of the cella wall within the colonnade. This frieze, almost 160 meters long, ran all the way around the building at the top of the wall. Phidias was in overall charge of the Periklean program on the Acropolis and of course made the cult statue for the building. Although his hand cannot be detected among the surviving sculptures, the elaborate and carefully planned program of decoration needed a single author, and one is probably right in seeing the sculptor's influence throughout.

Perikles' building program must have employed an army of artists of diverse

[23] The bibliography on the sculpture of the Parthenon is vast. A general survey is John Boardman and David Finn, *The Parthenon and Its Sculptures* (Austin, 1985). For the frieze: Martin Robertson and Alison Frantz, *The Parthenon Frieze* (New York, 1975), and Ian Jenkins, *The Parthenon Frieze* (Austin, 1994). For the Athena Parthenos: Neda Leipen, *Athena Parthenos* (Toronto, 1971).

8.35 Doryphoros. Museo Nazionale, Naples. Photo: Deutsches Archäologisches Institut, Rome.

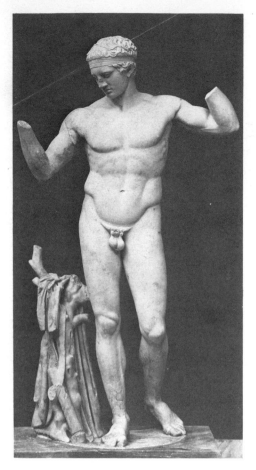

8.36 Diadoumenos. National Archaeological Museum, Athens. Photo: Deutsches Archäologisches Institut, Athens.

training and abilities. Diversity of quality and style are most clearly seen in the metopes. Most of the Parthenon's metopes have been destroyed; those that have survived are mainly from a series depicting Lapiths and centaurs in battle. Other groups included Greeks against Amazons, gods versus giants, and the sack of Troy. In the two metopes shown in Figures 8.38 and 8.39 the differences in composition and style can be clearly seen. The inclusion of long-bodied centaurs allowed the artist various imaginative possibilities in filling the available square space, but the composition of metope 31 (Fig. 8.38) is static and retarded. The linear treatment of the Lapith's chest muscles reminds one of the Severe style. It is generally held that the weaker metopes were the works of older artists, or of less accomplished ones not yet working in the style of the times. By contrast, metope 27 (Fig. 8.39) shows a successful composition and an advanced treatment of anatomy. The Lapith has seized the centaur with his left hand, and with feet braced and breath sucked in he stretches his right arm back to deliver the final blow. The Lapith's cloak, draped from both arms, hangs behind him, forming a background originally painted blue, against which the body stood out. The cloak serves as a device to emphasize the thrusting bodies and provide unity and balance for the diverging movements. The audacity of the composition and the powerful treatment of the bodies make one easily overlook the fact that the centaur's tail merges with one of the folds of the cloak.

Probably the most original and debated portion of the Parthenon's sculptural decoration is the frieze (Fig. 8.40 and Color Plate 10, following p. 96). Beginning at the west end, a procession moves along both the north and south sides of the building to the east front, where a ritual appears to be taking place. Most scholars agree that the procession on the frieze relates to the Panathenaic procession, the most important ceremony of Athens, in which a new peplos was solemnly carried up to the Acropolis in Periklean times to drape the old olive-wood statue of Athena in a building on the site later occupied by the Erechtheion. Whether the procession that is shown on the Parthenon frieze represents a specific occasion or is intended to be a general, idealized representation of all such processions, the people taking part in it are unmistakably citizens of Athens. The representation of human activity, no matter how solemn and idealized, on a religious building instead of a mythological scene is unparalleled in Greek art up to this time, and must surely reflect the attitude of Perikles and his circle; no doubt it was seen as arrogance and sacrilege by many others.

The task of fitting a procession into a long, relatively narrow strip some twelve meters above the floor of the temple presented many problems, not the least of which was visibility. To deal with this difficulty the sculpture was brightly painted and embellished with metal accouterments, and each frieze block was made thicker at the top than at the bottom. The scene was thus tilted toward the spectators below. Monotony, always a problem in a procession scene, was avoided by varying the spacing of the figures, turning some (such as officials controlling the procession) against the flow of traffic, and introducing variety in the details. Figure 8.41 shows one of the slabs from the north side, bearing a bunched group of horsemen. Horsemen are usually shown strung out in a line; here they have momentarily come together. The sculptor's ability to indicate overlapping figures in a maximum depth of less than six centimeters is astonishing. The horses appear small in relation to the human figures, and all the riders' heads are at approximately the same level, but these problems are hardly noticed unless they are pointed out. Note the slight variations in the figures, such as the way one rider soothes his mount by resting his hand on its neck. Figure 8.42 shows some of the sacrificial cattle from the north frieze being conducted by solemn youths. One of the animals acts up, a minor happening, but one that adds interest and helps to avoid monotony. A detail of one of the youths is shown in Figure 8.43. The idealized, solemn countenance is that of a miniature adult. Even very young children are shown as idealized adults in High Classical sculpture, and representations of old age and deformity are rare.

The problem of interpretation is most acute on the east frieze, where two figures, a larger and a smaller, handle what appears to be a large square of cloth (Fig. 8.44). The cloth is usually taken to be Athena's peplos, but whether it is the new one brought by the procession or the old one and just what is happening to it are debatable. Groups of figures conversing quietly together and seated Olympian gods are shown flanking the central scene, as if waiting for the procession to arrive. The gods are evenly arranged on either side of the peplos scene, but with their backs turned to it. They appear to be talking to one another, although one, Aphrodite (missing in our Figure 8.44), points toward a

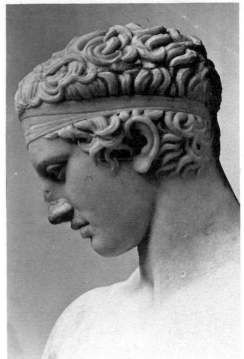

8.37 Diadoumenos: detail of head. National Archaeological Museum, Athens. Photo: Deutsches Archäologisches Institut, Athens.

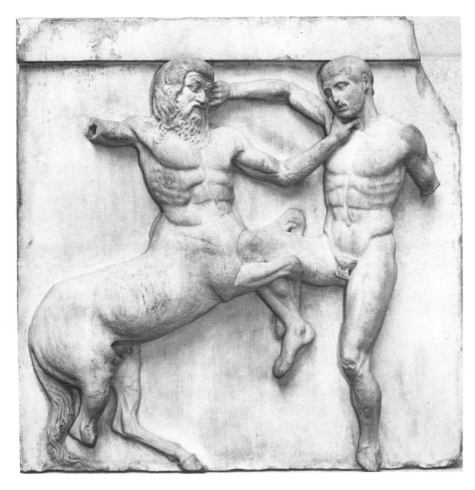

8.38 Parthenon metope 31: Lapith and centaur. Reproduced by courtesy of the Trustees of the British Museum, London.

227

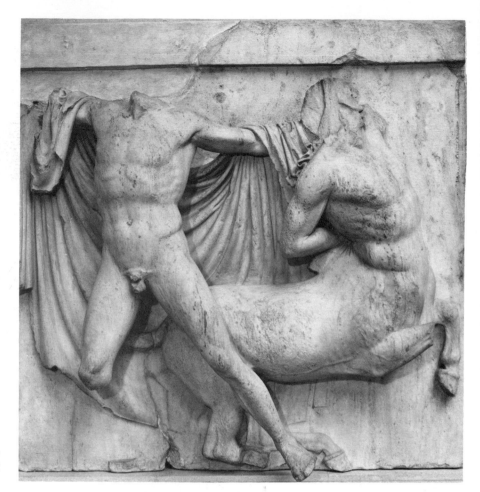

8.39 Parthenon metope 27: Lapith and centaur. Reproduced by courtesy of the Trustees of the British Museum, London.

group of standing men or perhaps beyond them to the procession. The seated god on the south end of the group clumsily overlaps the smaller mortal. Granted that the gods may be understood to be gathered somewhere removed from the principal scene, their large size and placement still seem peculiar; one expects something better in view of the masterful handling of the procession. The very placement of the Greek gods in the same scene with the people of Athens may have been considered enough of a departure from tradition, and conservatism, or perhaps political considerations, may have dictated the obvious attempt to separate god and mortal while still indicating a special relationship. We still do not fully understand the meaning of the Parthenon frieze.

The pediments, the last of the sculptural decoration to be completed, are dated between 437 and 432. They have unfortunately survived in extremely fragmentary condition. Although ancient sources tell us the general subject matter, various reconstructions are suggested for each pediment.

The subject of the west pediment is the contest between Athena and Poseidon for the land of Attica. The two gods are shown springing apart a moment after Athena has produced the miracle of her olive tree to win the contest (see Fig. 8.9). The pediment space was filled in a relatively crowded and conventional way, with horses and crouching, sitting, and reclining spectators.

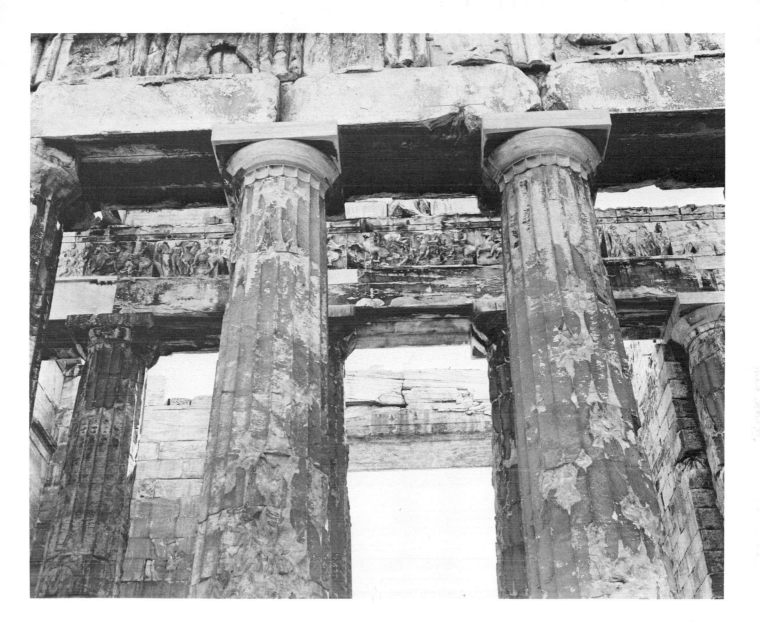

8.40 The Parthenon. Athens: view of west frieze from below. Photo: Alison Frantz.

More of the east pediment is preserved, although the central figures disappeared long ago when the building was turned into a Christian church. The subject is the birth of Athena, but without the central sculpture we cannot be certain how it was shown. Enough of the other figures are preserved to show that once again the moment immediately after the action was portrayed. Figure 8.45 represents a reconstruction of this pediment; Figures 8.46 and 8.47 show the remaining figures as they are preserved in the British Museum. As the news of the miraculous event radiates out from the center of the scene, the various figures react. At the right, or north side of the pediment, three female figures are seated facing outward, the one closest to the center looking back, just hearing of the event. To the left or south, a running figure communicates the news to a seated female figure, who raises her arms in excitement. Each end

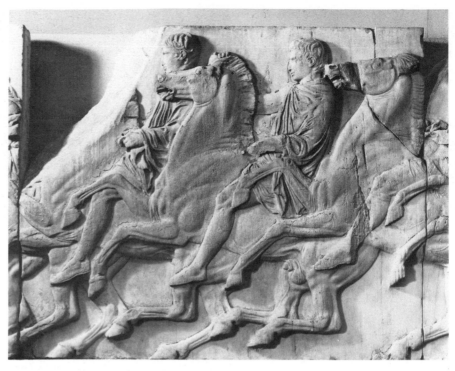

8.41 Parthenon frieze: horsemen. British Museum, London. Photo: Alison Frantz.

8.42 Parthenon frieze: sacrificial cattle. Acropolis Museum, Athens. Photo: Alison Frantz.

8.43 Parthenon frieze: detail of youth in cattle scene. Acropolis Museum, Athens. Photo: Alison Frantz.

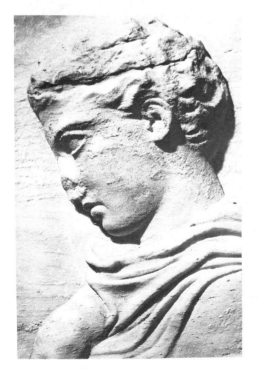

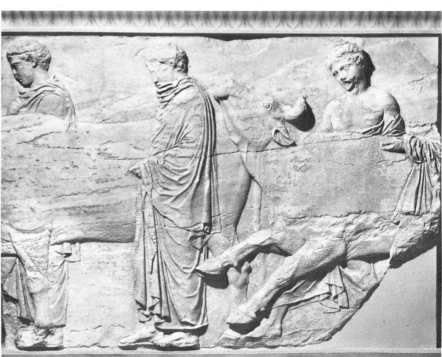

of the pediment is occupied by a reclining figure, back to the center, who has not yet heard the news and is intent on watching the new day dawn, or, more precisely, the departure of the chariot of the night at the north end and the arrival of the chariot of the sun at the south corner. The chariot of the sun

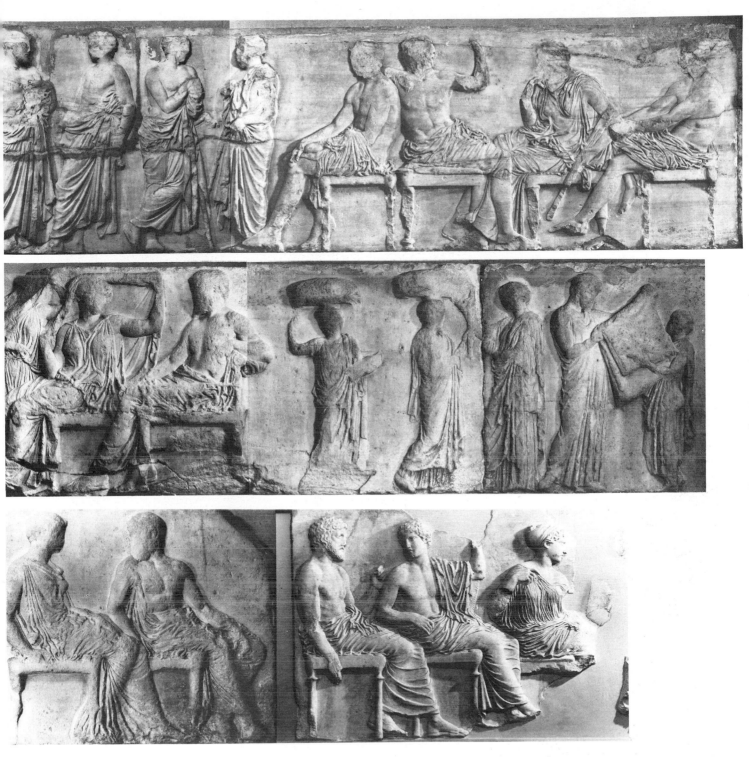

8.44 Parthenon east frieze: central portion as preserved in the British Museum. Photo: Alison Frantz.

actually rises up out of the floor of the pediment; only the heads of the four horses and the arms and head of the charioteer were shown. At the opposite corner the head of one of the horses of the moon goddess has been preserved,

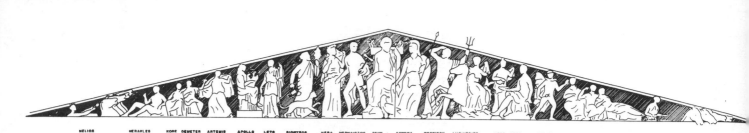

MELIOR   HERAKLES   KORE DEMETER ARTEMIS   APOLLO   LETO   DIONYSOS   HERA HEPHAISTOS ZEUS   ATHENA   POSEIDON AMPHITRITE   HEBE ARES   HERMES   HESTIA DIONE APHRODITE   SELENE

8.45 Parthenon: east pediment as restored by Evelyn B. Harrison. From Evelyn B. Harrison, "Athena and Athens in the East Pediment of the Parthenon," *American Journal of Archaeology* 71 (1967): 27–58, Plate 22, Fig. 30.

as has her torso, sinking through the floor. The sculptor has not only solved the pediment problem but gone beyond it to create the illusion of the rising sun and the setting moon, thus setting a time framework around his dramatic composition.

Details of the individual figures show the development in sculpture since the first half of the century. The reclining male figure, perhaps Dionysos or Herakles, although badly abraded by over two thousand years of weather, shows a full understanding of the body at rest, with swelling contours

8.46 Parthenon: preserved figures of south side of east pediment. Reproduced by courtesy of the Trustees of the British Museum, London.

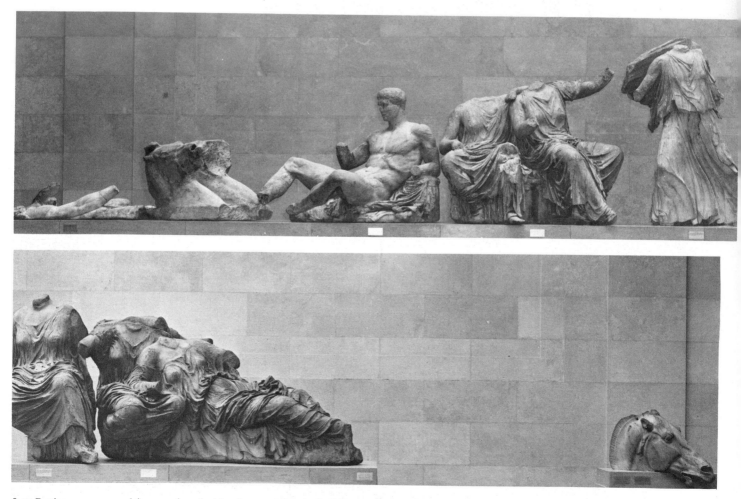

8.47 Parthenon: preserved figures of north side of east pediment. Reproduced by courtesy of the Trustees of the British Museum, London.

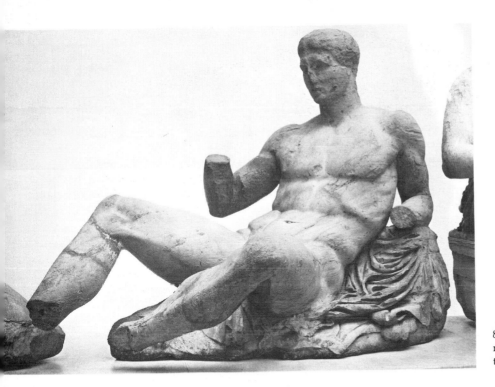

(Fig. 8.48). Heaviness and opulence can be seen in the seated and reclining figures on the other side of the gable (Fig. 8.49). Here the heavy forms are scarcely obscured by the elegant drapery, which is molded around them. The sculptor has finally learned to dig deeply into the marble, and the resulting

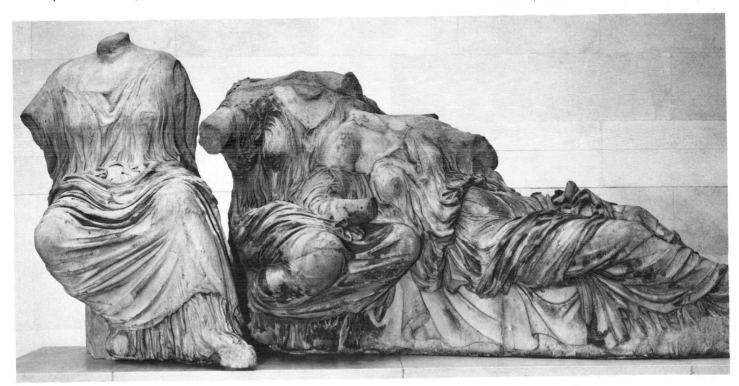

233

heavy folds and play of shadow suggest volume and modeling. The folds are still consciously arranged for decorative effect and the garments retain their own character, though they have become more transparent. The pediment figures are worked fully in the round, with a wealth of detail that could never have been seen from the ground. The overall quality of the carving is incredibly high, in fitting with the overall conception of the building.

This great elaborate building served as a house for Phidias' chryselephantine statue of the goddess, constructed on a wooden framework with removeable sheets of thin gold. We have some idea of the general nature of the figure from scanty descriptions and miniature representations of Roman times. The reconstruction, Figure 8.50, based on these sources, is a modern model of the statue

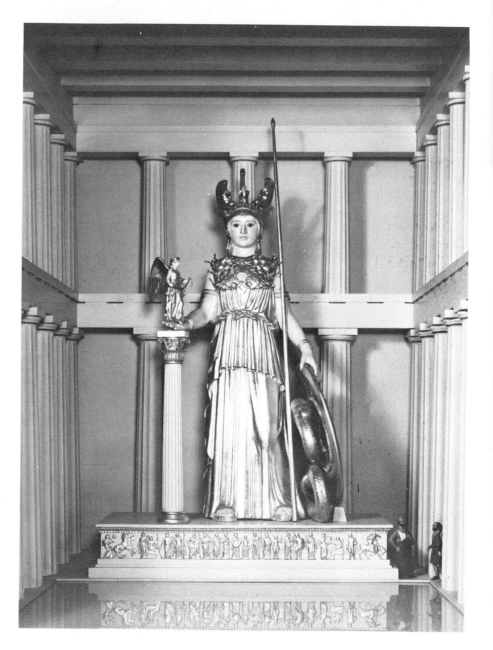

8.50 Model of the Athena Parthenos.ᴾ Photo: Royal Ontario Museum, Toronto.

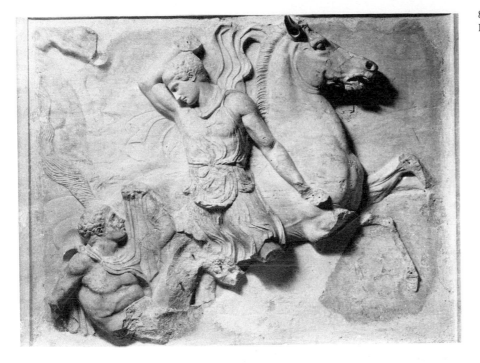

8.51 Relief from a monument. Villa Albani, Rome. Photo: Deutsches Archæologisches institut, Rome.

in the Royal Ontario Museum in Toronto. With only the light from the entrance to illuminate the statue, the effect on the visitor, stepping in from the bright sunlight, is not difficult to imagine.

The High Classical style of the Parthenon sculptures had great influence elsewhere. The relief in Figure 8.51, depicting a horseman about to strike an enemy, may have been a funeral monument and must have been carved by one of the masters who worked on the Parthenon frieze. The same detached monumental idealization is present in the human figures and the horse is very similar to those on the frieze.

Toward the end of the century, the restrained nature of High Classical art started to fade and more elaborate and highly decorated sculpture began to gain ascendancy. The frieze from the temple of Apollo at Bassai is as unusual as the architecture of the building. Battles of Greeks and Amazons (Fig. 8.52)

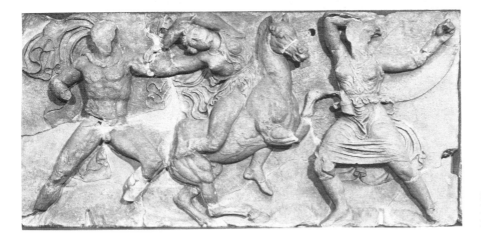

8.52 Amazonomachy on a frieze slab from Bassai. Reproduced by courtesy of the Trustees of the British Museum, London.

235

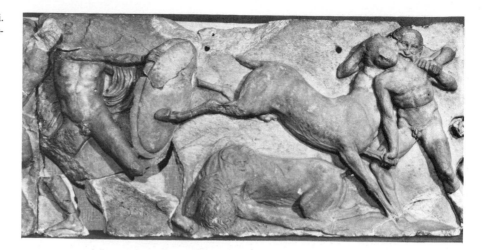

8.53 Centauromachy on a frieze slab from Bassai. Reproduced by courtesy of the Trustees of the British Museum, London.

and Greeks and centaurs (Fig. 8.53) are presented in high relief; some of the figures are actually modeled in the round. The quality of work is uneven, even crude in places, and the overall effect is one of ornate decoration somewhat divorced from the reality of battle, despite the undeniable brutality of the scenes. Visual references to the Parthenon sculptures abound and the figures' heads are generally idealized, but these sculptures differ noticeably from earlier works. Within a strict adherence to a frontal plain, which is never violated, the figures move back and forth and in and out of the background in twisted and agitated poses. The falling, whirling action is contained in set groups, making comprehension easy, and accented by flying drapery, sometimes only engraved. The drapery has now become quite transparent, emphasizing the plump bodies beneath.

The representation of clinging transparent drapery, the so-called wet-drapery style, was current at the end of the fifth century, and its most famous examples are found in Athens, on a parapet that surrounded the little Ionic temple of Athena Nike erected on the Acropolis in the last decade of the century. The relief depicts Victories (Nikai) erecting trophies or bringing sacrificial animals to Athena, and their elaborate draperies appear to have been the artist's main interest (Fig. 8.54).[24] When the fabric is pressed close to the body, its transparency is emphasized by shallow ridges; elsewhere it is deeply drilled to produce billowing folds independent of the anatomy beneath it. The emphasis on beautiful decoration is a departure from the style of the Parthenon sculptures, which show neither highly transparent draperies nor elegance and mannered gracefulness.

PAINTING AND MOSAICS

The fifth century produced wall paintings as well as sculpture. Our sources mention a number of painters, among whom Polygnotus and Mikon were outstanding. As their paintings are lost to us, we are reduced to reasoning back from the ancient sources and from painted scenes on some Red Figure vases.

Allied to painting is the art of mosaic, or the fitting together of colored stones

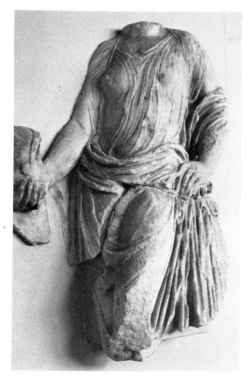

8.54 Standing Nike from the Nike Parapet. Acropolis Museum, Athens. By permission of the TAP Service, Athens. Photo: William R. Biers.

[24] The basic study of the parapet frieze is still Rhys Carpenter, *The Sculpture of the Nike Temple Parapet* (Cambridge, Mass., 1929).

236

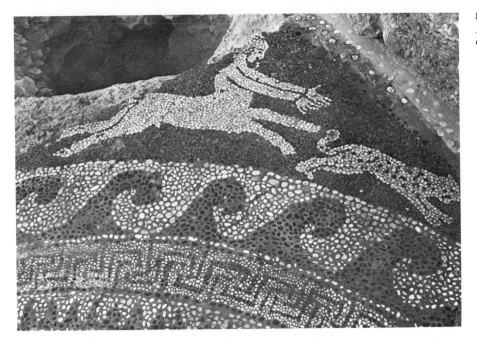

8.55 Corinth mosaic: centaur and feline. Photo: American School of Classical Studies at Athens: Corinth Excavations.

to form a picture or design. In Greece the technique was used to produce patterned floors. Stones were pressed into the still wet cement of the floor just after it had been laid. Often the finished floor was polished or cut down so that the surface would be as flat as possible. At first the stones were just natural pebbles, used as they were found. The earliest mosaic floors go back to the city of Gordion, in Phrygia, in the eighth and seventh centuries. The arrival of the technique in Greece is obscure, but by the fifth century isolated examples were in use. Floral patterns were popular, but by the end of the century figures began to appear. Modern excavations in Corinth have unearthed a pebble mosaic with a four-spoked wheel as a central motif and with figured scenes at the corners. At the northeast corner is preserved a centaur chasing a spotted feline (Fig. 8.55). Below them, bands of decoration border the wheel's rim. The color scheme is black and white, with a few red and tan pebbles spread at random in the background. Drawing is minimal; no anatomy is indicated, and the pebbles are not laid closely together. The impression is of an early example, as indeed it is: archaeological evidence indicates that the mosaic was laid in the last quarter of the fifth century.[25]

POTTERY

No drastic changes in shape are to be seen in the pottery of the fifth century, though subtle changes in profile and decoration allow the expert to recognize it. An interest in working the surface of plain black pottery developed in the first half of the century, and we find vertical ribbing on drinking cups, small amphoras, and lekythoi. After the middle of the century decorative incising

[25] On mosaics in general, see Peter Fischer, *Mosaic: History and Technique* (New York, 1971). Pebble mosaics in Greece and the Corinthian example are discussed in Martin Robertson, "Greek Mosaics," *JHS* 85 (1965): 72–89; C. K. Williams II and Joan Fisher, "Corinth, 1975: Forum Southwest," *Hesperia* 45 (1976): 113–115.

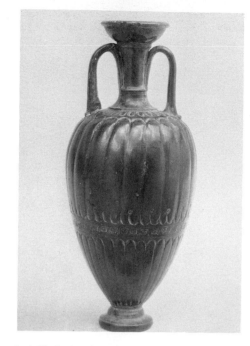

8.56 Black glazed amphora with a worked surface. The Metropolitan Museum of Art, Fletcher Fund, 1924.

and stamping appeared, often of palmettes. This interest in molding and working the surface rather than covering it with painted patterns finally eclipsed painted decoration in the Hellenistic period (Fig. 8.56).[26]

Red Figure painting in the fifth century was essentially a continuation of that of the previous period but there were fewer good painters; perhaps the major artistic undertakings of the period provided other employment. In the first half of the century several schools of painting may be recognized: some painters clung to the formulas of the Archaic period; some favored calm, quiet Classical compositions; some attempted more or less direct copies of wall paintings; and some experimented with innovations in technique and style. The Penthesilea Painter was one of the leading experimenters. In his elaborate Penthesilea cup in Munich of about 465, the crowded composition in which Achilles slays the Amazon hardly fits the circular space of the interior (Fig. 8.57). The artist employed an unusual technique in rendering the large figures, drawing the contours and musculature in dilute glaze and then tracing over them with relief line. Colored washes, shading, and bold foreshortening were also used, giving the scene an appearance of a full-sized painting crushed into a cup. The moment just before the death of Penthesilea is rendered especially poignant by the eye contact between the combatants.

The most ambitious vase painter of his time is the Niobid Painter, whose calyx krater in Paris, painted about 460–450, probably copies an ancient painting (Fig. 8.58). Instead of being grouped in a row, the figures are variously

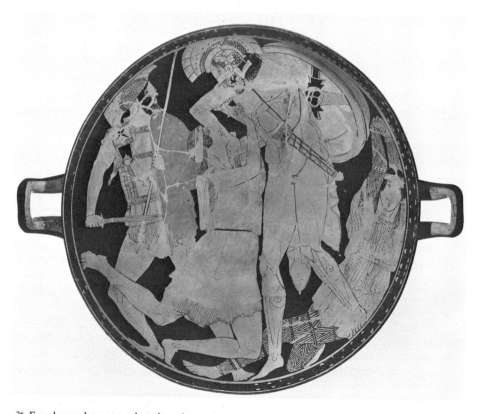

8.57 Tondo of a cup by the Penthesilea Painter:[P] Achilles slaying Penthesilea. Staatliche Antikensammlungen und Glyptothek, Munich. Photo: C. H. Krüger-Moessner.

[26] For shape changes and surface decoration, see Brian A. Sparkes and Lucy Talcott, *Black and Plain Pottery of the Sixth, Fifth, and Fourth Centuries*, Athenian Agora series, vol. 12 (Princeton, 1970), especially pt. 1, pp. 20–30.

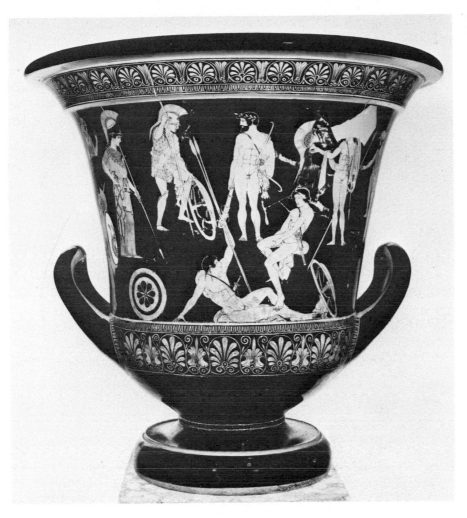

placed one above the other in a natural setting; one even partially disappears behind a rock. Clearly the artist was attempting to show distance but without diminishing the figures. Although Athena and Herakles are readily recognizable, the identities of the other figures and the explanation of the scene are fiercely debated.[27]

Even fewer good painters were at work in the second half of the century. The influence of contemporary Periklean sculpture is strong in the work of the Achilles Painter, so named after his vase in the Vatican (Fig. 8.59). One tall, quiet figure standing in the contrapposto pose illustrates all the technical advances of the time (Fig. 8.60). Note especially the rendition of the eye. The artist was probably trained in the workshop of the Berlin Painter. His quiet, idealized figures belong to the same serene world as do those on the Parthenon frieze.

Scenes from everyday life can still be found in the minor arts. The stamnos in Color Plate 5 (following p. 96) was painted by a contemporary of the Achilles

[27] Various attempts have been made to work back from vase paintings to major original wall paintings. A brilliant article by John P. Barron, "New Light on Old Walls: The Murals of the Theseion," *JHS* 92 (1972): 20–45, shows the methodology. See also Susan Woodford, "More Light on Old Walls: The Theseus of the Centauromachy in the Theseion," *JHS* 94 (1974): 158–165.

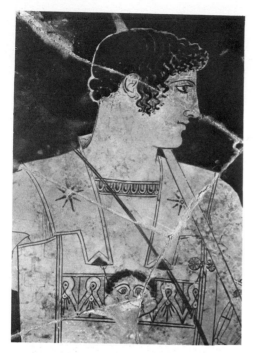

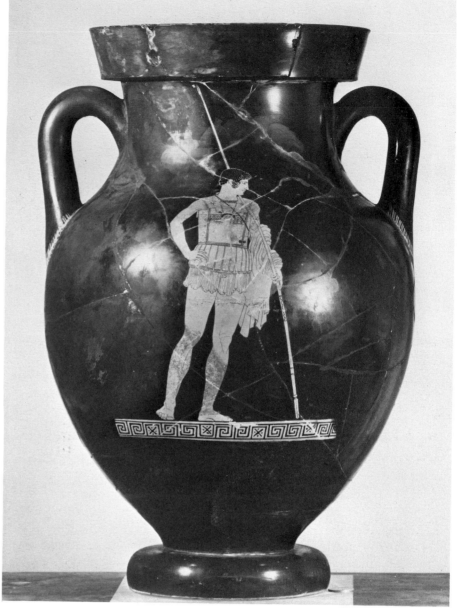

Painter. This painter produced fleshier figures than the Achilles Painter, yet the
same restrained idealism is evident even in a scene that shows a common
occurrence.

The highly decorative late-fifth-century style is also reflected in the work of
the Meidias Painter. On a hydria (water jar) in London an elaborate two-tier
composition is filled with small-scale, ornately dressed figures posed in lovely
attitudes (Fig. 8.61). Gilding was now used for details and attributes were
occasionally rendered in relief. At this point vase painting had entered a florid
stage. Painters turned toward pretty and petty subjects—domestic life, or alle-
gorical scenes filled with such personifications as "health" and "all-night feast-
ing." When a god appears, it is often Dionysos, Herakles, or some other deity

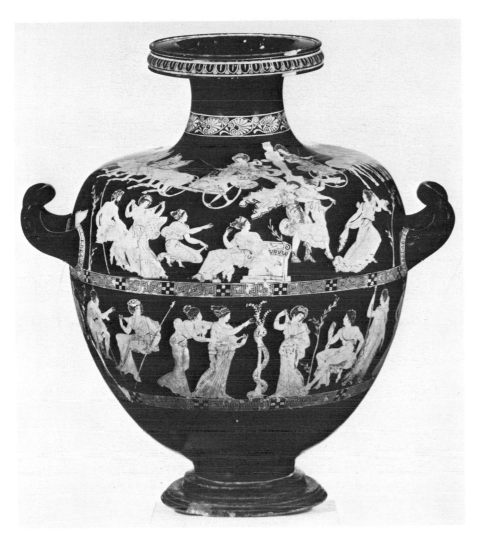

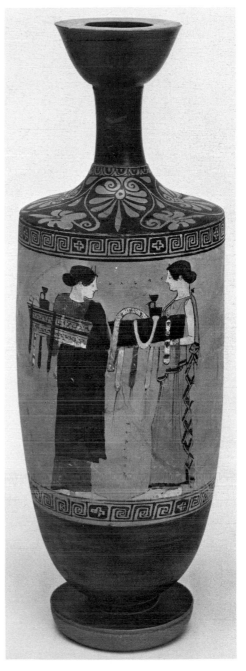

who could be connected to the pleasant side of life. Although scenes of battle, especially from mythology, do not disappear, there are fewer than before. Another hydria by the Meidias Painter (Color Plate 15), now in Florence, shows in detail how far this highly decorative style could go in the hands of a good painter. Here Phaon, an old ferryman turned into a handsome youth by Aphrodite, sits in a leafy bower with a lyre, accompanied by a woman named Demonassa. Observers of the scene are painted in the highly ornate style with a wealth of detail in the rich, transparent drapery. At this point, however, gilding and relief are used with some restraint. Characteristic of this painter are the softly rounded figures, who seem to have relatively boneless extremities. Note how they seem to grasp without holding and how Phaon's foot flows over the curved ground line on which it rests. This late-fifth-century style, with its soft, luxurious figures, appears escapist when one considers the reality of Athens at the end of the century.

In the latter part of the century the White Ground lekythos became popular as a funeral offering (Fig. 8.62). The White Ground style is so called because a coat of white clay slip covered the vase, on which a scene was painted in

8.62 White Ground lekythos.[P] Elvehjem Art Center, University of Wisconsin–Madison. Edna G. Dyar Fund and Fairchild Foundation Fund Purchase.

varying techniques, including occasionally polychrome decoration applied in flat washes. A tomb frequently occupies the center of the scene, with women carrying garlands to decorate the funeral monuments. Such scenes provide valuable information on funeral customs.[28]

The Achilles Painter chose a more subtle reference to death in a lekythos (Color Plate 11, following p. 96). A departure scene is depicted; presumably the warrior who is about to leave will not return. The quiet poses and the restrained treatment of the subject clearly belong to the High Classical style.

TRANSPORT AMPHORAS

Figure 8.63 shows a group of typical amphoras of the fifth century. In the third quarter of the century the shape of the Chian jars changed, assuming a more angular outline and dropping a characteristic swelling at the neck which had developed in the early fifth century. The old shape is shown on the left in Figure 8.63, the new on the right. The new-style jar was stamped with a Chian coin type that shows the old shape, presumably to identify it while the new shape was still unfamiliar. The distinctive, rounded amphora in the foreground held wine from the town of Mende in northeastern Greece, one of the most famous wine-producing areas in antiquity. The distinctive shape of the container clearly announced its contents.

TERRA COTTA FIGURINES

The typical fifth-century figurine is a standing or seated woman wearing chiton and himation. Attica was one of the principal centers of figurine production. By the middle of the century Archaic characteristics had been abandoned and hollow molded standing women with analogies to Severe-style sculpture were produced (Fig. 8.64). Similar parallels between the mass-produced figurines and sculpture can be made during the period of the Parthenon and the latter part of the century, as might be expected in such an artistic center.

Corinth, backward in comparison with Athens, continued to produce solid standing or seated female figures with molded fronts and flat backs. It was not until the latter half of the century that hollow molded figures were made. The types established in the fifth century continued to be produced with little change well into the fourth century (Fig. 8.65).

Other cities also produced figurines in simple classical style, such as that from Rhodes shown in Figure 8.66. These cheap, mass-produced objects, taken together with the more costly and grander dedicatory pieces whose style they emulate, help to provide us with a balanced view of Greek culture.

COINS

Metal vessels, figurines, armor, and other objects of course continued to be made and decorated in contemporary style, but aside from coins, no significant classes of metalwork unique to the fifth and succeeding centuries can be distinguished.

By the time of the Persian Wars the standard Greek coin, with the head of a

---

[28] Still basic is J. D. Beazley, *Attic White Lekythoi* (Oxford, 1938). A study concerned mainly with the subsidiary decoration on this class of vases, profusely illustrated, is Donna C. Kurtz, *Athenian White Lekythoi* (Oxford, 1975). For burial customs, see Donna C. Kurtz and John Boardman, *Greek Burial Customs* (Ithaca, N.Y., 1971).

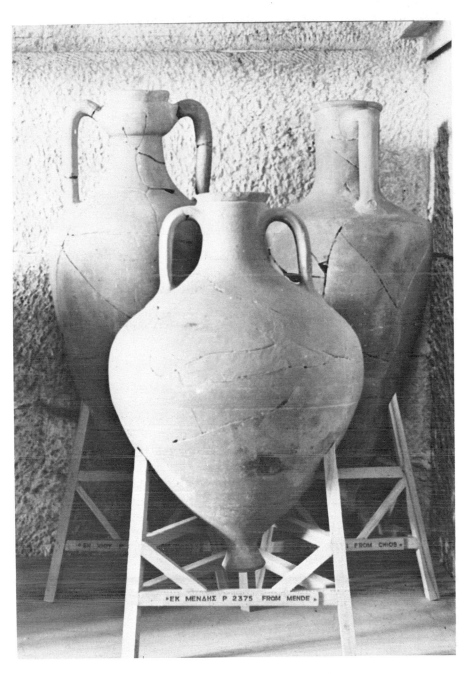

8.63 Typical fifth-century amphoras. Photo: American School of Classical Studies at Athens: Agora Excavations.

god or local divinity on one side and varying types on the other, had been established. The coins of Athens, the cultural and political leader of the time, were accepted throughout the Mediterranean. They bore a conservative Archaic head of Athena on the obverse, with stylized hair, frontal eye, and a profile head (Fig. 8.67). The reverse had an owl (Athena's attribute), an olive branch, and the first three letters of the city's name. The only change in this design came around 480, when olive leaves were added to Athena's helmet and a crescent moon to the reverse, perhaps to commemorate the defeat of the Persians. Except for this change, the same old-fashioned type was in use throughout the century, at a time when the Classical style had overtaken the other arts.

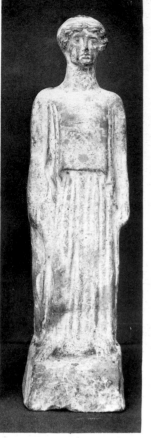

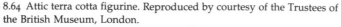

8.64 Attic terra cotta figurine. Reproduced by courtesy of the Trustees of the British Museum, London.

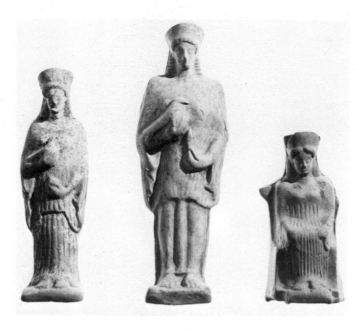

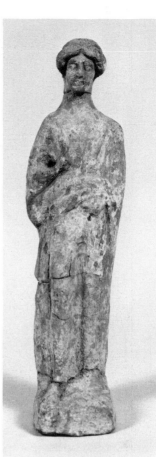

8.65 Typical molded female figurines of the fifth century, from Corinth. Photo: American School of Classical Studies at Athens: Corinth Excavations.

8.66 Common Rhodian terra cotta figurine. Photo: Museum of Art and Archaeology, University of Missouri–Columbia.

Athenian coins (known as "owls"), backed by an abundant supply of metal from mines in Attica, became the standard currency throughout the Greek world. Under the empire the allied states were forbidden to mint their own coins.

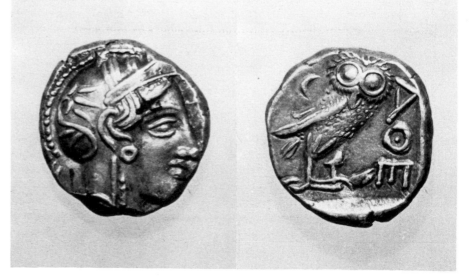

8.67 Fifth-century coin from Athens: obverse, Athena; reverse, owl. Photos: Museum of Art and Archaeology, University of Missouri–Columbia. Scale 2:1.

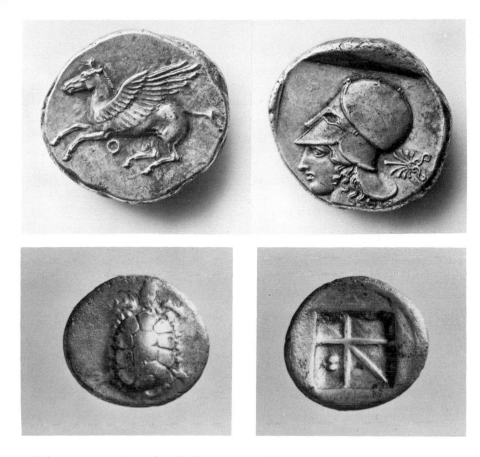

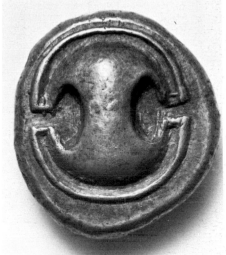

Other cities continued with the types established in the sixth century, such as the Pegasos and Athena head in Corinth and the distinctive Boiotian shield in cities of Boiotia (Figs. 8.68 and 8.69). An interesting change took place in the coins of Aigina around the middle of the century, when a land tortoise was substituted for the sea turtle on the obverse (Fig. 8.70). This change perhaps had something to do with the capture of the island by the Athenians in 456. By the second half of the century, coin art frequently reflected contemporary artistic styles, as can be seen in the Herakles coin from Thebes and especially in the handsome late fifth-century coin from Elis (Figs. 8.71 and 8.72).

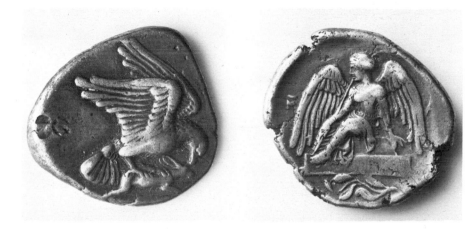

LAMPS

Lamps continued to develop slowly. As the bodies of lamps became increasingly enclosed, they tended to grow in length. A common variety of the first half of the century is shown in Figure 8.73*a*. This flat-bottomed type has a raised band around the filling hole, forming a rim. Some of these lamps have horizontal flat handles opposite the nozzle, others are handleless. Black glaze was applied in a band around the shoulder and on the rim; the area between the two bands of glaze was usually reserved.

The most common type of mid-century lamp is shown in Figure 8.73*b*. Now covered all over with black glaze and with a raised base and horizontal strap handle, this simple type was extremely popular and existed into the fourth century in a variation with a longer nozzle.

In the third quarter of the century emerged a slightly more decorative wheel-made type with an inward-sloping rim that has ornamental grooves or raised bands (Fig. 8.73*c*). The handles are horizontal or U-shaped, and base rings are often employed. These lamps are also wholly glazed except occasionally the base, which is sometimes striped.

8.73 Typical fifth-century lamps. After Richard Hubbard Howland, *Greek Lamps and Their Survivals*, Athenian Agora series, vol. 4 (Princeton: American School of Classical Studies, 1955). By permission of the American School of Classical Studies. Drawing by John Huffstot. Scale approx. 1:2.

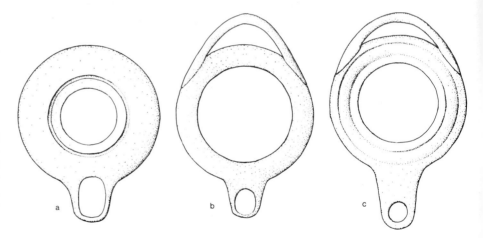

9

The Fourth Century

A POWER VACUUM was created by the dissolution of the Athenian Empire and various cities attempted to fill it, none with complete success. If there was any thought of returning to the earlier conditions of completely independent cities, it was soon quashed, and Sparta immediately attempted to take over the reins of power. The Spartans quickly proved that the cure of a Spartan empire was worse than the disease of an Athenian one, and very soon found themselves having to fight many of their former allies as well as their traditional enemies. A peace imposed by the Persians in 387 gave Sparta a free hand to try to assert its supremacy over the mainland Greek states.

The Second Athenian Sea League, formed by cities in European Greece and the islands under Athenian leadership, was established in 378 to oppose Sparta. The war dragged on until 371, when a peace was signed recognizing Athens' predominance on the sea, Sparta's supremacy on land, and the autonomy of all Greek cities.

By this time, however, another power had appeared, one that did not take part in the peace treaty. This was Thebes, powerful because of its gifted leaders, who a month after the signing of the peace treaty surprised the Greek world by defeating Sparta in the Battle of Leuctra. Alliances quickly shifted to oppose Thebes, whose short period of supremacy ended at the Battle of Mantinea in 362, when the last of its great leaders was mortally wounded.

Greece then lapsed into a general state of disarray as the various states jockeyed for position and power. The fatal divisiveness of the Greeks was not allowed to run long unchecked, for Macedon, a semi-Hellenic monarchy of northeastern Greece, soon stepped in. Under its king, Philip, its strength increased until, in the second half of the century, it became the dominant power.

An excuse was soon found for Philip to move south, and at least some of the squabbling city-states finally combined to face the danger. Thoroughly defeated by the Macedonians in 338 at the Battle of Chaironeia, they found unity once again imposed on them.

Philip, who liked to be considered the defender and champion of Greek culture and civilization, immediately called all the Greek cities together in a congress at Corinth. With a few exceptions he had treated them all well. Soon thereafter, Philip proclaimed a crusade against Persia to free the Greek cities of Asia Minor and punish the Great King for the invasions of the previous century. Philip did not live to see this expedition, for he was assassinated in 336 and his son, Alexander, took his place at the age of twenty.

Alexander's conquests in the East profoundly changed history. Crossing the Hellespont in 334, he conducted a remarkable series of campaigns that conquered the whole Persian Empire and carried Greek warriors and culture as far as northwest India. His death in 323 at Babylon, probably as a result of malaria but possibly of poison, left a huge legacy for his successors of the Hellenistic period.

The fourth century was, then, a period of almost constant warfare, culminating in the Persian expedition of Alexander the Great. It was a period of upheaval in which states rushed to align themselves against whichever city might be momentarily attempting to gain dominance. Cities also suffered internal strife as factions opposed each other for control.

This turmoil was also felt on an intellectual level. The city-state system seemed to have failed somehow, and the fourth century saw the rise of cosmopolitanism and individualism. A man's primary duty was no longer to serve the city, as it had been in Periklean times; now he could focus on his private interests. A symptom of the times was the rise of the military mercenary, who served any power that would pay.

The new power, Macedon, was a national monarchy with allegiance to the king rather than to the state, and the world its conquests forged was one of large nation-states. The fourth century was marked by the decline of the city-state system. The constant bickering and fighting that seem to have been endemic in this system led to its final submission to a stronger and united power.

ART

The art of the fourth century can be seen in various ways, depending on one's emphasis. In a sense it is a transitional period, with a lingering classicism in the first half and something new in the second half. Yet the fourth century exhibits enough differences from the fifth to signal a definite break. In this view, the fourth century and the succeeding Hellenistic period are seen as a continuum.

No historical marker indicates either the beginning or the end of fourth-century art, for the changes that occurred came gradually. Although the influence of High Classical style was strong in the early years of the century—as it was to a greater or lesser extent throughout antiquity—stylistic change clearly heralded the new age. Artists worked in highly individualized styles, almost as if reacting to the straitjacket of the Phidian style. Generally the same types of works were produced for the usual reasons, but the individuality of the times, expressed also in philosophy, is clearly visible. Realism increased as artists attempted to show emotion and states of mind. The strict bonds of idealism were slowly being loosened. In the second half of the century, Lysippos made great changes in almost all aspects of the representation of mortals and the gods, and the Hellenistic period dawned. The fourth century, then, may be seen as a bridge between the Classic and Hellenistic styles, not only in art but in civilization, yet it maintained an individuality of its own.

ARCHITECTURE

The exploration of the possibilities of the Ionic and Doric orders may be said to have reached its height in the temples of the fifth century. In the succeeding century fewer sacred buildings were constructed, owing in part to the unsettled nature of the times and in part to the fact that earlier buildings were still serviceable. The new temples that did arise were often rebuildings of earlier edifices that had been destroyed for one reason or another. Improvement of the Doric order was unlikely, perhaps impossible, so the architects experimented with the proportions of the plans, making the elevations more slender, and combining elements of the various orders in the same building. The results were often elegant but sometimes overloaded with decoration.

A good example of fourth-century Doric is the temple of Asklepios at Epidauros, built on a previously empty site early in the century, around 370, by an architect named Theodotus (Fig. 9.1).[1] Quite small, measuring only 23.06 by 11.76 meters on the stylobate (only one-ninth the area of the Parthenon), the building was also compact, with the normal six columns at each end but only eleven on each flank. A relatively deep pronaos led to a cella that contained a chryselephantine cult statue, perhaps not much larger than life-size. There was probably an interior colonnade but no remains survive; like many other fourth-century temples, this one had no opisthodomos. The building accounts of this temple add details that we would not be likely to divine from the remains—for instance, that some of the ceiling coffers were painted with masks. The temple, built of various types of limestone, had painted metopes on the outside but six sculptured ones in the pronaos frieze. The pediments were decorated with full battle scenes portraying Greeks fighting against Amazons and the fall of Troy. The nineteenth-century reconstruction shown in Figure 9.2 goes well beyond the evidence in the composition of the east pediment but gives a good overall view of the building.

A most interesting attempt to vary the Doric order is found in the temple of Athena Alea at Tegea in the Peloponnesos, built to replace the earlier temple

9.1 Plan of the temple of Asklepios at Epidauros.[P] From Georges Roux, *L'Architecture de l'Argolide aux IVe et IIIe siècles avant J.-C.* (Paris: E. de Boccard, 1961), Plate 28. By permission of the École Française d'Archéologie, Athens.

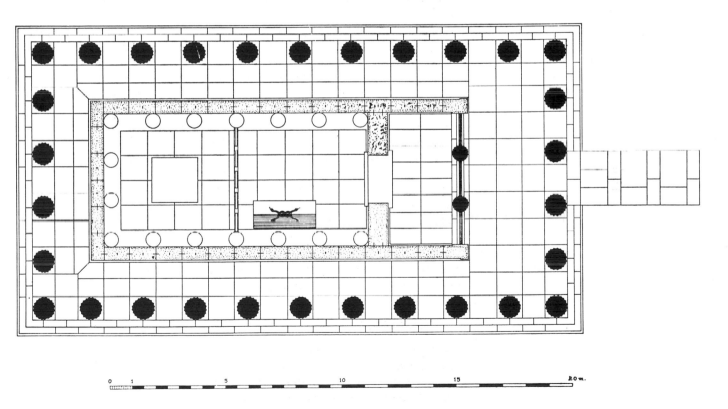

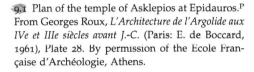

---

[1] A great amount of building went on in the sanctuary of Asklepios at Epidauros in the fourth century, and much technical information can be gathered from the numerous inscriptions that have been found there. Alison Burford, *The Greek Temple Builders at Epidauros* (Liverpool, 1969), deals with this material and produces interesting information on the methods of building.

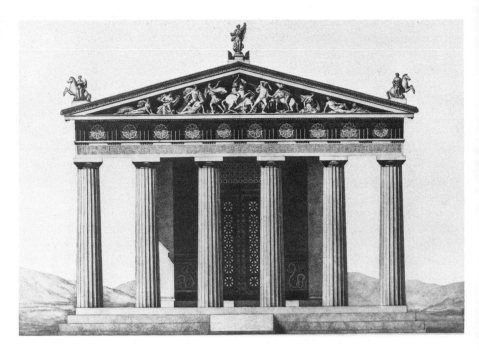

9.2 Reconstructed east facade of the temple of Asklepios at Epidauros. From Alphonse Defrasse and Henri Lechat, *Epidaure* (Paris: Libraires-Imprimeries Réunies, 1895), Plate 3.

9.3 Plan of the temple of Athena Alea at Tegea.[P] From Naomi J. Norman, "The Temple of Athena Alea at Tegea." *AJA* 88 (1984): Ill. 9. Reproduced by permission.

burned in 394 (Fig. 9.3). The present remains probably date to shortly after midcentury. The architect was Skopas of Paros, a famous sculptor who is discussed further below. The marble building measured 47.55 by 19.19 meters on the stylobate, with six columns across each end and fourteen on each flank. The columns were very slender, their height more than six times the lower diameter, and the entablature was low, giving the building a tall, thin appearance (Fig. 9.4). The unusual feature of this building is a long cella with a second

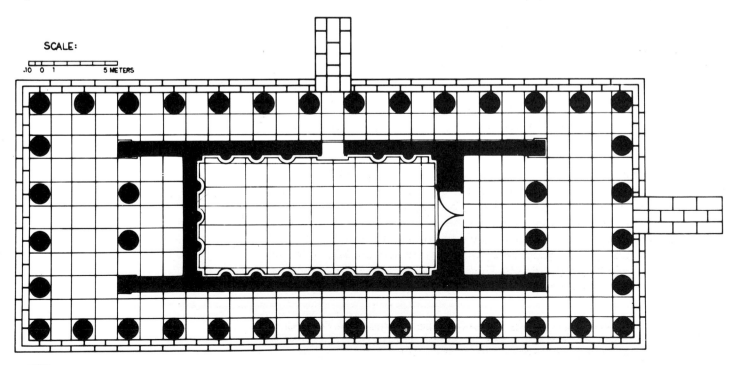

SCALE:

.10 0 1   5 METERS

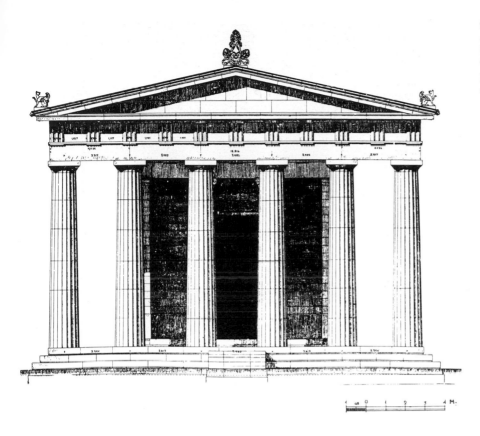

9.4 Reconstructed east facade of the temple of Athena Alea at Tegea. From Charles Dugas, *Le Sanctuaire d'Aléa Athéna à Tégée* (Paris: Librairie Orientaliste Paul Geuthner, 1924), Plates 12–14. By permission of the Ecole Française d'Archéologie, Athens.

entrance cut through the north wall, opening halfway down the colonnade. This elongated plan, which retains the opisthodomos, recalls Bassai and other Arcadian temples. The interior of the cella was treated with engaged Corinthian half columns with possibly an upper tier of Ionic pilasters or half columns above them, as in the later fourth-century temple of Zeus at Nemea. Thus the interior colonnade was pushed back almost flush to the wall and treated as decoration. The Corinthian capitals (Fig. 9.5) are quite squat and have two rows of acanthus leaves growing up the bell. Most of the remaining space on the bell is occupied by a vertical leaf rather than by the two spirals used at Bassai. By having the angle spirals emerge from a sheath displaying more leaves, the architect established what was to become a common element in subsequent Corinthian capitals.

In the fourth century the Ionic order reached a point of great refinement, as exemplified in the temple of Athena Polias at Priene, in modern-day Turkey (Fig. 9.6).[2] The small (37.20 by 19.55 meters) but elegant building was begun about 340 and was dedicated by Alexander the Great in 334. Though of standard plan, it had eleven columns on the flank, and the column bases sat on low plinths (square slabs) (Fig. 9.7), an unusual feature but one also known in the fourth-century rebuilding at Ephesos. The quality of carving on the building was very high and the plan consciously employed a specific canon of propor-

---

2 A good discussion of this temple appears in Helmut Berve, Gottfried Gruben, and Max Hirmer, *Greek Temples, Theatres, and Shrines* (New York, 1963), pp. 475–480. See also Joseph Coleman Carter, *The Sculpture of the Sanctuary of Athena Polias at Priene* (London, 1983).

9.5 Reconstructed Corinthian capital from the inner order of the temple of Athena Alea at Tegea. By permission of the American School of Classical Studies at Athens: Corinth Excavations.

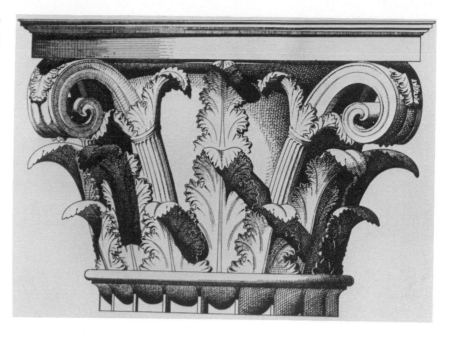

9.6 Plan of the temple and sanctuary of Athena Polias at Priene.[P] From Martin Schede, *Die Ruinen von Priene* (Berlin: Walter de Gruyter, 1964), p. 26, Fig. 27. Reproduced by permission.

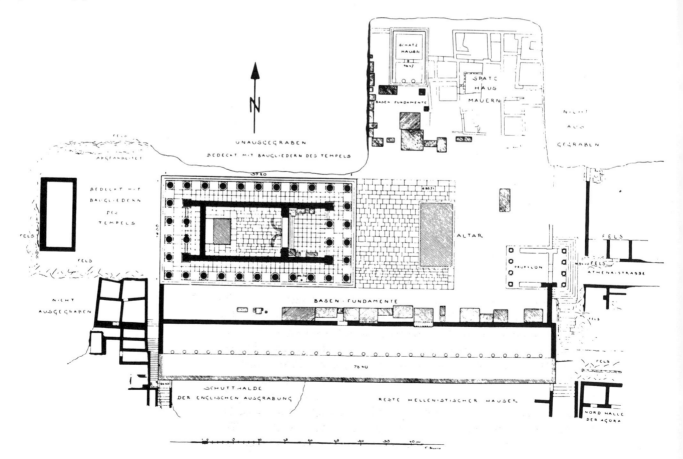

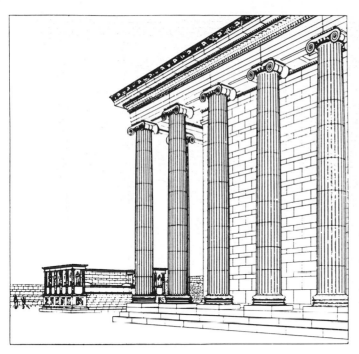

9.7 Reconstructed northeast corner and altar of the temple of Athena Polias at Priene. From Martin Schede, *Die Ruinen von Priene* (Berlin: Walter de Gruyter, 1964), p. 30, Fig. 33. Reproduced by permission.

tions based on multiples of the Ionic foot. Its architect, Pythios, wrote a book about it.

SECULAR ARCHITECTURE

Few new forms of secular buildings appeared in the fourth century, but many were built in nonperishable materials and so have been preserved. The center of Athens' life, the Agora (Fig. 9.8), underwent little change but a few additions were made, including a fountain house at the southwest corner; a square building with an interior colonnade, perhaps for the law courts, at the opposite corner; and minor additions and improvements elsewhere. Evidently there was no fundamental change in the functioning of the civic center.

Of the numerous monuments of varying types that adorned Athens, the Lysikrates Monument in the lower town east of the Acropolis merits attention because it is the first surviving example of the exterior use of the Corinthian order (Fig. 9.9). The monument, commissioned by a certain Lysikrates, was built to commemorate a victory won by a theater chorus in 334. It originally supported the prize, a bronze tripod, which stood on top of the spreading foliage that formed the peak of the roof. The circular monument of white marble stands on a square limestone base. Six elaborate and delicate Corinthian columns are engaged in the cylindrical wall, but there is some evidence that they were originally intended to be free-standing. It has been suggested that the building contained a statue, perhaps of Dionysos or a satyr. The Corinthian order, which had not yet settled into a canonical form, is not found again in later Athenian buildings until the temple of Olympian Zeus in the second century. Between the capitals of the Lysikrates Monument are reliefs of tripods; above the capitals are an epistyle, a sculptured frieze telling the story of Dionysos turning pirates into dolphins, a row of dentils, cornice, and roof. The combination of frieze and dentils in the entablature became common later; this

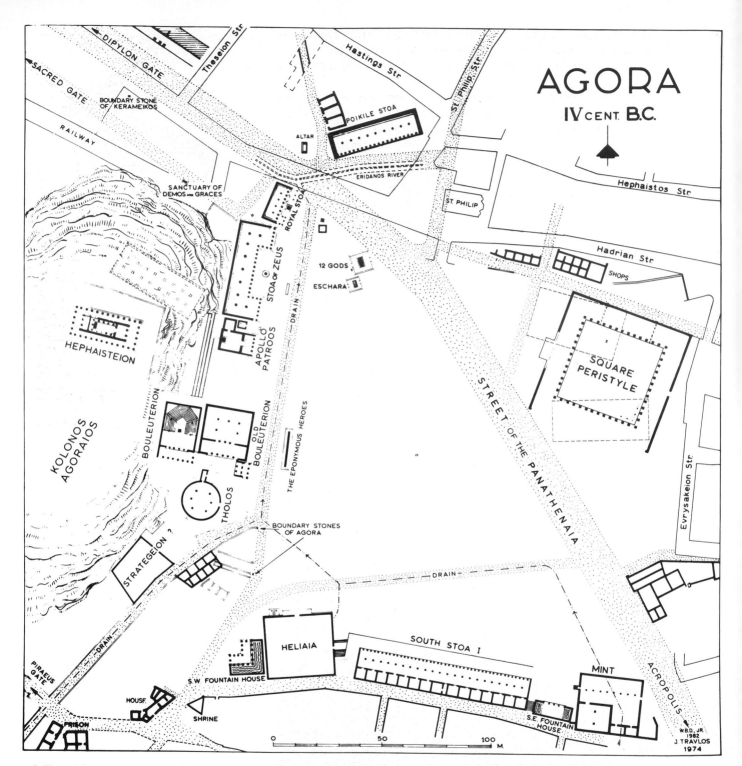

9.8 Plan of the Agora in Athens in the fourth century. Photo: American School of Classical Studies at Athens: Agora Excavations.

is one of the early examples. Perhaps the earliest is to be seen in the Philippeion at Olympia (see below). The Lysikrates Monument is now unique, but it stood on a street known for similar monuments, some of whose foundations still exist.

Another unique monument of the fourth century and one of the seven wonders of the ancient world was the Mausoleion at Halikarnassos, modern Bodrum on the Turkish coast. Here a great tomb was raised to a local dynast, Mausolos, who thus unwittingly gave his name to a particular type of building

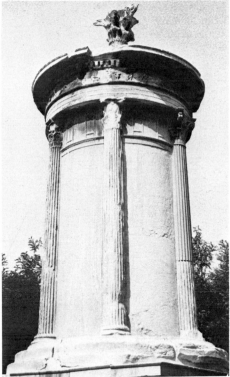

9.9 Lysikrates Monument, Athens. Photo: William R. Biers.

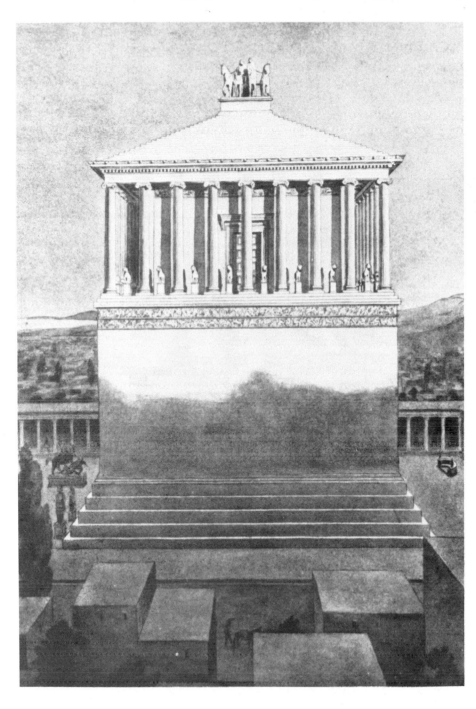

9.10 One reconstruction of the Mausoleion at Halikarnassos.[P] From Fritz Krischen, *Weltwunder der Baukunst in Babylonien und Jonien* (Tübingen: Verlag Ernst Wasmuth, 1956), Plate 26. Reproduced by permission.

in use for the entombment of the dead down to our own day. Mausolos died in 353 but work continued on the tomb until perhaps as late as 340. We have two ancient descriptions of the building, which unfortunately are open to varying interpretations, so that the many reconstructions of it tend to vary considerably. All have the same components, however: a rectangular building surrounded by an Ionic colonnade of thirty-six columns on a base that may or may not have been a stepped pyramid. Above this building all reconstructions place a stepped pyramid capped by a four-horse chariot. The building is said to have been some 45.11 meters high and the rock cuttings for its base measure 38.15 by 38.40 meters. The problems in reconstruction lie mainly in the arrangement of these components; one attempt is shown in Figure 9.10. Thrown down by an earthquake in the thirteenth century of our era, the building was thoroughly plundered in the sixteenth century by the Knights of St. John, who built much of it into one of their castles. Excavations in A.D. 1856 recovered many sculptures from the building; new investigations have recently been undertaken.[3] The sources indicate that the leading artists of the day were imported to work on the building, which was famous for the quality and amount of its sculpture. More will be said about the Mausoleion's decorations when we discuss fourth-century sculpture.

The Mausoleion was a personal monument to a foreign king who actually had little influence on Greece. Another absolute ruler who did have considerable impact was Philip of Macedon, who caused another unique building to be erected—the Philippeion in Olympia (Fig. 9.11). This round building was built after Philip's defeat of the Greeks at Chaironeia in 338 and may have been

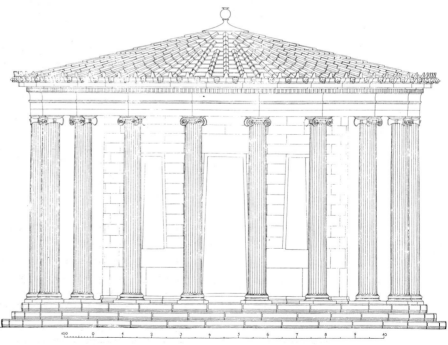

9.11 Restoration of the Philippeion at Olympia.[P] From Emil Kunze and Hans Schleif, *Olympische Forschungen*, vol. 1 (Berlin: Walter de Gruyter, 1944), Plate 1. By permission of the Deutsches Archäologisches Institut, Berlin.

[3] For a discussion of the building that includes the results of study of the mass of sculpture from the site, see Geoffrey Waywell, "The Mausoleum at Halicarnassus," in *The Seven Wonders of the World*, ed. Peter Clayton and Martin Price (London, 1988), pp. 100–123.

completed by the time Alexander left for his eastern campaign in 334. Eighteen Ionic columns stood around the exterior. The interior was ornamented by nine Corinthian half columns surrounding a base on which stood chryselephantine statues of Philip, Alexander, and Philip's father, according to Pausanias. As mentioned earlier, the building is the first preserved example of the use of dentils and a frieze in the same entablature, and it contains other peculiarities and innovations as well.[4] The Philippeion was evidently a votive offering, and it is interesting to note that it contained statutes of mortals (at least one of whom was still living) which were apparently made of gold and ivory, materials usually reserved for the gods. There is some evidence that the boundary of the sacred precinct was adjusted to admit the new building. These facts allow various interpretations of the meaning of the Philippeion, given the historical situation, but it certainly is symbolic of the change in the fourth century and the victory of a "foreign" absolute monarch.

One very characteristic type of Greek building, the theater, was now regularly built in nonperishable materials. The theater, associated with the cult of Dionysos, was an integral part of every Greek city.[5] Of the many theaters that were established or rebuilt in the fourth century, the most famous and best preserved is that at Epidauros (Fig. 9.12), built about the middle of the century. The designer was a man named Polykleitos—not the fifth-century sculptor, but perhaps his descendant, a talented architect also responsible for an ornate round building in the same sanctuary. The plan (Fig. 9.13) shows the principal parts of a developed Greek theater. Set into the slope of a hill, the vast auditorium extends around the circular orchestra like a fan. In the orchestra stood an altar to Dionysos (its base still remains), and here also the actors performed until a raised stage was introduced in the Hellenistic period. The rows of stone seats are interrupted by staircases that divide the seating area into a series of wedges. Part of the way up, a passageway (diazoma) divides the auditorium into two unequal portions. The total capacity was some 12,000, and such are the acoustics that a coin dropped from knee height on the altar base can be clearly heard from the top seats. Behind the orchestra, 24.38 meters in diameter, was a building in which equipment was stored and against which backdrops could be displayed. A passageway (parodos) separated the building from the auditorium on either side, permitting the actors and the audience to enter and leave quickly.

The Peloponnesian War and the succeeding turmoil of the fourth century left behind abundant remains in the utilitarian field of military architecture.[6] From this period on, military engineers produced increasingly elaborate fortifications to counter the growing sophistication of offensive warfare. Walls and towers carefully constructed of coursed masonry and often topped by wooden and mud-brick superstructures were built to surround cities and forts. An Attic border fort that stands between Attica and Boiotia is shown in Figure 9.14.

---

[4] An example of progress in the understanding of local styles of architecture can be found in an important article by Stella Grobel Miller, "The Philippeion and Macedonian Hellenistic Architecture," *Ath. Mitt.* 88 (1973): 189–218, in which the author connects the Philippeion with Macedonian architecture on the basis of archaeological evidence.

[5] The structural development of the Greek theater is an important and complex subject. The theater in all its manifestations is of course one of the great legacies of the Greeks. The basic overall treatment of the theater of the ancient world is Margarete Bieber, *A History of the Greek and Roman Theater*, 2d ed. (Princeton, 1971).

[6] The basic study of Greek military architecture is now F. E. Winter, *Greek Fortifications* (Toronto: 1971).

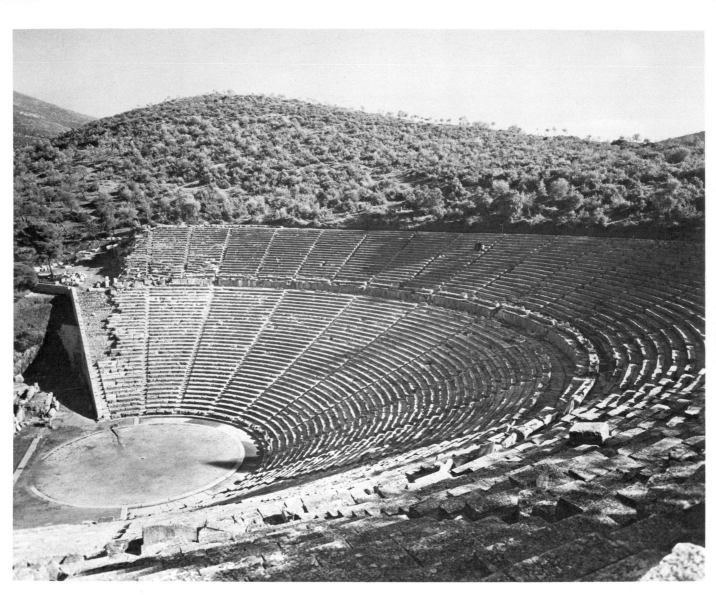

9.12 Theater at Epidauros.ᴾ Photo: Alison Frantz.

We are fortunate to have available for study an almost complete small city, built in the middle of the century to replace an earlier town on the slope of a hill overlooking the Maeander River in what is now Turkey. This tiny city, Priene, with a probable population of only some 4,000, had within its walls everything necessary for a city-state. German excavations at the end of the last century uncovered a great portion of the city (Fig. 9.15). The steep hill rising above the town to the north was used as an acropolis. A fortification wall enclosed this area as well as the lower town, which was carefully arranged in a modified Hippodamian plan. The east-west streets, running across the slope, were relatively level, while those running north-south were often simply staircases. The grid plan was carefully maintained for the residential quarters but was interrupted for the necessary public areas, such as the agora, which was situated off one of the major east-west streets. The principal temple, that of

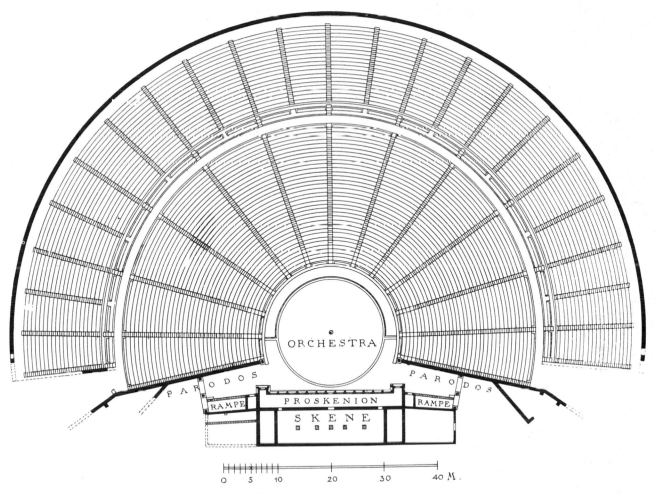

Athena Polias, which has already been discussed, stood on a terrace northwest of the agora; other sacred enclosures were scattered about the city. A theater and a small gymnasium were located to the north of the agora, while the major gymnasium and stadium were to the south. The council chamber and other city offices were conveniently placed close to the agora, to the north. Thus all the necessary parts of a Greek city are to be found in Priene.[7]

The houses of Priene date from the late fourth century into the Hellenistic period. Some vary from other contemporary dwellings in having a main large room fronted by a porch, often with two columns (Fig. 9.16). This megaron-like arrangement (unlike the true megaron, the central room is not completely independent) may show a revival of this ancient form, but lack of other domestic architecture makes it difficult to judge its significance. A few of the better houses in Priene were built of stone, but most city housing in older communities must still have been built entirely of wood and mud-brick. In plan they

---

7 Unfortunately, this fascinating little city has not received an exhaustive treatment in English. See George E. Bean, *Aegean Turkey* (London, 1966), pp. 197–216, and Ekrem Akurgal, *Ancient Civilizations and Ruins of Turkey*, 3d ed. (Istanbul, 1973), pp. 185–206.

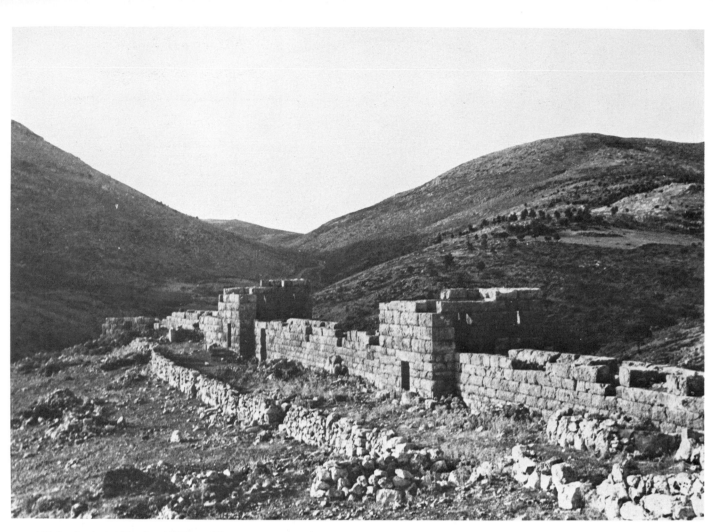

9.14 Attic border fort at Eleutherai.ᴾ Photo: Alison
Frantz.

must have resembled the sprawling types familiar from the fifth century
(Fig. 9.17), although some Athenian houses of the late fourth century had
pebble mosaics and other Olynthian features.

In the late 1960s a small (17.7 by 13.7 meters) country farmhouse was excavated at Vari in Attica. Careful excavation and study have given us much
evidence concerning this rather obscure type of building (Fig. 9.18).[8] Built
around a courtyard, the house was basically a pastas type but extended upward in a two-story tower at one corner, a defensive feature found in farm-
houses of more recent times in Greece and Cyprus. The excavators found
evidence to date the construction, occupation, and abandonment of this house
within the second half of the century. Continued isolated finds such as this
build up evidence on which a connected history of the house will someday be
written.

[8] J. E. Jones, A. J. Graham, and L. H. Sackett, "An Attic Country House below the Cave of Pan at
Vari," *BSA* 68 (1973): 355–452. For a more popular account, see John Ellis Jones, "Another Country
House in Attica," *Archaeology* 28 (1975): 6–15.

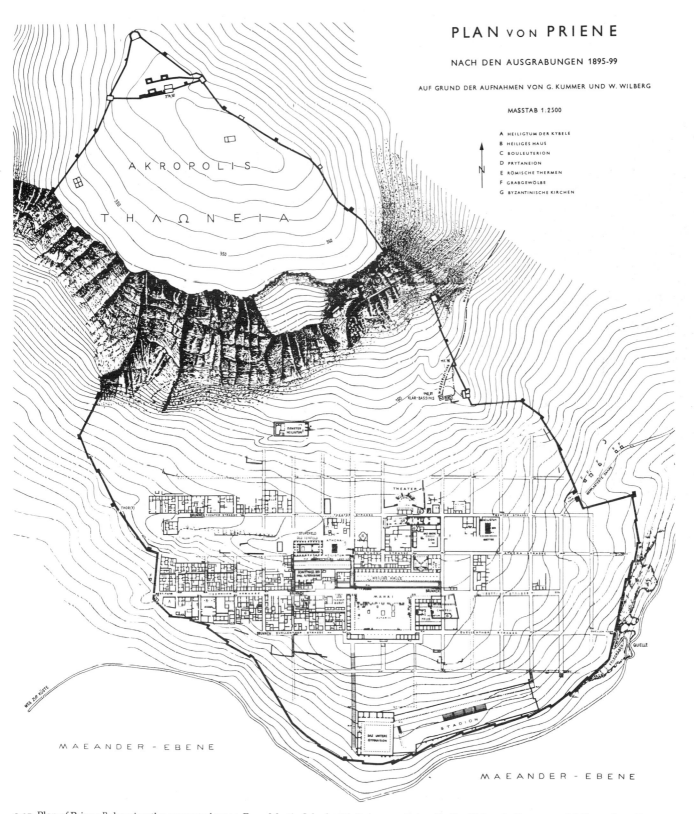

9.15 Plan of Priene,[P] showing the excavated areas. From Martin Schede, *Die Ruinen von Priene* (Berlin: Walter de Gruyter, 1964). Reproduced by permission.

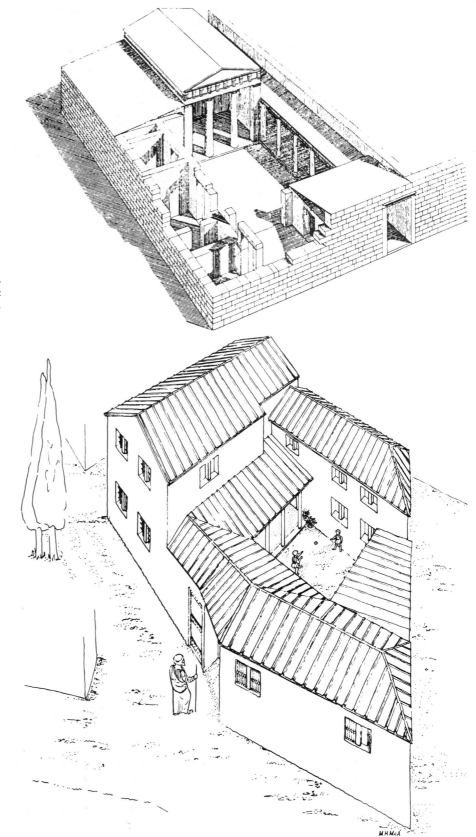

9.16 Reconstructed house complex at Priene. From Martin Schede, *Die Ruinen von Priene* (Berlin: Walter de Gruyter, 1964), p. 103, Fig. 120. Reproduced by permission.

9.17 Reconstruction of a fourth-century house in the Agora at Athens. Photo: American School of Classical Studies at Athens: Agora Excavations.

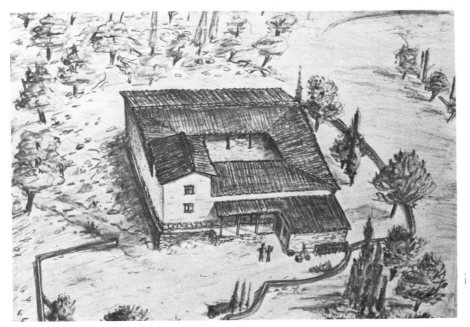

9.18 Reconstruction of a house at Vari.P From J. F. Jones et al., "An Attic Country House below the Cave of Pan at Vari," *Annual of the British School at Athens* 68 (1973): 355–452, Plate 82. By permission of the British School at Athens.

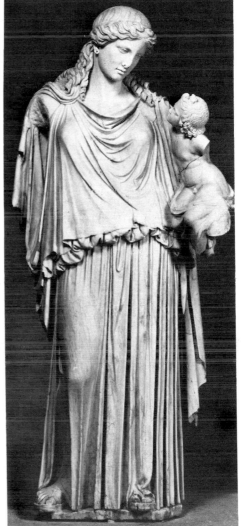

SCULPTURE

In one way the sculpture of the fourth century was a logical extension of that of the fifth: stylistically, many of its characteristics were direct continuations of previous practice. A change is noted in the treatment of subjects, however: sculptors moved away from the uniformity of High Classical art to depict emotional states.

The tendency toward the personification of abstract ideas which we have seen in the late fifth century is illustrated by the establishment in Athens of a cult of Peace. A statue of Wealth (Ploutos) in the arms of Peace (Eirene), mentioned in literary works and preserved in a number of copies, is attributed to the sculptor Kephisodotos, who was probably the father of the great Praxiteles. It is dated about 370. In a well-preserved copy in Munich (Fig. 9.19) the heavily clad Eirene gazes at the child Ploutos, whom she cradles in her left arm; her right probably held a now-vanished scepter. The heaviness of her peplos and cloak give her a massive appearance. A comparison of Eirene's drapery with that of the reclining female figures on the east pediment of the Parthenon (see Fig. 8.49) reveals the changes that have taken place in the treatment of drapery since the fifth century. Although derived from the earlier style, the fourth-century drapery falls in more complicated folds, which go in various directions, as they naturally do on articulated bodies, and transparency is shown where it would naturally occur. This increased naturalism and the massive quality of the drapery is representative of the fourth century. Eirene's head still shows a certain idealization but it is less stern than High Classical creations. It is the relationship of the adult to the child, however, that shows that a new age is dawning. The inclination of Eirene's head as she looks at her burden and the reaction of the child, who tilts his head to gaze intently at her, indicates a relationship between the two which would be alien to most High Classical sculpture. Moreover, an attempt has been made to treat the child as a child, not

9.19 Ploutos (Wealth) in the arms of Eirene (Peace), by Kephisodotos. Staatliche Antikensammlungen und Glyptothek, Munich. Photo: Hartwig Koppermann.

as a miniature adult. Thus realism, though still tempered by the idealism of the previous period, becomes one of the hallmarks of fourth-century sculpture.

The names of a number of fourth-century sculptors have come down to us both from comments in the works of ancient authors and from inscribed statue bases. Three represent distinct styles: Praxiteles, Skopas, and Lysippos.

Praxiteles (the "sculptor of grace"), whose career is usually given as stretching from about 370 to about 330, was one of the most famous of Greek sculptors. Three works that have been attributed to him will be discussed; all are generally dated to the period 350–330.

A statue of Hermes carrying the baby Dionysos was found in the Temple of Hera at Olympia by German excavators in A.D. 1877 (Fig. 9.20). The statue was immediately connected to Pausanias' statement that a marble statue of Hermes and Dionysos by Praxiteles was in the temple when he visited it. Subsequent technical studies, however, have thrown doubt on it as a work of the master,

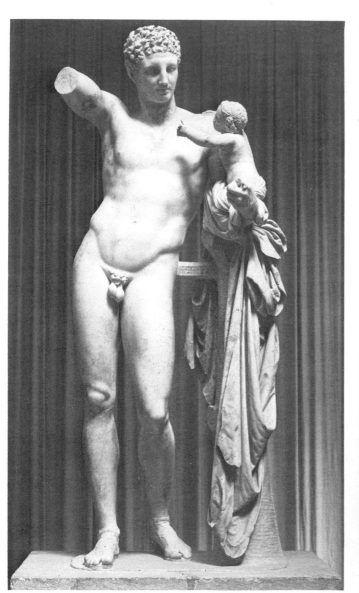

9.20 The Hermes of Praxiteles.ᴾ Archaeological Museum, Olympia. Photo: Alison Frantz.

9.21 Detail of the head of the Hermes of Praxiteles. Photo: Alison Frantz.

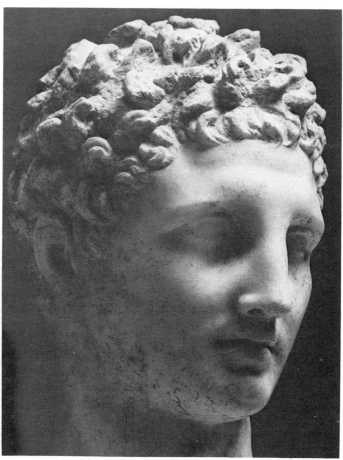

and most scholars no longer believe it to be an original. Several suggestions have been offered: that it is a copy of the fourth-century original made at a later date, or an original by another sculptor, or an original work by Praxiteles that was altered and reworked in Roman times.[9] Whatever the answer, the statue is an outstanding work of sculpture that awakens in the viewer a strong subjective reaction that can easily cloud judgment of its intrinsic merits. Although the right arm, the left leg below the knee, and the right leg between knee and ankle are missing (the legs have been restored), the statue is well preserved, especially the head (Fig. 9.21). The god is shown leaning on a tree trunk over which he has slung his cloak, holding the baby Dionysos in the crook of his left arm, which is supported by the tree trunk. His right arm is extended; he probably held a bunch of grapes, for which the baby wine god stretches out his chubby hand. The figure, with the flexed left leg and outthrust right hip, describes an S-curve, the so-called Praxitelean curve. Hermes' musculature is very softly treated: the various muscles and parts of the body flow into one another with few distinct divisions. A comparison with the sharply defined musculature of the Doryphoros (see Fig. 8.35) reveals a strong contrast in treatment. The softness is apparent in the head, whose features appear to be almost veiled. The god stares out into space with a dreamy expression, not looking at the child. The hair, which is worked in tufts, contrasts with the heavy brow, straight nose, and thick lips, but the contrast is not at all jarring.

In the Hermes of Praxiteles the gods have shed their Olympian grandeur and become soft and languid human beings. This almost effeminate figure is clearly far different from the gods of earlier Greek art.

We have several inferior copies of another Praxitelean work, the Apollo Sauroktonos, or Lizard Slayer, in which the Praxitelean curve of the body is more clearly accentuated (Fig. 9.22). The original bronze showed a limp young Apollo leaning against a tree, about to spear a lizard that is crawling up the trunk. The composition is different from that of the Hermes, but the musculature and the pose mark it as a product of the same hand. The body seems rather plump and the hair is treated differently from that of the Hermes, but these anomalies may be due to the copyist. The statue appears to have been made to be seen primarily from the front.

The most famous of Praxiteles' works is the Aphrodite of Knidos, probably the most popular statue in antiquity and perhaps the most difficult to appreciate. The Aphrodite was extravagantly praised for its beauty and survives in a great number of copies and representations in other media. The copy in the Vatican is the best known (Fig. 9.23). Unfortunately, the coarseness of the copies and the changing standards of feminine beauty hinder our appreciation of Praxiteles' work. The goddess is shown as if caught bathing. She does not lean, as do the Apollo and the Hermes, but strikes a rather complicated momentary pose. The broad planes of the body contrast with the drapery, as in the Hermes, but the overall sensuousness of the statue is lost on us. If not the first statue of a totally nude female, this is certainly the most famous. It started a seemingly endless line of nude Aphrodites in infinite variations of pose, which continue even today.

---

[9] These are only some of the interpretations of this statue. The question was debated in the 1930s; the symposium "Who Carved the Hermes of Praxiteles?" in *AJA* 35 (1931): 249–297, is interesting for the light it sheds on learned arguing. See Andrew Stewart, *Greek Sculpture* (New Haven, 1990), pp. 176–180, on Praxiteles in general and the Hermes in particular.

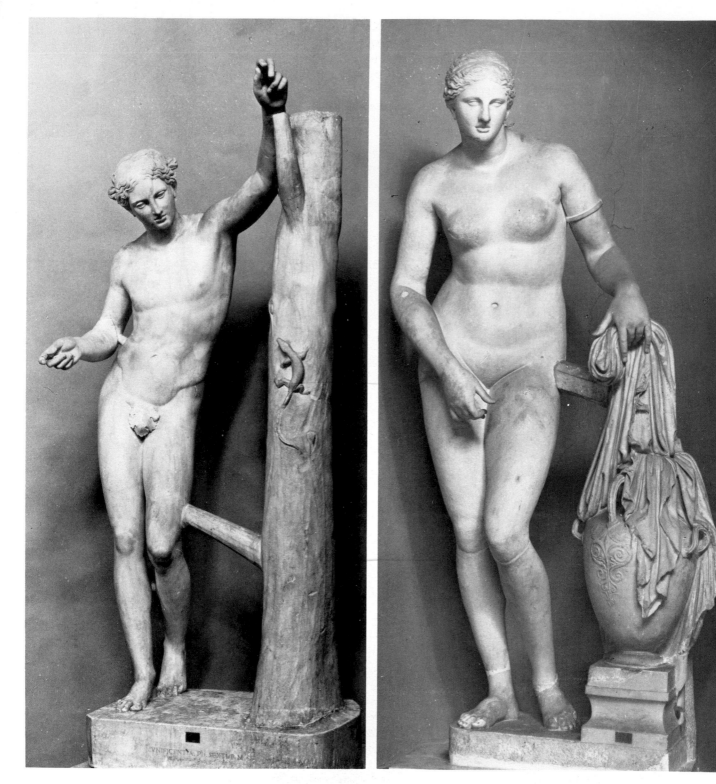

9.22 Apollo Sauroktonos.ᴾ Musei del Vaticano, Rome. Photo: Deutsches Archäologisches Institut, Rome.

9.23 Aphrodite of Knidos. Musei del Vaticano, Rome. Photo: Deutsches Archäologisches Institut, Rome.

A contemporary of Praxiteles was Skopas of Paros, whose style is marked by contorted poses and strong emotions. Apart from a few literary references that seem to indicate these elements of style among others in his repertoire, we are dependent on a rather thin thread of reasoning in assembling possible examples of his work.[10] As has been mentioned, Skopas is known to have been the architect of the temple of Athena Alea at Tegea. In the course of excavations, fragments of the pedimental sculpture were found, including a few extremely battered heads that show traces of a sturdy individual style that seems to fit the artist. One head (Fig. 9.24) exhibits a sharply turned square shape and distinctive deep-set eyes. Since these features are also found on a kneeling warrior on the Mausoleion frieze (Fig. 9.25), both the frieze slab and the Tegea heads are assigned to this artist, although there is no direct evidence for the authorship of

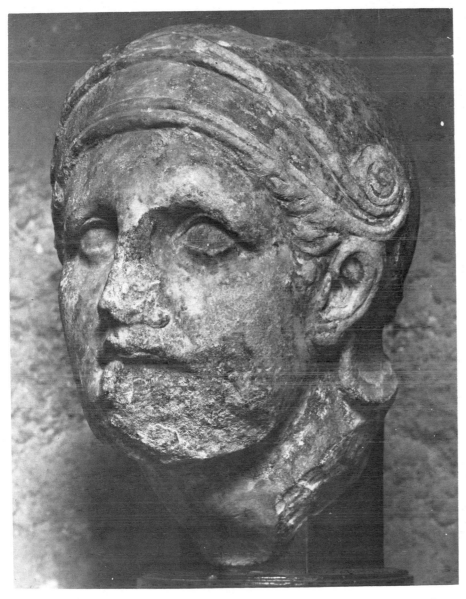

9.24 Head from the temple of Athena Alea, Tegea. National Archaeological Museum, Athens. Photo: Deutsches Archäologisches Institut, Athens.

---

10 A study of Skopas in English is Andrew Stewart, *Skopas of Paros* (Park Ridge, N.J., 1977).

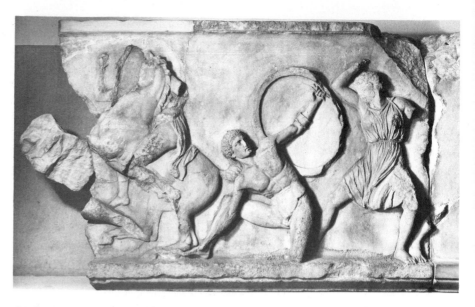

the latter and the attribution of the Mausoleion slab is not unanimously accepted. Further attributions to Skopas move outward from this group, depending primarily on the details that have been mentioned and the artist's general reputation for dramatic, twisted poses. If we may judge from what little is known of Skopas' style, he seems to owe something to the Polykleitan tradition while also introducing active, twisted poses and representations of emotion.

Skopas and at least three other sculptors of the day are associated with the sculptural decoration of the Mausoleion. The other sculptors—Bryaxis, Timotheos, and Leochares—are known from copies of their works, but evidence for a full and specific identification of their styles is lacking. Assignment of each artist to the surviving fragments of the frieze has been attempted by various scholars, for differences of style may be discerned, but no certainty has been attained.[11]

The third great sculptor of the fourth century was Lysippos, a native of Sicyon in the Peloponnesos.[12] He seems to have been working before the middle of the century, but the greater part of his career falls within the second half of the century. Alexander, who was born in 355, was one of his subjects while he was still a child, and in later years he appointed the artist court sculptor.

An extremely prolific sculptor, said to have produced 1,500 works, Lysippos belongs more to the coming Hellenistic period than to the Classical past. He was the first to introduce true three-dimensionality to sculpture, with open forms that can be viewed from more than one vantage point. One of his greatest innovations was his departure from the Polykleitan canon of proportions. Unfortunately, our knowledge of his works must depend on Roman

[11] A discussion of the various attributions is in Bernard Ashmole, *Architect and Sculptor in Classical Greece* (New York, 1972), pp. 147–191. For a different point of view, see Martin Robertson, *A History of Greek Art* (Cambridge, 1975), 1:447–463. For the huge number of free-standing sculptures associated with the monument, see Geoffrey Waywell, *The Free-Standing Sculptures of the Mausoleum at Halicarnassus in the British Museum* (London, 1978).

[12] An excellent set of lectures on Lysippos is Erik Sjöqvist, *Lysippos: Lectures in Memory of Louise Taft Semple,* University of Cincinnati Classical Studies no. 2 (Norman, Okla., 1973), pp. 1–50. What appears to be an original bronze statue of a young victor is discussed in Jiří Frel, *The Getty Bronze* (Malibu, Calif.: J. Paul Getty Museum, 1978).

copies that do not reproduce one of the qualities that made him famous—his treatment of surface and details.

One of Lysippos' most famous works was a bronze Apoxyomenos, or Youth Scraping Himself, which was especially prized by the Roman emperor Tiberius. A marble copy of it exists in the Vatican (Fig. 9.26). A comparison of this statue with the Doryphoros (see Fig. 8.35) clearly shows the change in proportions. Lysippos' youth appears taller and thinner, with a smaller head and longer legs than we find in the solid and close-knit Doryphoros. The young man is an athlete in the act of scraping oil and dust from his right arm with a metal instrument called a strigil, which is missing from the copy. His pose recalls the Polykleitan stance, but there is no alternation of tense and relaxed muscles in the body. The body is caught at a moment of overall action. The right arm is thrust out into space while the left crosses in front of the chest, thus partially obscuring it. This breaking of the frontal plane by the outthrust right arm is an important departure that foreshadows the more completely three-dimensional works of the Hellenistic period. Lysippos is quoted as saying that he portrayed men as they appeared to the eye, and the momentary quality of the Apoxyomenos shows this drive for naturalism.

A marble statue of a Thessalian prince from a group dedicated by a certain Daochos at Delphi is generally taken to be a contemporary copy of a Lysippan bronze whose signed base was found in Thessaly (Fig. 9.27). The distinguishing traits of the Lysippan style that we know from the Apoxyomenos are less evident in this much more traditional statue of a victorious athlete, though the small head, expressive face, and tentative turn of the torso are characteristic of Lysippos' works. It has been suggested that the Delphi statue may be a work of the sculptor's early years, when he was presumably still dependent on the Polykleitan tradition. The dating of this statue is disputed, some scholars bringing it well down toward the end of the century. The original bronze may well have been cast earlier. Unfortunately, we have no way of knowing how clearly the marble statue reflects the bronze. Even the approximate dating of a sculptor's works within his lifetime is very difficult when we have so little evidence at our disposal.

Lysippos produced numerous types of sculptured works: action groups, colossal figures, even table ornaments. He seems to have been particularly fond of portraying Herakles. One of his conceptions of the weary hero leaning on his club is preserved in an overblown Late Hellenistic copy in Naples (Fig. 9.28).[13] The pose, with one hand behind the back, exists in a number of other copies and will be seen again.

Portraits of Alexander exist in such profusion that it is difficult to identify one that might be attributed to Lysippos. Features said to be typical of Lysippos' portraits, a turning of the head and distinctive hair, are to be seen in a bust inscribed with the king's name (Fig. 9.29). It dates from Roman imperial times and is poorly preserved, but it may have been modeled on one of Lysippos' works. The reflection of personality in portrait was more fully developed in the Hellenistic period than in earlier years, but Lysippos may well have been an innovator in this area as well.[14]

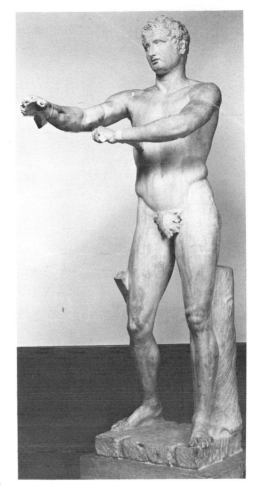

9.26 Apoxyomenos by Lysippos. Musei del Vaticano, Rome. Photo: Hirmer Fotoarchiv, Munich.

[13] The statue had a long life in antiquity. See Cornelius Vermeule, "The Weary Herakles of Lysippos," *AJA* 79 (1975): 323–332.
[14] Portraits of Alexander exist in tremendous numbers, representing various periods and artistic styles. See Margarete Bieber, "The Portraits of Alexander the Great," *Proceedings of the American Philosophical Society* 93 (1949): 373–427.

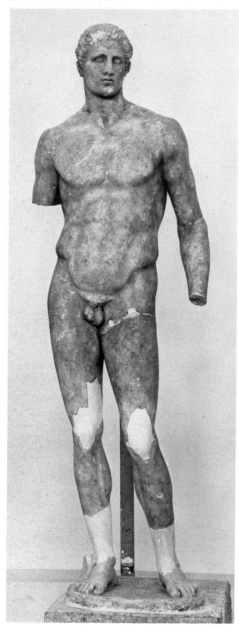

9.27 Agias from the Daochos Group in Delphi.[P] Delphi Museum. Photo: Deutsches Archäologisches Institut, Athens.

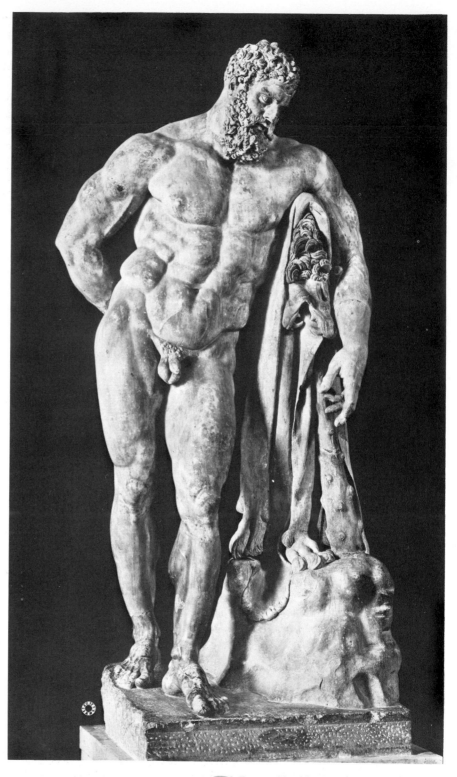

9.28 Farnese Herakles. Museo Nazionale, Naples. Photo: Anderson, Alinari.

A number of original works of the fourth century show the influence of the major artists. The Girl from Chios in Boston (Fig. 9.30), with her triangular forehead, straight nose, and distinctive lips, certainly reminds one of Praxiteles, especially in the extreme softness of the modeling. Dating to the end of the century, it is generally assigned to a follower of the sculptor.

A number of original bronze statues have been preserved. The Youth from Antikythera, found in an ancient shipwreck, seems to reflect two traditions (Fig. 9.31). Certainly the fifth-century Polykleitan influence is strongly indicated by the stance and the thick musculature, but at the same time the small head and the extension into space of the right arm suggest the fourth century and Lysippos. The figure has variously been interpreted as a ball player, although the pose is rather vapid for such an interpretation; as Paris displaying the golden apple of discord before awarding it to Aphrodite; and even as Herakles. It is dated about 340.

The artistic inspiration behind a bronze boy found in the sea near Marathon is more obvious (Fig. 9.32). The sinuous S-curve and the softness of the musculature inevitably recall Praxitelean work of the third quarter of the century. Indeed, some scholars have suggested that the Marathon Boy, who may be in the act of pouring a libation, is in fact an original work of the famous sculptor.[15]

In A.D. 1959 a cache of statues of various dates was found during building operations in Peiraeus. The statues, including an Archaic bronze kouros, were probably awaiting shipment when the warehouse that held them burned down. They may have been part of the loot from the Romans' sack of Athens in 87. Included in the cache was a larger-than-life-sized Athena (Fig. 9.33). It has been convincingly argued that a Roman marble copy of this statue provides interesting information on copying techniques, for the copy alters the position of one arm. The Athena has been attributed to Kephisodotos because of the similarities to the Eirene, but it has also been assigned to at least one other sculptor.[16]

The stylistic development of the sculpture of the fourth century can perhaps be best appreciated in a series of grave stelai from Athens.[17] Dating from the end of the fifth century to the end of the fourth, when a law restricting their production went into effect, these stelai provide good evidence of the artistic development of the times, with none of the uncertainties connected with copies. Although often formulaic and produced in great numbers, these intensely personal monuments chronicle the changes in style and content.

The stele of Hegeso (Fig. 9.34), dating from the late fifth century, shows the deceased seated in a chair. In front of her stands her maid, rendered in smaller scale. The maid holds a jewel box, which her mistress also supports with her left hand. The seated woman gazes at a piece of jewelry that she has just taken

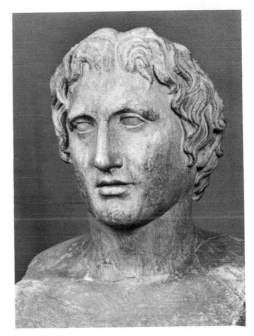

9.29 Portrait of Alexander the Great. Musée du Louvre, Paris. Photo: Giraudon/Art Resource, New York.

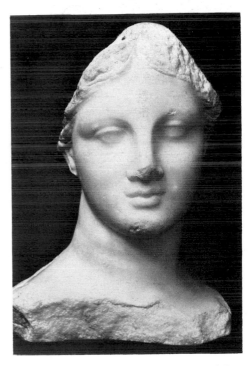

9.30 Girl from Chios. Courtesy, Museum of Fine Arts, Boston. Gift of Nathaniel Thayer.

15 More pictures and commentary on both the Antikythera youth and the Marathon boy may be found in Reinhard Lullies and Max Hirmer, *Greek Sculpture* (New York, 1960), pp. 92–93, Plates 218–222.
16 The connection between the Athena from Peiraeus and the copy of Roman times known as the Athena Mattei has been made by Geoffrey Waywell in "Athena Mattei," *BSA* 66 (1971): 373–382. In this article the bronze is attributed to Kephisodotos. It is attributed to the artist Euphranor in Olga Palagia, "Euphranoros Techne," *AAA* 6 (1973): 323–329. An alternate theory may be found in Ross Holloway, "Athena Archegetis in the Piraeus," *AJA* 67 (1963): 212. Details of Athena's sandal may indicate that she is in fact a Hellenistic copy; see Brunilde S. Ridgway, *Hellenistic Sculpture I: The Styles of ca. 331–200 B.C.* (Madison, Wis., 1990), p. 363.
17 A great many late fifth- and fourth-century gravestones have been found. See Christoph W. Clairmont, *Classical Attic Tombstones* (Kilchberg, Switzerland, 1993).

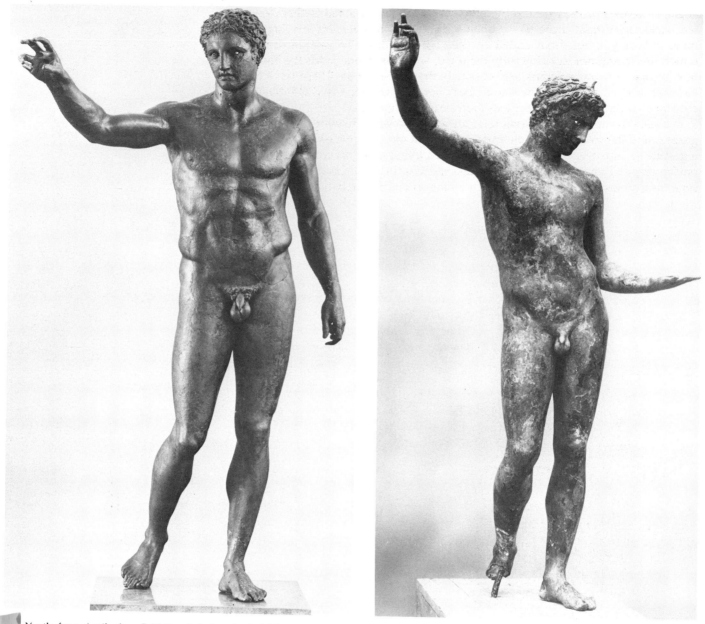

9.31 Youth from Antikythera.ᴾ National Archaeological Museum, Athens. Photo: Deutsches Archäologisches Institut, Athens.

9.32 Marathon Boy. National Archaeological Museum, Athens. Photo: Deutsches Archäologisches Institut, Athens.

from the box, and which was rendered in paint. The two figures, posed in front of an architectural frame, essentially form a single unit, joined by the jewel box. The decorative, slightly transparent drapery reminds one of the Parthenon sculptures, as do the idealized heads and quiet poses. The attitude of sorrow is merely suggested by the composition; the mistress is linked to the presumably living maid by the objects and tasks that linked them in life.

Figure 9.35 shows another stele, this time from Peiraeus and dated about 370. The scene is similar but a subtle shift in emphasis has taken place. The figures are now isolated from one another, and the seated woman is placed at a slight angle, with one foot drawn back. Both figures are larger and stand farther from the background than those of the Hegeso stele. The heavier drapery hangs more naturally about the rounded curves of the bodies. The gesture of the seated figure and her isolation from the maid, who now alone holds the jewel box, begins to show a pathos not present in the Hegeso stele. These tendencies—separation of figures, increased depth of relief, and increased emotional content—can be seen to intensify as the century progresses.

In a relief from the Ilissos River (Fig. 9.36), a nude youth leaning on a pillar gazes out of the scene toward the viewer, while an old man, his hand raised in a gesture of sorrow, gazes at him. At the man's feet is a dog. A child is seated on the stepped base of the pillar, apparently weeping. The central figure is separated almost completely from the old man, who is probably his father, and

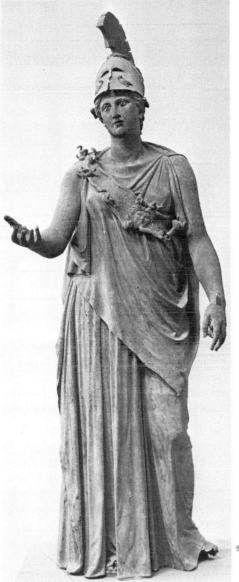

9.33 Bronze statue of Athena found in Peiraeus.ᴾ National Archaeological Museum, Athens. Photo: Deutsches Archäologisches Institut, Athens.

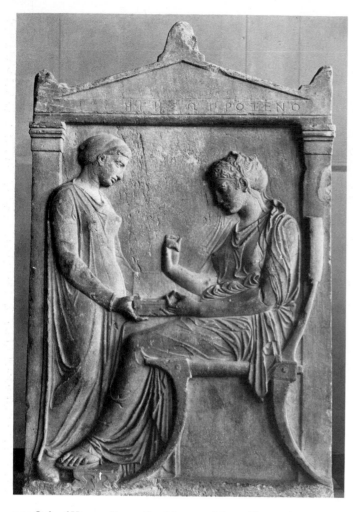

9.34 Stele of Hegeso. Kerameikos Museum, Athens. Photo: Alison Frantz.

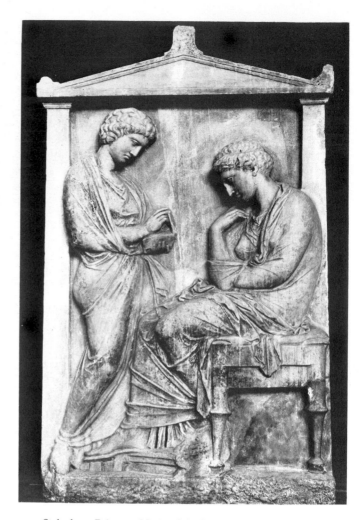

9.35 Stele from Peiraeus. National Archaeological Museum, Athens. Photo: Deutsches Archäologisches Institut, Athens.

by looking out of the scene induces a sympathetic reaction in the viewer. The sorrow of the old man and the child and the presence of the dead man's favorite hunting dog lend poignance to the scene. The proportions of the central figure and the depth of relief place this sculpture within the second half of the century; it is usually dated about 340. By this time the figured scene and the architectural frame had become separate entities.

A stele from Rhamnous in Attica (Fig. 9.37) is dated somewhat later, about 330–320. Here the two figures are linked by clasped hands. The male figure shows the same gesture of grief as did the father in the previous example. The woman, although looking at him, is actually fully frontal. She is probably his wife, taking her husband's hand in a last farewell. The two tall figures touching for the last time express an understated depth of emotion.

The statue in Figure 9.38 is from the grave monument of Aristonautes, which must have been carved just before the restrictive law of 317. The figure, almost in the round, portrays the deceased as a warrior moving into battle. The elaborate carving and exuberance of motion make one wonder what direction the

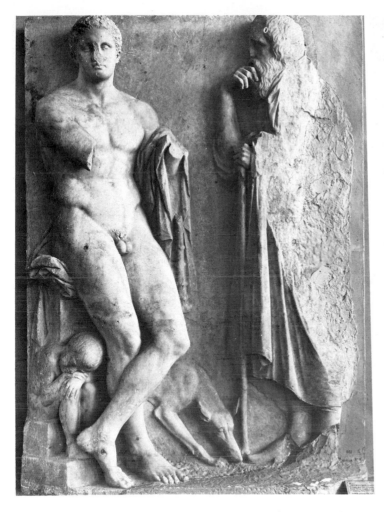

9.36 Relief from the Ilissos River. National Archaeological Museum, Athens. Photo: Deutsches Archäologisches Institut, Athens.

9.37 Relief from Rhamnous. National Archaeological Museum, Athens. Photo: Deutsches Archäologisches Institut, Athens.

development of grave monuments would have taken if their production had not been curtailed.

PAINTING AND MOSAICS

Greek painting appears to have reached its zenith in the fourth century. We hear of a great number of famous artists, but once again nothing is left of their work. We are dependent on reflections in a few early-fourth-century vases and mosaics, such as the Alexander Mosaic from Pompeii, discussed in the next chapter. Both wall paintings and movable paintings were made, presumably much like those in the Pinakotheke in Athens. The luck of excavation has preserved for us a fragment of Greek painting on wood from the early fourth century. Found in the 1971/72 season by the English Egypt Exploration Society at Saqqara in Egypt, the panel of a box or other small wooden object is now in the British Museum (Fig. 9.39). A seated woman is shown in bright colors against a light background, holding an object, perhaps a kind of tambourine, in

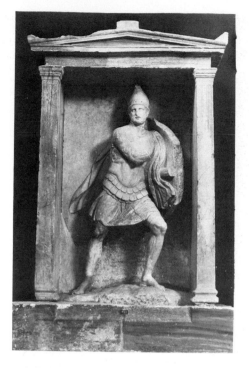

9.38 Statue of Aristonautes. National Archaeological Museum, Athens. Photo: Deutsches Archäologisches Institut, Athens.

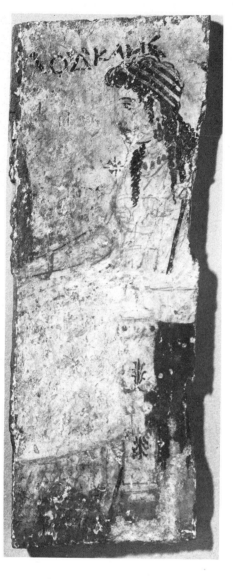

9.39 Painted plaque from Saqqara, Egypt. Reproduced by courtesy of the Trustees of the British Museum, London.

front of her. Her flesh is painted pink; the throne on which she sits is red; white bands encircle her black hair; the object she is holding is yellow. An enigmatic inscription is painted above the figure. This is a minor object from a site far from Greece, but it is important for its rarity.

In the first half of the century mythological scenes began to appear in pebble mosaics, as in the central figures of Bellerophon and the Chimaira in a house mosaic from Olynthos (Fig. 9.40). The color scheme was essentially still black and white, but the drawing had been done with some care (compare the rendering of the wave pattern with that on the fifth-century example from Corinth shown in Fig. 8.55), and some attempt has been made to show detailed inner markings.

At the end of the century a series of magnificent pebble mosaics was laid at Pella, the capital city of the Macedonian dynasty. One of the best, signed by a certain Gnosis, is probably quite similar to contemporary wall painting (Fig. 9.41). The scene still stands out against a dark background but now details

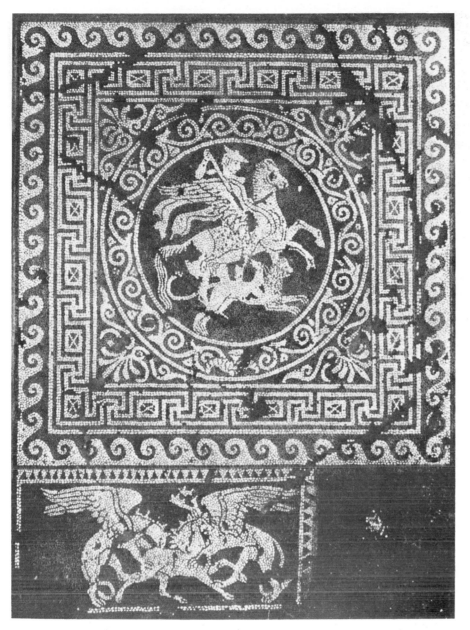

9.40 Mosaic of Bellerophon and the Chimaira at Olynthos.[P] From David M. Robinson, *Mosaics, Vases, and Lamps of Olynthus Found in 1928 and 1931.* Excavations at Olynthus series, vol. 5, Plate 12. Copyright 1933, The Johns Hopkins Press.

are picked out in red, yellow, and other bright colors. The stance of the figures—no longer in profile—the use of shading, and the interest in anatomy indicate that the mosaicist was abreast of all the contemporary developments in painting. In the best of these mosaics the artists outlined the figures with strips of lead or terra cotta to emphasize contours. They also saw to it that the pebbles were more closely packed and graded than before.

POTTERY

The fourth century was a transitional period for pottery, and especially for its decoration. The bell and calyx krater, the hydria, the pelike, the lekanis, and

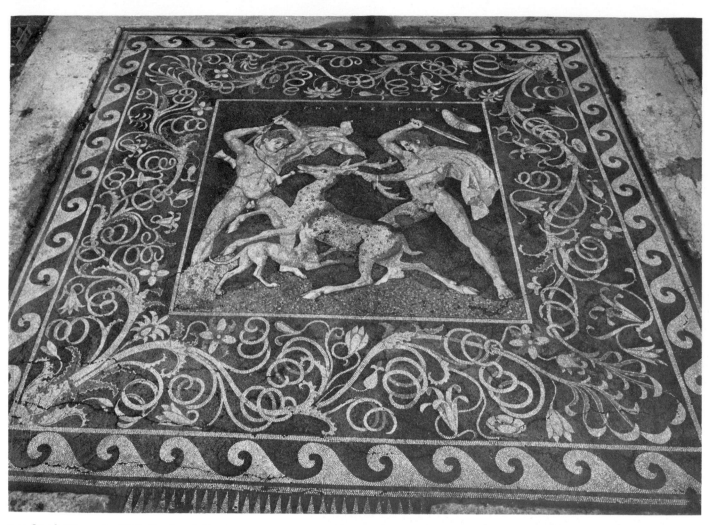

9.41 Stag-hunt mosaic at Pella,[P] as found. Courtesy of Ph. M. Petsas.

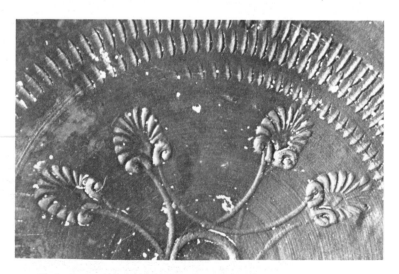

9.42 Rouletting and stamped decoration on a black glazed plate. Photo: Museum of Art and Archaeology, University of Missouri–Columbia.

the skyphos were the most popular shapes. The stemmed kylix, the squat lekythos, and a number of other shapes dropped from use in the course of the century. All shapes continued to elongate.

The interest in working the surface of the vase rather than painting it, which began with impressed decoration and ribbing in the fifth century, gained in popularity, and rouletting was added in the early years of the fourth: a strip of metal was held against a pot while it rotated, thus forming incisions in the clay at desired intervals. Rouletting was often employed in combination with stamps (Fig. 9.42). The surfaces of some fourth-century vases were covered with painted clay reliefs.

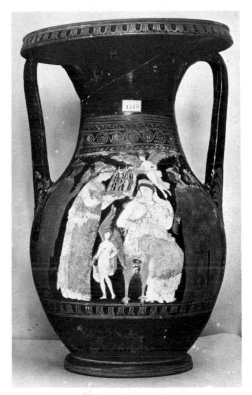

9.43 Typical Kerch style amphora. National Archaeological Museum, Athens. Photo: Deutsches Archäologisches Institut, Athens.

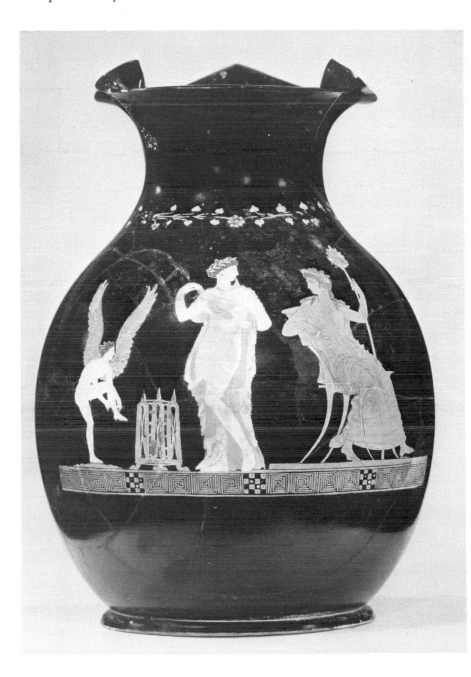

9.44 Red Figure oinochoe. The Metropolitan Museum of Art, Fletcher Fund, 1925.

279

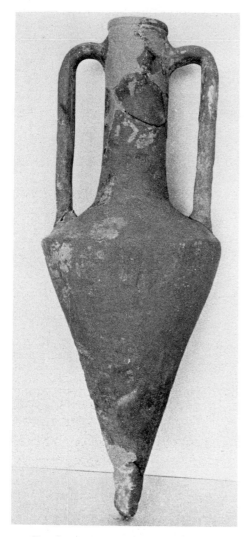

Fourth-century Red Figure painting at first was a continuation of an ornate style that began at the end of the fifth. Large figures painted with bright subsidiary colors—white, red, yellow—and often shaded, gilded, and embellished with relief work, were pushed into crowded compositions. Religious and domestic scenes were popular. A typical example of a fourth-century painting style, the so-called Kerch style (named after the city in southern Russia where examples were first found), is shown in Figure 9.43. More simple examples have also been found, such as the often-illustrated oinochoe from the middle of the century now in New York (Fig. 9.44). All the gilding and polychromy of the time are present in the figures of Pompe (the personification of a festal procession), Dionysos, and an Eros, but the composition is more quiet and elegant than the ornate Kerch examples. The oinochoe has a band of ivy around its neck, a harbinger of things to come, for by 320 the figured style in Attic vase painting had given way to the simplified designs of Hellenistic pottery.

9.45 Fourth-century transport amphora from Chios. Photo: American School of Classical Studies at Athens: Agora Excavations.

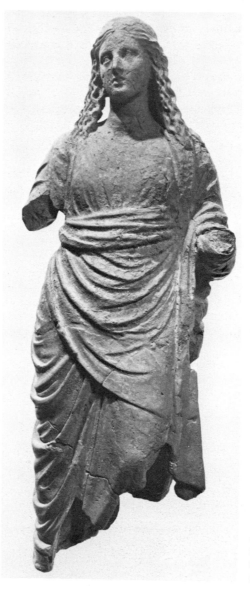

9.46 Standing female figurine from the sanctuary of Demeter and Kore at Corinth. Corinth Museum. Photo: American School of Classical Studies at Athens: Corinth Excavations.

TRANSPORT AMPHORAS

The continued elongation of transport amphoras in the fourth century can be seen in another Chian example, Figure 9.45. The button toe of the fifth-century predecessor has been eliminated and the neck has become longer, with the mouth projecting father above the lip. Perhaps ease of storage and transport was the principal factor in the changes, but the trend toward taller and thinner shapes is noticeable in fine pottery too.

TERRA COTTA FIGURINES

The transitional nature of the fourth century is well illustrated by the terra cotta figurines produced during the period. Most of them reproduced the handmade and mold-made types already established, though realism constantly increased until, about 330, the famous Tanagra style was developed. This style, named for the place in Boiotia where the first examples were found, was probably developed in Athens and is to be seen primarily in draped standing women and girls, dancing figures, and genre scenes. It is a style of complete naturalism and belongs in spirit to the Hellenistic age. It is further discussed in Chapter 10.

Although many of the figurines produced in the fourth century remained close to their classical models, some more original work was done. A tall (0.275 meters preserved height) standing woman in heavy fourth-century drapery, found at the site of a sanctuary of Demeter and Kore in Corinth, is a forerunner of the elegant Tanagras (Fig. 9.46). Figure 9.47 shows a standing actor portraying a woman, perhaps pregnant, dressed in a chiton and himation that cover him almost entirely except for the upper part of the face. Figurines inspired by Greek comedy were very popular in Athens, but this example was also found in the Demeter and Kore sanctuary in Corinth.

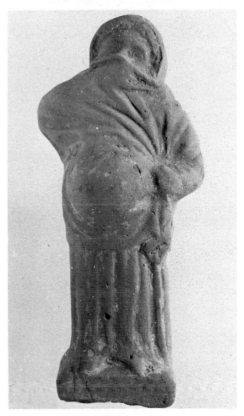

COINS

Coins, like figurines, continued the traditions of the fifth century for a time, but as the century progressed, High Classical idealism gradually waned. In many ways the fourth century, with its great variety of interesting types, was the high-water mark of Greek coin production, before a certain regimentation set in with the establishment of portrait types of the various Hellenistic rulers.

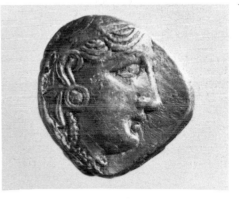

9.48 Fourth-century coin from Athens: head of Athena. Photo: Museum of Art and Archaeology, University of Missouri–Columbia. Scale 2:1.

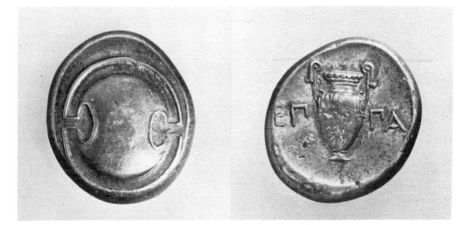

9.49 Fourth-century coin from Thebes: obverse, shield; reverse, amphora. Photos: Museum of Art and Archaeology, University of Missouri–Columbia. Scale 2:1.

281

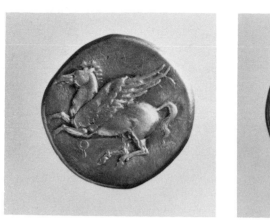

9.50 Fourth-century coin from Corinth: obverse, Pegasos: reverse, Athena Chalinitis. Photos: Museum of Art and Archaeology, University of Missouri–Columbia. Scale 2:1.

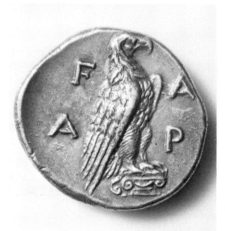

9.51 Fourth-century coin from Elis: obverse, head of Zeus; reverse, eagle. Photos: Hirmer Fotoarchiv, Munich. Scale 2:1.

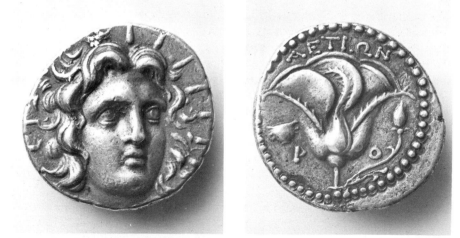

9.52 Third-century coin from Rhodes: obverse, head of Helios; reverse, rose. Photo: Hirmer Fotoarchiv, Munich. Scale 2:1.

The greatest producer of coins in the previous century, Athens, fell on evil days after its defeat, and for a while was unable even to mint in silver at all. By 393, however, silver coinage was revived. Fifth-century types reappeared, but now Athena's eye was drawn correctly in profile (Fig. 9.48). Other mainland centers

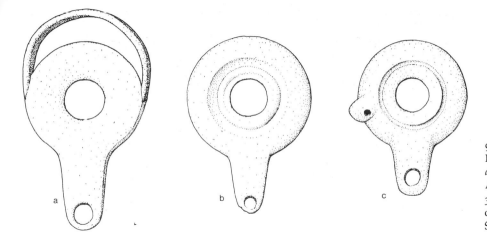

9.53 Typical fourth-century lamps. After Richard Hubbard Howland, *Greek Lamps and Their Survivals*, Athenian Agora series, vol. 4 (Princeton: American School of Classical Studies, 1958), Plates 36 and 38. By permission of the American School of Classical Studies. Drawing by John Huffstot. Scale 1:2.

continued to mint coins with more or less up-to-date designs (Figs. 9.49 and 9.50). In this period the new freedom and elaboration derived from contemporary artistic currents often combined to produce masterpieces in miniature through the development of old types and the invention of new ones. The series from Elis has a magnificent head of Zeus on the obverse and an eagle on the reverse (Fig. 9.51). In the city of Rhodes, which was founded only at the end of the fifth century, coins with a three-quarter head of Helios and a rose on the reverse (a punning reference to the city's name) became famous. Some feel the style reached its acme in the third century—an example is pictured in Figure 9.52—although the types were fully established soon after the founding of the city.

LAMPS

Lamps continued to grow in height, and rims broadened to enclose more of the interior. Nozzles grew longer and narrower, with holes progressively closer to the ends. Figure 9.53a is a shape common in the first half of the century, with a simple raised base, a horizontal band handle, and a covering of shiny black glaze. More globular bodies were popular in the second half of the century and well into the third (Fig. 9.53b). These lamps, which are distinguished by their high curving sides separated from the rim by groove, have a long, narrow nozzle with a small wick hole at the end. They may be glazed or unglazed (Figure 9.53b is an unglazed type) and with or without handles, but handles seem to be an early feature. Figure 9.53c illustrates a slightly different development of the second half of the century: the handle has been replaced by a pierced lug on the left side. Perhaps a lug was less susceptible to damage than a handle. The hole is thought to have been provided so that the lamp could be hung up by a cord passed through the lug when it was not in use. An alternate theory is that the pierced lug served as a place to store a thin instrument for use in poking up the wick, but the first explanation seems the likelier one.

10

The Hellenistic Age

WHEN ALEXANDER DIED in Babylon, he left neither will nor heir. The gigantic empire he had conquered was suddenly without its conqueror, and it was left for his generals to divide up the prize so suddenly given to them. The inevitable result was some forty years of struggle and bloodshed while men vied for power and territory. By the second quarter of the third century, three major divisions of Alexander's empire had become more or less established.

One kingdom, the smallest, was based on the old Macedonian capital of Pella and included European Greece. Ruled by the Antigonid dynasty, Macedonia maintained its authority over the old Greek cities through garrisons and alliances but constantly had to fight off various combinations of states seeking their freedom. For this purpose a number of small cities joined together in leagues hostile to Macedon. The Antigonids eventually came into conflict with Rome, and after a long struggle their kingdom was destroyed at the battle of Pydna in 168.

Athens was now politically unimportant but became a university town and cultural center. As such it benefited materially from the gifts of buildings and sculpture lavished upon it by Hellenistic kings who had studied in the city in their youth. Athens avoided active involvement in most of the conflicts of the Hellenistic world until the early first century, when it opposed Rome's attempt, ultimately successful, to subjugate the East. The city was sacked by the Roman general Sulla in 88.

The Seleucid kingdom, with its capital at Antioch, on the Orontes, included much of the eastern territory conquered by Alexander. This huge area was governed through a network of settlements, most of them newly founded, which stood as Greek outposts in a foreign land. Many of these settlements began as military colonies and evolved into more or less independent cities. They were Greek in culture, and through them a veneer of Hellenic civilization spread over the empire. The Seleucid kingdom thrived on trade, and the assimilation of Oriental and Greek elements can be seen in the arts and artifacts of some of the trading settlements on the fringes of the empire. The Seleucid kingdom fell to the Romans in 65.

Egypt was taken by one of the more astute of Alexander's generals, Ptolemy, who founded a stable dynasty that lasted until the last queen, the famous Cleopatra, lost her throne to the Romans in 30. The rule of the Ptolemies differed from that of the Seleucids, since their prize was an already organized country of ancient traditions. Greek rule here consisted primarily of adapting existing machinery to the systematic exploitation of the country. Greek settlers poured in to form the upper stratum of a society that never became wholly Hellenized. As time went on, some assimilation took place, but in general the great mass of the people lived under their own laws and religions. Ruling from the new capital city of Alexandria on the Mediterranean, the Ptolemies aspired to head a maritime empire and thus inevitably came into conflict with the other states.

The Hellenistic period was an age of constant conflict among the great states, most notably between the Ptolemies and the Seleucids over the Syria/Palestine area. During these struggles a city could often seize an opportunity to become independent and prosperous. Pergamon, on the northwestern coast of modern Turkey, was a spin-off from the struggles of Alexander's successors, and became rich as a result of a good commercial situation. It also became the center of some of the most original Hellenistic art, inspired by Pergamon's defense of Hellenism against invading Gallic tribes. Another city that owed its fortune to trade was Rhodes, which grew to become one of the foremost commercial centers of the age.

Clearly the Hellenistic period was very different from previous centuries. The most obvious difference was the great size of the political units and the variations among and within the nation-states. Cities that varied in size, age, ethnic composition, and religion were joined together by a common language, Greek, and varying degrees of Greek culture. This extension of Greek culture to other lands is a distinguishing feature of the time and the quality that gives the period its name. Essentially a new culture was formed, more secular and cosmopolitan than the old. It was this culture that so influenced Rome, and through it the Western world.

The Hellenistic world was more "modern" than any up to that time. The tremendous increase in population, the rise of urban centers, the emphasis on manufacturing and commerce, the growth of foreign and ecstatic religions, growing separation of rich and poor, bureaucracy, scientific investigation, reverence for the past, taxes—all these characteristics of the Hellenistic age are familiar to us today.

The Hellenistic kingdoms were ultimately absorbed by Rome, whose empire was greater than Alexander's and which gave the civilized world over two hundred years of relative peace, a feat that the warring kingdoms of Alexander's successors were unable to accomplish and which, in fact, has not been repeated to this day.

ART

The new world created by Alexander demanded a new art. Various factors combined to form this art, including the changing way in which people thought of themselves and their relationships with others. Also important was the increased contact between the Greeks and other lands and peoples. The artistic needs of the Hellenistic kingdoms were different from those of the earlier city-states. Artistic creations still had to be dedicated to the gods— the traditional gods as well as new ones—and monuments still had to be erected for the dead, but a growing wealthy class in the great cities now wanted art for decoration to an extent not known before. Houses were decorated with mosaics and gardens with statuary, and the rich collector became a force in the art world. Individual tastes can be detected in some Hellenistic works, especially in sculpture. The occasional artistic tour de force is to be found in this period also. But Rome, the biggest collector of them all, dominated the latter part of the period, and the Romans' appetite for old works stimulated artists and sculptors to produce works with the Classical and Archaic qualities they prized.

The variety of art in the Hellenistic age is staggering, stretching in time over almost three hundred years and in space from India to Egypt. It is a tremendously rich and vibrant field, but one that is exceedingly difficult to understand fully and impossible to condense into a few short pages. In order to appreciate the range of Hellenistic art, one must look beyond mainland Greece, for in this period Greece was fast becoming a provincial backwater.

The period may be divided artistically into three phases. The second century—perhaps the most original period, with its powerful Pergamene-Baroque style—is bracketed by two periods with roots in the past, the earlier a continuation of fourth-century styles and the later incorporating some characteristics of the past in contemporary artistic expressions.

In the history of Greek art we have seen a relatively constant development toward the realistic representation of nature. In the Hellenistic period this development reached a certain climax, then occasionally lapsed into stale repetition or exaggeration. For the first time all classes of society and all gradations of physical condition were realistically shown, and often caricatured. Technically, Greek art had never reached such heights as those attained by Hellenistic practitioners. It was this art that had such influence on the Romans, and through them on the Italian Renaissance.

ARCHITECTURE

The conquests of Alexander and the subsequent founding of new cities spawned much new building. It is in the East, where opportunity and funds were abundant, that most new examples are to be found. Architects of the Hellenistic age had freedom to experiment. The Ionic order reigned supreme in its homeland and was developed to a height of elaboration. The Doric order continued to be used for traditional temples and utilitarian secular constructions, but in the second century it fell into neglect. The Corinthian order was slow to develop. It was first used as an exterior free-standing order only in the third century, and was left for the Romans to explore fully. New orders were invented, and at the very end of the Hellenistic age an attempt was made to revivify the orders by physically combining them. Thus one can find Ionic volutes superimposed on the bell of a Corinthian capital.

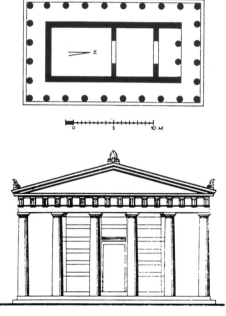

10.1 Plan and elevation of the temple of Athena Polias Nikephoros at Pergamon.[P] From Gottfried Gruben, *Die Tempel der Griechen* (Munich: Hirmer Verlag, 1966), p. 403. Figs. 322/323. Reproduced by permission.

The traditional Doric temple of Athena Polias Nikephoros (Bringer of Victory) (Fig. 10.1) was one of the earliest buildings erected on the hill at Pergamon during the reign of the city's founder, Philetairos (282–263). Later, in the first half of the second century, its terrace was surrounded by a colonnade. A short building (21.77 by 12.27 meters), the temple continued the fourth-century tendency toward slimness and lightness: the height of its widely spaced columns, six on each end and ten on each flank, was seven times their lower diameter. The wide spacing of the columns allowed three metopes between each pair of columns instead of the canonical two, a fashion begun in the fifth century. The columns were fluted only immediately below the capitals; they were never finished, not even when the later stoa was built. This lack of interest in completing the columns has been interpreted as a loss of interest in the order itself. The cella had the normal pronaos but no opisthodomos; it may have been divided into two rooms by a wall across its width.

The temple of Artemis Leucophryene (white-browed) at Magnesia on the Maeander (Figs. 10.2 and 10.3) demonstrates the new freedom to experiment with plans. It was built by one of the most famous architects of the age,

Hermogenes of Priene. He was renowned as a theoretician and is said to have devised a new system of proportional relationships for the Ionic order that was based, at least in part, on the relationship between the height and diameter of columns to the distance between them. A glance at the plan (Fig. 10.2) shows the architect's originality. Set on a high podium of seven steps, the marble temple measured 57.90 by 31.61 meters on the stylobate with eight columns across each end and fifteen on each flank. The Ionic columns were evenly arranged, except at the central space at both ends, where they were more widely spaced. The Ionic bases sat on square plinths. Although there was room for a second row of columns behind the outer row, the space was left free, thus

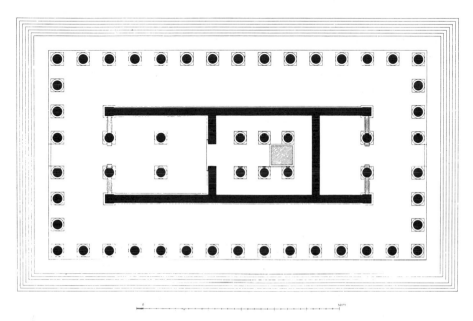

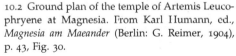

10.2 Ground plan of the temple of Artemis Leucophryene at Magnesia. From Karl Humann, ed., *Magnesia am Maeander* (Berlin: G. Reimer, 1904), p. 43, Fig. 30.

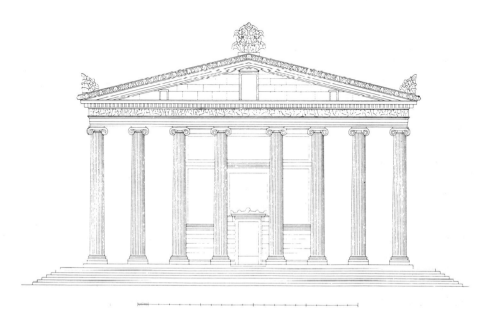

10.3 Restored west front of the temple of Artemis Leucophryene at Magnesia. From Karl Humann, ed., *Magnesia am Maender* (Berlin: G. Reimer, 1904), p. 47, Fig. 32.

forming a pseudo-dipteral plan. In front of the cella was a pronaos of the same depth as the cella; the opisthodomos was more shallow. On the exterior a sculptured frieze ran above the epistyle, but no sculpture adorned the pediments. Instead there were apparently openings or windows at each corner and over the central intercolumniation. The reason usually given for these openings, or at least for the central one, was a desire to reduce the weight over the wide central intercolumniation. Attic influence can be detected in this building, from both fifth-century and later buildings. The temple of Artemis has been dated to the first half of the second century.

Probably the Hellenistic temple most often cited is the temple of Apollo at Didyma, near Miletos (Figs. 10.4–10.6). Work began about 300 on a great new temple in the tradition of the huge religious buildings of archaic Ionia. The temple is one of the largest (109.38 by 51.14 meters) and most grandiose ever built. Work continued on it until the second century of the Christian era but it was never finished. Raised on a high podium, the cella was surrounded by some 120 columns, 19.70 meters high, standing in two rows (dipteral columniation). Ten columns stood on each end and twenty-one along each flank. The cella itself was open to the sky along most of its length, providing a setting for a small tetrastyle, free-standing Ionic shrine for the cult statue of Apollo (Fig. 10.5). Apollo spoke through an oracle, and the whole ornate pile was designed to surround this open court, which was originally planted with trees and contained an oracular spring and a shrine that was considered to be the original home of the oracle. The walls of the court were ornamented with pilasters, and opposite the little temple, a massive staircase of twenty-four steps led up between two semidetached Corinthian columns to a rectangular room whose ceiling was supported by two free-standing Corinthian columns. It was probably from the threshold of this room, which was at chest height above the floor

10.4 Plan of the temple of Apollo at Didyma.[P] From Gottfried Gruben, *Die Tempel der Griechen* (Munich: Hirmer Verlag, 1966), p. 345, Fig. 274. Reproduced by permission.

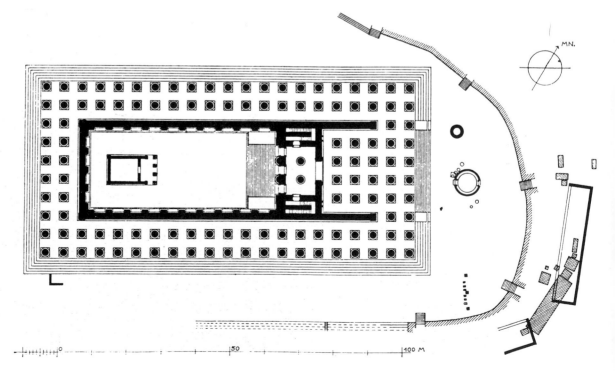

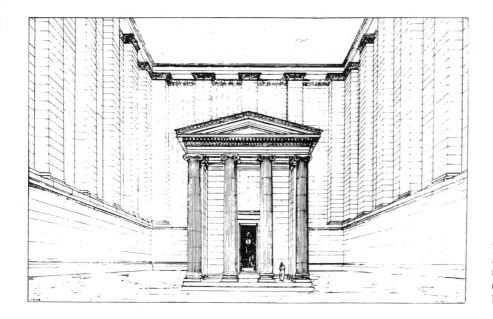

10.5 Restored inner Ionic shrine of the temple of Apollo at Didyma. From Fritz Krischen, *Weltwunder der Baukunst in Babylonien und Jonien* (Tübingen: Verlag Ernst Wasmuth, 1956), Plate 33. Reproduced by permission.

10.6 Ruins of the temple of Apollo at Didyma, from the north. Photo: Hirmer Fotoarchiv, Munich.

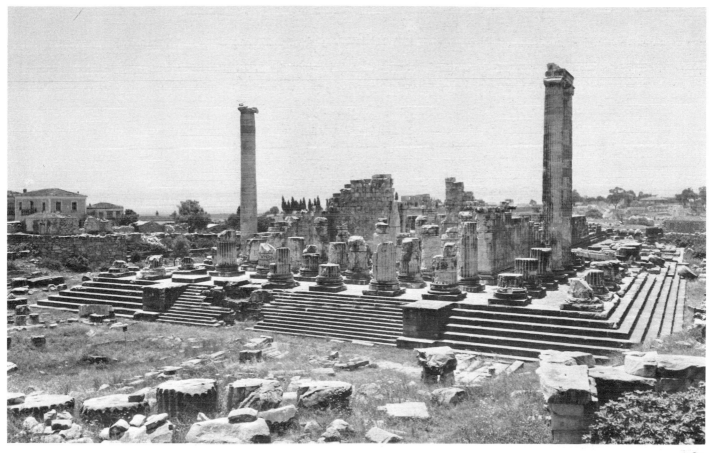

of the deep pronaos, that the oracle spoke. Small doors on either side of the pronaos led to sloping barrel-vaulted passageways that led down to the court-yard, while staircases from the rectangular room led to the roof, perhaps for ritual purposes. The building was loaded with ornament, much of it dating from the last years of the building's construction. The ornamentation and the interest shown by the architects in working with space are characteristics of Hellenistic architecture. Interesting evidence for construction methods has been revealed by the discovery that working drawings of architectural details were inscribed on the walls of the temple to guide the construction workers.[1]

Another colossal temple, this time in Athens, was worked on in the Hellenistic age. The sons of Peisistratos had begun a large temple to the east of the Acropolis in the sixth century in emulation of the great buildings being erected by tyrants in Asia Minor and Samos. It was originally to have been built in the Doric order but was never completed. One of the Hellenistic kings, Antiochos IV, engaged a Roman architect, Cossutius, to rebuild it in 174 in the more modern Corinthian order. Some of its columns still stand today (Fig. 10.7). The great building, 108.00 by 41.12 meters, with three rows of eight columns on each end and two rows of twenty along each flank (Fig. 10.8), is notable for the Corinthian capitals designed for it (Fig. 10.9). Coming out of the Greek tradition, they may have had a strong effect on the Roman Corinthian order, for

10.7 Temple of Olympian Zeus at Athens, with the Acropolis in the background. Photo: William R. Biers.

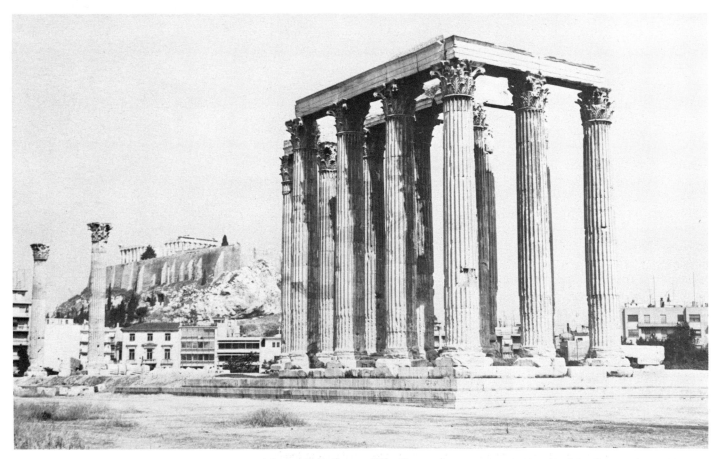

[1] Lothar Hasselberger, "The Construction Plans for the Temple of Apollo at Didyma," *Scientific American* 253 (1985): 126–132.

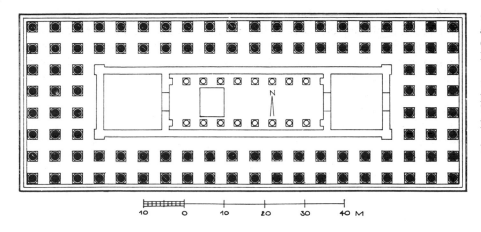

10.8 Ground plan of the temple of Olympian Zeus at Athens. From Gottfried Gruben, *Die Tempel der Griechen* (Munich: Hirmer Verlag, 1966), p. 226, Fig. 173. Reproduced by permission.

10.9 Corinthian capital from the temple of Olympian Zeus at Athens. From Gottfried Gruben, *Die Tempel der Griechen* (Munich: Hirmer Verlag, 1966), p. 227, Fig. 174. Reproduced by permission.

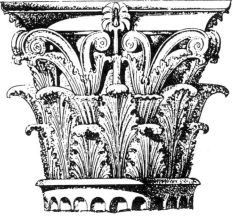

after the sack of Athens in 86, some were removed to Rome by the Roman general Sulla. In these capitals the bell is almost covered by acanthus leaves. Work on the temple stopped with the death of the king, and it was completed only under the Roman emperor Hadrian in the first half of the second century of the Christian era.

SECULAR ARCHITECTURE

In the course of the second century considerable changes were made in the plan of the Athenian agora (Fig. 10.10). Apart from the reconstruction of the old Bouleuterion to house the cult of the Mother of the Gods and of the state archives (the building now being called the Metroon), the changes essentially took the form of the addition of long stoas. To the south a subsidiary square, called the South Square, was created by the construction of two long stoas to the north and south and a short building connecting them to the east. This complex is associated with the law courts by the excavators. The east side of the Agora square was closed by the erection of the Stoa of Attalos, a two-story building given to Athens by King Attalos II of Pergamon (159–138), who had studied in the city in his youth. The building was destroyed in a barbarian raid in A.D. 267 and then incorporated in a late fortification wall. So much of the fabric was preserved that it was possible to rebuild the building with a high degree of accuracy. The reconstruction was carried out between A.D. 1953 and 1956 by the American School of Classical Studies at Athens to serve as a museum and workrooms for the Agora excavations. Thus a complete reconstruction of an ancient building containing much of the original material can be seen today standing where it stood over two thousand years before (Fig. 10.11).[2]

The Stoa of Attalos is a fine example of an advanced form of Hellenistic stoa, measuring 116.50 by 20.05 meters and utilizing Pentelic marble for facade and columns. Stoas were designed to provide protection from the sun and cold winds, as informal gathering places, and as shopping centers. The colonnade on each floor was backed by a series of shops. The Doric order was used on the ground floor on the outside, with Ionic columns on the inside (Color Plate 16). The upper story had piers with Ionic half-columns on each end and marble

[2] The reconstruction of the Stoa of Attalos yielded a fascinating glimpse of building methods in Greek times. See Homer A. Thompson, *The Stoa of Attalos II in Athens*, Agora Picture Books no. 2 (Princeton, 1959), and the various reports on the building in *Hesperia*, 1950–1959.

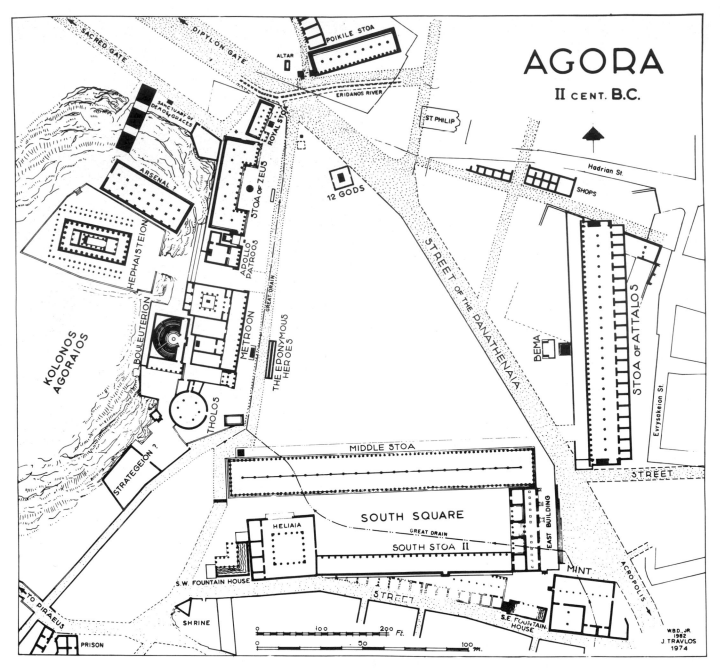

10.10 Plan of the Agora at Athens in the second century. Photo: American School of Classical Studies at Athens: Agora Excavations.

balustrades between them. The interior order was the new Pergamene order, which had capitals in the form of curving petals supporting the abacus (Fig. 10.12).

The Pergamene order, which was probably adapted from an Egyptian palm capital, was a typical feature of Pergamene architecture. Another common Hellenistic device, used mainly in secular buildings where a good deal of traffic was expected, was the faceting of the lower portions of the exterior

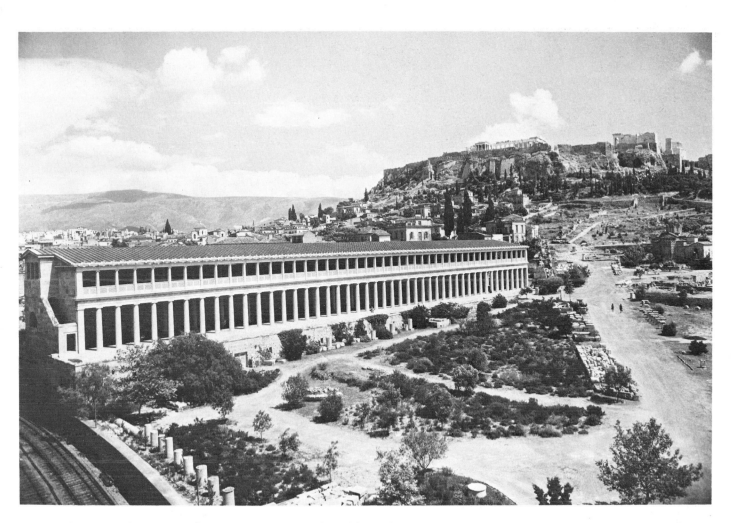

10.11 The reconstructed Stoa of Attalos in Athens, from the northwest. Photo: American School of Classical Studies at Athens: Agora Excavations.

Doric colonnade. Flutes, even flat Doric ones, are vulnerable to damage. For a similar reason the interior Ionic columns were left plain, with neither flutes nor facets.

Thus in the second century the Athenian agora took on a more ordered look, with stoas defining the south and east boundaries. This use of the stoa to surround or define a space reflects the contemporary interest in space and planning.

Stoas played a great part in the unified complexes that are found where new Hellenistic cities or sanctuaries were laid out. A concern for the relationship of buildings in structural settings together with an interest in visual effects developed in the Hellenistic period and led to the orchestrated architecture of Roman times. This new tendency to place buildings in architectural settings can be seen in the Asklepieion on Kos, built in the third and second centuries (Fig. 10.13). Here the most important building, the temple, was placed at the highest point, at the head of a flight of stairs, and framed on three sides by stoas. Below it stretched two large terraces, more or less formally laid out and serving to emphasize the temple above them. Although cult requirements dictated the placement of some of the buildings and although the lowest terrace was not exactly in line with the temple, the builders clearly took care to

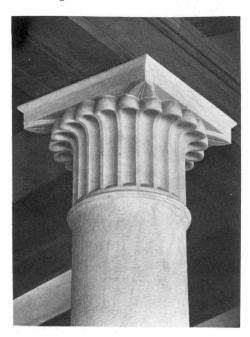

10.12 A Pergamene capital in the Stoa of Atalos. Photo: American School of Classical Studies at Athens: Agora Excavations.

relate elements of the sanctuary to one another, rather than simply adding new structures wherever space was available.[3]

A similar concern is evident in the plan of the great city of Pergamon, whose principal portion was built on a steep hill. A series of large terraces connected by a broad street ascends the hill, on the slope of which is a great theater (Fig. 10.14). Below lie an agora, gymnasium, and two sanctuaries. The major monuments of the city are on the fortified hill, however, including three terraces that are arranged around the top of the hill and placed so as to give unobstructed views out over the valley. The Pergamene kings considered themselves to be the standard-bearers and protectors of Hellenic civilization, and this concept was clearly expressed in the great monument that occupied the lowest of the three terraces. The Pergamon Altar bore a relief of the battle of gods and giants as a victory monument to the Pergamenes' defeat of the Gauls, which they equated with the Athenians' defeat of the Persians (see below). The altar was linked visually with the temple of Athena on the next highest terrace by the alignment of its first step with the flank of the temple. To the north of the two-story stoa that surrounded the court of the temple stood a great library, where the Pergamene rulers kept what they considered to be their written heritage and works of art. Another terrace, farther to the north, is now adorned with the remains of a temple built by the Roman emperor Trajan. It is uncertain what was there in Hellenistic times. Opposite, on the east side of the hill, was the modest palace of the kings of Pergamon and some barracks. Pergamon was

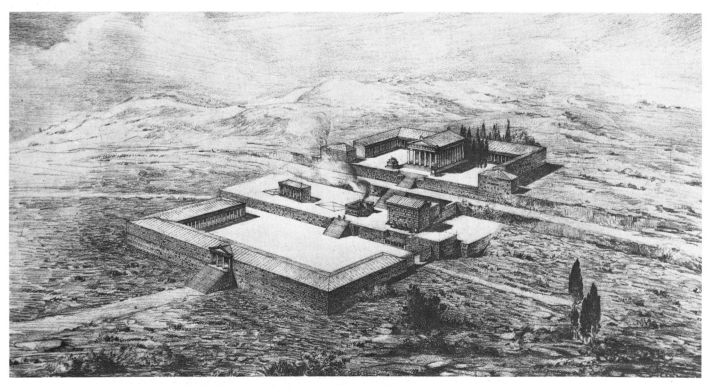

10.13 The Asklepieion on Kos.[P] From Paul Schazmann, Kos (Berlin: Heinrich Keller, 1932), Plate 40. By permission of the Deutsches Archäologisches Institut, Berlin.

[3] Phyllis Williams Lehmann, "The Setting of Hellenistic Temples," Journal of the Society of Architectural Historians 13 (1954): 15–20.

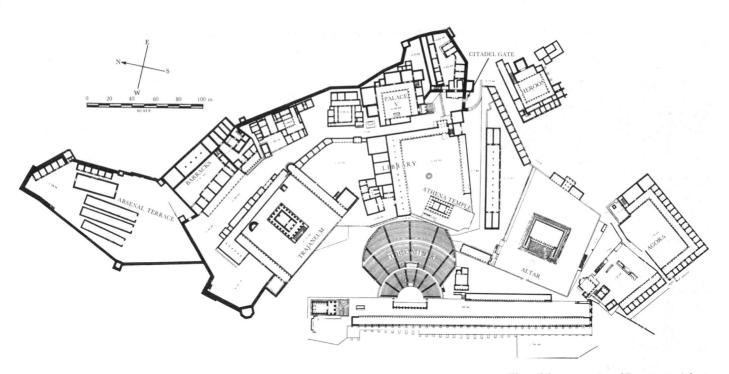

thus a carefully planned citadel and a grandiose monument to the power and culture of the age.[4]

The five second-century buildings at Delos whose plans are shown in Figure 10.15 are typical of Hellenistic houses. The house still faces inward. The central courtyard is now a complete peristyle, usually with elongated Doric columns; the water basin in the center often has a mosaic pavement. Beneath this basin, or impluvium, is a cistern to hold rainwater. The main rooms of the house are grouped around the courtyard. One room is usually larger than the others and more finely appointed (*c* in Fig. 10.15). Many houses had two stories and some had three. Some were very elegant indeed, decorated with fine mosaics and marble. Delos was a great mercantile center at this time and its wealth is evident in its houses. The same general plan, however, executed in a less costly manner, was common throughout the Hellenistic world.

SCULPTURE

Sculpture in the Hellenistic age presents a wealth of examples and an abundance of problems.[5] The new cities demanded sculpture in great quantities and of many kinds, giving unprecedented opportunities to working artists. Many of their works have been preserved, and more are known from Roman copies. The great centers supported schools of artists, but as both artists and their finished works traveled, it is probably best to consider sculpture chronologically, according to the hallowed scheme of early (323 to about the middle of the third century), middle (mid-third to mid-second century), and late (mid-second century to the Roman conquest in 31). The dating of Hellenistic works

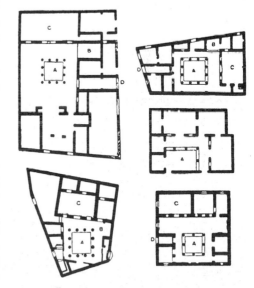

10.15 Plans of houses in Delos:[P] *A*, courtyard; *B*, sheltered area (*exedra*); *C*, main room; *D*, entrance. From W. B. Dinsmoor, *The Architecture of Ancient Greece*, 3d ed. rev. (New York: W. W. Norton, 1975), p. 324, Fig. 118. Reproduced by permission.

[4] Pergamon and the Pergamenes are discussed in Esther V. Hansen, *The Attalids of Pergamon*, 2d ed. (Ithaca, N.Y., 1971).
[5] The basic handbook is R. R. R. Smith, *Hellenistic Sculpture* (London, 1991).

is notoriously difficult, especially as one nears the Roman period. One characteristic that runs through the works of the period, continuing from the fourth century, is the realistic reproduction of nature. The interest in realism can be seen in uncompromising fidelity to natural models in dramatic, emotional works.

The influence of the past—both of the recent past of Lysippos and of the fifth and fourth centuries—was still strong in the early Hellenistic period. It must be remembered that the Classical style remained alive, although in a stale and repetitive form, throughout the Hellenistic period and on into Roman times. At some times it exerted more tangible influence than at others, but it was always present. The statue of the goddess Themis from the Attic town of Rhamnous, by the otherwise unknown artist Chairestratos, shows a repetition of classical formulas (Fig. 10.16). The artist's interest was clearly focused on the drapery of the goddess, and some ingenuity was used in rendering the contrasting surface textures. The treatment of the drapery clashes somewhat with that of the head, which owes much to fourth-century Classical prototypes. The Themis, dating to the beginning of the third century, has a formulaic and sterile quality that is not seen in more original Hellenistic creations.

The influence of Lysippos can be seen in the work of his pupil Eutychides, who was commissioned in the early third century to make a bronze statue of the personification of the city of Antioch, the capital of the Seleucid Empire. A number of reproductions of this work are known, including a small marble statue in the Vatican (Fig. 10.17). The Tyche or Fortune of Antioch is shown as a draped, seated woman wearing a turreted crown, which represents the city's walls. In her right hand she holds wheat stalks, which symbolize abundance. She rests one foot on a male swimmer, representing the Orontes River. This statue, with its detailed and systematic symbolism, sets the style for the personification of cities. The twisted pose of Tyche and the extended arms of the swimmer show Lysippos' influence. The essentially closed group is enlivened by the motion within it as Tyche and her drapery seem to move toward the right while the swimming figure looks to the left. Complex groups, often in pyramidal compositions, were a specialty of the Hellenistic age; the Tyche of Antioch is an early example, although the pyramidal form is not clearly seen.

A portrait statue of Demosthenes was set up in the Agora of Athens in 280, some forty years after the orator's death. The sculptor was a certain Polyeuktos. Demosthenes was shown standing with clasped hands, as if pausing during an oration. A large number of copies of this statue exist, including a full-length statue in Copenhagen (Fig. 10.18). Many true-to-life portraits were produced in the Hellenistic period. Before this time, as far back as the sixth century, statues of famous people had been produced, but their actual resemblance to the individuals depicted is debated. Idealization and the many problems connected with Roman copies make the study of portraiture extremely difficult. Certainly, however, uncompromising realism is to be found in the Hellenistic period, though the date of its first appearance is a matter of controversy.[6]

In the tall, spare figure of Demosthenes that we see in the copy in Copenhagen, portraiture is not confined to the head. The stance and realistic musculature of the entire body form an individualized representation of the

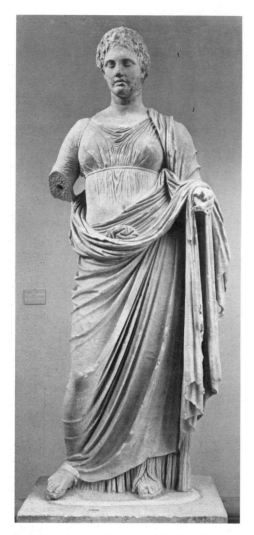

10.16 Themis from Rhamnous. National Archaeological Museum, Athens. Photo: Deutsches Archäologisches Institut, Athens.

[6] See two works by G. M. A. Richter: *The Portraits of the Greeks*, 3 vols. (London, 1965), and *Greek Portraits*, 4 vols., Collection Latomus, vols. 20, 36, 48, 54 (Brussels, 1955–1967).

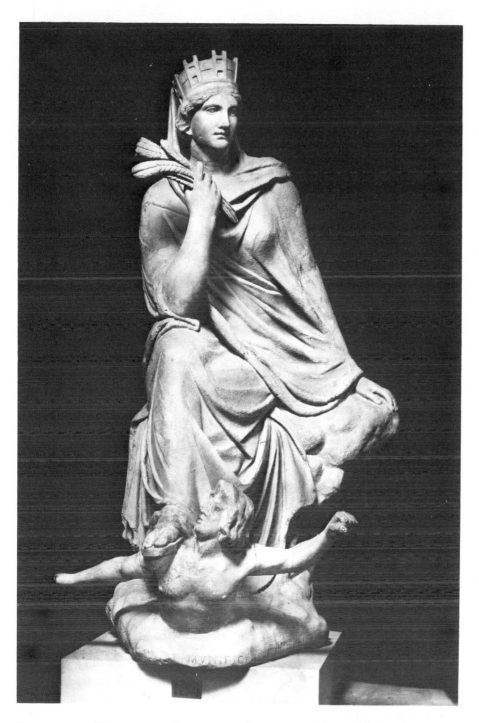

10.17 Tyche of Antioch, Musei del Vaticano, Rome. Photo: Anderson, Alinari.

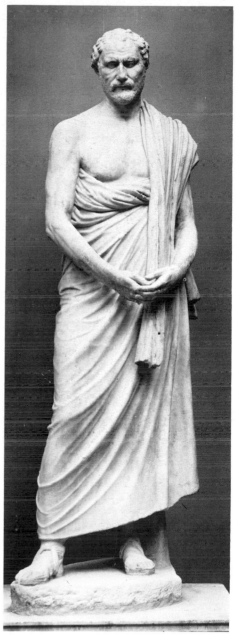

famous man. The common Roman practice was to add portrait heads to mass-produced bodies. If this copy, then, is a correct rendition of the original statue, we are probably justified in assuming that faithful portraits were being produced in the early third century.[7]

[7] Christine Mitchell Havelock, *Hellenistic Art,* 2d ed. (New York and London, 1981), pp. 39–40, sees the statue as a "modernized" copy produced in the first century.

10.18 Statue of Demosthenes. Photo: The Ny Carlsberg Glyptothek, Copenhagen.

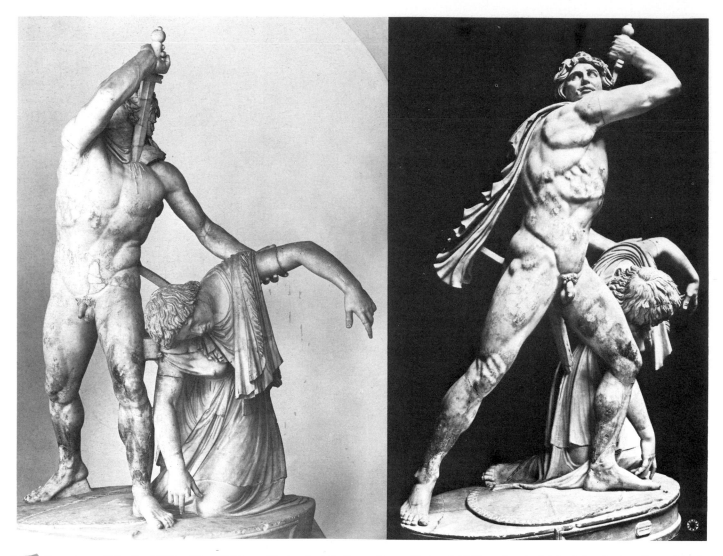

10.19 Two views of The Gaul Killing Himself. Museo Nazionale delle Terme, Rome. Photos: (left) Deutsches Archúologisches Institut, Rome; (right) Anderson, Alinari.

In the middle phase of Hellenistic sculpture, a dramatic quality appeared. The most original art of the time radiated from Pergamon, in a style that has been called Hellenistic Baroque—an ornate and flamboyant style quite different from anything that had gone before. The impetus for this style was the defeat of invading Gallic tribes in the second half of the third century. In celebration the Pergamenes erected a number of great monuments, some of which we know through literary references and Roman copies. Part of one of these great sculptural groups is preserved in a copy in Rome known as The Gaul Killing Himself (Fig. 10.19). The Pergamene artists chose to represent the Gauls as noble in defeat, thus elevating their own victory to noble triumph. The Gallic chieftain is committing suicide at the approach of the victorious Greeks. He has already killed his wife, whose body he holds up with his left hand. The heroic Gaul and his dead wife form a typical Hellenistic three-dimensional pyramidal group, whose composition can be fully appreciated only when it is

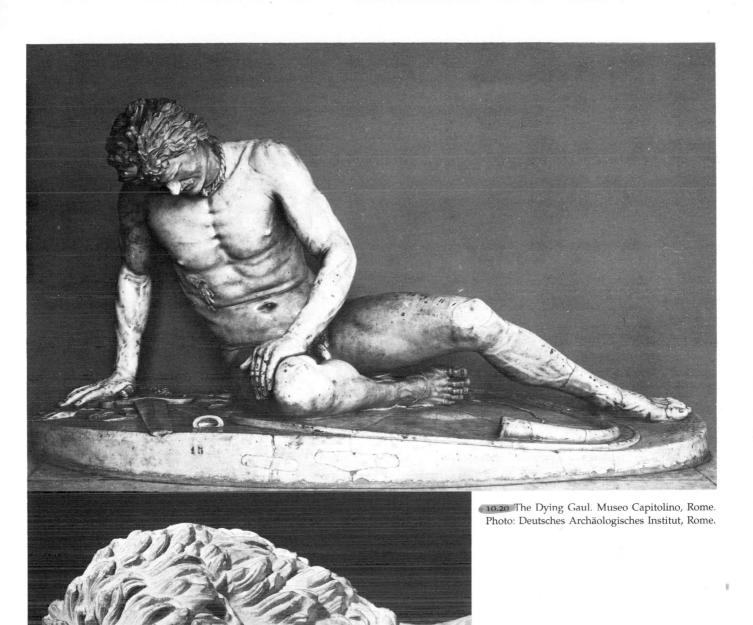

10.20 The Dying Gaul. Museo Capitolino, Rome.
Photo: Deutsches Archäologisches Institut, Rome.

10.21 The Dying Gaul: detail of head. Photo:
Alinari.

viewed from all sides. The exaggerated musculature, the twisted pose, and the wild, barbarian features add to the dramatic quality of the work.

Another statue, perhaps from the same monument, is the so-called Dying Gaul or Dying Trumpeter (Fig. 10.20). The Gaul, who wears a torque around his neck, is shown supporting himself on one arm while a wound in his side realistically spurts blood. His body is three-dimensional, the legs projecting in different directions while the torso is turned to one side and the head is lowered. The head bears the same ethnic characteristics that we saw in the previous group (Fig. 10.21). The hair, drooping mustache, and general cast of features are obviously not Greek. Although differences may be discerned between The Dying Gaul and The Gaul Killing Himself, perhaps attributable to different sculptors or copyists, they are related to each other by the despair and pain to be seen in their faces and the similarity of their situations.

The greatest monument of the Hellenistic age is the Pergamon Altar erected about 180 as a memorial to the victories of Attalos I (241–197) and dedicated to Zeus and Athena. The high platform to hold the altar was erected on a terrace of the acropolis. A giant central staircase, 20 meters wide, was framed on three sides by a podium bearing an Ionic colonnade (Fig. 10.22). The podium was decorated with a great sculptured frieze some 2.3 meters high depicting the battle of gods and giants. The theme, an old one that had appeared in the sixth century on the frieze of the Siphnian Treasury of Delphi (see Figs. 7.22 and 7.23), was appropriate for a war memorial and also suggested a parallel between the triumph of the gods and the victories of the Greeks—both the defeat of the Persians by the Athenians and the defeat of the Gauls by the Pergamenes, who viewed themselves as the champions of Hellenism. Fully seventy-five gods and their adversaries are shown in the frieze. In addition to the usual twelve Olympians, we see a host of divinities, including heavenly lights and earth and water deities. The giants are shown mainly in human form, but often winged or with snakes for legs.

The movements of Zeus and Athena, who would have been seen first by a visitor to the altar (Figs. 10.23 and 10.24), clearly were inspired by the pediment sculpture of the Parthenon, and it is thought that the Athena probably resembles the lost Athena from the east pediment. Similar visual references to earlier works are to be found throughout the frieze.

The Zeus and Athena scenes, although badly battered, clearly show the style. Zeus fights three giants, one collapsing to the left with a flaring thunderbolt through his thigh. In the companion piece Athena pulls a winged giant by the hair. The giant Alkyoneos stretches toward his mother, Ge, or Earth, for he cannot be killed if he maintains contact with her. She is shown as a large figure rising from the ground. Athena will conquer, however, for a Nike swoops in from the right bearing a wreath of victory.

As can be seen from these two slabs, the old rules no longer apply in this new world. The large figures use up all available space and on the sides adjacent to the steps actually writhe out of the frieze, putting an arm or a leg on the staircase. All is action, with a multitude of details and dramatic incidents. The deep-set eyes and agonized expressions on the giants' faces show depths of emotion not seen before, and perhaps just bordering on exaggeration. The massive anatomy of the Zeus is typical of this style; muscles and veins stand out as if pumped up with air. Despite the ferocious action of the battle, individual figures of great beauty appear, such as the figure usually identified as the goddess Nyx (night) about to throw a snake-covered jar (a representation of

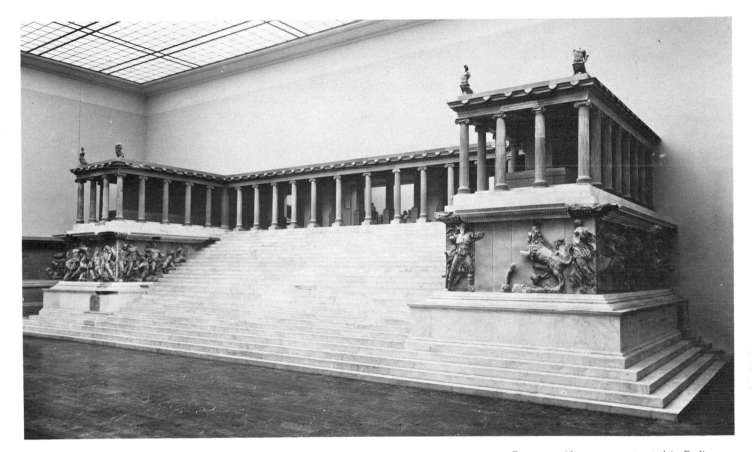

a constellation) at a giant, whose shield she pulls down with her left hand (Fig. 10.25). All the technical ability of the time is lavished on her swinging garments, which fail to hide the strong feminine body. These large, opulent figures with a wealth of detail and movement are representative of the developed Pergamon style, whose influence can be seen in the art of later times.[8]

The groups of battling Gauls contained many figures who were dead or close to death. The representation of sleep and death was a Pergamene specialty. The Sleeping Satyr (also known as the Barberini Faun) in Munich is dated about 200 and may be an original work (Fig. 10.26). It was found in Rome in the seventeenth century and restored. The drunken satyr sprawls on a rock with his legs wide apart. His right leg has been restored too sharply flexed. The musculature connects this piece with the Pergamon school, as do the sensual quality, the three-dimensionality, and the open form. The satyr represents a new class of sculpture, works produced to decorate the home or garden of a private patron. We also find individual pieces that might be considered "art for art's sake," for it is difficult to imagine that they appealed to a large public.

---

[8] Diether Thimme, "The Masters of the Pergamon Gigantomachy," *AJA* 50 (1946): 345–357. For the altar itself see Max Kunze, *The Pergamon Altar: Its Rediscovery, History, and Reconstruction* (Mainz, 1991).

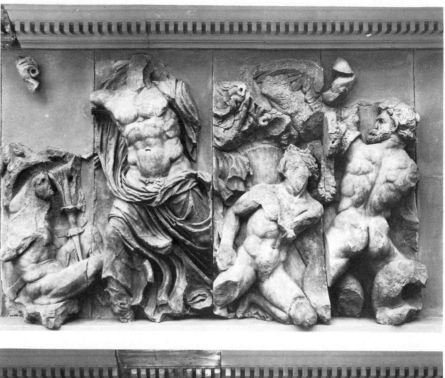

10.23 Zeus slab from the Pergamon Altar. Photo: Staatliche Museen zu Berlin.

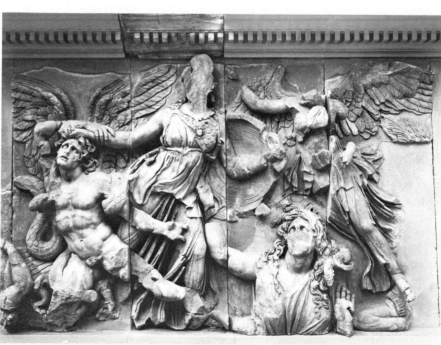

10.24 Athena slab from the Pergamon Altar. Photo: Staatliche Museen zu Berlin.

Realistic portraiture is well represented in Hellenistic sculpture. Figure 10.27 shows a bust of a ruler of Bactria, an eastern state founded by Alexander which was independent of the Seleucid Empire. Euthydemos I (230–190) is shown in stark realism, wearing a type of sun hat that also appears in other works. The bust has been touched up in modern times, especially the sun hat and the nose, which we know from coin portraits was somewhat less bulbous. The bust may date from the king's lifetime or may be a later Roman copy.

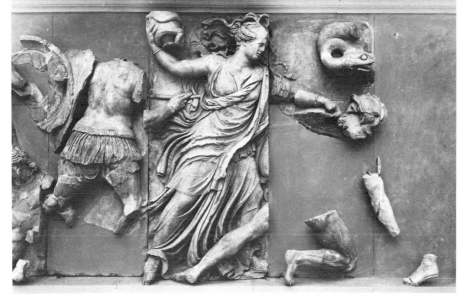

10.25 The goddess Nyx (Night) from the Pergamon Altar. Photo: Staatliche Museen zu Berlin.

Observation of everyday life and interest in various types of people are evident in Hellenistic sculpture. A sculpture of a boy playing with a goose (Fig. 10.28) shows the typical plump child of the period. Children were now clearly shown as children, engaging in childish occupations. This one is playing rather roughly, and the goose, a household pet in antiquity, seems not to be enjoying the game. The subject is known in a number of marble copies, such as this one in Munich, which may go back to an original of the third century by a certain Boethos of Chalcedon, a city in Asia Minor south of the Bosporos. The back-and-forth movements of the child and the goose are shown in the form of a pyramid, with the four corners of its base formed by the feet of the combatants and the tail of the goose.

At the other end of the scale is the Drunken Old Woman (Fig. 10.29), one of a number of marble copies of a figure mentioned in literary sources as a work of a sculptor named Myron. A Myron of Thebes is known from an inscription in Pergamon, and the statue is attributed to this third- or second-century sculptor. The best copy is in Munich and is shown here. The woman sits on the ground cradling a wreathed wine bottle as if it were a child. The extreme aging of the face and neck and the position of the head, thrown back in a drunken stupor, make a powerful impression on the viewer; photographs do not do the figure justice. Some scholars have seen a discordance in the rather elegant drapery, fastened over the shoulder with a pin, and the rings and earrings the woman wears, and have read a morality message into the work; others have suggested a religious context connected with the worship of Dionysos.[9] The bottle she holds, incidentally, is a common Hellenistic shape, a lagynos (see Fig. 10.46).

The Nike or Victory of Samothrace in the Louvre is one of the most famous statues of antiquity (Fig. 10.30). Originally a part of a dramatic composition that included a reflecting pool and the prow of a ship, on which Victory was alighting, she was erected to celebrate a naval victory; exactly which one is

[9] The problem of the meaning of such genre figures is discussed by J. J. Pollitt in his *Art in the Hellenistic Age* (Cambridge, 1986), pp. 141–147.

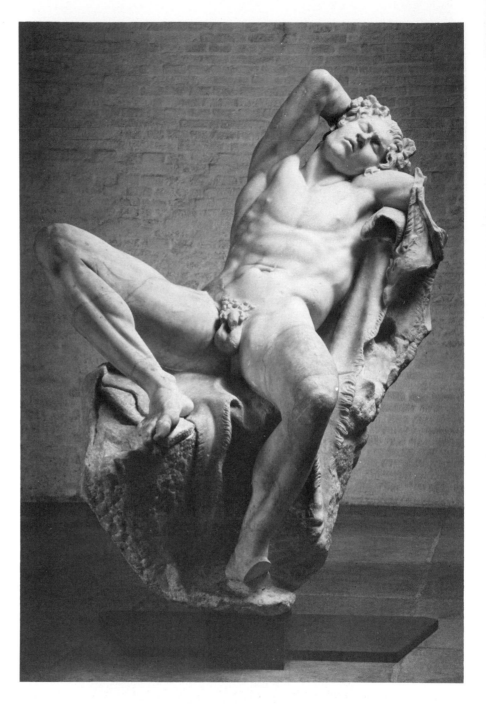

debated. Excavation evidence has provided a date around 200 for the erection of the base, and it is generally agreed that the work was made by a Rhodian sculptor. The large figure (2.45 meters high) is shown sweeping through the air with her drapery blown back against her body, imparting a strong sense of motion. The treatment of the folds is reminiscent of some of the figures on the Pergamene frieze, on which we know Rhodian sculptors were engaged. This mighty Victory indicates that the Hellenistic age could render traditional subjects in original ways.

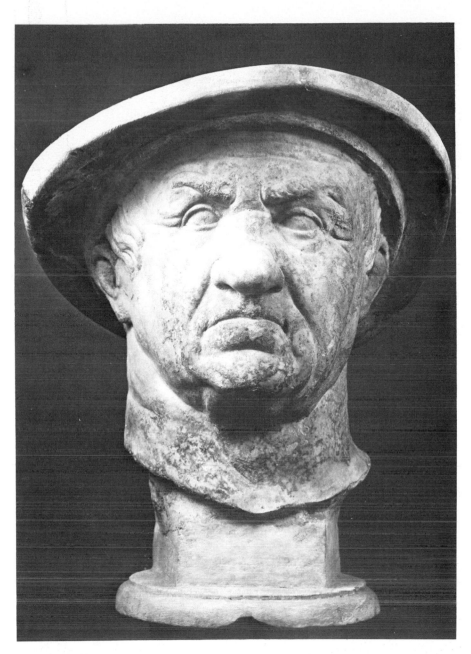

In the Late Hellenistic period the influence of Classical art of the fifth and fourth century was again felt, in part because of the increasing demand of the Roman market for Greek sculpture of the "best period" and in part as a response to contemporary local taste, which also favored the works of earlier periods. Earlier features could be introduced to a particular piece in a greater or lesser degree to give it life and variety, or it could be executed in an earlier style while retaining modern characteristics. Actual copies of earlier works were made by the pointing process, and outright fakes were probably also produced to feed the voracious Roman market.[10] Genre subjects and complex

[10] A possible example of an ancient forgery is discussed in Brunilde Sismondo Ridgway, *The Bronze Apollo from Piombino in the Louvre*, Antike Plastik, vol. 7 (Berlin, 1967), pp. 43–75.

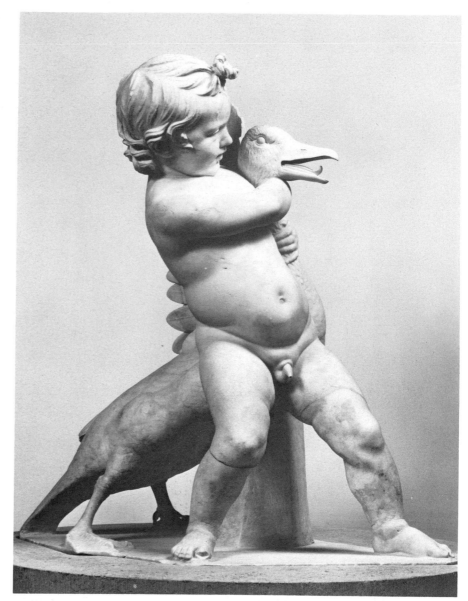

dramatic groups were popular as well. The baroque realism of the earlier period gave way to an exhibitionistic, almost theatrical style in which much was sacrificed so that an impact might be made. Eroticism and florid sweetness also found admirers. All of these varied forms were rendered with a high degree of technical skill.

Many of the artistic currents of this period can be seen in three Aphrodites of the many produced during the Hellenistic age. The Aphrodite of Melos (Fig. 10.31) was found on that island in A.D. 1820 and is accepted today as the personification of feminine beauty, at least for the ancient world. The larger-than-life-sized figure (2.04 meters in height) probably leaned on a pillar originally, a presumption that would account for the almost Praxitelean S-curve of the heavy torso. The drapery wound around the hips appears unstable, and

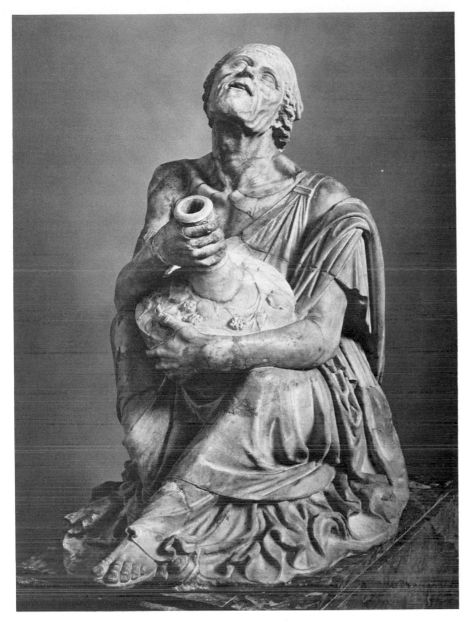

there is a marked discrepancy between the fleshy, matronly body and the head, which is coldly classical. These features have been cleverly joined together, however, and the curved, leaning pose imparts a freshness to the figure that perhaps accounts for its fame. But it must be recognized that the figure incorporates a number of features derived from various periods. The Aphrodite of Melos belongs to the second half of the second century.

A small marble Aphrodite (Fig. 10.32), only 49 centimeters high, was found on the island of Rhodes. The slender figure is shown in the act of washing her hair and holding it out at both sides. The position of the body—the lower part is in profile to the viewer while the upper half is almost frontal—has led to the speculation that the figure is a combination of the standing and crouching

10.30 Nike of Samothrace. Musée du Louvre, Paris. Photo: Chuzeville.

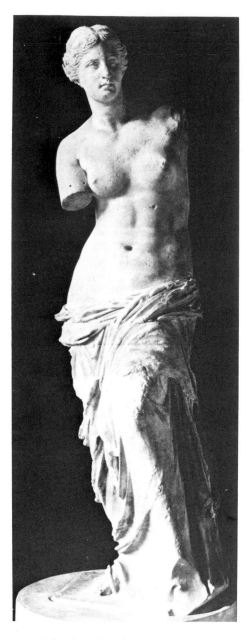

10.31 Aphrodite of Melos. Musée du Louvre, Paris. Photo: Chuzeville.

types. The composition is flat and is seemingly meant to be seen from one vantage point. It is probably a product of the first century.

Playful eroticism is evident in the Pan and Aphrodite group created about the year 100 for a Syrian merchant on Delos and now in Athens (Fig. 10.33). This small group, sometimes known as The Slipper Slapper, depicts the smiling goddess of love being accosted by a smaller Pan, whom she seems to be threatening with her slipper. A chubby Eros pushes the goat man's head as if to

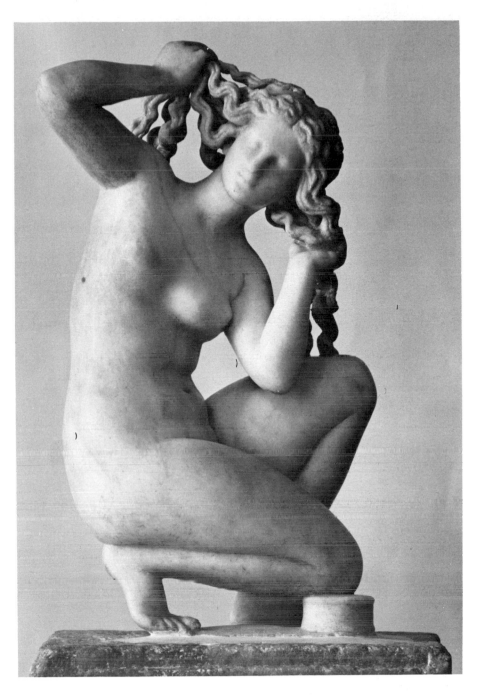

10.32 Aphrodite of Rhodes. Archaeological Museum, Rhodes. Photo: Hirmer Fotoarchiv, Munich.

help the goddess avoid him. Although the group is technically well done, the cute eroticism of the scene is distasteful to many scholars.[11]

[11] An interesting interpretation of the action of Aphrodite, attributed to Bernard Ashmole, is given in Martin Robertson, *History of Greek Art* (New York, 1975), 1:556. Aphrodite's display of her sandal is seen as an allusion to the fact that prostitutes had the word "follow" picked out on the soles of their sandals. Thus she is welcoming Pan's advances, not shunning them (although the action of the figures does not seem appropriate). Robertson further comments that it is probably not coincidental that ritual prostitution was practiced in temples of Aphrodite in the Levant, and that the owner of the group was a Syrian.

10.33 Aphrodite and Pan from Delos. Photo: National Archaeological Museum, Athens.

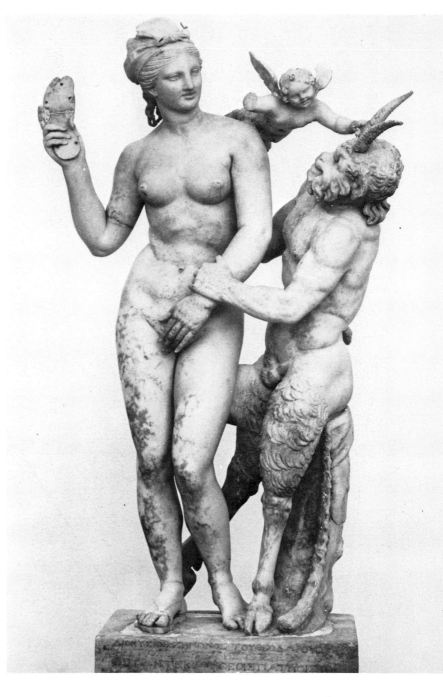

An original bronze of great power is the seated boxer in Rome (Fig. 10.34). The figure combines a theatrically realistic body—cauliflower ears, smashed nose, open wounds—with neatly arranged hair and beard derived from classical models. The small head sits uneasily on the great body, which seems too large for it. Despite the mixture of characteristics, the figure has an emotional impact on the viewer, as do many of the late eclectic works.

The original bronze head of an unknown man from Delos of the late second or early first century (Fig. 10.35) is representative of the portraiture of the Late Hellenistic period. Carefully modeled, the expressive face looks to the left and

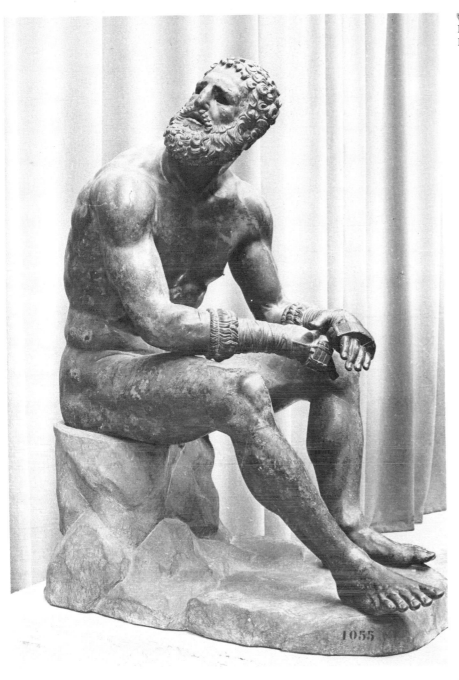

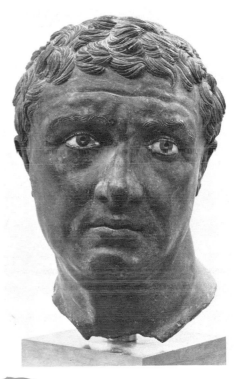

10.34 Seated boxer. Museo Nazionale delle Terme, Rome. Photo: Deutsches Archäologisches Institut, Rome.

10.35 Man from Delos. National Archaeological Museum, Athens. Photo: Deutsches Archäologisches Institut, Athens.

upward. One is in no doubt that a specific individual is portrayed. The despairing expression has a typically Hellenistic theatricality. Note the treatment of the hair, close to the skull as in earlier times. This intensely alive portrait seems to reflect its time as well as the character of the subject.

The calm stare of the child in Figure 10.36 also shows that Late Hellenistic art was not entirely derivative. Although earlier characteristics may be traced here, their appearance in combination with Hellenistic realism produces a masterpiece. The head in Figure 10.36 is actually a modern tin copy of the original, which when found was smashed out of shape and too fragile to be

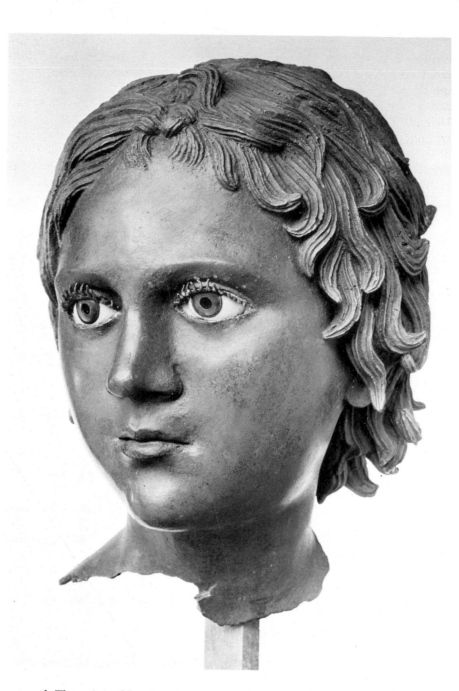

10.36 Modern tin copy of a child's head, from Olympia. Olympia Museum. Photo: Deutsches Archäologisches Institut, Athens.

restored. The original head was found in Olympia; this copy is faithful to it in every way.

The problem of archaizing in Greek sculpture, especially in the sculpture of the Hellenistic age, is too complex to go into here.[12] Suffice it to say that a number of sculptors employed Archaic stylistic devices either to give variety to their figures or simply because they and their patrons liked the patterns and the suggestions of antiquity they evoked. In a number of works of the Hellenistic age, the earlier characteristics appear not as obvious anomalies but as parts of a well-conceived whole.

[12] An excellent discussion is given in Pollitt, *Art in the Hellenistic Age*, pp. 175–184.

An example of a definite archaizing style as late as the second half of the first century A.D. has been found in Corinth. A sculptured triangular base is decorated with three figures in relief, one of which, a Zeus, is shown in Figure 10.37.[13] The archaistic characteristics of the drapery, with its zigzag folds, can be seen clearly. The modeling of the face and neck, however, is Late Hellenistic. So, in fact, is the drapery, which only approximates Archaic folds without actually reproducing them. The two female figures on the other sides of the base wear chitons and himations in the manner of the korai, and their drapery shows similar flat and sharp folds. The combination of naturalistic Hellenistic forms with imitation Archaic characteristics is typical of this style.

The great group known as the Laocoon (Fig. 10.38), found in Rome in

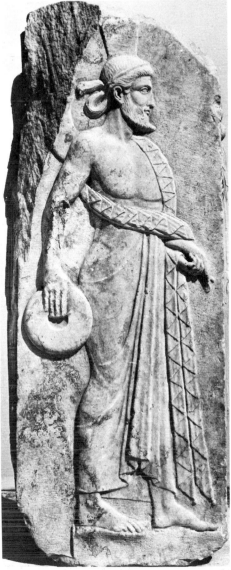

10.37 Zeus on a triangular base, from Corinth. Photo: American School of Classical Studies at Athens: Corinth Excavations.

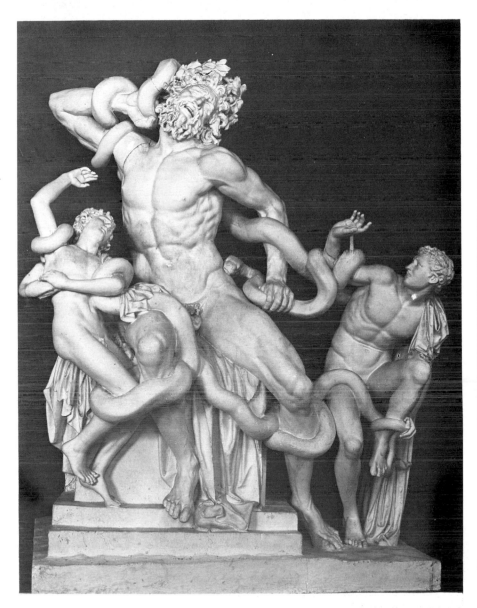

10.38 Laocoon (modern plaster reconstruction). Musei del Vaticano, Rome. Photo: Deutsches Archäologisches Institut, Rome.

13 Charles K. Williams II discusses this sculpture in *Zeus and Other Deities: Notes on Two Archaistic Piers*, Studies in Athenian Architecture, Sculpture, and Topography (Hesperia suppl. 20) (Princeton, 1982), pp. 175–181.

A.D. 1506 with Michelangelo in attendance, has had a great influence on Western art. Although it has seemed at first glance to be the group mentioned by an ancient source as made by three Rhodian artists, Hagesandros, Athenodoros, and Polydoros, modern scholars have moved its date up and down from the second century B.C. to the first century of the Christian era, and have even moved the elements of the composition about.[14] Most recently they have settled for a date late in the first century B.C. or early in the first century A.D., on the basis of evidence from the Sperlonga cave (see below). A modern reconstruction is shown here. Fully 1.84 meters in height, the work depicts the death of the Trojan priest Laocoon and one of his sons as a result of his advice to the Trojans not to bring the Trojan Horse within the walls of their city. Laocoon and his two sons were attacked by giant snakes, and their struggles are graphically presented. Laocoon struggles against the enveloping coils, reacting to a savage bite with a distorted, despairing face. The heavy musculature and distorted features remind one of the Pergamon frieze, especially the young giant in the Athena slab (see Fig. 10.24). To his right, Laocoon's younger son already collapses in death while to his left the older is extricating himself from the coils but looks back in horror at the other two. The composition can be easily taken in from a frontal vantage point, a characteristic of late groups, and can be interpreted as presenting a series of contrasts: man versus beast, maturity versus youth, life versus death.

In A.D. 1957 a cache of ancient sculpture was found in a great cave at Sperlonga on Italy's west coast. An inscription described groups that stood inside the partially artificial grotto in Roman times, including great compositions of

10.39 Colossal group of the Blinding of Polyphemos. Museo Archeologico, Sperlonga. Photo: Deutsches Archäologisches Institut, Rome.

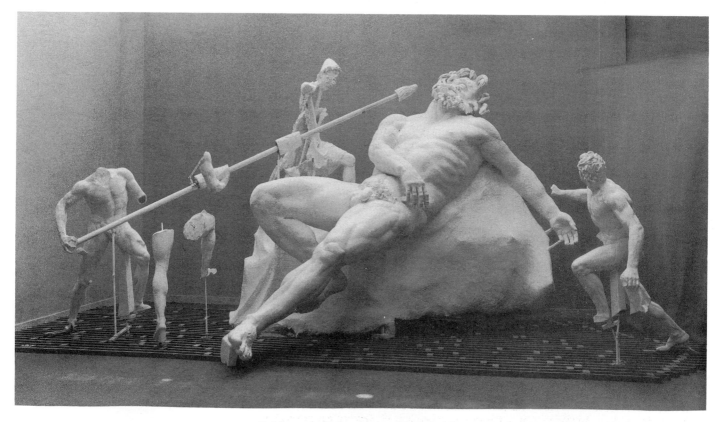

[14] Margarete Bieber, *Laocoon: The Influence of the Group since Its Rediscovery* (New York, 1942).

the blinding of Polyphemos (Cyclops) (Fig. 10.39) and the wreck of Odysseus' ship. Literally thousands of fragments of sculpture, many of heroic size, were recovered, and their interpretation will continue for some time to come. Many of the fragments are in Hellenistic style, with similarities to both the Laocoon and the Pergamon Altar (Fig. 10.40). The names of the Rhodian sculptors associated with the Laocoon were found inscribed on the ship from the cave, and many scholars assume that their workshop may have been responsible for all the sculpture found there. The general consensus now is that both the Sperlonga sculpture and the Laocoon were carved perhaps as late as the early first century A.D. or a little earlier, but were based on Hellenistic originals. Just how these superior copyists changed or adapted their models provides endless grounds for speculation.[15] Thus does Hellenistic sculpture shade into Roman sculpture.

PAINTING AND MOSAICS

Although the high point of Greek painting was said to have been reached in the late fourth and early third centuries, it naturally continued to flourish in the later Hellenistic period. Some original paintings have come down to us, mainly from tombs, but most of those that have been reported are of inferior workmanship. Others are known but have never been reported in print. A number of large underground tombs in Macedonia and elsewhere have been found with paintings of floral and funerary subjects (see below). Painted grave stelai are known from a number of sites, including Pagasai (Volo) in northeastern Greece. Most of the works from this series show the usual seated or standing figures in farewell scenes, but one painted by a superior artist shows some depth both spatially and psychologically. In the stele of Hediste (Fig. 10.41), from the first half of the second century, a woman lies on a couch; at its foot is a man, gazing at her. Behind stands a woman with a child in her arms, and a young girl appears in an open door in the background. Here we see an attempt at depicting depth which is not paralleled in the other stelai from the site.[16] Moreover, the depth of feeling expressed in the unhappy husband and the appearance of the doomed child (the accompanying inscription indicates that the child died soon after the mother) well illustrates Hellenistic emotionalism. Studies have shown that the paintings on the Pagasai stelai were produced not by the encaustic method, in which heat is used to fix the colors, but by a tempera technique that probably used egg as a binding medium.

A distinctive feature of mainland Hellenistic architecture is the Macedonian tomb. Many of these vaulted tombs were adorned with wall paintings, which preserve some glimpses of the painter's art in the Hellenistic period. Color Plate 17 shows the north wall of the burial chamber of a tomb built around 200 B.C. for two brothers, whose names, Lyson and Kallikles, were inscribed over the entrance.[17] The tomb held the cremated remains of four generations of

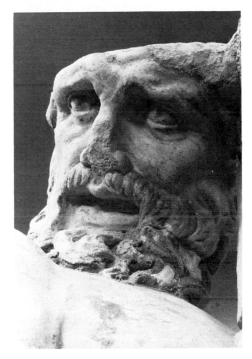

10.40 Head of Odysseus' steersman. Museo Archeologico, Sperlonga. Photo: Deutsches Archäologisches Institut, Rome.

---

[15] These matters are well summarized in Smith, *Hellenistic Sculpture*, pp. 108–111. A popular account of the find and the work of restoration is presented in D. J. Hamblin, "Italy's Marvelous Marble Jigsaw Puzzle with 20,000 Pieces," *Smithsonian* 3, no. 11 (1973): 54–61.

[16] For an overall study of perspective, see G. M. A. Richter, *Perspective in Greek and Roman Art* (New York and London, 1970).

[17] Several tombs await publication and study. The one illustrated here has received careful examination, however, and the publication also serves as the best survey in English of the whole subject of the Macedonian tombs: S. G. Miller, *The Tomb of Lyson and Kallikles: A Painted Macedonian Tomb* (Mainz am Rhein, 1993). An overall view of the art and archaeology of Macedonia is provided in René Ginouvès, ed., *Macedonia: From Philip II to the Roman Conquest* (Princeton, 1994).

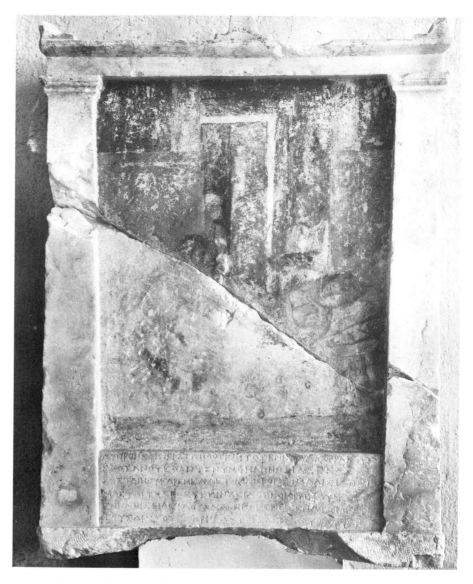

the same family; niches that once held the ashes now gape open after depredations by tomb robbers. The stuccoed wall was painted to represent pillars; painted shadows give an illusion of depth to the flat wall. A garland is draped across the pillars, and they support an architrave that serves as the base of a crescent-shaped space below the vault, a lunette, in which military equipment is displayed, symbolic of that used in life by the men buried in the tomb. The careful representations provide the military historian precious contemporary illustrations of armor, and the whole scheme of decoration appears to echo contemporary domestic interior design known to us from the remains of palatial Macedonian houses. The illusionistic effects are later to be seen in Roman wall paintings, where they are carried to greater development.

The problem of differentiating Greek works from Roman is as difficult in Hellenistic painting as in sculpture, if not more so. A large number of wall paintings of Roman times have been found in Italy, especially in the towns of Pompeii and Herculaneum, destroyed by the eruption of Vesuvius in A.D. 79.

Many of these murals are thought to reproduce Greek works or portions of Greek works, but the paintings are essentially Roman productions that show the influence of earlier paintings in greater or lesser degrees.[18] We know that Greek wall paintings were copied by the Romans, but the copies were necessarily less exact than those of sculpture, which could be produced by mechanical means. Roman wall decorations often contain scenes that appear to be copies of Greek originals of which we have heard in the sources, but the existence of more than one version of a given scene is a warning that it is impossible to know what the original looked like. The painter could and obviously did combine individual groups or figures from a number of paintings in various ways. It is an academic exercise to try to pick out the Greek element in a given painting, and one that leads to endless disagreements. A painting from Herculaneum (Fig. 10.42), however, has won general agreement as a copy of an original Pergamene painting of the second half of the second century. The subject is the discovery of the child Telephos by his father, Herakles. Telephos was a minor figure mentioned in the Trojan War stories whom the learned scholars of Pergamon adopted as the mythical founder of their city.[19] He had been exposed on an Arkadian mountain as an infant and had been saved by wild beasts. Here he is shown being suckled by a deer while Herakles looks on. To the left, and taking up much of the scene, is the colossal personification of Arkadia, who stares into space while a satyr child pauses in his flute playing just behind her. Herakles is assisted in finding his child by a winged being who points him out. A basket of fruit, an eagle, and a shaggy lion complete the composition, probably as references to the wild land of Arkadia and its guardian deities.

The figure of Arkadia is particularly impressive and has inspired a number of artists, including Ingres, who reproduced her pose in his Madame Moitessier. It is interesting to note the difference in technique between Arkadia and Herakles. Arkadia's form is defined by line, whereas the Herakles figure depends more fully on color. Arkadia's linear quality, together with her heavy drapery, has been interpreted as indicating that she belongs to an older tradition of Greek painting, perhaps of the fourth century, while Herakles is considered to be in a more contemporary style, relying on color contrasts. The pose of the Herakles, however, is similar to that of the Farnese Herakles (see Fig. 9.28), and a similar scene of the hero and child is to be found on the Telephos frieze on the Pergamon Altar. The extent to which the composition of the painting reproduced the presumed original is difficult to tell, but the subject and at least parts of the composition are appropriate to a Pergamene origin.

Early in the third century, mosaic technique underwent a major change. Instead of natural river pebbles, small squares (tesserae) cut from stones of various colors were used. This change allowed figures to be more clearly defined and increased the artist's control in following trends in representation already evident in the stag-hunt mosaic of Pella (Fig. 9.41). A corner of a floor

---

[18] A good survey of Roman painting can be found in Roger Ling, *Roman Painting* (Cambridge, 1991).

[19] His story was told in a small frieze that adorned the upper part of the inner wall of the colonnade of the Altar of Zeus at Pergamon. The frieze, incidentally, told the story in a continuous narrative, with the same figures reappearing in various scenes. This is the only time that continuous narrative occurs in Greek sculpture, though it is common in Roman historical relief. The Telephos frieze is generally attributed to the period just before the middle of the century, slightly later than the gigantomachy. See Hansen, *Attalids of Pergamon*, pp. 338–348; Kunze, *Pergamon Altar*, pp. 45–47.

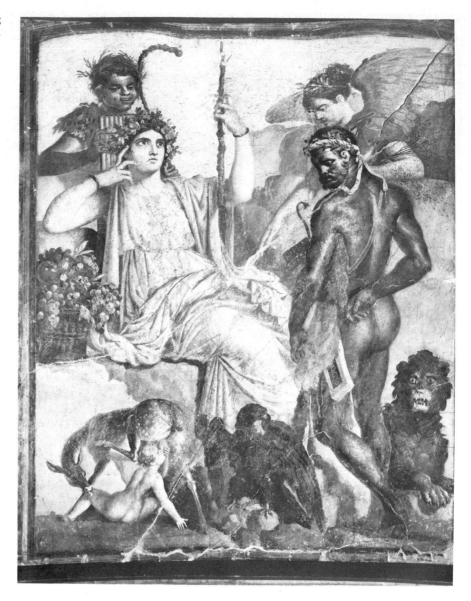

mosaic from the House of the Dolphins at Delos (Color Plate 9, following p. 96) shows clearly how the new technique can be used to indicate shading and color changes, and even to create the illusion of depth (below the black-and-white wave pattern). In the fully developed Hellenistic style, marble, onyx, enamel, and clay were also used. Some scenes in mosaics from Pompeii are thought to be copies of earlier paintings.[20]

Much of the famous Alexander Mosaic from the House of the Faun in Pompeii (Fig. 10.43) has been obliterated, but luckily the main figures are relatively intact. Probably laid when the house was built, in the second century, it is quite exceptional in composition, for most other Hellenistic floor mosaics consist of

[20] Tessera mosaics in Pompeii and elsewhere are discussed in Robertson, *History of Greek Art,* 1:578–581, and Havelock, *Hellenistic Art,* pp. 221–224.

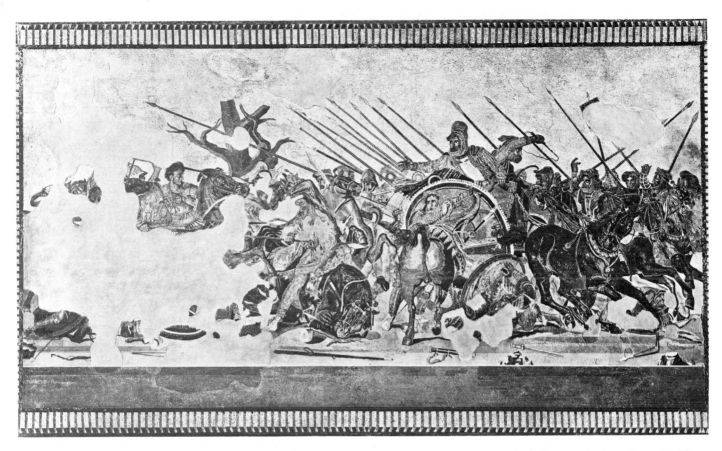

10.43 Alexander mosaic from Pompeii. Museo Nazionale, Naples. Photo: Anderson, Alinari.

small central designs surrounded by border patterns. Here nearly the whole floor is taken over by a scene over five meters long and two meters wide, composed of minute stone and glass tesserae. The scene depicted is one of Alexander's battles against the Persian king Darius, probably the battle at Issos in 333. The elaborate and grandiose composition is centered on the two protagonists, the bareheaded Alexander charging in from the left and the king about to flee in his great chariot. Their eyes meet as Alexander runs through with his spear a Persian who has tried to block the way to his enemy. Another Persian offers his horse to the king as the charioteer frantically tries to turn the unwieldy vehicle away from the encircling Greeks, whose spears can be seen behind the Persian horsemen. It is the moment of victory for the Macedonians. Only four colors were used, black, white, red, and yellow, alone and in combination. All the crowded action takes place in the foreground. Only a gnarled tree, the wreck of battle, and a few stones form a setting.

The characterization of the figures, the use of four colors, the accurate knowledge of military equipment, and other bits of evidence have led scholars to believe that the Alexander Mosaic is a direct copy of a famous painting of the late fourth century. A number of artists known to have produced such paintings have been put forth as candidates. The most likely artist is generally believed to have been Philoxenos of Eretria, who painted for Kassander of Macedon (327–319). We are not certain, however, nor do we know what liberties the copyist may have taken with the original. The quality of the work and the astonishing use of light, foreshortening, and details bring home to us again how much of major Greek painting must have been lost.

A virtually intact royal burial in a Macedonian tomb at Vergina in Macedonia was a major archaeological find in A.D. 1977. In addition to many small finds and the cremated remains of two individuals, the excavators found a painted scene on the facade (Fig. 10.44). Apparently the tomb had been buried before the paint had dried and the scene is badly preserved, but clearly it represents a hunt in a wooded landscape and shows obvious similarities to the Alexander mosaic—the leafless tree, for instance, and the positions of some of the mounted hunters. The background of hills is surprising at such an early date. The excavator of the tomb has suggested that the painting may be an early work of the painter responsible for the design of the Alexander mosaic. As an undoubted original from the fourth century, this painting is of first importance for our understanding of the development of mural painting, but its exact date is controversial, for the tomb it adorns was assigned by the excavator to Philip II, Alexander's father, who was assassinated in 336. Others would date it later in the century.[21]

10.44 Facade of Tomb 2 at Vergina. Courtesy of M. Andronikos.

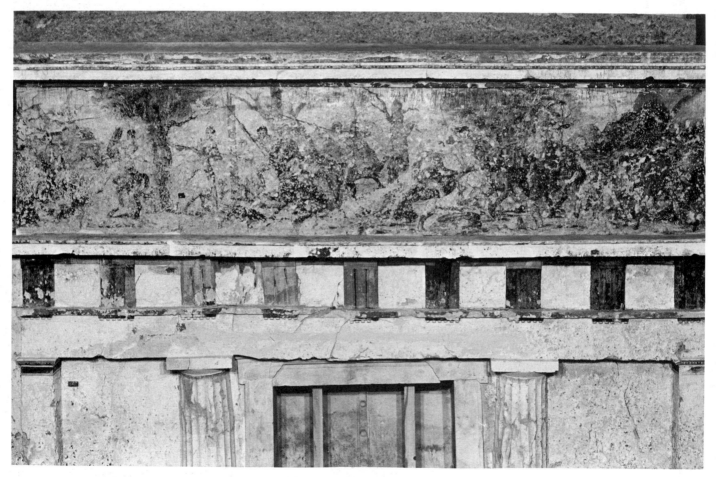

[21] Manolis Andronikos, the excavator, describes these discoveries in *Vergina: The Royal Tombs* (Athens, 1984); other views are expressed in Eugene N. Borza, *In the Shadow of Olympus: The Emergence of Macedon* (Princeton, 1990), pp. 256–268, 311–313 (pb. ed.).

POTTERY

New, instantly recognizable pottery shapes appeared in the Hellenistic period while the survivors of the previous period changed their proportions.[22] Some shapes became low and clumsy, others tall and slim, and the influence of metalware increased.

When painted decoration appears, it takes the form of such simple subjects as wreaths, festoons, and abstract patterns in white and yellow on a black background. The squat neck amphora in Figure 10.45 was found in Athens and works in this style have come to be called West Slope ware, for the first examples were found on the west slope of the Acropolis. Similar ware, known as Gnathian, was in use in the West. Unusual styles were also found, including Centuripe ware—a group of large polychrome funeral pots decorated with figured scenes and embellished with decorations applied in clay in the form of architectural details.

The pot in Figure 10.46 is a new shape, a lagynos, a squat, long-necked jug. This example represents an alternate decorative form, a simple dark decoration on a light surface. Such decorations are usually simple wreaths, but sometimes animal figures, musical instruments, or other objects appear. A number of other small pottery groups with dark-on-light decoration are also known. A group of hydriae known as Hadra ware, used as ash urns in Alexandria, often have datable inscriptions.

Plain black pottery continued to be produced in the Hellenistic period, but by the late second century several centers in the East were producing pottery with a red surface. This Sigillata ware, with its shiny red surface, originated in Syria. Its manufacture spread to Italy and later to Gaul, where mold-made vessels covered with low relief decoration were most popular. Other popular decorative devices were floral appliqués and lead-glazed wares, which were produced at several sites in modern Turkey in the first centuries B.C. and A.D.

Relief wares were very common in the Hellenistic age, and many fragments of deep bowls decorated with relief figures or designs have been found in sites of the period. These bowls, once called Megarian bowls from their presumed place of origin, were actually made in molds that had been imprinted with clay stamps. The designs thus stand out in relief on the surfaces of the bowls (Fig. 10.47). They were made in many places, and the stamps for the molds may themselves have traveled. Some decorations were floral, as here; others reproduced scenes from literature or the theater.

Other pottery often found in Hellenistic excavation contexts includes such shapes as the spindle-shaped unguentarium (Fig. 10.48) and the fish plate which has a small cup in the center for oil or fish sauce, and is often painted with representations of the seafood it was meant to hold (Fig. 10.49).

TRANSPORT AMPHORAS

The great and small states of the Hellenistic age relied more than ever before on trade and commerce, and transport amphoras appear everywhere in Hellenistic excavations. Four typical shapes of the first century are shown in Figure 10.50. Perhaps the most common Hellenistic transport amphoras are those from Rhodes, the great commercial state of the period. Their distinctive shape

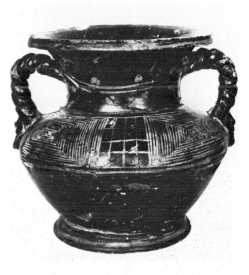

10.45 Amphora decorated in West Slope style. Agora Museum, Athens. Photo: American School of Classical Studies at Athens, Agora Excavations.

10.46 Lagynos. Photo: Museum of Art and Archaeology, University of Missouri–Columbia.

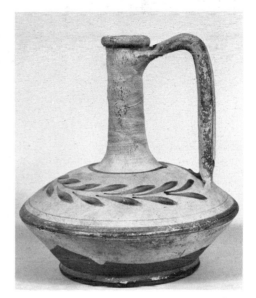

---

[22] Hellenistic pottery has not received its due in publications in English. A good short treatment of the fine wares is J. W. Hayes, "Fine Wares in the Hellenistic World," in *Looking at Greek Vases*, ed. Tom Rasmussen and Nigel Spivey (Cambridge, 1991), pp. 183–202.

321

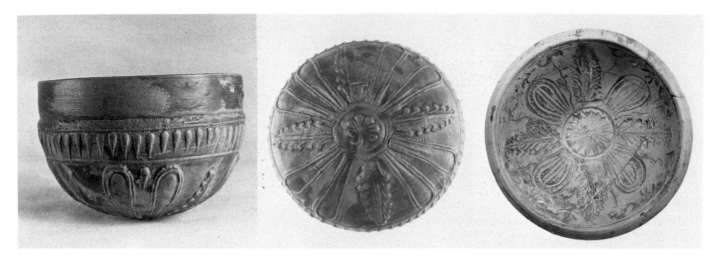

10.47 Side and bottom views of a Hellenistic relief bowl, and mold from which such bowls were made. Photo: Museum of Art and Archaeology, University of Missouri–Columbia.

and angular handles are easy to recognize. Figure 10.51 shows two typical Rhodian stamps. Such stamps appear in pairs on the handles of the amphoras and usually show a symbol of the city where exported produce originated, such as the head of Helios or a rose, as here. They also generally give the name of the manufacturer, the date expressed as the term of a magistrate, whose name is given, and the name of the month.

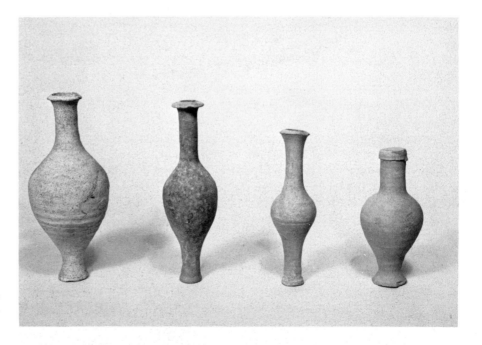

10.48 Spindle-shaped unguentaria. Photo: Museum of Art and Archaeology, University of Missouri–Columbia.

TERRA COTTA FIGURINES

Great masses of Hellenistic terra cotta figurines have been found, but little diversity of style can be noted until the latter half of the period. Part of the reason for this lack of diversity is the dominance of the Tanagra style, which, as has been mentioned, originated at the end of the fourth century. The style is

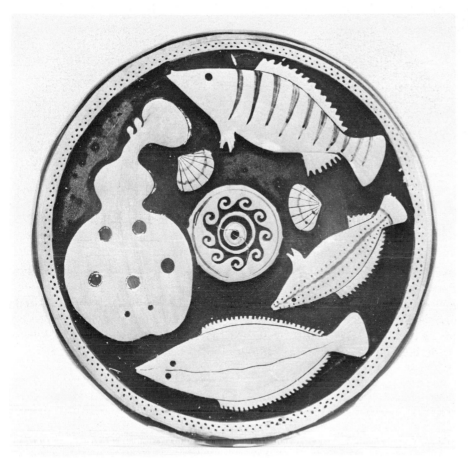

10.49 Typical Hellenistic fish plate. Courtesy, Museum of Fine Arts, Boston. Seth K. Sweetser Fund.

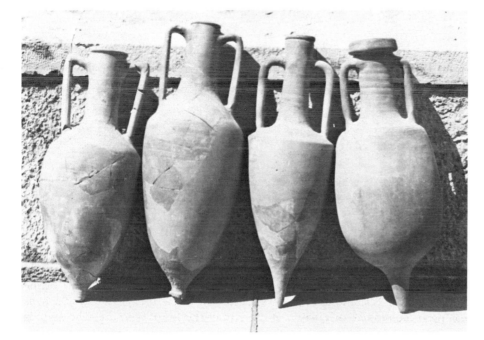

10.50 Typical Late Hellenistic amphoras from the debris of the destruction of Athens in 86. Left to right: Rhodian, Knidian, Chian, Roman. Agora Museum, Athens. Photo: American School of Classical Studies at Athens: Agora Excavations.

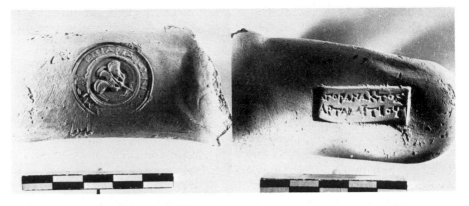

10.51 Rhodian amphora stamps of the manufacturers Hellanikos (with rose) and Agoranax. Photo: American School of Classical Studies at Athens: Agora Excavations.

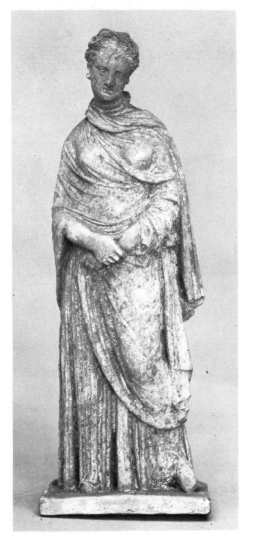

10.52 Typical Tanagra figurine of a standing woman. Reproduced by courtesy of the Trustees of the British Museum, London.

realistic, even approaching a certain sweetness in its later years. The favorite subjects were elegantly dressed women (Fig. 10.52), standing, seated, dancing, or playing games. Men and boys were also portrayed, as were figures of Eros flying, shown as a chubby Hellenistic child (Fig. 10.53). The relaxed poses and sweet expressions together with the distinctive, carefully treated drapery compare well with the best sculpture of the period. These figures were made by a more elaborate method than that used previously. Instead of being made in a single mold, they were formed in many partial molds and then assembled, with some handmade parts often added. They were also painted in softer shades than had been preferred earlier.

In the Late Hellenistic period, after 200, more local types emerged, and the figurines closely followed contemporary sculptural styles. So did the Tanagras,

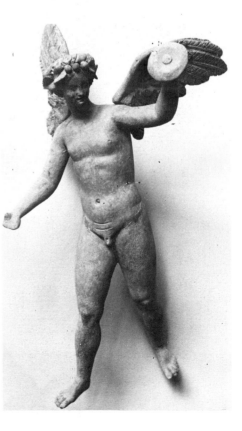

10.53 Flying Eros figurine. National Archaeological Museum, Athens. Photo: Deutsches Archäologisches Institut, Athens.

324

though to a much lesser extent. The Tanagras continued to be produced but in a repetitive and weakened version. Copies of statues, genre scenes, and grotesques (Fig. 10.54) are typical of the Late Hellenistic period.

COINS

As the conquests of Alexander the Great affected all branches of the arts, so coins underwent a great change. Alexander's gold coins featured Athena on the obverse, but a young Herakles appeared on his large silver issues, which became the most common throughout the Greek world (Fig. 10.55). A seated Zeus, the god of all Greeks, appeared on the reverse. The first portrait of Alexander seems to have appeared after his death on silver coins from Alexandria, which show him wearing an elephant scalp as a symbol of his victories in India (Fig. 10.56). The reverse of some of the coins in this series have an archaizing Athena that may represent the goddess of Pella or perhaps the victorious Athena depicted on vases given as prizes during the Panathenaic Festival in Athens. In the upheavals following Alexander's death, other portraits of him were used on coins issued by various claimants to his rule. On one series he is shown with the horns of Zeus Ammon (Fig. 10.57), in whose sanctuary in Egypt Alexander was said to have been declared divine. This coin portrait, in which idealization and realism combine in a harmonious whole, is

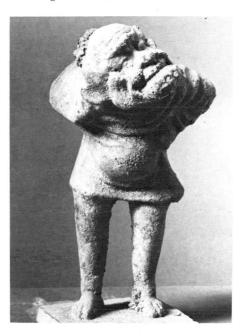

10.54 Typical grotesque figurine. National Archaeological Museum, Athens. Photo: Deutsches Archäologisches Institut, Athens.

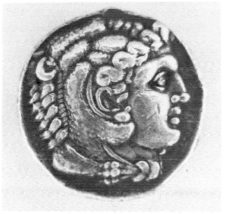
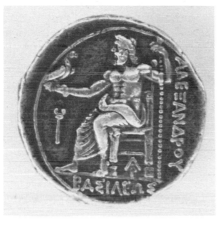

10.55 Silver coin of Alexander: obverse, Herakles; reverse, seated Zeus.

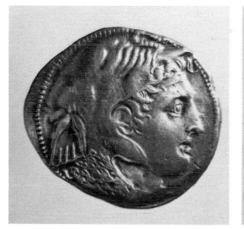
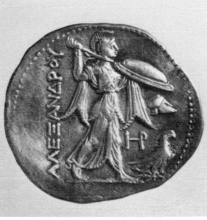

10.56 Silver coin of Ptolemy I, from Alexandria: obverse, Alexander; reverse, striding Athena. Photos: Museum of Art and Archaeology, University of Missouri–Columbia. Scale 1.7:1.

325

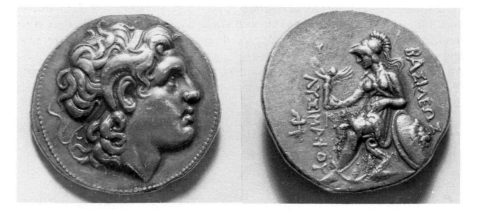

10.57 Coin of Lysimachos: obverse, Alexander; reverse, seated Athena Nikephoros. Photos: Museum of Art and Archaeology, University of Missouri–Columbia. Scale 1.7:1.

considered by some to be one of the most beautiful of Greek coins. It was not until the first quarter of the third century that one of his successors had his own portrait placed on a coin. This portrait started a series of coin types that extends to modern times.

Portrait coins of varying periods and quality are shown in Figures 10.58 and 10.59. Quality began to decline toward the end of the period. Reverse types

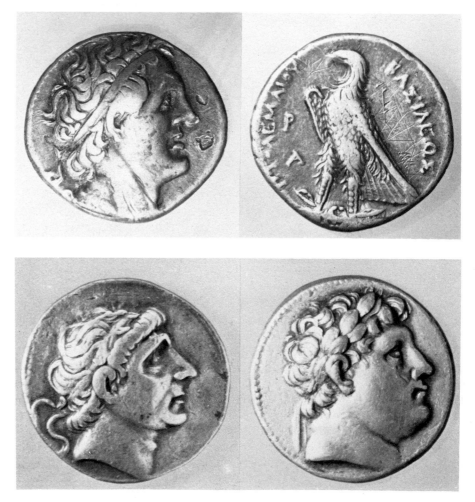

10.58 Coin of Ptolemy II: obverse, Ptolemy I; reverse, eagle on thunderbolt. Photos: Museum of Art and Archaeology, University of Missouri–Columbia. Scale 2:1.

10.59 Hellenistic portrait coins: Antiochus I (left) and Philetairos (coin of Attalos I). Photos: Museum of Art and Archaeology, University of Missouri–Columbia. Scale 1.9:1.

varied for political or personal reasons; some, such as the eagle of Zeus seated on a thunderbolt, were repeated by succeeding dynasts. At the same time such free cities as Rhodes and Athens minted their own coins. Rhodes had the rose and head of Helios, the sun god (see Fig. 9.52), while Athens had a modernized Athena and owl (Fig. 10.60). The mainland leagues also issued their own coins (Fig. 10.61). The great variety of the age is thus reflected in its coinage, as it is in the other arts.

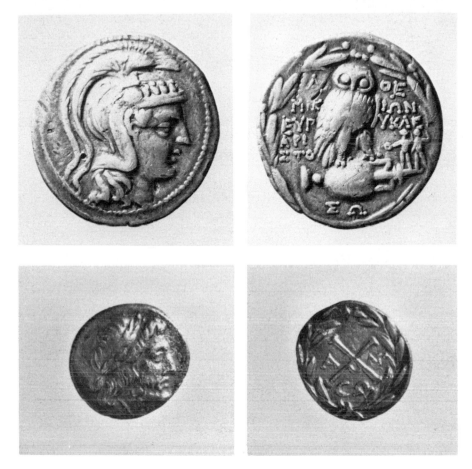

10.60 Second-century coin of Athens: obverse, Athena; reverse, owl. Photos: Museum of Art and Archaeology, University of Missouri–Columbia. Scale 1.7:1.

10.61 Coin of Antigoneia: obverse, Zeus; reverse, symbol of the Achaean League. Photos: Museum of Art and Archaeology, University of Missouri–Columbia. Scale 2:1.

LAMPS

As one might expect, the production of lamps mushroomed in the Hellenistic period. Many local types were produced, but we shall confine our attention to those from the Athenian agora, which are typical of the period.

Early Hellenistic lamps, from the end of the fourth century and into the third, continued in the general line of development seen in earlier fourth-century lamps. A common type with a lug in place of a handle, shown in Fig. 10.62a, is broad and flat, with a distinct angle between the upper and lower halves. It is covered with black glaze. Some lamps of this shape bear a simple wreath on the upper surface—essentially West Slope decoration.

In the early years of the third century a major innovation took place with the introduction of lamps made in molds rather than on a wheel or by hand. Two molds were used, an upper and a lower; the joint between them was sealed

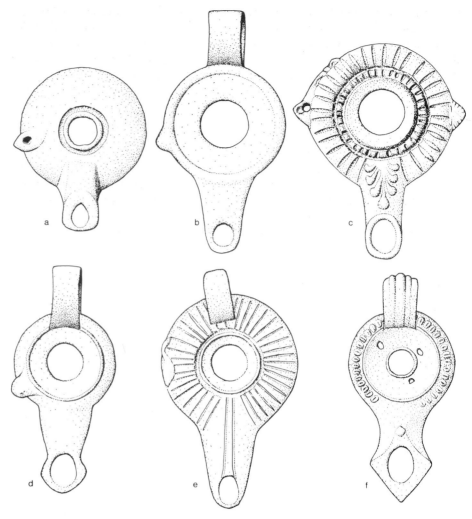

10.62 Typical lamps of the Hellenistic period. After Richard Hubbard Howland, *Greek Lamps and Their Survivals*, Athenian Agora series, vol. 4 (Princeton: American School of Classical Studies, 1958), Plates 41, 43, 46, 47, and 48. By permission of the American School of Classical Studies. Drawing by John Huffstot. Scale 1:2.

and worked over so that it was difficult to detect. Wheel-made lamps continued to be made alongside the new types into the first century of the Christian era. Figure 10.62b shows a typical molded lamp with an angular design and flat, depressed top around the filling hole. This is a clear and sharp design, suited to a mold. Its shape may have been influenced by metal lamps. Lamps of this type may or may not have flat ribbon handles, as seen in our example. Lugs are pierced, unpierced, or partially pierced.

Some molded lamps were made with elaborate relief decoration. Lamps imported from the east appear to have provided the major inspiration for Athenian production of such lamps in the third century. Figure 10.62c shows an Athenian handleless version—many such lamps do have handles—with two lugs, one in the shape of a shell and the other, pierced, in the shape of a knuckle bone. The top of the lamp is decorated with a design of rays in relief; the nozzle bears a palmette—a typical design for this type. Both the inside and the outside of the lamp were originally covered with black glaze.

A circular wheel-made lamp of the first century is shown in Figure 10.62d. It has tall inward-sloping sides above the angle and broad, low, outward-sloping sides below. The deeply sunken top, or discus, became popular late in the period and anticipated Roman types. Our example has a handle, a solid lug, and a distinctive long nozzle that widens and flattens around the wick hole.

Molded relief decoration continued to be popular; a typical example from the late third to the last quarter of the second century is shown in Figure 10.62e. It has a double convex body with a typical long nozzle ending in an oval. The nozzle is decorated with a pair of lines on its rounded upper side. One unpierced lug and a vertical ring handle are also common in this type. The tops are usually decorated with rays or ridges.

A distinctive nozzle is found on an extremely common Late Hellenistic type called the Ephesos lamp because of the great number of examples found at that site (Fig. 10.62f). Imported to Athens after 125, these lamps were made in molds but had a handmade collar around the top to stop oil from spilling down the sides. Small holes, usually three in a triangular pattern, allowed the oil to drip back into the lamp rather than draining back through the filling hole, which is protected by a raised ring. The sides are in a double convex shape with a sharp angle between the two halves. Various relief designs usually decorate the body. The triangular nozzles are typical of this large group of Late Hellenistic lamps, which owe their shape to metal prototypes.

Epilogue

Limitations of space make it impossible to treat the neglected Roman period in Greece to the extent it deserves. Greece became a small part of the mighty Roman Empire and receded into relative insignificance. New cities became prominent, as did some old ones, such as Corinth, refounded in 44 B.C. as capital of the province of Achaia, but in general old Greece was even less important than it had been under the Hellenistic rulers. Athens continued as a university town whose greatness lay in the past, but which was adorned with new buildings and monuments through sentimental attachment to that past. Greek art was still popular among Roman collectors, and many originals, copies of originals, originals in ancient styles, and fakes flooded out of the old sanctuaries and cities to the imperial capital. At the same time, typically Roman monuments, often in Greek style, were established in Greece.

Roman buildings were added throughout Greece, and both the excellent materials available and the Greek tradition had their effect on the Roman forms. The Romans' employment of concrete, which could be laid in vaults and domes, and their use of brickwork gave their buildings a decidedly Roman flavor, though Greek architectural orders and details were used as decoration. Typical Roman baths, aqueducts, triumphal arches, and basilicas appeared throughout the country, employing monumental and often exaggerated Greek forms in their decoration. At the same time direct architectural copies of earlier Greek buildings were erected and earlier monuments, such as the door of the north porch of the Erechtheion, were restored (Fig. E.1). The restored upper portion can be distinguished from the Greek work by the carved, solid centers of the decorative rosettes.

A good example of Roman monumentality and elaboration can be seen in the reconstruction of a fountain house in Corinth known as Peirene. In the Hellenistic period this natural spring was faced by seven piers, which held up the overhanging rock and formed chambers. In these chambers water could be taken from parapets that fronted rectangular rock-cut reservoirs extending back under the hill (Fig. E.2). In the second century of the Christian era, during Roman times, the spring was monumentalized with a high walled court decorated with statues, including some of the imperial family (Fig. E.3). Although more elaborate than the Hellenistic form, Roman architecture in Greece tends to be somewhat subdued by the simpler Greek tradition and does not reach the heights of overloaded decoration that can be seen in Roman architecture elsewhere.

In Greece of the Roman period wealthy private donors renovated a number of buildings and built new ones as gifts for various cities and sanctuaries. The emperor Hadrian, who completed the temple of Olympian Zeus at Athens, was another benefactor. As in the Hellenistic period, when the princes of the time gave gifts to their old university town, Greece was largely dependent on philanthropy in the Roman period.

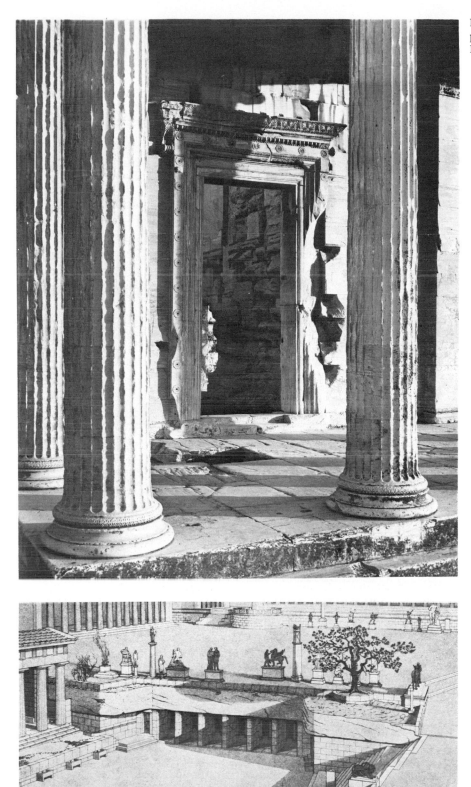

E.1 North door of the Erechtheion, Athens; upper portion restored in Roman times. Photo: Alison Frantz.

E.2 Peirene, Corinth, as it appeared in the Hellenistic period. From Gorham P. Stevens, *Restorations of Classical Buildings* (Princeton: American School of Classical Studies, 1958), Plate 19. By permission of the American School of Classical Studies.

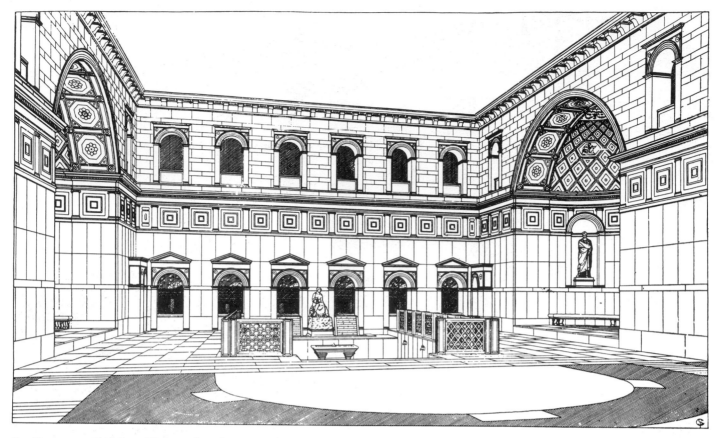

E.3 Roman reconstruction of Peirene, Corinth, in
the second century of the Christian era. From
Gorham P. Stevens, "The Fountain of Peirene in
the Time of Herodes Atticus," *American Journal of
Archaeology* 38 (1934): 55–58, Plate 7.

A glance at a reconstruction of the Athenian agora of the second century of
the Christian era shows the great changes that took place as the central area
was gradually filled with buildings (Fig. E.4). Most commercial activity was
probably moved to the east, where a colonnade surrounded a marketplace,
next to which stood a great library building erected by Hadrian. The center of
the old Agora was dominated by a large music hall, first erected about 15 B.C.
by Agrippa, and a fifth-century temple of Ares moved into the area by the
Romans in the first century of the Christian era. Much further elaboration of
existing buildings and the erection of two small temples, an elaborate fountain,
a library, and other small buildings attest to the further adornment of the
Agora in the Roman period.

Roman statuary abounds, particularly portrait statues of members of the
imperial family and others. Greek influence is also seen in elaborate copies and
adaptations of earlier types, such as the large karyatids used to support the
porch of a gateway built at the sanctuary of Eleusis in 50 B.C. (Fig. E.5). The
concept is obviously Greek and the maidens stylistically relate to the fifth
century, though they are definitely Roman. The sanctuary of Eleusis, incidentally, has another gateway built in the second century of the Christian era as an
accurate copy of the central portion of the Propylaia in Athens. The pediment
of the Roman gate, however, is decorated with a bust of a Roman emperor,
probably Marcus Aurelius.

Perhaps one of the best examples of the mixture of Hellenistic Greek and

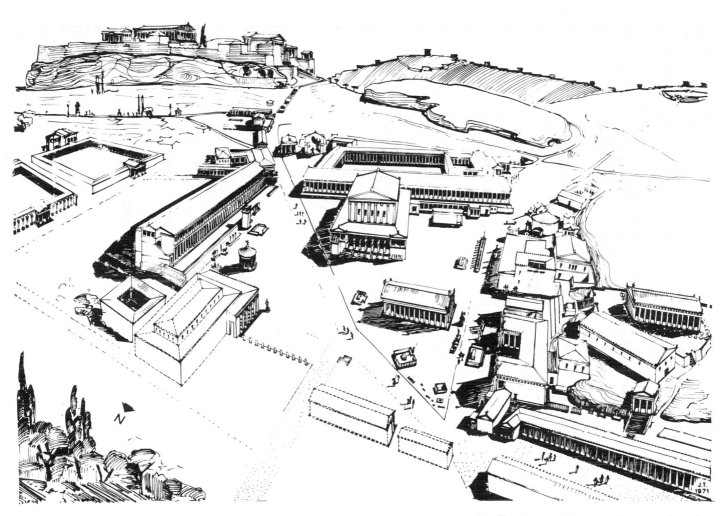

E.4 The Agora, Athens, as it appeared in the second century of the Christian era. Photo: American School of Classical Studies at Athens: Agora Excavations.

Roman styles is a monument on the Hill of the Muses, southwest and close to the Acropolis (Fig. E.6). Dated between A.D. 114 and 116, the monument was actually the tomb of C. Julius Antiochos Philopappos, an exiled prince who settled in Athens and adopted Athenian citizenship. Philopappos, the son of Antiochos IV of Commagene, an Eastern kingdom, was a Roman consul in A.D. 109 and an Athenian magistrate. The curving facade, originally decorated with niches, pilasters, and sculpture in the Roman fashion, had three units, one of which is now missing. The relief in the lower portion of the monument, showing Philopappos in his consular chariot, is Roman in style and subject matter and has been seen to be related to the reliefs on the Arch of Titus in Rome. The technique of carving can be paralleled in Athenian sculpture of the time. In the upper level of the monument, statues stood in three niches separated by two Corinthian pilasters. The central niche holds a seated, partially draped statue of Philopappos, now unfortunately headless, in the pose of a divinity or philosopher. To his right is a seated statue of King Antiochos, wearing Greek chiton and himation. To Philopappos' left was a statue of his ancestor King Seleucus I, which is now completely missing. Two inscriptions on the monument gave the details of Philopappos' career, one in Latin, the

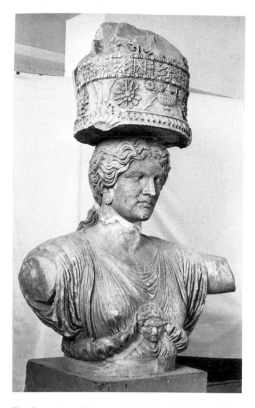

E.5 Remains of a karyatid in Eleusis.ᴾ Eleusis Museum. Photo: Deutsches Archäologisches Institut, Athens.

other in Greek. The mixture of honors, titles, architecture, and sculpture is a fine example of the blending of Greek and Roman traditions in Greece in the Roman period.

The Greco-Roman civilization was the beginning of our Western civilization. Many of the concepts, ideas, and artistic forms invented by the Greeks are still with us today. It is possible to take any of a number of Greek compositions—

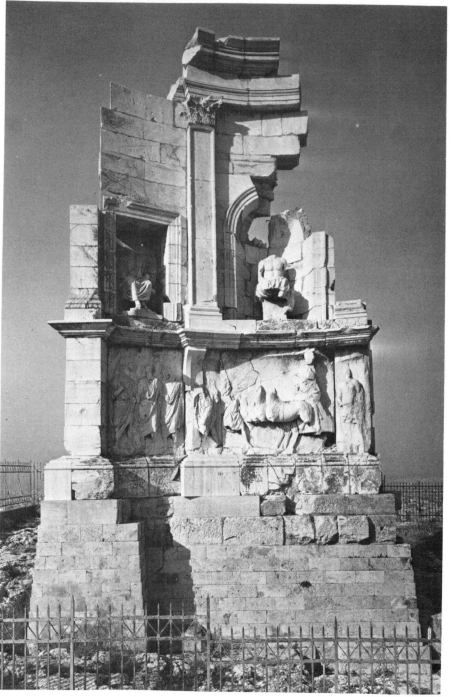

E.6 Philopappos monument, Athens. Photo: Alison Frantz.

for instance, the Three Graces—and trace them from their Hellenistic birth through Roman art to the Renaissance, and then forward through the works of various artists to our own time. Such an academic exercise emphasizes and reflects the essential unity of Western civilization and the debt that we today owe to those people in a small land far away and long ago.

Suggestions for Further Reading

1. ARCHAEOLOGY IN GREECE

Paul MacKendrick, *The Greek Stones Speak* (New York, 1962; paperback ed., 1966), deals with Greek archaeology from a basically topographical point of view. A wide overall coverage can be found in John Griffiths Pedley, *Greek Art and Archaeology* (Englewood Cliffs, N.J., 1993). A general handbook of archaeology in the Bronze Age, arranged by subject rather than chronologically, is Oliver Dickinson, *The Aegean Bronze Age* (Cambridge, 1994).

Old, but something of a monument, is Harold North Fowler and James Rignall Wheeler, *A Handbook of Greek Archaeology* (New York, 1909). A definite monument of scholarship and learning is the even older translation and commentary on the traveler Pausanias by J. G. Frazer, *Pausanias's Description of Greece,* 6 vols. (New York, 1898; reprinted New York, 1965); it should at least be looked into by anyone interested in the subject of ancient Greece.

2. THE MINOANS

The two basic works are still Arthur J. Evans, *The Palace of Minos at Knossos* (London, 1925–1935; reprinted 1964), and J. D. S. Pendlebury, *The Archaeology of Crete* (London, 1939; reprinted New York, 1963). Many of the finds from Kato Zakro are to be found in Nicholas Platon's *Zakros* (New York, 1971). The best recent overall survey is Sinclair Hood, *The Minoans* (New York and London, 1971). R. A. Higgins's *The Archaeology of Minoan Crete* (London, 1973) emphasizes the early excavations. A short and readable description of the palaces may be found in Gerald Cadogan's *Palaces of Minoan Crete,* rev. ed. (London, 1980). J. Walter Graham's *Palaces of Crete,* 3d ed. (Princeton, 1987), deals with Minoan architecture; a more detailed study is J. W. Shaw, "Minoan Architecture," *L'Annuario della Scuola Archeologica di Atene,* n.s. 33 (1971):4–256. Also useful are Stylianos Alexiou, *Minoan Civilization* (Heraklion, 1969), and R. W. Hutchinson, *Prehistoric Crete* (Harmondsworth, 1962), which also surveys post-Bronze Age Crete.

General works that deal with the Minoan and Mycenaean civilizations jointly are described in the section on Chapter 3.

3. THE MYCENAEANS

William A. McDonald and Carol G. Thomas, *Progress into the Past: The Rediscovery of Mycenaean Civilization,* 2d ed. (Bloomington, Ind., 1990), is a readable account primarily of the Bronze Age on the mainland. A similar but more popularly written book by Joseph Alsop, *From the Silent Earth* (New York, 1964) concentrates on Pylos. The background of the author, who is the well-known political reporter, gives him a new angle from which to attack the problems. Several good general surveys of the Mycenaeans have appeared. The later chapters in Emily Vermeule's *Greece in the Bronze Age* (Chicago, 1972) deal in some detail with the Mycenaeans, while Lord William Taylour's *The Mycenaeans* (London, 1964; New York, 1971) deals mainly with the Late Helladic period. George E. Mylonas's *Mycenae and the Mycenaean Age* (Princeton, 1966) emphasizes Mycenae but also describes other sites, in many instances giving information unavailable in English elsewhere. Spyridon Marinatos and Max Hirmer's *Crete and Mycenae* (London, 1960) is a lavishly illustrated survey with a good text. A compendium of sites and finds arranged chronologically with little text but a great deal of information and many illustrations can be found in Hans-Günter Buchholz and Vassos Karageorghis, *Prehistoric Greece and Cyprus* (London, 1973).

Several books cover the art of both Crete and the mainland. R. A. Higgins's *Minoan and Mycenaean Art*, 2d ed. (London and New York, 1981) and Friedrick Matz's *Crete and Early Greece* (London, 1962; New York, 1965) are probably the best of the group. Also useful is Peter Warren, *The Aegean Civilizations from Ancient Crete to Mycenae*, 2d ed. (New York, 1989). A highly illustrated handbook in the Pelican History of Art series is Sinclair Hood, *The Arts in Prehistoric Greece* (Harmondsworth and New York, 1978).

4. THE DARK AGES

Two excellent surveys of the Dark Ages are A. M. Snodgrass, *The Dark Age of Greece* (Edinburgh, 1971) and V. R. d'A. Desborough, *The Greek Dark Ages* (New York, 1972). Desborough's earlier work, *The Last Mycenaeans and Their Successors* (Oxford, 1964), is the standard work for the period from about 1200 to 1000.

Several of the works cited for Chapter 5 deal with the period covered by this chapter also.

5. THE GEOMETRIC PERIOD

Snodgrass's *Dark Age of Greece* also deals with the Geometric period. More specific and a good overview of the period and its regional developments is J. N. Coldstream, *Geometric Greece* (New York, 1977). Jane Carter, "The Beginning of Narrative Art in the Greek Geometric Period," *BSA* 67 (1972): 25–58, and Gudrun Ahlberg-Cornell, *Myth and Epos in Early Greek Art: Representation and Interpretation* (Jonsered, 1992), also consider artistic representations of the succeeding period. James Whitley, *Style and Society in Dark Age Greece* (Cambridge, 1991) exemplifies the new approaches to the evidence from the early periods of Greece, including the time period covered in Chapter 4. A good selection of illustrations can be found in Bernhard Schweitzer's *Greek Geometric Art* (London, 1971). The exhibition catalogue *From Pasture to Polis: Art in the Age of Homer*, ed. Susan Langdon (Columbia, Mo., 1993), is also useful.

6. THE ORIENTALIZING PERIOD

The Orientalizing period is usually included in studies of the Archaic period, which are described in the section on Chapter 7. A few studies, however, focus on the important overseas connections: Ekrem Akurgal, *The Birth of Greek Art: The Mediterranean and the Near East* (London, 1963); John Boardman, *The Greeks Overseas*, 2d ed. (London, 1973); and Sarah Morris, *Daidalos and the Origins of Greek Art* (Princeton, 1992). Karl Schefold, *Myth and Legend in Early Greek Art* (London, 1968), deals with early artistic representations.

7. THE ARCHAIC PERIOD

A good discussion of the Persian Wars can be found in A. R. Burn, *Persia and the Greeks* (London, 1962). For general surveys, see L. H. Jeffery, *Archaic Greece: The City-States, c. 700–500 B.C.* (London and Tonbridge, 1976), and A. M. Snodgrass, *Archaic Greece: The Age of Experiment* (London, 1980). A number of works deal specifically with Archaic Greek art; Jean Charbonneaux, Roland Martin, and François Villard, *Archaic Greek Art, 620–480 B.C.* (London, 1971), is one of the most comprehensive treatments. Also useful is Ernst Homann-Wedeking's *The Art of Archaic Greece* (New York, 1968). For the period from the end of the Bronze Age to the end of the Archaic period, see Jeffrey M. Hurwit, *The Art and Culture of Early Greece, 1100–480 B.C.* (Ithaca, N.Y., 1985). Also useful is Roland Hampe and Erika Simon, *The Birth of Greek Art: From the Mycenaean to the Archaic Period* (New York, 1981). The decade of the 1980s was enlivened by a challenge to the generally accepted chronology for the Archaic period. The primary presentations of the two sides are E. D. Francis and Michael Vickers, "Signae Priscae Artis: Eretria and Siphnos," *JHS* 103 (1983): 49–67, and John Boardman, "Signa Tabulae Priscae Artis," *JHS* 104 (1984): 161–163. The arguments are summarized in R. M. Cook, "The Francis-Vickers Chronology," *JHS* 109 (1989): 164–170.

8. THE FIFTH CENTURY *and* 9. THE FOURTH CENTURY

A lavishly illustrated study of the art and architecture of the fifth and fourth centuries is to be found in Jean Charbonneaux, Roland Martin, and François Villard, *Classical Greek Art* (New York, 1972). A slightly different approach is taken in J. J. Pollitt's *Art and Experience in Classical Greece* (Cambridge, 1972). Illuminating essays on the changes of styles between the Archaic period and the succeeding fifth century can be found in C. G. Boulter, ed., *Greek Art: Archaic into Classical* (Leiden, 1985).

T. B. L. Webster, *Art and Literature in the Fourth Century* (London, 1956), is a basic study of the fourth century. A discussion that treats the problem of the interpretation of this period is Blanche R. Brown, *Anticlassicism in Greek Sculpture of the Fourth Century* (New York, 1973).

10. THE HELLENISTIC AGE

A great number of works have been published about the Hellenistic age. William W. Tarn, *Hellenistic Civilization,* 3d ed. rev. by G. T. Griffith (New York, 1961), is still basic. Good introductions are John Ferguson, *The Heritage of Hellenism* (New York, 1973), and F. W. Walbank, *The Hellenistic World* (Cambridge, Mass., 1981). John Onians, *Art and Thought in the Hellenistic Age: The Greek World View, 350–50 B.C.* (London, 1979), is also useful.

Three surveys of the arts of the period stand out: Christine Mitchell Havelock, *Hellenistic Art,* 2d ed. (New York and London, 1981); Jean Charbonneaux, Roland Martin, and François Villard, *Hellenistic Art* (New York, 1973); and J. J. Pollitt, *Art in the Hellenistic Age* (Cambridge, 1986).

EPILOGUE

Scholars are now studying Roman remains in Greece, but these remains have been quite neglected in the past. Among works reflecting the relatively new interest is Susan Walker and Averil Cameron, eds., *The Greek Renaissance in the Roman Empire,* Papers from the Tenth British Museum Colloquium (London, 1989). A more recent overall view based to a great extent on the results of surface survey is provided by Susan Alcock, *Graeca Capta: The Landscapes of Roman Greece* (Cambridge, 1993). Among regional studies is *The Corinthia in the Roman Period,* ed. Timothy E. Gregory, *Journal of Roman Archaeology,* suppl. ser. no. 8, ed. J. H. Humphrey (Ann Arbor, 1993).

Select Bibliography

THIS BIBLIOGRAPHY contains selected English-language handbooks and surveys of the art and archaeology of Iron Age Greece. General works on archaeology are listed in the Suggestions for Further Reading for Chapter 1. Works on the Bronze Age are listed in the Suggestions for Further Reading for Chapters 2 and 3. Basic studies dealing with the minor objects discussed in the text may be found in the footnotes. Unfortunately, limitations of space make it impossible to comment on all categories of minor finds, so a short list of works dealing with classes of objects not mentioned in the text is appended.

LITERARY SOURCES

Pollitt, J. J. *The Art of Greece: Sources and Documents.* Cambridge and New York, 1990.
——. *The Ancient View of Greek Art.* New Haven and London, 1974.

ART

Boardman, John. *The Diffusion of Classical Art in Antiquity.* Princeton, 1994.
——. *Greek Art.* 3d ed. London and New York, 1987.
—— et al. *The Art and Architecture of Ancient Greece.* London and New York, 1967.
——, ed. *The Oxford History of Classical Art.* Oxford, 1993.
Brilliant, Richard. *Arts of the Ancient Greeks.* New York, 1973.
Cook, R. M. *Greek Art: Its Development, Character, and Influence.* 2d ed. London and New York, 1976.
Moon, Warren, ed. *Ancient Greek Art and Iconography.* Madison, Wis., 1983.
Richter, G. M. A. *A Handbook of Greek Art.* 9th ed. London, 1994.
Robertson, Martin. *A History of Greek Art.* 2 vols. Cambridge, 1975.
——. *A Shorter History of Greek Art.* Cambridge, 1981.
Sparkes, Brian. *Greek Art.* Oxford, 1991.
Woodford, Susan. *An Introduction to Greek Art.* Ithaca, N.Y., 1986.

ARCHITECTURE

Coulton, J. J. *Ancient Greek Architects at Work.* Ithaca, N.Y., 1977.
Dinsmoor, W. B. *The Architecture of Ancient Greece.* 3d ed. rev. New York, 1975.
Lawrence, A. W. *Greek Architecture.* 4th ed., rev. R. A. Tomlinson. Harmondsworth, 1983.
Robertson, D. S. *Greek and Roman Architecture.* 2d ed. Cambridge, 1969.
Tomlinson, R. A. *Greek and Roman Architecture.* London, 1995.
Winter, Nancy A. *Greek Architectural Terracottas.* Oxford, 1993.

SCULPTURE

Barron, John. *Greek Sculpture.* London, 1981.
Beazley, J. D., and Bernard Ashmole. *Greek Sculpture and Painting.* 2d ed. Cambridge, 1966.

Carpenter, Rhys. *Greek Sculpture*. Chicago, 1960.
Lullies, Reinhard, and Max Hirmer. *Greek Sculpture*. New York, 1960.
Richter, G. M. *A Sculpture and Sculptors of the Greeks*. 4th ed. rev. New Haven, 1970.
Stewart, Andrew. *Greek Sculpture: An Exploration*. 2 vols. New Haven, 1990.

PAINTING (INCLUDING VASE PAINTING)

Arias, P. E., Max Hirmer, and B. B. Shefton. *A History of Greek Vase Painting*. London, 1962.
Bruno, Vincent J. *Form and Color in Greek Painting*. New York, 1977.
Cook, R. M. *Greek Painted Pottery*. 2d ed. London, 1972.
Noble, J. V. *The Techniques of Painted Attic Pottery*. Rev. ed. London, 1988.
Rasmussen, Tom, and Nigel Spivey, eds. *Looking at Greek Vases*. Cambridge, 1991.
Robertson, Martin. *The Art of Vase-Painting in Classical Athens*. Cambridge, 1992.
——. *Greek Painting*. Geneva, 1959.
Sparkes, Brian A. *Greek Pottery: An Introduction*. Manchester, 1991.
Swindler, Mary Hamilton. *Ancient Painting*. New Haven, 1929.
Trendall, A. D. *Red Figure Vases of South Italy and Sicily*. London, 1989.

MISCELLANEOUS MINOR FINDS

Boardman, John. *Greek Gems and Finger Rings*. London, 1970.
Barber, E. J. W. *Prehistoric Textiles*. Princeton, 1991.
Burnett, Andrew. *Coins*. London, 1991.
Calinescu, Adriana. *The Art of Ancient Jewelry*. Bloomington, Ind., 1994.
Cook, B. F. *Greek Inscriptions*. London, 1990.
Grose, David Frederick. *Early Ancient Glass: Core-Formed, Rod-Formed, and Cast Vessels and Objects from the Late Bronze Age to the Early Roman Empire*. Toledo and New York, 1989.
Higgins, Reynold. *Greek and Roman Jewelry*. 2d ed. Berkeley and Los Angeles. 1980.
——. *Greek Terracottas*. London, 1967.
Lang, Mabel, and Margaret Crosby. *Weights, Measures, and Tokens*. Athenian Agora series, vol. 10. Princeton, 1964.
Richter, G. M. A. *The Furniture of the Greeks, Etruscans, and Romans*. London, 1966.
Snodgrass, Anthony. *Arms and Armour of the Greeks*. London, 1967.
Strong, D. E. *Greek and Roman Gold and Silver Plate*. Ithaca, N.Y., 1966.
Vermeule, Cornelius, and Mary Comstock. *Greek, Etruscan, and Roman Bronzes in the Museum of Fine Arts, Boston*. Boston, 1971.
Webb, Virginia. *Archaic Greek Faience*. Warminster, 1978.
Williams, Dyfri, and Jack Ogden. *Greek Gold*. New York, 1994.

Glossary

GEOGRAPHICAL AND PERSONAL NAMES are omitted. Architectural terms are illustrated on pp. 134–135; pottery shapes are illustrated on p. 105.

abacus   A block-shaped member of a column capital which provides transition between the swelling echinus and the epistyle.

alabastron   A slim oil container with rounded end, narrow neck, and flaring mouth.

amphora   A two-handled vase used for storage of liquids.

anta (pl. **antae**)   A thickened extension of the cella walls forming the sides of the pronaos or opisthodomos of a temple.

apsidal   Having a curved end, as an apse.

archaizing style   A style that combines archaic and contemporary forms.

architrave   The Latin term for an epistyle.

arris   The area between the flutes on a column shaft.

aryballos   A round, narrow-necked bottle for oil or perfume.

ashlar construction   Construction of blocks of squared stone laid in regular courses.

bilingual vase   A vase painted in Black Figure style on one side and in Red Figure style on the other.

black figure technique   A style of pottery painting in which black silhouette figures are decorated with incision and added color.

cella   The central structure that housed the cult statue in a Greek temple.

Centuripe ware   Large polychrome funeral pots of the Hellenistic period, adorned with figured scenes and relief decoration.

chamber tomb   A rectangular chamber cut into the side of a hill and approached by a long entrance passage (dromos); typical of the Mycenaean period.

chiton   A light, one-piece garment fastened with buttons or pins.

chronology   The arrangement of events in time.

chryselephantine   Constructed of gold and ivory. Chryselephantine statues usually had a wooden core.

contrapposto   Opposition of contrasted masses achieved by a pose in which the body's weight is supported by one leg, so that the tension of one side is contrasted with the relaxation of the other.

corbel   An architectural member projecting outward from a wall and bearing the weight of the next course above it. Each course projects slightly beyond the one below.

cyclopean construction   A type of construction characterized by the use of large, often unworked boulders; typical of the Mycenaean period.

dado   The lower portion of a wall, distinctively decorated.

dentil   A rectangular, toothlike projection, as on an Ionic epistyle.

dressed masonry   Stone construction of blocks cut and finished in regular shapes.

dromos   The entrance corridor to a tomb of the Mycenaean period.

echinus   The swelling member of a column capital beneath the abacus.

ekphora   A ritual transportation of a corpse for burial; a common subject on Geometric pottery.

encaustic technique   A painting technique in which the colors are fixed with heat.

entasis   The vertical, convex curve of a column.

epigraphy   The study of inscriptions and letter forms.

epistyle   A line of blocks that extend from column to column and support the upper parts of the building.

faience   An opaque glaze made mainly of crushed quartz.

fibula   A dress pin with a clasp.

flute   One of a series of vertical concave channels serving as decoration on a column.

flying gallop   A rapid, springing gait of a four-footed animal, conventionally indicated in art by a representation of an animal stretched out with all four feet off the ground.

fresco   The technique of creating a wall painting by applying pigments to wet or dampened plaster; a painting so created.

frieze   The zone above the epistyle, decorated with triglyphs and metopes (Doric order) or sculpture or dentils (Ionic order).

geison   The horizontal course above the frieze, its undersurface decorated with mutules and guttae in the Doric order.

Gnathian ware   Pottery of the Hellenistic period decorated with simple designs in yellow and white; a western equivalent of West Slope ware.

guttus (pl. **guttae**)   A circular projection from a mutule or regula.

gypsum   Soft stone used in Minoan architecture.

half-timbered   Constructed of wooden framework with spaces filled by stone, rubble, or mud brick.

hieroglyphic script   A writing system based on pictures.

himation   An outer mantel or cloak.

hydria   A three-handled vase used for carrying water.

ideogram   In a writing system, a picture that represents an idea.

kantharos   A drinking cup with high swung handles.

kore (pl. **korai**)   An Archaic statue of a draped female figure.

kouros (pl. **kouroi**)   An Archaic statue of a nude standing male figure.

krater   A vase used for mixing wine and water.

kylix   A tall, stemmed, shallow drinking cup.

lagynos   A squat, one-handled Hellenistic bottle.

lebes   A rounded, handleless vase used for mixing wine and water.

lebes gamikos   A special vase used in marriage rituals.

lekanis   A covered dish.

lekythos   A tall, one-handled oil bottle.

linear script   A writing system employing simplified pictures.

loutrophoros   A vase of a special shape used to hold water in a marriage ritual.

megalithic architecture   A type of construction characterized by the use of large blocks of stone.

Megarian bowl   A bowl of the Hellenistic period adorned with relief decoration.

megaron   A free-standing, more or less square room entered at one side through one or more anterooms and a two-columned porch. It generally contains a round, fixed hearth.

metope   A slab, usually blank but sometimes decorated, between two triglyphs of a Doric frieze.

Minoan civilization   A prehistoric civilization based on the island of Crete; named after the legendary king Minos.

mud brick   A brick made of sun-dried mud.

mutule   A projecting slab, decorated with guttae, on the underside of a geison.

Mycenaean civilization   A prehistoric civilization of the Greek mainland and adjoining areas; named after its most famous site, Mycenae.

niello   A black compound of copper, lead, sulfur, and borax used as inlay in metalwork.

numismatics   The study of coins and coinage.

oinochoe   A vase used for pouring liquids.

olpe   A jug with round mouth and sagging belly.

opisthodomos   The back porch of a Greek temple.

orthostate   The bottom course of a wall, generally two to three times higher than the upper courses.

pediment   The triangular space formed by the pitched roof at the end of a Greek temple.

pelike   A two-handled vase used for storage.

peplos   A heavy, one-piece garment worn by women. It was fastened at the shoulders with pins and was often worn with an overfold.

peristyle   A covered colonnade surrounding a building or a court.

polos   A round, hatlike headdress.

pommel   A rounded protrusion on the handle of a sword or dagger which prevents the hand from slipping.

post-and-lintel system   An architectural system based on vertical supports for horizontal members.

pronaos   The front porch of a Greek temple.

prothesis   The lying in state and ritual mourning of a deceased person; a common subject on Geometric pottery.

psykter   A bulbous vase used as a wine cooler.

radiocarbon dating   A method of dating that relies on measurement of the rate of decay of carbon 14 in organic remains.

red figure technique   A style of pottery painting in which the background is painted black and the figures are left in the natural color of the clay and decorated with dilute glaze paint and some added colors.

regula (pl. **regulae**)   A raised panel containing guttae placed on the underside of a geison block.

relief sculpture   Sculpture in which figures project from a sunken background.

relieving triangle   A space, often triangular, left above a lintel in megalithic construction to relieve the weight of the superincumbent masonry.

repoussé technique   A metalworking technique in which a design is raised by hammering on the reverse of a metal sheet.

resistivity survey   A geophysical survey technique involving the measurement of the resistance of subsurface layers to a flow of electricity.

rubble masonry   Stone construction in which rubble is used as building material.

shaft grave   A communal grave at the foot of a shaft dug from the surface; typical of the earlier Mycenaean period.

Sigilata ware   Red ceramics that began to be produced in the Hellenistic period.

sima   A crowning gutter at roof level.

skyphos   A deep two-handled drinking cup.

sphyrelaton technique   A method of constructing figures in which thin plates of metal are hammered over a core and then nailed to a wooden form.

spindle whorl   A weight attached to the end of a spindle to facilitate manipulation of the thread in spinning.

stamnos   A two-handled vase used for storage.

stereobate   The stepped foundation of a stone temple.

stirrup jar   A rounded vase with a double handle and a narrow spout; common in Mycenaean civilization.

stoa   A long, rectangular construction with a roof extending from the back wall to a row of supports at the front.

stylistic development   Change in shape and decoration over time.

stylobate   The portion of the floor of a building on which the columns rest.

syllabic script   Writing that employs signs representing syllables.

taenia   A horizontal flat molding along the top of the epistyle, decorated with regulae and guttae.

tempera technique   A painting technique in which a colloidal medium (such as egg yolk) is used to bind the colors.

terra cotta   Baked clay.

tesserae   Small squares of stone used in mosaic compositions.

thalassocracy   Supremacy on the sea.

thermoluminescence dating   A method of dating pottery that depends on measurement of the amount of radiation absorbed since a vessel was fired.

tholos tomb   A round, corbeled stone tomb, perhaps royal, characteristic of Mycenaean civilization.

triglyph   A grooved slab in the frieze course of the Doric order.

type   In numismatics, the design on the face of a coin.

West Slope ware   Pottery of the Hellenistic period decorated with simple designs.

xoanon (pl. **xoana**)   A primitive statue made of wood.

Index

Pagasai, stele of Hediste, 315, *316*
Painting (other than on pottery): archaic,
    96 / 97, 178–79, 187–88, *188*; on buildings,
    135, 138; fifth-century, 236; fourth-century,
    275, *276*; Hellenistic, *96/97*, 315–18, *316, 318,
    320, 320*; Minoan, 40–42, *43–49, 46–47, 49–51*;
    Mycenaean, 73, 80–84, *81–85*; on statues,
    96/97, 143,169, 226; Theran, *96/97*, 51–52,
    52–54. See also Pottery
Painting styles. *See* Black Figure style; Floral
    style; Kerch style; Marine style; Outline style;
    Palace style; Pattern style; Pictorial style; Pro-
    to-Attic style; Red Figure style; West Slope
    style; White Ground style
Palaces, mainland, 64; Mycenae, *66, 68, 69, 70*;
    Pylos, *67, 71, 73, 73–75*; Tiryns, *71, 72*
—Minoan: features of, 30, 31; Gournia, 42, *44*;
    Kato Zakro, 29, 32, *33*; Knossos, 23, 26, 28, 29,
    30, 32–42, *34–42*; Mallia, 31, *31, 34*; Phaistos,
    23, 29, 31–32, *32*
Palace style, 54–55, *55–56*
Parthenon. *See* Acropolis: Parthenon
Pattern style, 54, 55, *85, 86*
Pediments, 134; sculpture in, *156, 171–74, 173–
    74, 176–77, 177,* 218–19, *219,* 228–34, *232–33,*
    249–50, *250,* 267, *267*
Peiraeus: plan of, 211; statues from, 271, *273*;
    stele from, 272–73, *274*
Pella, 276, 284; stag-hunt mosaic from, 276–77,
    278
Pendlebury, John, 107
Penthesilea Painter, cup by, 238, *238*
Peplos kore, 169–70, *170*
Perachora, 113; model from, 113, *113*
Pergamene order, 292, *294*
Pergamon, 285, 294–95, *295*; temple of Athena
    Polias Nikephoros, 286, *286*
Pergamon Altar, 294, 300–301, *301–3*
Perikles, 194, 196, 226; building program of,
    200–207, *225–26*
Perseus and Medusa, *96/97,* 147, *148,* 180
Persian Empire: defeat of, 247; destruction by,
    194, 209; development of, 155; wars, 155,
    247–48
Phaistos (Crete), palace at, 29, 31–32, *32*
Phidias, 196, 222, 234–35; attributions to, 222;
    cult statues by, 196, *197,* 234–35, *234*; cup of,
    22; style of, 196
Philip of Macedon, 247, 256
Philippeion (Olympia), 256–57, *256*
Philopappos monument (Athens), 332–34, *334*
Phrasikleia, *96 / 97, 169*
Phylakopi (Melos), 45
Pictorial style, 85–86, *88*
Pins: in Dark Ages, 107–9, *109*; Geometric, 128–
    29, *129*; Orientalizing, 151–52, *152. See also*
    Fibulae
Pithoi, Minoan, *35, 36, 43, 54, 55*
Pitsa, wooden plaque from, *96 / 97,* 178–79
Ploutos in arms of Eirene (Kephisodotos), 263–
    64, *263*
Polis: definition of, 110; development of, 132,
    154; failure of, 248
Polykleitos, 222–24; canon of, 224, 269; Di-
    adoumenos, 223–24, *226–27*; Doryphoros,
    222–23, *225*; influence of, 271
Polykrates, temple of (Samos), 159
Pompeii, Alexander mosaic from, 318–20, *319*
Porto Cheli (Peloponnesos), 18
Portraiture, 269, *271,* 296–97, *297,* 302, 305, 310–
    12, *311–12*

Poseidon: on Parthenon pediment, 228, *232*;
    temples of, 136–37, *137*
Post-and-lintel system, 29 134; "relieving trian-
    gle," 68, *68, 70, 77, 78*
Pottery: Archaic, *96/97,* 179–88, *181–84, 186–
    88*; Dark Ages, 103–6, *105, 107*; fifth-century,
    96/97, 237–42, *238–41*; fourth-century, 277–
    78, *278–79*; functions of, 103; Geometric, 121–
    26,*122–26*; Hellenistic, 321–22, *321–22*; Min-
    oan, 52, 54–55, *54–56*; Mycenaean, 85–86, *86–
    88*; Orientalizing period, *96/97,* 143–48, *145–
    49*; Protogeometric, 105–6, *107*; relief wares,
    278, 279, 321–23; shapes, 54, *87,* 103–4, *105,*
    321, *321–23*; use of, in dating, 16, *27–28. See
    also* Amphoras; Aryballos; Caldrons; Cups;
    Fish plate; Kantharos; Kraters; Kylix; Lagynos;
    Lekythos; Olpe; Pithoi; Stirrup jars; Unguen-
    tarium
Praxiteles, 264–65; Aphrodite of Knidos, 265,
    266; Apollo Sauroktonos, 265, *266*; curve of,
    265, 271, 307; Hermes, 264–65, *264*
Priene: city plan, 258–59, *261*; temple of Athena
    Polias, 251, 253, *252–53,* 259
Propylaia. *See* Acropolis: Propylaia
Propylon: at Knossos, 35; at Samos, 159, *160*
Proto-Attic style, 145–48, *147–48*
Protogeometric style, 105–6; shapes, 106, *107*;
    rise of, 104–5
Pylos (Peloponnesos), 24; palace at, *67, 71, 73,
    73–75*; Procession fresco, 83 *84, 84*; Tarzan
    fresco, 84, *85*

Red Figure style, *96/97,* 184–87,*186–87,* 238–41,
    238–41, 279, 280
Religion: attitudes toward, 143n; cult prac-
    tices, 70, 113; Minoan, 26–27; Mycenaean, 64–
    65
Rhamnous: statue of Themis, 296, *296*; stele
    from, 274, *275*
Rhodes, 285; Aphrodite of, 307–8, *309*; coins
    from, 283, *282,* 327; destruction in, 28; trans-
    port amphoras from, 321–22, *323–24*
Rhoikos and Theodorus, 159; temple designed
    by, 159, *160*
Rhytons: Minoan, 56, 58, *58–59*; Mycenaean,
    94–95, *95*
Riace, bronze statues from, 222, *225*
Roman copies: mosaics, 318–20; paintings, 316–
    17; sculpture, 214–15, 295–96
Roman period in Greece: buildings, 330–32,
    331–33; influence, 330–35; restorations, 330,
    331; statuary, 332–34, *334*
Rome: as collector, 215, 285
Royal Stoa, 162, 164, *164, 165*

Samos, temples at: Heraion I, 113–14, *116* ; Her-
    aion II, 138–39, *140, 141*; Polykrates, 159;
    Rhoikos, 159, *160*
Santorini, 27–28; excavations on, 51
Saqqara (Egypt), painted plaque from, 275–76,
    276
Satyrs (silenoi), *182, 183, 184,* 303, *304*
Schliemann, Heinrich, 21, 62, 64, 75, 94
Sculpture: Archaic, *96/97,* 165–77, *167–80*;
    Daedalic, 140–43, *143–44*; fifth-century, 214–
    36, *215–36*; fourth-century, 263–65, *263–64,*
    267–75, *267–76*; Geometric, 119, *120–21, 121*;
    Hellenistic, 295–98, *296–99,* 300–315, *301–15*;
    Mycenaean, *68,* 78–79, *80–81*; in Orientalizing
    period, 140–43, *142–44*; Roman, 332, *334*
Seated Boxer, 310, *311*

349